Ethics and Science

Who owns your genes? What does climate science imply for policy? Do corporations conduct honest research? Should we teach intelligent design? Humans are creating a new world through science. The kind of world we are creating will not simply be decided by expanding scientific knowledge, but will depend on views about good and bad, right and wrong. These visions, in turn, depend on critical thinking, cogent argument, and informed judgment. In this book, Adam Briggle and Carl Mitcham help readers to cultivate these skills. They first introduce ethics and the normative structure of science, and then consider the "society of science" and its norms for the responsible conduct of research and the treatment of human and animal research subjects. Later chapters examine "science in society" – exploring ethical issues at the interfaces of science, policy, religion, culture, and technology. Each chapter features case studies and research questions to stimulate further reflection.

ADAM BRIGGLE is Assistant Professor in the Department of Philosophy and Religion Studies and Faculty Fellow in the Center for the Study of Interdisciplinarity at the University of North Texas. He is the author of *A Rich Bioethics: Public Policy, Biotechnology, and the Kass Council* (2010).

CARL MITCHAM is Philosopher of Science and Technology in the Division of Liberal Arts and International Studies at Colorado School of Mines. He is the author of several books, including *Thinking through Technology* (1994), and coauthor of *Humanitarian Engineering* (with David Muñoz, 2010). He is coeditor (with Stephen Cutcliffe) of *Visions of STS: Counterpoints in Science, Technology and Society Studies* (2001), and editor of the four-volume *Encyclopedia of Science, Technology, and Ethics* (2005).

Cambridge Applied Ethics

Titles published in this series:

ETHICS AND BUSINESS *Kevin Gibson*
ETHICS AND CRIMINAL JUSTICE *John Kleinig*
ETHICS AND THE ENVIRONMENT *Dale Jamieson*
ETHICS AND ANIMALS *Lori Gruen*
ETHICS AND THE MEDIA *Stephen J. A. Ward*
ETHICS AND WAR *Steven P. Lee*
ETHICS AND SCIENCE *Adam Briggle and Carl Mitcham*

Ethics and Science

An Introduction

ADAM BRIGGLE
University of North Texas

and

CARL MITCHAM
Colorado School of Mines

CAMBRIDGE
UNIVERSITY PRESS

University Printing House, Cambridge CB2 8BS, United Kingdom

Cambridge University Press is part of the University of Cambridge.

It furthers the University's mission by disseminating knowledge in the pursuit of education, learning and research at the highest international levels of excellence.

www.cambridge.org
Information on this title: www.cambridge.org/9780521878418

First published 2012
3rd printing 2014

Printed in the United Kingdom by Clays, St Ives plc.

A catalog record for this publication is available from the British Library

Library of Congress Cataloguing in Publication data
Briggle, Adam.
Ethics and science : an introduction / Adam Briggle and Carl Mitcham.
pages cm. – (Cambridge applied ethics)
Includes bibliographical references and index.
ISBN 978-0-521-87841-8 (hardback) – ISBN 978-0-521-70267-6 (paperback)
1. Research – Moral and ethical aspects. 2. Science – Social aspects.
I. Mitcham, Carl. II. Title.
Q180.55.M67B75 2012
174'.95–dc23 2012018836

ISBN 978-0-521-87841-8 Hardback
ISBN 978-0-521-70267-6 Paperback

For Mom and Dad, who gave me the gift of a love for learning.

– Adam

For all my students, who (strangely enough) often seem like parents in the ways they stimulate my love for learning.

– Carl

Zwei Dinge erfüllen das Gemüt mit immer neuer und zunehmenden Bewunderung und Ehrfurcht, je öfter und anhaltender sich das Nachdenken damit beschäftigt: *Der bestirnte Himmel über mir, und das moralische Gesetz in mir.*

Two things fill the mind with ever new and increasing wonder and awe, the more often and persistently I reflect on them: the starry heavens above me and the moral law within me.

–Immanuel Kant, *Kritik der praktischen Vernunft* II, Beschluß
(*Critique of Practical Reason*, II, Conclusion) 1788

Contents

Figures and tables

Figures

Tables

Preface

This volume aims to introduce students of science and philosophy to issues that are sometimes thought peripheral to real science or real philosophy. As an introduction, it necessarily simplifies, hopefully in a manner that stimulates further reflection. With regard to those who doubt the centrality of ethics to science or science to ethics, our claim for centrality is argued from multiple perspectives. But most importantly, given the central influence of science on the character of the contemporary world and of ethics in human affairs, not to reflect on the ethics–science relationship is to limit self-understanding in the technoscientific human condition.

A brief word is in order here about how we conceive of both science and ethics as actors on the social stage. As for science, since the 1970s the interdisciplinary field of science, technology, and society (STS) studies has been arguing that science cannot properly be understood solely as a cognitive enterprise or method of knowledge production. Science is situated in economic, cultural, and political contexts that it both reflects and influences. Science and society co-construct each other through ideas and scientifically based technologies in ways that make ethics all the more relevant, even crucial, to the self-understanding of scientists. From an STS perspective, science must be recognized as technoscience, a view implicit in many of the arguments to be explored.

Ethics too is something more than theory and analysis. In the chapters that follow, ethics is understood to involve two mutually related tasks. First, it seeks to make explicit certain beliefs about human conduct in and in relation to science in order to commend efforts to live them out. This is what might be called inspirational ethics. As Aristotle says, ethics is concerned not just with knowing the good but in becoming good (*Nicomachean Ethics* II, 2, 1103b29). What is wrong with calling attention to important beliefs about the good and then encouraging oneself and others to work toward enacting those beliefs?

Well, one might retort, how do we know those beliefs are the right ones to enact? There are, after all, a variety of beliefs about the good and about right conduct. This is where the second understanding of ethics comes into play. It might be called critical ethics. It points out that moral beliefs, including scientific norms, are themselves socially and historically constructed. This forces us to challenge our beliefs. With a different history or social context would they be the same? The possibility of alternatives promotes philosophical work to transform belief into knowledge – classically defined as justified true belief – by reflection and criticism. We can appeal to Aristotle again here, who was all too aware of the challenge that perhaps moral beliefs "exist only by convention and not by nature" (*Nicomachean Ethics* I, 3; 1094b17).

Yet to recognize the challenge need not lead to relativism or a skeptical rejection and paralysis. To replace unquestioned beliefs by questioned and questionable ones can also give birth to efforts to appreciate and enact their salience in new ways. Existential uneasiness about the foundations of belief need not give rise to nihilism, although it will commonly replace aggressive certainty in commitment with more nuanced action. One way of living out beliefs is exchanged for another. In its questioning, philosophy can sponsor taking up the good with deeper courage. Doubt can be an antidote to fanaticism that nevertheless grounds its own convictions.

At the close of the nineteenth century, William James contrasted science with ethics along these lines. In science, there is no pressing need to act, so it is better to remain skeptical and not make up our minds than risk believing a falsehood. But "moral questions" often cannot wait for "sensible proof." Here it may be necessary to risk error and act rather than continue to reflect. Of course, the extent to which this science–ethics contrast still holds in the context of twenty-first-century "Big Science" is itself something that should give pause.

There is thus at the heart of this book a paradox about the phenomenon or experience of becoming good: the more one wants to be good, the more one finds it difficult – the recognition of which, if one avoids cynicism and despair, is precisely part of becoming good. In some measure, the paradox was discovered in the writing itself, as we were forced to face the difficulties of being good in and with science. Our desire to do so grew in proportion with our reflection on what this entails. It is a paradox learned rather than assumed, and one with a pedigree of learned ignorance that traces back to Socrates. Socrates never failed to ask questions.

To restate a point of importance: The practice of science or technoscience will depend on guiding ethical visions. The strength of these visions will depend, in turn, not solely on acceptance or affirmation but on reflective thinking, cogent argument, and informed judgment. The book in hand aspires to help cultivate these skills among people living today in a tangled web of ethics and science. To this end, *Ethics and Science: An Introduction* aspires

- to provide an informative (though necessarily selective) snapshot of emerging engagements in the co-construction of an ethical science, broadly construed;
- to promote critical reflection that brings science and its practices more deeply into the presence of ethics and philosophy; and
- to foster greater understanding, critical thinking, and open-minded dialogue among scientists and nonscientists alike, so as to contribute to a more self-aware and responsible democratic citizenry in a technoscientific age.

There are two near antecedents of this volume. One is the *Encyclopedia of Science, Technology, and Ethics*, a four-volume work edited by Mitcham with over 700 entries, many of which are obviously related to the present text. The other is Briggle's *A Rich Bioethics*, a monograph dealing in depth with one special aspect of the ethics–science relationship. Our collaboration began at one moment with the encyclopedia and on another, with early work that eventuated in the monograph. Briggle served as a research assistant on the encyclopedia; Mitcham was a member of the committee advising the dissertation that eventually became *A Rich Bioethics*. The fruitfulness of these endeavors led us to imagine collaboration on the present project.

A diversity of other articles and books also witness more extended origins. Over the course of the last decades both authors have ventured numerous discussions regarding science, technology, and ethics. No doubt arguments, ideas, and perhaps even phrases have been picked up from these other works – but with an effort to rethink and integrate them enough into the present volume that they do not require rigid citation.

Our initial idea was to do a monograph to bridge ethics, science, and technology. We continue to think such an interdisciplinary, synthetic book is needed. But after writing within that framework for two years it became too unwieldy. The result is that – given the intensity of an academic life overly blessed with opportunities for teaching, research, and service – we have worked on this project for more than five years, much longer than once anticipated. We credit the forbearance of Cambridge University Press as we worked our way slowly toward the volume in hand in the midst of many other activities and responsibilities.

This book has taken shape within a growing constellation of similar texts. Roughly, we see three types of books dealing with ethics and science:

- First, there are textbooks on specific aspects of ethics and science such as bioethics and research ethics. Construing science more broadly adds works on engineering ethics, computer ethics, environmental ethics, and more. Some of these, especially in the area of research ethics narrowly construed, are the product of commissions formed to draft reports, proposals, or curricula to promote ethics in science; others are anthologies.
- Second, there are extended monographic studies of particular cases and issues. A significant number of these deal at length with high-profile events. Examples include Gary Taubes' *Bad Science: The Short Life and Weird Times of Cold Fusion* (1993), Daniel Kevles' *The Baltimore Case: A Trial of Politics, Science, and Character* (1998), Eugenie Samuel Reich's *Plastic Fantastic: How the Biggest Fraud in Physics Shook the Scientific World* (2009), and Rebecca Skloot's *The Immortal Life of Henrietta Lacks* (2010).
- Third are more general analyses and arguments regarding the ethics of science or technoscience. This is a category with roots in the Enlightenment defense of modern science against religious or political control, but that began to take on new life and form in the twentieth century. Examples range from Henri Poincaré's *La valeur de la science* (1905) through Jacob Bronowski's *Science and Human Values* (1956), Everett Hall's *Modern Science and Human Values: A Study in the History of Ideas* (1956), and Hans Jonas's *The Imperative of Responsibility: In Search of an Ethics for the Technological Age* (1984) to Philip Kitcher's *Science, Truth, and Democracy* (2001).

Although the present book belongs primarily to the first category, more than most in that set it also incorporates perspectives from the second and third by placing research ethics in broad historical, sociological, and policy contexts. It considers responses to the challenges of scientific research as these have emerged in North America, Europe, and beyond - an especially important point given the increasingly global setting of scientific research and technological development. It regularly links science with its engineering and technological involvements, to the point of including a chapter on engineering ethics. It is also unique in its chapter on the place of science in culture and its chapter on attempts to give a scientific account of ethics.

Indicative of the importance we place on case studies, each chapter opens and closes with a case of some sort: initially to set the stage, finally to promote continuing reflection. These references to imaginative or real-world cases are designed to illustrate, in concrete fashion, the types of questions discussed in each chapter. References to the opening case are often woven into multiple sections of a chapter; end-of-chapter cases are designed at once to reflect back and to move reflection forward. At the ends of chapters there are also a few questions designed to stimulate further deliberation. All cases and questions can be further used as the basis for classroom discussions, quizzes, or research papers. The bibliography at the end of the book includes, for each chapter and case study, a few suggested texts we recommend for anyone wishing to learn more about the issues. Suggestions for Chapter 4 also include video and online resources that we have found helpful in teaching about the responsible conduct of research and research misconduct.

Chapters often cross-reference one another to lend coherence to the overall discussion. Yet each chapter is written so that it could be used independently. Chapters may thus be read in an order different than that in which they appear here. As explained in Chapter 1, chapters are also clustered in ways that suggest other use blocks.

One particular pedagogical practice we especially recommend is to make use of codes of ethics and other ethics declarations. The Appendix ("Ethics Codes") points readers to sixteen of the most influential codes and declarations. Ethics codes are sometimes frowned on by philosophers as simplifications that impede ethical reflection and by scientists as unnecessary. In a provocative study of medical and other procedural checklists, however,

Atul Gawande argues persuasively that clear directions and guidelines can improve performance of technoscientific tasks. Although Gawande does not extend his moral argument for checklists to include ethics checklists such as codes of conduct, the extension is easily made. In our experience, asking students to construct their own ethics codes or checklists can be a salutary conclusion to a class on ethics and science.

Another suggestive connection would be to link codes of conduct in the form of manifestos and constitutions with the formation of social movements. Ron Eyerman and Andrew Jamison, for instance, have argued for understanding social-movement behavior in terms of "cognitive praxis" – a term they use "to emphasize the creative role of consciousness and cognition in all human action, individual and collective."[1] The conscious articulation of codes of conduct can make its own contribution to such creativity.

For encouragement and assistance in writing *Ethics and Science* we first thank our students. Many chapters, sections, arguments, and ideas received trial runs in classes conducted at the Colorado School of Mines and the University of North Texas as well as in special classes and seminars at the University of Colorado, Boulder, University of Twente (Netherlands), Universidad Internacional Menéndez Pelayo and Universidad del País Vasco–Donostia/San Sebastian (Spain), European Graduate School (Switzerland), and Tshinghua University and Dalian University of Technology (China). Among scholar colleagues who have made special contributions through discussions or critical readings, the following deserve special recognition: Andoni Alonso, Thomas Boyd, Keith Brown, Sarah Fredericks, Robert Frodeman, Britt Holbrook, Thomas Kowall, Robert Mackey, René von Schomberg, Roel Snieder, and Katinka Waelbers. Douglas Dupler provided a critical reading of most chapters. Our copy editor James Thomas deserves further thanks. Doris Schroeder suggested the map metaphor in Chapter 2.

Finally, Hilary Gaskin, our editor at Cambridge University Press, has from start to finish exercised a strong guiding hand and contributed measurably to the character of the volume. In this age of too much self-edited electronic publishing, we are fortunate to have had an editor who worked with us at every step of the way to make the book better than it would have otherwise been.

[1] Eyerman and Jamison 1991, p. 3.

1 Introduction and overview

This book differs from many other introductions in philosophy, and even more so from those in science. It does not so much summarize existing knowledge – although it does some of that – as attempt to open a space for critical reflection on a spectrum of questions that were rarely asked until the late twentieth century. Philosophy and ethics deal with perennial questions, but here they are associated with new issues that nevertheless promise to become perennial in a world increasingly dependent on science and technology. By means of case references and interpretative arguments, the chapters that follow invite philosophical attention to the relationship between ethics and science, on the part of students and practitioners in the fields of both philosophy and science. The introductory chapter provides a quick intellectual geography of the terrain to be explored.

Setting the stage: the Manhattan Project

On August 2, 1939, Nobel Prize physicist Albert Einstein signed a letter (written by the Austro-Hungarian physicist Leó Szilárd) addressed to US President Franklin D. Roosevelt. The world's preeminent scientist felt a moral responsibility to inform the president of recent developments in nuclear physics. Scientific advances had raised the possibility of creating nuclear chain reactions that could unleash vast amounts of energy. This new knowledge might lead to the construction of bombs more powerful than any previously imagined, and Einstein concluded that Nazi Germany might already be pursuing such weapons. Roosevelt responded with an initial allocation of US$6,000 for preliminary research. This was the beginning of what became the "Manhattan Project," a massive, secret effort by the United States to build the atomic bomb. The project eventually employed 160,000 people working at centers in remote locations including Hanford, Washington; Knoxville, Tennessee; and Los Alamos, New Mexico. The push to build "the gadget" (as the scientist-engineers called it) was the most expensive research and development (R&D) project to that point in history.

Scientists and engineers overcame enormous challenges, and the first nuclear weapon exploded on July 16, 1945, over the desert sands near Alamogordo, New Mexico. Scarcely three weeks later, on August 6, 1945, the US *Enola Gay* bomber dropped "Little Boy" (a 90-kilogram uranium-239 device) on Hiroshima, Japan. Three days later another bomber dropped "Fat Man" (a plutonium bomb) on Nagasaki. Both cities had previously been spared attack and kept as "virgin targets" in order to test the devastating effects of the new weapons. The bombs leveled each city in turn, vaporized entire structures and human beings, burned thousands of people, and sowed radiation poisoning in flesh, water, and soil. Japan surrendered less than a week after the initial bombing. But radiation effects continued into the twenty-first century.

Upon viewing the test explosion the month before in New Mexico, J. Robert Oppenheimer, scientific director of the Manhattan project, quoted to himself, from the *Bhagavad Gita*, words spoken by the Hindu god Vishnu, "I am become death, destroyer of worlds."[1] He would later argue that as a result of their role in developing the atomic bomb, physicists had "known sin" and had a responsibility to educate the public about nuclear science. Indeed, many scientists associated with the Manhattan Project were appalled by the use of the bomb and wrestled morally with their degree of responsibility. Some created organizations such as the Emergency Committee of Atomic Scientists to lobby against the proliferation of nuclear weapons and to educate the public about the associated dangers. According to Einstein, "the unleashed power of the atom has changed everything," requiring a "new type of thinking" by humans. "We scientists who released this immense power have," he thought, "an overwhelming responsibility in this world life-and-death struggle to harness the atom for the benefit of mankind and not for humanity's destruction."[2] He also confessed that had he "known that the Germans would not succeed in producing an atomic bomb, [he] would never have lifted

[1] Rhodes 1986, p. 676. [2] Einstein 1968, p. 376.

a finger" to call the potential of the bomb to the attention of President Roosevelt.[3]

Other scientists and engineers continued to work on nuclear weapons, arguing that the weapons rendered their use too horrific to contemplate, thereby actually saving lives. Edward Teller, the "father of the hydrogen bomb," was especially vocal in defending nuclear weapons as a necessary deterrent to the Soviet Union, a totalitarian Communist state that after World War II had subjugated his home country of Hungary and threatened to invade the rest of Europe. Teller even went further, envisioning nuclear explosives as a means for pursuing such geoengineering projects as harbors in Alaska and a new canal between the Caribbean and Pacific. In the late 1950s, one of his scientific colleagues, Samuel Cohen, sought to turn the hydrogen bomb into a more clearly moral device by redesigning it as a "neutron bomb" that would kill people while minimizing destruction to buildings and physical property. As Cohen is quoted 50 years later in his obituary, the neutron bomb is "the only nuclear weapon in history that makes sense in waging war. When the war is over, the world is still intact."[4]

Soviet Premier Nikita Khrushchev, however, criticized the neutron bomb as one designed to "kill a man in such a way that his suit will not be stained with blood, in order to appropriate the suit."[5] US President Ronald Reagan, by contrast, accepted Cohen's argument and ordered production of 700 neutron weapons, although they were never deployed. Additionally, on the advice of Teller and others, Reagan established the Strategic Defense Initiative in the belief that technology could become a shield against ballistic missiles and protect the United States from nuclear attack.

By 1949, the Soviet Union had tested its first nuclear weapon and the world was locked in the Cold War. Recognizing how modern science and technology had come profoundly to influence global affairs and daily life, US President Dwight D. Eisenhower commented in his 1953 Inaugural Address:

> Man's power to achieve good or to inflict evil surpasses the brightest hopes and the sharpest fears of all ages. We can turn rivers in their courses, level mountains to the plains. Oceans and land and sky are avenues for our colossal commerce. Disease diminishes and life lengthens.

[3] "The Man Who Started It All," *Newsweek* (cover story), March 10, 1947. Cited in Isaacson 2007, p. 485.

[4] McFadden 2010, p. A35. [5] Shapiro 2010, n.p.

> Yet the promise of this life is imperiled by the very genius that has made it possible. Nations amass wealth. Labor sweats to create, and turns out devices to level not only mountains but also cities. Science seems ready to confer upon us, as its final gift, the power to erase human life from this planet.[6]

Beyond the issue of nuclear weapons, since the mid-twentieth century science has continued to expand the power of human beings to create and to destroy. On every continent, in the oceans, and even in outer space people now possess abilities to control and alter nature and human beings themselves to an extent unprecedented in history, through both intended and unintended consequences of advances in physics, chemistry, and biology. Such powers and the challenges they present make it incumbent on scientists and all citizens of contemporary society to bring ethics to bear in and on science.

Relations between ethics and science

It is common to think of science as objective and value neutral. If this is true, then ethics – as the systematic study of norms and values in human conduct – would seem to have only an external relationship to science. But the value neutrality of science is a myth that critical reflection readily challenges. Even as we assert the value neutrality of science, we often claim that science is a morally admirable enterprise that frees from superstition, discloses reality, speaks truth to power, and opens new pathways to material progress. Investments in science are justified by the goods science is alleged to bring, including not just knowledge but increased health and wealth, along with serving as a basis for better personal and public decision-making. Indeed, scientific knowledge is linked to moral imperatives for action. Once we know from science that smoking is harmful, is it not the case that there is an obligation to do something about personal behavior and public policy with regard to smoking?

Scientific knowledge is also often seen as an intrinsic good, valuable in its own right and as an expression of the human spirit of wonder

[6] "First Inaugural Address: Tuesday, January 20, 1953," Inaugural Addresses of the Presidents of the United States, Bartleby.com, 1989, www.bartleby.com/124/pres54.html.

and curiosity. Some see the practice of scientific inquiry as an activity that depends on and cultivates intellectual and moral virtues such as honesty, integrity, trust, fairness, perseverance, sound judgment, and open-mindedness. Ethical standards of right conduct are intrinsic to science (e.g., one must not fabricate or falsify data), making the canons of epistemological objectivity themselves constituents of an ethical ideal.

How can science be at once neutral and good? Perhaps it is good in one sense, precisely because it is neutral in another.

But why is it important for students of both philosophy and science to think critically about the relationships between ethics and science? In the first instance, this is simply because we live in a world that is increasingly distinguished by the presence and influence of science. To emphasize this point, consider seven often overlapping trends in science that invite ethical concern.

First trend: the increasing power of science

The first trend is the growing scale and power of science symbolized by the fiery, boiling mushroom clouds of atmospheric nuclear explosions. Indeed, we began with the Manhattan Project because this episode serves as a nodal point in cultural awakening to the profound ability of science to extend human power. Prior to the mid-twentieth century, science progressed with mostly celebration of its expanding powers because of the assumption that the new powers were always under the control of and proportionate to human understanding, which could be expected to use them wisely. By the end of World War II, however, suspicions began to arise that the powers of science might actually go beyond human abilities always to appreciate and manage them. It is one thing to understand and be concerned about the effects of science on a few people in the present. It is something else to understand and appreciate how new scientific powers might affect the planet or people thousands of years in the future. This suspicion about the powers of science becoming disproportionate to human capacities has only increased as science has (at the macro level) begun to consider geoengineering of the planet Earth and (at the micro level) to manage biological conception, reconfigure DNA, create hybrid organisms, and undertake the nano-scale designing of new materials. Can science so practiced continue to be thought of as proportionate to human understanding and control?

Second trend: threats and risks from science

Second, and connected with the growing power of science, has been an increasing awareness of its potential to generate knowledge with harmful implications and unintended consequences. Of course, tales about dangerous knowledge are as old as the stories of Prometheus and Adam and Eve. But by the last third of the twentieth century, the idea of dual-use knowledge of promise and risk began to pose real questions for the governance of science. As one dramatic example, nuclear science and engineering seem inextricably to enfold the potential benefits of nuclear electric power generation with the fearful risks of nuclear weapons, warfare, and accidents. In another example, in the 1960s Rachel Carson and other conscientious scientists deflated the utopian promises of "better living through chemistry" by connecting synthetic pesticides to biodiversity destruction, human illness, and environmental degradation.

In 1975, an international group of molecular biologists held a special conference at Asilomar, California, to draft new protocols for further work in the rapidly advancing field of recombinant DNA. The first instance of splicing genes into organisms raised not only hopes about improved drugs and crops, but also concerns about biohazards from biological weapons or super-organisms that escape control. Preceding the conference, in an unprecedented call for self-restraint, prominent scientists led by Paul Berg called for a temporary moratorium on such research. This trend has continued with concerns about R&D across a number of scientific fields, from information and computer science (enhanced communication linked with threats to privacy and cyberterrorism) and genetically modified foods (superfoods that undermine family farms or pose risks to health) to nanoscience and synthetic biology (new materials linked to threats of new toxins or even out-of-control self-replicating nano-bots). Can the potential goods of science ever be pursued without potential risks of harm? If not, how are risks to be controlled or managed and who should make such decisions?

Third trend: humans and animals as research subjects

A third trend fueling reflection on the ethical dimensions of science also had its origins in World War II. This pertains to the treatment of human subjects in research. Dr. Josef Mengele and other Nazi research physicians in Germany along with Japanese scientists in the infamous Unit 731 performed atrocious experiments on concentration camp inmates and prisoners of war, which included vivisection, research on the effects of hypoxia, nerve gas, freezing, high pressure, the ingestion of sea water, and more.

The immoral treatment of human subjects was not, however, confined to the Hitler and Tojo regimes. In the United States, biomedical researchers working in Tuskegee, Alabama, refrained for forty years (1932–72) from treating poor African-American men for syphilis in order to observe the long-term effects of the disease. Not until 1997 did President Bill Clinton make a formal apology for such treatment. Then in 2010 it was revealed that related US-sponsored human experiments had also been carried out on prisoners in Guatemala in the late 1940s.

Since the conclusion of the Doctors' Trial in Nuremberg in1947, numerous national and international bodies have drafted laws and guidelines to require the free and informed consent of human subjects of research. Indeed, in some cases the term "human participants" replaces that of "human subjects." Yet the interpretation and enforcement of these rules continue to pose ethical dilemmas, especially across cultural contexts. Additionally, since the mid-nineteenth century in England the use of nonhuman animals in scientific experimentation has sparked controversy about whether the benefits are sufficient to justify the animal suffering. The ability to replace some animal models with computer program models has only intensified this issue.

Fourth trend: scientific misconduct

A fourth trend is the continuing occurrence of scientific fraud and misconduct and questions about research integrity. This issue attracted prime-time publicity in the United States during the 1980s through several high-profile cases of misconduct, including fraudulent research on the treatment of mental retardation (by Stephen Breuning, University of Pittsburgh), disputes over credit for discovery of the AIDS virus (Luc Montagnier, Institute Pasteur, Paris, versus Robert Gallo, National Institutes of Health, Washington, DC), and allegations regarding data fabrication in the laboratory of Nobel Prize molecular biologist David Baltimore (of MIT and Rockefeller University). Government investigation of the third case, which was eventually judged not to be the fraud alleged, raised serious due-process issues of its own. Though numerous studies claim that the frequency of misconduct is low compared with other professions, instances of fabrication, falsification, and plagiarism (FFP) in science continue to grab headlines. They also pose difficult questions about how to define good science or the responsible conduct of research, adjudicate allegations of misconduct, treat whistle-blowers, and reduce instances of dishonest practices. Research misconduct threatens the integrity of science, undermining the trust essential to its operation and social value.

Fifth trend: commercializing science

A fifth trend is the increasing interdependence of science with business and industry. There is great potential here for good, as the resources and creativity of the private sector can foster beneficial research. But there are also dark sides to the "academic-industrial complex." Scientific values of free inquiry and open sharing can clash with corporate interests in protecting intellectual property for competitive advantage. Researchers working for private corporations often face scenarios where financial interests conflict with professional obligations. As public funding declines relative to private investments in many countries, questions arise as to whether nonmarket and common interest goods are adequately served by privately funded research. This can be especially problematic in developing countries, where opportunities for commercialization are often limited. Pharmaceutical companies naturally tend to invest in research on diseases that afflict the wealthy, who will be able to afford the resulting drugs. But this leaves underfunded research on malaria and other diseases that primarily afflict the poor. Moreover, when commercialization does occur in developing contexts it may unfairly exploit local people and resources.

Sixth trend: science in cultural and political controversies

Sixth, scientific methods, theories, and research often clash with other sets of ideas and values in multicultural societies. Historically, those who criticized some scientific claims – such as Christians who challenged heliocentric astronomy or biological evolution – did so in defense of traditional cultural beliefs that they saw as undermined by science, often claiming that science was overstepping its proper bounds. This argument has regularly been deployed to oppose an alleged tendency of scientific reductionism to weaken moral commitments. Indeed, the clash of civilizations that historian Samuel Huntington has used to characterize international affairs in the post-Cold War era could also be described as a clash between scientific and nonscientific cultures. Controversies surrounding embryonic stem cell research and prospects for human cloning, genetically modified organisms, the teaching of evolution in public schools, and global climate change are but the more prominent examples.

This trend can be broadened to include the entanglement of science and scientists in ethical and political controversies. Scientific advances often create "policy vacuums," or situations that demand choices. But the right path is seldom clear. For example, who should be allowed access to the information contained in an individual's genes? To what extent should the benefits of science be shared with "passive contributors" such as tissue donors or indigenous peoples whose practical knowledge is used in pharmaceutical development? Furthermore, public policy debates on everything from vaccinations to endangered species often pivot on claims about "what the science says." Determining precisely what science says can itself become a moral or political act of choosing which authorities to believe and how scientists convey levels of certainty and agreement to decision-makers or the public. Related questions surround the use of humanistic as well as traditional or indigenous forms of knowledge for public policy. On occasion, might certain ways of knowing other than scientific be appropriate guides for environmental, health, and other policies?

Seventh trend: science and technology

Finally, the atomic bomb aptly symbolizes a seventh trend, the increasing interdependence of science, engineering, and technology. Engineering and technology may in some sense be described as applied science; but science is also both applied and theoretical technology. Indeed, some claim the two realms are now so tightly coupled as to constitute a compound "technoscience" enrolled in socioeconomic innovation. Likewise, the distinction between nature (as studied by science) and material culture (constructed by technology, then studied by science) is increasingly replaced by the hybrid "nature–culture" (simultaneously studied and constructed).

Questions about ethics within scientific practice easily shade into questions about the ethical implications of the resulting products, both cognitive and material. This poses difficulties in thinking about the extent of their responsibilities for both scientists and engineers, with the two becoming increasingly difficult to disaggregate. For example, Hans Bethe – who led the theoretical physics division of the Manhattan Project – originally argued that scientific research should proceed even when it might be used for immoral purposes. It is only at the point of application, he contended, that people should debate whether to proceed, but "pure science" should not be stopped. Later in life, however, Bethe concluded that scientist-engineers had an obligation to cease further research on weapons that had proliferated beyond what he had originally imagined possible. A critical observer might wonder whether there is any bright line or easily controlled valve between research and application; science and application have perhaps become science–application and application–science. If so, how far do scientists' responsibilities extend?

Responses: professional, industrial, governmental

Uniting these trends is a common theme: science is such an integral and important part of society that it can no longer be – if ever it were – a refuge from ethical issues, challenges, and ambiguities. Reactions to this state of affairs have taken multiple forms. Across all disciplines, scientific institutions and societies have held conferences, produced publications, and drafted codes of conduct to bolster their capacities for self-governance. (For a selection of websites with ethics codes see the Appendix.) As one explicit manifestation of the relationship between science and ethics, we will often reference various codes of conduct throughout the book, beginning with the famous Nuremberg Code for the protection of human subjects in research.

The Nuremberg Code was imposed on science from outside. Other responses have come from within. In the mid-1970s, for instance, an American Association for the Advancement of Science (AAAS) Committee on Scientific Freedom and Responsibility recommended establishing a permanent committee of the same name to study "the general conditions required for scientific freedom and responsibility" and to respond to "specific instances in which scientific freedom is alleged to have been abridged ... or responsible scientific conduct is alleged to have been violated."[7] This committee has become part of a larger program on scientific responsibility, human rights, and law. Another example is the "Responsible Care" initiative launched in 1985 by the International Council of Chemical Associations. This program improves the health, safety, and environmental performance of the products created by chemists.

In one more instance, the US National Academy of Sciences, following a report on *Responsible Science* (1992), drafted the short textbook *On Being a Scientist*, which has now gone through multiple editions to become one of the most widely used resources for the ethics education of scientists. Additionally, governments have created numerous bioethics commissions in the United States and Europe that have served to stimulate reflection on issues related to medical research.

Still more responses have taken the form of state action oriented toward regulation and external oversight. Since the 1970s, countries throughout the world have created regulatory agencies to protect the environment. The 1970s also witnessed the awarding of grants by the US National Science Foundation (NSF) to support ethics and values research related to science and engineering. In the 1980s, the federally funded Human Genome Project set aside 3–5 percent of its budgets for consideration of ethical, legal, and social implications (in so-called ELSI grants) raised by genetic research. In 1990 the UK Human Fertilisation and Embryology Act set limits on the kinds of research that could be performed in privately as well as publicly funded biomedical science. In 1991 the European Commission established what has become the European Group on Ethics in Science and New Technologies and in 2010 published a *European Textbook on Ethics in Research*. In 2007 the US Congress extended to researchers funded by NSF a mandate for ethics education that had, since the 1980s, applied to all researchers funded by the National Institutes of Health.

As scientific research grows, it continues to influence our lives in surprising ways – sometimes hopeful, sometimes frightening, often ambivalent or unclear. There is thus an ongoing need for critical assessment of the relationship between science and society. Sometimes this has been framed as a need to move beyond an outdated "social contract" that grants the institutions of science support and autonomy in return for the many societal

[7] Edsall 1975, p. 687.

benefits research may yield. The justification is that these benefits (free from negative side effects) result automatically from the self-regulating knowledge market within science. But reality is far more complex. The years since Einstein's letter have witnessed a growing chorus of calls for increased accountability and oversight in the conduct of science. All such arguments must be cautiously measured in order to protect the status of science as an institution capable, at least ideally, of transcending politics and ideology to improve human lives - without allowing scientism to dominate or distort culture.

The way science is conducted and used and the magnitude and type of scientific research performed - research that holds increasingly important implications for society - are the result of choices. These choices present profound ethical questions: What ideals should inform the practice of science and for what reasons? How are these ideals best operationalized? Who should exercise authority or responsibility in and over scientific practices? How can progress in science be defined and measured in the context of broader ethical norms and social goals? Both individually and as a society, what research should we pursue and how? Is it sufficient to appeal to the pursuit of truth or curiosity as motives or to an "invisible guiding hand" that turns independent research programs to the common good? Or are scientists and nonscientists alike responsible for managing the link between research and social goals? Whose interests do, and should, research projects serve? How should conflicts between science and society be adjudicated? Are there some things we should not research and some aspects of life or existence that should not be manipulated?

In sum, human beings are in the midst of constructing a new world through science, technology, engineering, and medicine. This is taking place both in developed and developing countries - in Europe, the Americas, Australia, Asia, and Africa - among peoples in opposition and in dialogue with each other. The global governance of science manifests both collaborating and clashing cultures. The kind of world we create will be decided not simply by the expanding knowledge of science or the increasing powers of technology. It will depend more significantly on our visions, implicit or explicit, about good and bad, right and wrong, justice and injustice - and by our abilities to enact ideals in the face of limited knowledge and temptations to ease or arrogance. Effective vision will depend, in turn, on reflective thinking, cogent argument, and informed judgment.

This book aspires to contribute to the cultivation of informed thinking, argument, and judgment among philosophically reflective (and occasionally democratic) publics facing the tangled web of ethics and science. For such a citizenry, including citizen scientists, ethics is no longer just an option; it has become an obligation.

Course of the argument

Conceptually the book is divided into three sections. The first section, comprising this and the following two chapters, introduces the central phenomena of ethics and science. The following two sections explore interrelationships between these fundamental aspects of culture, selectively engaging the trends sketched above. Chapters 4, 5, and 6 (as the second section) focus on the "society of science" – the standards of practice internal to science, influences on their origins, and how they sometimes break down. Chapter 7 functions as an appendix to this discussion. After a transitional Chapter 8, Chapters 9 through 12 (as the third section) focus on "science in society" – exploring ethical issues at the interfaces of scientific and nonscientific practices, institutions, and ideals. This section is further divided into discussions about science and politics (Chapters 9 and 10), science and culture (Chapter 11), and science, engineering, and technology (Chapter 12).

We nevertheless chose not to explicitly partition the chapters, because such separations would inevitably suggest a greater degree of distinction than really exists. For example, although we need to begin with working definitions of ethics and science, these terms should remain open for adjustment throughout the book. Furthermore, there is too much overlap between science and society to rest comfortably with sections pretending to deal solely with the internal or external governance of science. The ethics of research, especially on humans and animals, is critical to, but transcends, the boundaries of science. Indeed, in sparking media attention and government regulation, human and animal research has made the ostensible boundaries for the society of science quite porous. External influences on science – such as regulations or engineered instrumentations – can become constitutive of the internal workings of science, just as the internal structures of science can influence societies in which science is practiced. Although these divisions are useful heuristics for structuring discussion, they are ultimately too artificial and fragile to warrant any stronger status. Having provided a sense of overarching themes and structure, it is appropriate briefly to summarize the flow of argument in more detail.

Chapter 2. Ethical concepts and theories

The challenge throughout will be to promote critical thinking about ideals for individual and group conduct. In short, the aim is to do ethics in contexts created or influenced by science. Ethics or moral philosophy is a systematic effort to reflect on the virtues and vices in agents, rightness or wrongness of actions, and goodness or badness in results or states of affairs, to promote both deepened understanding and better action. In this sense, ethics is like science itself, which aspires to understand the world in a manner that may also transform our way of being in the world. Chapter 2 emphasizes those normative concepts and theories most pertinent to discussions of ethics and science. The basics are treated somewhat pragmatically as tools that aid in the thinking of evaluative judgments in relation to science. The chapter highlights relations between ethics and convention, historical moments in the relationships between ethics and science, the special character of moral knowledge, and three major ethical theories with their implications for science. In keeping with the pragmatic approach, the normative theories are treated as maps, each highlighting different layers of the moral landscape and thus each useful in different contexts.

Chapter 3. Science and its norms

Science is a process or method, a human activity and social institution, as well as a set of theories and knowledge. Chapter 3 emphasizes what might be termed idealized descriptive ethics. It concerns the norms of science in a general sense – as these have developed historically and become implicitly constitutive of science as a knowledge-producing activity. It reviews the historical and philosophical roots of science in the emergence of natural philosophy as distinct from myth. It then proceeds to examine the importance of the institutionalization of science in the early modern period. The last sections survey the epistemological and social norms that appear to be intrinsic to the conduct of science, as these have been explicated by sociologists of science and scientists themselves.

Chapter 4. Research ethics I: responsible conduct

To what extent are scientists really living up to the normative ideals they appear to espouse? Why and how might they do better? Addressing such questions, Chapter 4 considers the adequacy of the idealized norms in science – adequacy in both descriptive and prescriptive senses. The outcome is a review of efforts within science to articulate its ideals, recognize those circumstances in which they fail to be enacted, and develop ways to more effectively enjoin their practice. To this end, it briefly surveys a suite of cases of research misconduct ranging from physics through biomedical and environmental science to psychology, anthropology, and other social sciences – from the mid-1800s to the early 2000s. These short case studies call attention to a spectrum of questionable research practices across the flow of research, from anticipating to practicing and disseminating science. Each phase in the research spectrum manifests important ethical issues faced by scientists, from conflicts of interest, data management, and biases, to trust, peer review, authorship, and the allocation of credit. The chapter also discusses the globalizing context of research. In sum, it identifies the basics of all good science or the responsible conduct of research, which is what mostly concerns scientists themselves when they talk about research ethics.

Chapter 5. Research ethics II: science involving humans

A second basic set of issues that arise in discussions of ethics within the society of science concerns the treatment of human subjects. No ethical issue has sparked more controversy or had greater influence on research conduct than experimentation on humans. Chapter 5 opens with a description of the most common type of human experimentation, namely, clinical drug trials. It then provides a historical survey of landmark cases, highlighting the problematics of human subjects research and the almost inevitable clash between ethical standards in science and in the societies in which science exists. The chapter pays particular attention to the rise of the principle of free and informed consent, the establishment of related protocols, and difficulties in their application. Special challenges arise when efforts are made to take standards of free and informed consent, originally developed for adults participating in biomedical research in a European context, and extend them to research on children, on vulnerable populations, and in diverse cultures. Globalization presents special puzzles for this critical dimension of research ethics.

Chapter 6. Research ethics III: science involving animals

This chapter turns to related questions raised by experiments on non-human animals, including whether such experimentation is useful or justified, and whether different ethical principles might apply to different types of animals. It situates animal research broadly in relation to animal treatment in other contexts, from farms to wildlife preserves, and offers a historical survey of key moments in the development of scientific attitudes toward animals and their use in science. Another section compares three ways to think about the moral status of animals: whether animals deserve moral consideration because they are capable of feeling pain (sentience), experiencing subjects of a life (purposiveness), or fellow creatures constituted by relational bonds (shared narratives). A concluding section reflects on three normative principles of animal research – Replace, Reduce, and Refine (also known as the 3Rs).

Chapter 7. The science of ethics

Chapters 4, 5, and 6 constitute the core of most discussions concerning good science and responsible conduct in the society of science. But just as ethics has been brought to bear on science, so science has been used to try to understand ethics. In a supplement to the three core chapters, Chapter 7 reviews various efforts to complement the promotion of ethics in scientific research with scientific research on ethics – that is, attempts to explain ethical principles by using sciences such as game theory, psychology, neuroscience, and evolutionary biology. Whether and to what extent such scientific understandings of ethics can facilitate good science and the responsible conduct of research are topics conspicuous by their absence in most attempts to address issues in the ethics of science.

Chapter 8. Transition: from ethics to politics and policy

Traditionally, textbooks on the ethics of science have focused almost exclusively on the kinds of procedural issues addressed in Chapters 4 through 6. This suggests that the ethics of science begins and ends with the delivery of a product that is quality-controlled by scientific peers and intellectually sound. Seen through this frame the pursuit of good science only captures conduct within the society of science and not the relationship of science to the larger society. Yet in an age that is demanding accountability from science, Chapter 8 considers the extent to which scientists must not only police their own intellectual integrity, but also monitor and assess their roles in contributing to societal goods and goals. The chapter argues for the importance of thinking about the broader social and political implications of science, which then forms the substance of the remaining chapters.

Chapter 9. Science and politics I: policy for science

Following the transition, Chapter 9 focuses on ethical issues related to policies for the promotion, practice, and regulation of science. It begins with a debate between those who argue that scientists should be free to pursue knowledge with minimal external interference and those who affirm a need for some measure of external social control over science. Given the expense of social investments in science and the ethical problems often associated with science, the latter position is in ascendance, although not among scientists. This leaves unsettled questions about how and how much to manage the various practices of science. Chapter 9 considers, for instance, the ethics of science budgets and issues such as intellectual property rights, the democratization of science, and policies that would integrate ethics education into scientific training.

Chapter 10. Science and politics II: science for policy

In a democracy, elected officials have – or are at least commonly expected to have – a moral responsibility to base decisions on sound principles and warranted evidence. What counts as sound principles and warranted evidence, however, can vary widely; and different principles can sometimes call for turning to different kinds of evidence. Religious traditions, for instance, may invoke the principle of appeal to scripture or institutional authority. Yet in a wide variety of situations, governments claim to rely on science to inform and legitimize policy decisions on issues ranging from food and drug regulation to natural resource management. When this happens, scientific uncertainty and disagreement can cause political gridlock. What ethical guidance can be provided for scientists when called on to inform public policies? What roles should scientists - as experts in a democracy - play in policy formation? How should uncertainty be communicated and managed, and how do norms embedded in research design affect policy decisions based on the science? Who should speak as the authoritative voice of science and what role should "lay experts" play? Chapter 10 also touches on the politicization of science, the scientization of politics, and the use of science in courtrooms and by the media and the military.

Chapter 11. Science and ideational culture

Beyond politics and practical culture, science has enormous ethical implications for ideational culture or the human lifeworld of experience and ideas. Science directly impacts the beliefs, values, and identities of individuals, especially through the social institutions of formal education. What science does and should mean for culture is often controversial. Examples of such debates include the human meaning of the theories of evolution and relativity and whether physicochemical causation counts against free will. Such discussions pose questions about the proper relationship between scientists and the media and how individuals should interpret and use science. Chapter 11 identifies four basic ways of conceiving and evaluating the relationship between modern science and other aspects of culture: independence, conflict, dialogue, and integration.

Chapter 12. Science applied: ethics and engineering

Science and technology are increasingly linked, especially through the practices of engineering and design. Indeed, it is the scientific nature of modern engineering that distinguishes it from craft or trial-and-error making. Thus the ethics of engineers and scientists are tightly coupled, even though the social separation of these two professional communities means the two subjects are seldom pursed in tandem. As a natural complement to any discussion of ethics and science, Chapter 12 surveys the history of ideals in engineering ethics, discusses influential cases, and considers perspectives from a variety of countries. It concludes with remarks on the role of ethics in design processes such as those related to computer programs and argues for a special imperative for engineers to "take more into account" – an imperative that can serve as a general obligation in science as well.

As the outline indicates, the book covers diverse ground, from internal conduct in the society of science to the interfaces between science, politics, culture, and technology. Uniting these various considerations are certain fundamental ethical themes: the proper roles of scientists and science in society, the kinds of science deserving public or private sector support, how science should be conducted, and who should have which responsibilities in making different decisions. Throughout, the goal is to raise and initiate critical reflection on the most important issues, without claiming to exhaust their complexity or reach consensus with regard to appropriate responses. No introductory text can be fully comprehensive; *Ethics and Science* nevertheless aspires to stimulate exploration and to provide orientation in an expansive intellectual geography.

Extending reflection: scientific controversies and the Nobel Prize

Since 1901, the Nobel Prize (established by the Swedish chemist and inventor of dynamite, Alfred Nobel) has been awarded annually to those who have made outstanding achievements in the fields of physics, chemistry, and physiology or medicine. As the most prestigious award in those fields, it is highly scrutinized and often becomes the center of criticisms and controversies. Surveying some of these incidents provides an indication of the breadth of issues that will be encountered throughout the chapters that follow.

Reminiscent of the questions raised by the Manhattan Project, some Nobel Prize controversies have been about the link between science and war and the responsibility of scientists for the social uses of their work. The 1918 Nobel Prize in Chemistry, for instance, was awarded to the

German chemist Fritz Haber for his research on synthesizing ammonia, a process important for developing fertilizers and bombs. Haber's prize was controversial, because during World War I he had partnered with German chemical companies to develop methods for deploying chlorine gas against enemy soldiers. Indeed, many considered Haber to be the "father of chemical warfare."[8]

Other controversies have hinged on disputes over priority in discovery. For example, in 1903, the Nobel Prize in Physics was awarded to the French physicist Henri Becquerel (with Pierre and Marie Curie) "in recognition of the extraordinary services he has rendered by his discovery of spontaneous radioactivity." Yet some scientists maintained that Becquerel had only rediscovered a phenomenon that the French photographic inventor Claude Félix Abel Niépce de Saint-Victor had investigated much earlier. The 1945 Nobel Prize in Physiology or Medicine was awarded to Alexander Fleming for isolating the active antibacterial substance, which he named penicillin, from the *Penicillium* mold. Yet some claimed that this too was a rediscovery, and that others had much earlier documented the medicinal properties of the mold. Additionally, with this award several contemporaneous researchers doing similar work were left unrecognized. This case suggests that the moment of a scientific discovery is often hard to pinpoint, given the collective and cumulative nature of scientific research.

Still other controversies have hinged on questions about appropriate scientific procedures. The American experimental physicist Robert Millikan was awarded the 1923 Nobel Prize in Physics for measuring the charge on the electron and for his work on the photoelectric effect. Controversy still lingers about his oil-drop procedure and selective use of data. Some contend that Millikan claimed he had reported all of his observations when in fact he omitted data from his final paper. As another case in point, the Austrian zoologist Karl von Frisch shared the 1973 Nobel Prize in Physiology or Medicine for his explanation of the "dance language" of bees. But von Frisch's theory was never tested directly, which led some to question it and propose alternative explanations. Over thirty years later, however, research performed with radar vindicated von Frisch's theory about dancing as a complex form of communication between bees.

[8] See Haber 1986.

Perhaps both Millikan's and von Frisch's prizes were awarded too early. Even though they later proved to be right, questions remained at the time about the integrity and adequacy of their methods and validity of their theories. Another controversy surrounded a case where the Nobel Prize recipient was quickly proven wrong. The 1962 Nobel Prize in Physiology or Medicine went to the Danish scientist and physician Johannes Andreas Grib Fibiger for his alleged discovery of a microbial parasite that Fibiger claimed was the cause of cancer. His finding that cancer is a communicable disease was soon discredited by other scientists, but it was never suggested that his prize be rescinded or returned.

Another controversy highlights scientific competitions and conflicts of interests in the commercialization of science. The 2008 Nobel Prize in Physiology or Medicine was awarded jointly to the French team of Luc Montagnier and Françoise Barré-Sinoussi for identifying the virus that causes AIDS and to the German virologist Harald zur Hausen for work on the link between cancer and the human papillomavirus (HPV). The AIDS virus award excluded the American Robert Gallo, who in the 1980s had been accused of improperly acquiring samples from Montagnier's laboratory, although the charge was later dropped. The HPV award raised a different issue: the pharmaceutical and biologics company AstraZeneca had sponsored Nobel Media and Nobel Web (which manage the official Nobel Prize media portfolio). This caused the Swedish police anticorruption unit to investigate zur Hausen's prize, since AstraZeneca held a stake in two HPV vaccines and thus stood to gain financially from the prize. Two senior members in the process that chose zur Hausen as the Nobel Prize recipient also had strong ties to AstraZeneca.

Questions for research and discussion

1. Is there any scientific research that should be restricted or even banned on principle? Why or why not? More generally, are there any societal values that justifiably limit the quest for knowledge?
2. What is the relationship between concerns for integrity in science and the dangers of science (as exemplified by the Manhattan Project)? How can misconduct in science threaten to harm society and not just science itself?

3. Are there differences between ethics in science, ethics in engineering, ethics in legal practice, and ethics in medicine? If so, how might they be described and how important are they?
4. What constitutes a conflict of interest for scientific researchers? How common are cases like that of zur Hausen, the Nobel selection process, and AstraZeneca?

Further reading about the cases

Feldman, Burton (2001) *The Nobel Prize: A History of Genius, Controversy, and Prestige*. New York: Arcade.

Hewlett, Richard G., and Oscar E. Anderson Jr. (1962) *The New World: A History of the United States Atomic Energy Commission, Volume 1: 1939–1946*. University Park: Pennsylvania State University Press.

Kelly, Cynthia C., ed. (2007) *The Manhattan Project: The Birth of the Atomic Bomb in the Words of Its Creators, Eyewitnesses and Historians*. New York: Black Dog and Leventhal.

2 Ethical concepts and theories

Following the Chapter 1 high-altitude overview of the whole terrain to be covered, Chapter 2 begins with an inventory of key concepts and theories. This is not a book focused primarily on theory. But concepts indicate a geological-like foundation for thinking important distinctions in the landscape, while theories function like maps, which can call attention to different features in a geography – features which might otherwise be overlooked or obscured. Political maps reveal jurisdictional boundaries, road maps help navigate driving distances, and "worldmapper cartograms" can resize images to give abstract phenomena graphic representation. Consider, for instance, the maps in Figures 1 and 2.

The land area map provides one perspective on the world, the population map another. Each may be described as a theory of, or way of looking at, the world. Indeed, the word "theory" comes from the Greek *theorein*, to look at or observe. Theories are ways of observing our experience. Like spectacles or glasses, ethical concepts and theories assist us in seeing the world in which we live – although they can on occasion also distort it.

Following the Chapter 2 introduction to ethical theory, Chapter 3 describes the normative cartography of scientific practice as presented in social science theory. This complement to ethical theory analyzes the morality often deemed by scientists as essential to their identity and practice. Together, these two opening chapters prepare the way for critical reflection on the core areas of research ethics, which are explored in more detail by Chapters 4, 5, and 6.

Setting the stage: the miracle drug thalidomide

William McBride was growing increasingly concerned. The young Australian obstetrician had delivered several babies with malformed or

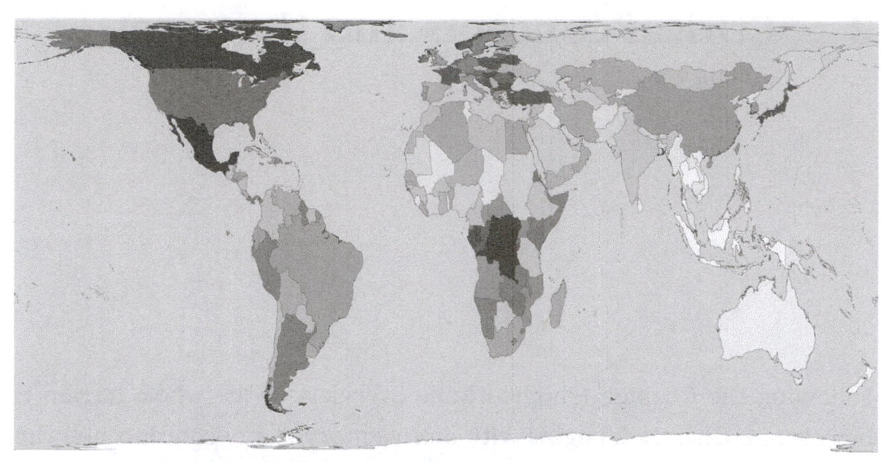

Figure 2.1 *World map sized to represent land areas of the various countries (as of 2000). © Copyright SASI Group (University of Sheffield) and Mark Newman (University of Michigan)*

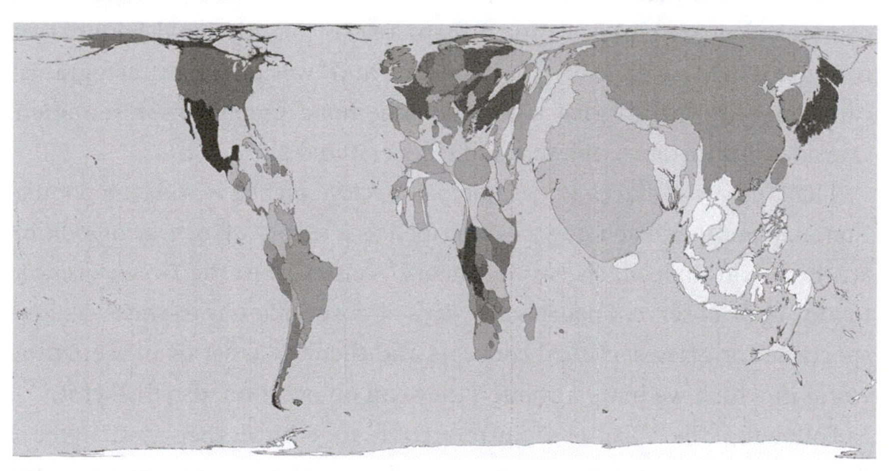

Figure 2.2 *World map sized to represent populations of the various countries (as of 2002). © Copyright SASI Group (University of Sheffield) and Mark Newman (University of Michigan)*

missing limbs. Indeed, for the past few years thousands of babies in over forty other countries had been born with similar birth defects. What was causing the deformities? Doctors and scientists hypothesized the culprit as a new virus or radioactivity from nuclear weapons testing and atomic reactors. But in 1961, McBride examined the medical records of three patients with deformed babies and discovered they had all taken thalidomide early in pregnancy.

Thalidomide is a sedative-hypnotic drug discovered accidentally in 1954 by chemists working at a German pharmaceutical firm. It was widely used beginning in 1957 for a variety of minor symptoms, including the "morning sickness" nausea often experienced by pregnant women. Further research by the German scientist Widukind Lenz found the deformities to be a direct consequence of thalidomide use in early pregnancy.

The drug was withdrawn from use in 1962, but by then over 8,000 children had been harmed. In the United States, thalidomide was not widely available due to the valiant efforts of Frances Kelsey, a Food and Drug Administration (FDA) examiner, whose suspicions about the drug led her to repeatedly reject applications to market it. Despite pressure from the drug manufacturer, Kelsey insisted on additional testing to explain some puzzling results from research and a study that linked thalidomide to a nervous system side effect. Even with repeated appeals to Kelsey's superiors, the Merrell Company was unable to sway her or the FDA. For modeling courage, judgment, and integrity in the service of public safety, Kelsey received the prestigious President's Award for Distinguished Federal Civilian Service.

Many countries responded to the thalidomide tragedy by creating more stringent regulations for the development, testing, prescription, and sale of drugs. In the US, for example, the 1962 Kefauver-Harris Amendment put the burden on drug companies to demonstrate safety and efficacy, required informed consent from patients in clinical trials, and introduced a much more exacting drug review process. It required that drugs be tested for potential teratogenic (birth-defect-causing) properties and eliminated the prescription of experimental drugs while approval for marketing was still pending (a practice that led to some birth defects in the US from thalidomide).

As a result of these new laws, drug regulations are now often criticized for their glacial pace – wasting valuable time before potentially life-saving pharmaceuticals can be used. In the case of thalidomide, simply prohibiting use in all circumstances also proved problematic. Although a relatively simple molecule, thalidomide has a surprising range of biological effects; some are harmful, others beneficial, often depending on context. As the story of thalidomide continued, it posed the question of whether and how compounds with dangerous side effects still can be used therapeutically with appropriate controls and precautions.

Around 5 percent of leprosy patients develop painful skin lesions as part of an immune response to the bacterial infection. Three years after it was taken off the market in 1965, Jacob Cheskin found some old bottles of thalidomide and gave it to a few patients at his clinic in Jerusalem in an attempt to ease their suffering. Surprisingly the drug worked therapeutically to eliminate the skin lesions. Extending Cheskin's experience, over the next few decades thalidomide was discovered to be effective in treating Behcet's disease (an autoimmune condition causing ulcers of the mouth and genitals), multiple sclerosis, and some cancers such as multiple myeloma. As a result, in 1998 the FDA approved the application of Celgene to market thalidomide for treatment of leprosy, while research continued on other potential therapeutic applications and ways to modify the drug to eliminate some negative side effects, which in cancer treatment include neuropathy or tingling in fingers and toes.

This has brought renewed pressures to make thalidomide more widely available. But regulators must take into account the teratogenicity of the drug when crafting policies. This became apparent in Brazil, where in the 1970s and 1980s a new generation of deformed children was born. Pregnant women were taking thalidomide without understanding the risks. Many were illiterate and thus could not read the warning labels. Seeking to avoid this situation, the FDA exercised extreme precaution, requiring that only doctors registered with an educational program be allowed to prescribe thalidomide. As of the early 2000s, its decision to license the drug had not led to any birth defects in the United States.

But risk can never be eliminated. The question of thalidomide remains: How can society best wield this double-edged sword? It is in many respects the same question raised by the Manhattan Project, since nuclear fission too can be used both to make atomic bombs and to generate electricity. When we praise the research of McBride, Cheskin, and others, what precisely is it that is being honored? The results of their work? The actions themselves? Or the researchers as persons?

Distinctions and definitions

Although circumstances limit their options, human beings regularly face choices. Having to make choices is a basic feature of the human condition and a precondition for ethics. If all action were determined by instinct or reflex – if no one could choose otherwise – then there would be no sense to discussions of how things should be different or attempts at reflective decision-making. There could be no moral agency or responsibility for being virtuous, acting right, or realizing good outcomes.

Many versus few

Many choices are, of course, trivial or easy. We make them every day. Examples include deciding what to eat for breakfast or which clothes to wear. Others are difficult, because they are made in response to serious dilemmas or because of the uncertainties associated with the choices themselves. There are fewer of these, but they engage human existence in multiple ways. Dr. Kelsey found herself in one such situation: Should she grant or reject the application for FDA approval of thalidomide? How many tests is it reasonable to require before taking action? Where does the burden of proof lie – with regulators to prove risk or with manufacturers to guarantee safety? What evidence is sufficient to satisfy safety concerns?

Dr. Kelsey herself is also among the few in any society who, because of having to face such issues, receive education to help address them. Although everyone practices some kind of morality in making important choices for themselves, not everyone is called to think about these things in any systematic manner. In a general sense we can distinguish between the many (not deeply involved with ethics) and the few (seriously involved) in terms of both decisions and people. The few people involved with ethics in a serious and extended manner are sometimes called intellectuals, thinkers, scholars, or philosophers. Scientists (including medical scientists) are intellectuals of this type who, along with their technical knowledge and skills, are also often called on to think ethically about their work.

Ethics or moral philosophy aims to help everyone but especially intellectuals think through serious choices and arrive at sound, although often provisional, judgments. It concerns judgments as to the rightness or wrongness of actions, goodness or badness of results or states of affairs, and the virtues and vices of agents. Ethics poses the fundamental questions: How should we live? What is the right thing to do? Though ethics will never dispel the difficulties and anguish of moral dilemmas, it can provide useful tools for learning to live with the burdens of the human condition. It supplies a normative vocabulary and a grammar, assisting in the framing of problems and formulating of moral standards. These in turn are useful for evaluating options and for articulating and critiquing moral intuitions. The present chapter introduces ethics in this sense, beginning with some definitions and distinctions.

From convention to ethics

One important distinction is between convention (what people *do* value) and ethics (reflection on what people *should* value). Convention pertains to the customs, manners, habits, cultures, and laws of a group of people (their *ethos* or *mores*). It is a descriptive matter of how people behave and what people believe. By contrast, ethics is a normative matter of critically reflecting on conventions and articulating reasons about how people should behave and what they ought to believe. For example, slavery or the incarceration of peoples based on their religious beliefs or sexual orientation may be legal in some societies (part of their conventions), but this does not make such practices morally right. The drug regulation process prior to 1962 was part of social convention, but in light of the thalidomide disaster it was subjected to ethical criticism for being too lax – just as current processes are sometimes criticized for being too stringent. To be ethical is not simply to do what one is told or to conform to the ways of one's group. Ethics concerns the reasons for and against the conventions of a society. It demands thinking, not conformity.

The careful articulation of convention is called descriptive ethics. Such description is necessary, because it is not always easy to know what people believe. For instance, people sometimes say they think one thing (e.g., they want to protect the environment) but behave differently (e.g., they purchase polluting products). There is a difference between expressed and revealed preferences or beliefs. In contrast to descriptive ethics, metaethics involves analysis of the meanings of central terms in ethics such as "justice," "virtue," and "obligation." It examines the logic of moral reasoning. A third type of ethics, normative ethics, is the attempt to formulate and defend basic understandings of the good, principles of right conduct, and the character of virtue. This is the kind of ethics that articulates reasons for what people should do and what they ought to believe.

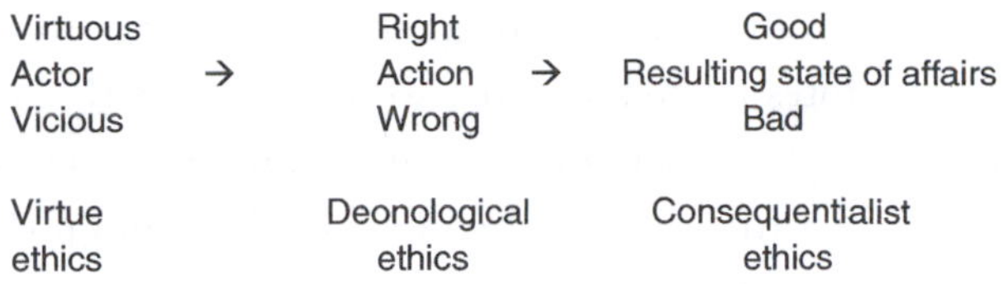

Virtuous		Right		Good
Actor	→	Action	→	Resulting state of affairs
Vicious		Wrong		Bad
Virtue ethics		Deonological ethics		Consequentialist ethics

Figure 2.3 *Graphic illustration of relations among three normative ethical theories*

Much of normative ethics consists of theories about what makes persons, states of affairs, and actions, virtuous or vicious, good or bad, and right or wrong. There are three main ethical theories. Virtue ethics emphasizes the character of persons who perform actions, that is, actors or agents. Consequentialism stresses the goodness or badness of states of affairs that result from actions. Deontology emphasizes the intrinsic rightness or wrongness of actions themselves. Figure 2.3 provides a simple illustration of relations among these three basic ethical theories.

Normative ethics and politics

A key distinction within normative ethics is between theoretical and applied ethics, where the latter draws on the resources of the former to identify morally appropriate courses of action within a given context. Many fields of applied ethics – such as bioethics, computer ethics, environmental ethics, and research ethics – focus on ethical issues raised by science and technology. The relationship between theory and contextual practices in ethics is contested. Some prefer the term "practical ethics," arguing that moral reasoning is not as simple as "applying" principles or methods in a deductive fashion. Others defend casuistry, a case-based form of moral reasoning that begins with the particulars of context rather than with a predetermined theory. These all could be thought of as simply pointing out different ways to use maps: using them as guides for travel, as graphics that are continuously being drawn to help us remember the richness of a trip we are taking, or as lots of small maps that are being examined and fitted together like pieces of a puzzle as the trip unfolds.

Finally, it is common to distinguish between ethics, pertaining to the conduct of individuals, and politics, pertaining to the action of groups or social institutions. Moral and political philosophy are not easily disentangled. Because humans are social beings, questions for individuals about living well and acting rightly are ultimately inseparable from questions about what constitutes a good and just social order. As the opening case demonstrates, the well-being of mothers and their children is inextricable from the institutions that develop, market, regulate, and prescribe pharmaceuticals. More generally, questions about apportioning responsibility to individuals or institutions, how much and what kinds of science should be funded, or how scientists ought to relate to policymakers are simultaneously ethical and political. Later chapters thus treat politics and policy matters as deeply implicated in ethics. The balance of this chapter, however, surveys the historical coevolution of ethics and science, examines the metaethical quandary about the possibility of moral knowledge, and then focuses on three basic normative ethical theories.

Ethics and science: a brief relational history

The history of philosophy developing out of the European tradition is customarily divided into classical, medieval, and modern periods. From the perspective of ethics and science, this can be simplified further as follows.

A science of ethics among the Greeks

According to the philosophers of classical Greece (*c.*400–300 BCE), ethics is a science – a science focused on human affairs. It is also a technique, because we study ethics not simply to know, but also to become, good. Ethics rejects both authority and custom as sufficient sources of moral guidance. The systematic or scientific use of reason is necessary to acquire the knowledge to distinguish between what people *do* value and what they *should* value.

By the time Socrates was conversing with fellow Athenians in the agora, increased travel was raising awareness of other cultures. This situation acted – in a manner similar to contemporary globalization – to challenge traditional conventions. People began to either assert that their conventions were the only truly human ones ("Greeks are humans, all others are barbarians") or to believe that all conventions are relative ("When in Rome, do as the Romans do"). In light of increasing knowledge about alternative conventions people began to doubt that convention is ever rational: either convention has to be asserted with a strong will or people are free to do whatever they can get away with.

The two responses of willfully asserting the truth of one's own conventional values or simply accepting the absence of any true values are two kinds of nihilism or the denial of any transconventional sense of the good. The former has been described as active nihilism, the latter as passive nihilism. But in opposition to the responses of active and passive nihilism, it is also possible to consider whether the differences between cultural conventions might not be exactly what they appear to be. Instead of succumbing to nihilism, it is possible to seek clarification about whether the conventional disagreements are real or only apparent, and if real then trying to determine the correct belief. Often disagreements are superficial, as when one person says the Moon is made of dirt and another that it is made of rock; both may mean to imply the same thing, that there is no water on the Moon. But if a disagreement is real, because one claim is that the Moon is made of cheese and another is that it is made of rock, then we are naturally stimulated to try to identify the correct belief. Disagreement can be the beginning of philosophical ethics, not its termination; it can lead to both conceptual clarification and substantive argument. So Socrates faced a question: Each society appeared to have its own conventions, but insofar as the conventions really differ, which are best? Is there some standard underlying all conventions that can be used to assess them?

This question prompted Aristotle to argue that philosophical ethics begins once knowledge about conventions is replaced with knowledge about nature. Unlike convention, nature does not vary. Although Greeks speak a different language than the Persians, fire burns in Greece the same way as in Persia. According to Aristotle, the study of natures, as the distinguishing functional features of entities that do not vary from place to place, provides insight into how things are and in some cases to how they might be better or good. Fire produces heat, so simply as fire it would seem that the best fire produces the most heat. When it comes to living things, what Aristotle called their *teloi* (plural of *telos*) or ends become even more significant. The *telos* of an acorn is to grow up into an oak tree, so a good acorn is one that has not been so deformed that it cannot produce a tree. When a living entity performs some function well so as to realize a *telos*, this is called its *arete* or virtue. The nature of a thing is both descriptive and prescriptive – identifying what it is (*telos*) and what it means for it to flourish (virtue).

In the Roman adaptation of the traditional science of ethics, the four cardinal (or most important) virtues are *fortitudo* (courage), *temperantia* (moderation), *prudentia* (practical wisdom), and *iustitia* (justice). All such virtues were further understood to be guidelines for how to act in harmony with the order of nature – or what would later be called natural law.

There are, however, problems with this teleological approach to ethics. Sometimes things appear to have multiple *teloi*. The acorn both grows up into an oak tree and provides food for squirrels. But the first is internal to the acorn, the second external. The Aristotelian approach is to privilege the internal over the external, since without the internal *telos* the external one would not be possible. Virtues lead to the flourishing of entities in themselves and make it possible for them to become part of or fit in with larger contexts. Without oak trees squirrels would run out of food.

In the case of humans, there appear to be multiple internal *teloi*. Some humans function as farmers, others as politicians and soldiers, still others as scientists and philosophers. How does one assess these alternative human *teloi* of pursuing physical well-being, social recognition and honor, and knowledge – along with their associated virtues? Although farmers are necessary to support politicians and philosophers, there is another sense in which philosophers are superior to farmers. Philosophers can understand the lives of farmers, while to farmers the lives of philosophers may look irrational if not worthless. On a physical basis, farming is superior to philosophy, but on a cognitive basis philosophy is a higher *telos* than farming. Additionally, philosophy or rationality is something that appears to separate humans from other animals more than providing food or social engagements. By means of such multiple arguments, Aristotelian science seeks to respond to the knowledge of variation in conventions and the challenges of nihilism.

Ethics: medieval and modern

During the Middle Ages (*c.*500–1500 CE), natural law ethics as theory (science) and practice (technique) was enclosed within the framework of revelation. In the theology of Thomas Aquinas, for instance, the universal laws that govern nonhuman reality take special form in the natural law found in human beings, moving them to seek the good through the establishment of human or social laws. The basic content of natural law, which the few can know by reason but about which the many may be less sure, is confirmed and fulfilled in divine law as revealed by God through scripture and the church. Although humans can discover on their own through the use of reason that, for instance, murder is wrong (because it destroys a particularly noble manifestation of nature), the Ten Commandments conveyed to Moses by God make it clear to anyone who might lack sufficient intelligence to reach this conclusion or be tempted to think otherwise. "God said … thou shall not murder" (Exodus 20:13). Furthermore, according to revelation, human nature is molded in the image of God, and the natural world is the word of God written in flesh, rock, and leaf. This era introduced the new virtues of faith, hope, and love and emphasized the salvation of individual souls. But the task of ethics remained one of identifying and interpreting nature in both the nonhuman and human worlds as a guide to proper conduct.

The development of modern natural science in early modern Europe profoundly challenged this approach to ethics. The scientific understanding of nature came to focus, no longer on the natures of different kinds of entities, but on laws that are quite different from premodern natural law. Modern laws of nature are purely physical, transcend all particulars and kinds, and are indifferent to any order of human meaning. The modern scientific understanding of nature no longer claims to answer the question of ends or "what for" for each kind of thing. Nature is composed not of entities with ends to be realized so much as of matter and energy in space and time. Values that had once been inscribed in the order of things collapse into the human will. The moral order does not precede human acts, and the task is not to align acts with that order. Rather, the moral order emerges from human acts, and the task is to weigh and balance those acts against one another.

Classical nihilism, which was derived from historical knowledge and the apparent lack of agreement among cultures, is replaced by a new form of nihilism, derived from science and its positive denial of any good in nature. In response, according to a modern philosopher of values such as Friedrich Nietzsche, the passive nihilist simply goes along with the flow of convention – in nineteenth-century Europe, the bourgeois convention of industrial production for physical convenience – while the active nihilist takes the opportunity to creatively assert human freedom. Humans create, not discover, values. In this way, the world of science (facts) was divorced from ethics (values).

Facts and values

The fact/value dichotomy is open to a variety of criticisms. The most radical, of course, is to challenge nihilism and the alleged denial of any connection between nature and the good. The philosophical interpretations of biology advanced in the thought of John Dewey, Hans Jonas, and Leon Kass all take this approach. But even on a less problematic or radical level, there are many links between science and ethics other than those of the extremes of passive and active nihilism. Four linkages in particular merit mention.

First, as modern science became the paragon of inquiry, ethics strove for scientific precision. This took shape in the development of technical approaches to metaethics and in normative theories that seek precise rules for human action and decision-making. Some ethical systems maintain that such rules are best determined by the outcomes of actions (consequentialism), while others argue for rules grounded in the intentional features of the actions themselves (deontology). Another way to render ethics scientific is to subsume it under evolutionary or cognitive science. This move treats the origins and functions of human morality as amenable to scientific explanation and can even attempt to justify ethical norms (e.g., about right and wrong actions) on the basis of science. (The scientific approach to ethics is examined more in Chapter 7.) A further move is for a given science to appropriate territory that once belonged to ethics or theology. This occurs, for example, when bad behavior by children is redefined as a medical condition, thereby shifting the problem from the moral tasks of parenting and education to the scientific tasks of drug development or therapy.

Second, from its origins modern science has been defended with fundamentally ethical justifications. For example, Francis Bacon argued that the new scientific method would culminate in "the conquest of nature for the relief of man's estate."[1] René Descartes felt obliged to share the methods of

[1] The conquest of nature for the relief of man's estate" is often attributed to Bacon. Though not his exact words, it is a legitimate summary statement of his vision. See *Novum Organum* I, 3 and 129; and *Advancement of Learning* I, 3.

science, because they would promote "the general good of all mankind" and render humans "masters and possessors of nature" (*Discourse on Method*, VI). Auguste Comte argued that modern science rationalizes the political order. Others, such as Karl Popper and Michael Polanyi, have defended science on the ground that it fosters free, open, and democratic societies. Such ethical justifications of science continue through claims, for example, about the role of scientific research in treating diseases, informing public policies, and shaping a critically minded democratic citizenry. Indeed, any society that publicly funds science education at least implicitly advances an ethical claim that citizens ought to be guided by scientific knowledge and emulate the methods of scientific reasoning in their daily lives. The constitution of India even states that it is a duty of every citizen to develop a "scientific temper."

Third, ethics is engaged in questioning and criticizing science. Modernity is not a straightforward ethical commitment to science and technology. Since the dawn of Romanticism in the late eighteenth century, it has indeed been a reflexive questioning of this commitment – including ambivalence and outright resistance – in response to social injustices, cultural dislocations, and unintended consequences. This ethical questioning of science has drawn from a variety of normative theories. It is occasionally holistic, but more often analytic.

Holistic assessments of science and technology often draw from existentialism, phenomenology, feminism, or Marxism. They tend to conceptualize modern science as a uniform and radically new way of perceiving, experiencing, and interacting with the world. For example, some have claimed that modern Western science is a form of power that hides cultural hegemony (the imposition of one value system over another) behind a mask of "objectivity." By contrast, analytic assessments of science focus on individual practices considered in relative isolation, with the aim of generating solutions to well-defined problems. There are many sciences featuring a variety of practices, actors, and institutions. Analytic ethical assessments of science can be conducted upstream prior to research (e.g., should it be funded?), midstream during research (e.g., how should it be conducted?), or downstream after research (e.g., how should the results be disseminated or regulated?). Recent efforts strive not only to critically comment on the conduct of science but to integrate ethical inquiry into scientific practices, with the goal of modulating their trajectory in light of insights into the ethical issues at stake.

Fourth, ethics and science are intermingled in the question of responsibility. Who is responsible for identifying and addressing the ethics of science? In particular, how much responsibility can reasonably be ascribed to scientists? In 1961, the English scientist and writer C.P. Snow argued that scientists often appealed to a moral division of labor based on a view of science as value neutral. Such a scientist would say,

> *we* produce the tools. *We* stop there. It is for *you* - the rest of the world, the politicians - to say how the tools are used. The tools may be used for purposes which most of us would regard as bad. If so, we are sorry. But as scientists, that is no concern of ours.[2]

By contrast, Snow argued for an enlarged professional responsibility of scientists beyond the simple production of tools. As producers of tools, scientists are oriented toward improving the world, and thus have an implicit commitment to make sure their work actually does make the world better. But is it fair to extend the scientists' responsibility this far? And does their progressive orientation toward knowledge production give scientists a rightful authority to project their progressivism into politics in regard, for example, to the adoption of genetically modified crops to address needs for increased agricultural productivity? Do we risk something in conceiving social and human problems as always amenable to fixes with scientific means?

From moral knowledge to ethical reasoning

To the extent it seeks systematic knowledge, ethics is a science. In this sense there are many sciences. Even astrology, insofar as it purports to systematic information about how the stars affect human lives, can claim to be a kind of science. One thing that distinguishes ethics is the kind of knowledge it seeks: not just knowledge about what is the case (although descriptive knowledge is often crucial to moral reasoning), but knowledge about what should be the case, the purposes or goals of action. In the face of modern nihilism, is such knowledge possible?

In order to secure any knowledge, we require some standard for distinguishing true from false claims. What might this standard be with respect

[2] Snow 1961, p. 256.

to moral knowledge? As already noted, it cannot be convention. Claims about virtuousness, rightness, or goodness cannot be based on appeals to custom. It will not do to claim, "This is right because it is the way of my people." Such a claim begs the question, because what we wish to know is precisely whether the way customary to a particular group is in truth to be affirmed as right. What is required is some standard that transcends local custom so that it can be used to validate or legitimize valuation claims made by members of any culture.

This is what Aristotle meant by "nature." But as already noted, modern science divorces valuation claims about what *should be* from empirical claims about what *is*. As the Austrian and British philosopher Ludwig Wittgenstein remarked, if we take an inventory of all the (scientific) *facts* in the universe, we will not find in it a *fact* that killing is wrong. A complementary claim has been advanced by philosopher of science Carl Hempel: science can verify instrumental statements about how best to achieve goal X. But it can neither confirm nor falsify any answer to the question of whether goal X ought to be pursued.

One response is termed emotivism, the argument that ethical claims are no more than statements of individual preference: to claim that "X is right or good" is the same as saying "I like X"; to say "You stole my money and that is wrong" is equivalent to saying "You stole my money!" or "You stole my money and I don't like it one bit!"

One alternative to emotivism is an appeal to God. For example, in Sophocles' *Antigone* the eponymous protagonist defies the king's order. When she is asked to justify her defiance, she argues that the king's law is unjust because it contradicts the law of Zeus. Similarly, in his struggle against racist laws in the southern United States, Martin Luther King Jr. argued that a "just law is a man-made code that squares with the moral law or the law of God."[3] But equating ethics with the law of God has multiple problems. Not everyone believes in the same God or interprets revelation in the same way. Even a divine command theory of ethics requires arguments to support it.

Still another alternative is to argue that ethics is not to be grounded in custom, nature, emotion, or religion but in a deeply personal inner sense often termed conscience. Ethical inquiry may entail leaving public dogma

[3] King 1963, n.p.

(customs or religious commands) for that essentially private knowledge called conscientious conviction. Ultimately, only personal experience can determine what is right or wrong, good or bad. Socrates arguably justified the ethical claim that death should not be feared (*Apology* 29a) by appeal to an inner voice (*Apology* 31c). For Socrates, to disobey this inner voice and create an unsettled conscience is far worse than any wrong that someone else could perpetrate against him.

The notion of conscience captures something profound about ethics, its deeply personal nature, but is ultimately unsatisfying. When a person does not have any inner sense of the wrongness of some action that others think is clearly wrong, what is to be done? What is most commonly done is to try to use argument or reason to awaken the wrongdoer's conscience. This certainly appears to be Socrates' approach. Yet even if we assume that everyone possesses the same conscience which, when activated, gives accurate insight into ethical quandaries, people remain adept at rationalizing their actions, deceiving themselves, or ignoring any inner voice of ethical compunction. Again, in this situation it is common to resort to moral reasoning with such a person – or even with ourselves. Additionally, the standard we are seeking needs to be reliably intersubjective – clearly shareable by and applicable to everyone. My conscience may advise something contrary to your conscience, and at that point we are back at square one: How do we tell who is right? We need a way to scrutinize our convictions together.

This is why the interpersonal practice of reason-giving is recognized as basic to ethical reflection. Reliance on reason does not solve all problems; it is procedure more than product. But as procedure it does identify a pathway that may in some instances lead to agreements, however provisional. In science, too, propositions are true only to some degree provisionally, insofar as they are accepted by an intersubjective consensus.

Ethics is the effort to guide one's conduct with careful reasoning. One cannot simply claim "*X* is wrong." Rather, one needs to claim "*X* is wrong because (fill in the blank)." Filling in the blank is called justification, and is at the heart of ethics. To justify a valuation claim is to furnish adequate grounds for it. It involves strength and cogency in producing premises and drawing conclusions in arguments. Indeed, we have already been appealing to this standard by offering various reasons to question the adequacy of appeals to convention, science, emotion, religion, or conscience in the justification of ethical claims. Just as importantly, ethics involves the open-mindedness and humility necessary to revise one's beliefs and actions in light of good reasons. In this way, ethics is analogous to science.

The role of theory

What role does theory play in reason-giving? This question is more difficult than it may appear, and is widely debated. One extreme theory of theory argues that theories are just summaries of experience that enable us to anticipate future experience; another theory of theory is that theories are innate and make experience possible. Some philosophers think of theory as a form of knowledge or understanding valuable in its own right; others take theory as valuable only in practical or instrumental terms. Theories about what it means to be human have been argued to move people to historical action (witness the French revolutionary ideals of *liberté, égalité, fraternité*), at other times to mislead them into illusion (as with the theory of the divine right of kings). To some extent, of course, what theory is depends on the type of theory being considered. Scientific theory may not function in exactly the same way as ethical, political, or aesthetic theory.

In the present context, however, we can begin to respond to the basic question by using a simplified schema from science. In science, theories are sometimes described as propositions that are more general than laws, which are in turn more general than observations. For example, analyses of electrical phenomena led to Ohm's law that current is directly proportional to voltage and inversely proportional to the resistance; similarly, observations of the phenomenon of magnetism led to the formulation of Gauss's law that magnetic monopoles do not exist. Subsequently these and related laws were unified in Maxwell's electromagnetic theory. Once in place, such a theory provides a kind of unifying perspective that synthesizes or relates multiple phenomena, that is, constitutes knowledge. Additionally, such a theory offers guidance in thinking about any particular instance covered by it. It provides concepts for identifying different aspects of some phenomenon (e.g., resistance, current, and voltage) and answers questions about relationships between different types of phenomena (e.g., electricity and magnetism). A theory creates, as was suggested earlier, a perspective that helps us see things that might otherwise be overlooked or underappreciated.

In an analogous simplification, ethical theory can be thought of as synthesizing moral rules, which in turn generalize diverse moral experiences. Embedded in a culture we discover that telling parents we did not do something that we in fact did is punished, that telling friends we did something that we did not do winds up undermining friendship, and in multiple other instances speaking in ways that do not properly represent our behaviors is associated with negative results. This leads to the formulation of the concept of lying and the rule, "It is wrong to tell lies." (Of course, since in some instances lying is also associated with positive experience, we either refine the concept or introduce exceptions into the rule. Morality is more complex than electromagnetism.) Upon noticing other rules, such as "It is wrong to break promises," there is an inclination to develop theories that can synthesize or relate them and in so doing provide both understanding about what it means to be human and guidance for making future decisions.

Of course, there are also fundamental differences between scientific and ethical theories. The most obvious is that there is usually only one widely accepted candidate for a unifying scientific theory, whereas there are often multiple competitors for some unifying ethical theory. One way of accounting for this difference is to suggest still another analogy: the hierarchical structure of a social organization with a CEO at the top, managers in the middle, and individual employees at the bottom. Theories in ethics may be thought of as functioning more like leadership in some social organization. Leadership can be exercised in different ways: by visionary inspiration, strong rule-setting, personal coaching, and more – none of which, it is important to note, are mutually exclusive. Just as organizational leadership can be explained by and structured according to multiple theories, so can moral behavior. It is possible to be a pluralist in ethics in ways that are not so easy in science.

Nevertheless, organizations ultimately depend on leadership, however it may be understood or exercised. Without leadership, social orders flounder and fail. The ethics equivalent is that attempts to behave morally often fail without some reason-giving guidance, and this reason-giving guidance or justification is (consciously or not) ultimately undertaken using some theory. It thus becomes important to identify and become conscious of the basic theoretical alternatives within which people make ethical arguments. Reason-giving achieves its highest level when it becomes self-conscious about the frameworks it adopts and thereby can undertake to reason even about these frameworks. Part of reason-giving involves becoming reflexive about giving reasons.

There are many basic ethical theories, but for present purposes it will be sufficient to describe and consider three of the most currently influential, especially when it comes to advancing ethical reasons that engage with science. In historical order of their appearance these are virtue theory, consequentialism, and deontology. The three theories also represent some of the highest-order achievements of human culture, so that to become aware of them can have value in its own right – just as becoming aware of different types of government or religion can have value independent of which government or religion one chooses as best. To become aware of ethical theories is to appreciate diverse efforts to understand the complexities of the human lifeworld and thus of the richness of that lifeworld itself. One does not have to use any particular map to appreciate the enormous achievement of map-making as a human activity. Although each of these ethical maps has already been introduced, it is beneficial to provide a comparative review of the theories as such.

Virtue ethics

Virtue ethics received passing attention earlier in the overview of the history of relations between ethics and science, both because of its presence at the origin of the development of ethics in European culture and because of the way it seeks to bridge science and culture. Like any ethical theory, virtue ethics offers a distinctive map for thinking through the fundamental question of ethics: How should we live? From the perspective of virtue theory, the aim of life is to fare well or flourish, which takes distinctive forms in different organisms. Organisms exhibit a special type of being that includes growth and reproduction. Virtue is just another name for the proper operation of such functions in particular species. For example, *Danaus plexippus* spins a cocoon and becomes a monarch butterfly. It has a distinctive anatomy and physiology, a hierarchy of needs, and internal principles of development. These constitute its nature and determine what it is for this organism to flourish. When internal debilities or external impediments thwart the exercise of its particular way of flourishing then it is said to have failed to realize its potentialities. Realization of its potentiality can be described as its virtue or power – also as its excellence or perfection.

Human beings too have a distinctive nature, and it is reasonable to think of human life at the biological level as oriented toward its own type of flourishing. For Aristotle, the name for human flourishing is *eudaimonia*, a term often translated as "happiness." But happiness in Aristotle's sense is not a subjective experience; it is an objective quality, more like health. Indeed, since the Greek word is composed of *eu* (well or good) and *daimon* (divinity or spirit), and is used interchangeably with *eu zen* (well living), an alternative translation is "well-being" or "welfare," yet in a more than simply physiological sense. In order for humans to live well or flourish, according to Aristotle, they must develop certain potential character traits, capacities, skills, or excellences in their behaviors or conduct. Insofar as these skills become ingrained into a person and facilitate flourishing they are called good habits or virtues.

One difficulty with virtue theory, as Aristotle already recognized, is that humans, unlike other organisms, flourish in more than biological ways. Human beings think and argue about what constitutes true human flourishing. Disagreements arise among those who propose that the pursuit of pleasure (physical well-being), honor (social well-being), and knowledge (cognitive well-being) constitute true human flourishing (*Nicomachean Ethics* I, 5). Aristotle himself defended knowing as the most distinctive and highest of these forms of flourishing for humans, because knowing is their fully distinguishing feature, that which they do only or best. At the same time, Aristotle saw these different types of virtue as biology based.

Aristotle's argument has at least two serious difficulties. One is biologism, another elitism. In the Aristotelian tradition, biology is much more function based than modern biology, and Aristotelians think biology determines the good in a manner that leaves humans little freedom to interpret the meaning of or alter biology. Because women possess the special function of being able to bear children, they are often described as virtuous primarily insofar as they do so. Among humans in general, Aristotle describes some as "by nature" slaves (*Politics* I, 5). Aristotelians also tend to see Greeks or the heirs of Greek culture as realizing their biological potential to a greater extent than other humans.

Contemporary efforts to revive and defend virtue theory have thus sought to replace biological functions with social and historical traditions of practice as the foundations of the virtues. Practices or traditions of practice, such as music or science, are well realized through acquired skills that are independent of any particular practitioner but to the understanding of which any dedicated practitioner is able to contribute. The contemporary Scottish-American philosopher Alasdair MacIntyre debiologizes virtue in precisely this manner. For MacIntyre, virtues are the realization of potential excellences present in practices. Practice is defined as "any coherent and complex form of socially established cooperative human activity through which goods internal to that form of activity are realized in the course of trying to achieve those standards of excellence which are appropriate to, and partially definitive of, that form of activity, with the result that human powers to achieve excellence, and human conceptions of the ends and goods involved, are systematically extended."[4]

The virtues enable their possessor to live a good life because they are just those character traits that make their possessor good qua some human practice. There is nothing mysterious about this; all societies honor the development and expression of virtues in practices. The award given to Dr. Kelsey for her virtuous behavior is an example. But practices are more ingrained in human life than the occasional ceremony. The entire process of maturation – and the parenting and teaching that aid it – is a long study in the acquisition of virtues.

Virtue is the concept of something that makes its possessor good: a virtuous person is a morally good, excellent or admirable person who acts and feels well, rightly, or as she should. Some important virtues include compassion, courage, honesty, justice, patience, and thoughtfulness. Virtues thus pertain both to one's own happiness and acting rightly toward others. Aristotle distinguishes two kinds of virtue: intellectual virtue or excellence in thinking, where reasoning constitutes the activity itself, and moral virtue or excellence in activities carrying out the precepts of reason. Both kinds of virtues are acquired through habituation or practice. This entails witnessing the acts of a virtuous person, reflecting on that experience, and attempting to emulate those acts appropriately modified for new situations.

Virtue ethics has been subjected to several criticisms. First, some claim that the definitions of "virtue" and "vice" must be relative to the cultures

[4] MacIntyre 2007, p. 187.

defining them. For example, what Aristotle considered to be human nature may only be a predominant bias in his culture, one that differs with the evaluations of other cultures. Perhaps Aristotle's "flourishing human" is merely the leisured, male philosopher of classical Greece. In response, one could argue that certain virtues are universal, underwritten not by variable conventions but by a shared human nature. In any human group, it is hard to imagine that friendliness, courage, and honesty will not be valued, simply because a group that did not value such virtues would languish or even perish rather than flourish. It is true that there are more goods than can be pursued in any one life, so the virtues one develops will depend on circumstances and choices about one's plan of life. The shape of individual lives will differ; there is not a single mold for *the* virtuous person. Nonetheless, every life path worthy of pursuit demands the cultivation of some set of virtues, and it seems likely that a certain set of core virtues will be central to any such path.

Second, some have claimed that virtue ethics relies on a refuted teleological metaphysics. As noted earlier, modern natural science holds that nature is not prescriptive. Values are imposed on nature by humans and their conventions, not derived from nature. So, how could human nature be a normative standard for conduct? In response, one can note that modern science supports various claims about how humans are creatures of a certain type with certain needs that must be satisfied in order to flourish. Physiologically, we require specific nutrients and psychologically we require caring relationships. The opening case study is an example of science discovering something necessary for human flourishing, namely, the absence of thalidomide in the early stages of embryo development. Indeed, science helps us to understand what we are naturally fit for, capable of, and adapted to, and this helps us to know what is good for us. In other words, modern science often derives values claims from the study of our "factual" nature.

Finally, some have argued that virtue ethics provides no action guidance. Its emphasis on character, the claim goes, does not provide insight into what we should *do*. In response, one can argue that virtue ethics does pertain to morally right actions. It just frames them in a unique way. Actions are still assessed as right or wrong by reference to the reasons that can be given for or against them. But the reasons cited will be connected with the virtues. The reasons for doing an act will be that it is fair, prudent, loyal, and so on. The reasons against doing an act will be that it is unfair, imprudent, an act of betrayal, and so on. In other words, the right thing to do is whatever a virtuous person would do.

We have already indicated the ways in which modern science may or may not challenge the very intelligibility of virtue ethics. There are several other ways in which virtue ethics is relevant to science. First, virtue epistemology is an attempt to understand the epistemic justification of beliefs (i.e., knowledge claims) on the model of virtue ethics. Just as virtue ethics understands the normative properties of actions in terms of the normative properties (virtues) of moral agents, virtue epistemology understands the normative properties of beliefs in terms of the virtues of cognitive agents. In other words, justified belief or knowledge is not the result of following a reliable method. Rather, knowledge is belief arising from epistemic or intellectual virtue. Putting the agent at the center of the justification of belief has implications for how we understand science. Is it primarily a matter of following methods or actively practicing skills (virtues)?

Thinking about science in terms of virtues also highlights the importance of training processes and mentor–mentee relationships. Aspiring scientists require mentors who can model not just intellectual, but also moral virtues such as honesty, fair-mindedness, humility, and respectfulness. Virtue ethics is well positioned to criticize the rise of Big Science and its tendency to attenuate the bonds between senior and junior researchers. As a profession, science also relies on virtuous practitioners who will not seek to advance their careers in unethical ways that undermine the credibility of the scientific community. Furthermore, society must often trust in the virtuous character of scientists who receive public grants or possess potentially dangerous knowledge.

Virtue ethics has also provided resources for normative critiques of some scientific research. In particular, normative appeals to human nature are commonly used as an argumentative strategy to question the wisdom of pursuing certain physical or cognitive enhancements. For example, perhaps research on certain mood brighteners should not proceed, because their use will estrange emotions from the way life actually is, thereby preventing fitting or virtuous responses to experience. Would it really be good to be happy no matter what? Would it not, rather, be a distortion of the human condition – a failure to recognize its sometimes tragic nature?

Finally, though it has broad relevance to science, virtue ethics has its limitations. Most importantly, as it focuses on individual agents, it is less well-suited for the evaluation of institutions and collective policymaking. The FDA needs virtuous scientists as drug reviewers, but it also needs general rules or principles – for example, about how to weigh costs and benefits – to guide its regulations. For such general social policies, utilitarianism is often seen as a more pertinent normative theory.

Consequentialism

Virtue ethics focuses on agents as a whole (their character). By contrast, consequentialist ethics focuses on states of affairs that result from an agent's actions. An act is right or wrong according to its consequences; it has no moral value apart from outcomes. An act is right if and only if it is reasonably expected to produce the greatest good or least harm in comparison with alternative action choices. Consequentialism thus also requires some account of what counts as good.

The strong version of consequentialism known as utilitarianism was first systematized in the nineteenth century by Jeremy Bentham and John Stuart Mill in an effort to develop a decision-making rule capable of guiding social policies in a world being transformed by science, technology, and the Industrial Revolution. In 1781, Bentham formulated the "principle of utility," which "approves or disapproves of every action whatsoever, according to the tendency which it appears to have to augment or diminish the happiness of the party whose interest is in question" (*An Introduction to the Principles of Morals and Legislation* I, 3). Five years earlier Bentham had used the phrase with which the principle of utility is most often associated, when he proposed as a "fundamental axiom" that "*it is the greatest happiness of the greatest number that is the measure of right and wrong*" (*A Fragment on Government*, preface, Bentham's emphasis). Then in 1861, Mill put it this way: "Actions are right in proportion as they tend to promote happiness, wrong as they tend to produce the reverse of happiness, i.e., pleasure or absence of pain" (*Utilitarianism* II, para. 2). Historically, utilitarianism contributed to democratic development and social reform. Additionally, because of its compatibility with democratic decision-making in the public realm, utilitarianism has become incredibly influential. In one version or another it is the basis of virtually all contemporary economics and much public policy formation. Policymakers at various governmental agencies, for instance, commonly weigh the benefits and harms that may accrue from alternative regulatory actions and adopt those judged to produce the greatest overall benefits.

Despite basic agreements, there are two important differences between Bentham and Mill. Bentham proposes that each individual action be evaluated on the basis of a "felicific calculus" that subjects all outcomes to a common metric. This is known as act utilitarianism. Mill proposes instead that what should be evaluated are not actions but rules for action, and that these be assessed in recognition of qualitative differences in their outcomes. This is called rule utilitarianism. Qualitative differences are recognized by people on the basis of experience; anyone who has experienced two different kinds of outcome will be able to discern which one is best. In Mill's words,

> It is better to be a human being dissatisfied than a pig satisfied; better to be Socrates dissatisfied than a fool satisfied. And if the fool, or the pig, are of a different opinion, it is because they only know their own side of the question. The other party to the comparison knows both sides. (*Utilitarianism* II, para. 5)

Thus, although Bentham and Mill use the same word, "happiness," to name the good or morally relevant outcome in terms of which actions or rules are to be evaluated, they mean somewhat different things. For Bentham, happiness is physical pleasure, so that his theory is often termed hedonic utilitarianism; for Mill, happiness includes any need, desire, or interest that a person chooses to pursue, so that his theory is termed "preference utilitarianism."

Mill's preference utilitarianism has generally been adopted as the more rationally defensible – although not always. But in the early twentieth century, preference utilitarianism underwent a bifurcation, becoming, on the one hand, more abstract and, on the other, more concrete. On the abstract side, the British philosopher G.E. Moore argued that the good at which consequentialism aims cannot be reduced to happiness, however understood. Goodness, for Moore, is a "nonnatural" property. For any natural property such as pleasure or psychological happiness, it is always possible and meaningful to ask, "But is it good?" In place of hedonic and preference utilitarianism, Moore argued an "ideal utilitarianism" that privileges phenomena with intrinsic value such as aesthetic appreciation and friendship.

On the more concrete side, utilitarianism merged with liberal economic theory, in which market activity is argued to be the most effective means for assessing outcomes in terms of preferences and maximizing preference-producing actions. By the end of the twentieth century, economics had transformed many ethical questions about how to reach the best consequences into questions about how to increase market efficiency. In some instances this argument has been applied to, for instance, assessing the best regulatory regime for pharmaceuticals and investments in science.

As the most widely adopted ethical theory, utilitarianism has also played host to a number of extended public discussions, many of which are especially relevant to ethics in science. One concerns conceptual issues related to the greatest happiness of the greatest number. Which is it – greatest happiness or greatest number? The two are not necessarily the same. One response is to argue that the greatest happiness principle means the greatest average happiness. By analogy, would the greatest science education for the greatest number, which might be a reasonable statement of the goal for science education, imply the greatest average science education? Would this not tend to militate against the gifted and talented in science?

Another issue in the economistic version of utilitarianism is the phenomenon of declining marginal utility of preference goods. Put simply, although both the poor and the rich will express a preference for £100 over £10, £100 means a lot more to the person making £1,000/month than to someone making £100,000/month. One hundred pounds sterling declines in happiness-producing (or utility) value as it becomes a smaller proportion of income. Something similar appears to occur in most preferences. Adding one room to a ten-room house is a lot less significant than adding one room to a one-room house. In scientific research, questions arise with regard to a declining marginal utility in repeating experiments or collecting more data.

Still a third issue concerns the difference between expressed and revealed preferences. Often people say that some good *X* has a certain value, but then act as if it had a different value. Statements that safety is important are often belied by behavior that increases risk. The same people who seek one level of safety in airplanes accept a much lower level of safety in automobiles. This paradox occurs not only in everyday life but in the laboratory. Which kind of behavior should utilitarianism endorse, that which increases expressed or revealed preferences?

Finally, there is the problem of discounting the future. Since actions have consequences that in turn have consequences, how far into the future should consequentialism project? As a methodological principle, with economistic utilitarianism future costs and benefits are given less weight than present-day ones. The future is discounted, with debates about how much over how long. Since futures are more often probable than simply necessary, future discounting can overlap with risk analysis, which presents still more challenges to consequentialism. In relation to science, relevant questions arise with regard to laboratory practices, as when lowering safety (or any other) standards might have only long-range and low-risk consequences. Additionally, why become too concerned about making sure all contributors read, understand, and sign off on every single word of a multiauthored paper, since one can project a future in which there is a diminishing likelihood of failures to do so making any significant difference?

Independent of such problematic issues, the late twentieth century has witnessed a revival of classic utilitarianism via the science-related work of Australian philosopher Peter Singer. According to Singer, what is distinctive about ethics is that "we go beyond our own likes and dislikes" and adopt "the standpoint of the impartial spectator or ideal observer." In this commitment to impartiality, "I am accepting that my own needs, wants and desires cannot, simply because they are my preferences, count more than the wants, needs and desires of anyone else." Such moral reasoning "points towards the course of action that has the best consequences, on balance, for all affected."[5] Singer uses this restatement of preference utilitarianism to defend equality of consideration not just for all humans irrespective of class, race, sex, ethnicity, and more, because "an interest is an interest, whoever's interest it may be."[6] Indeed, extending an argument from Bentham, Singer defends giving animals, insofar as they have interests in avoiding pain, moral consideration as well.

Singer's brief for the moral considerability of animals leads him to a controversial defense of abortion. According to Singer, an antiabortionist

[5] Singer 2011, pp. 11–12. [6] Singer 2011, p. 20.

concern for embryos and fetuses is based on a biased concern for our own species, sometimes termed "speciesism." Drawing on scientific descriptions of prenatal development, he argues that "On any fair comparison of morally relevant characteristics, like rationality, self-consciousness, awareness, autonomy, pleasure and pain and so on, the calf, the pig and the much derided chicken come out well ahead of the fetus at any stage of pregnancy – whereas if we make the comparison with an embryo … a fish shows much more awareness." On the basis of such an analysis, he suggests "that we accord the fetus no higher moral status than we give to a nonhuman animal at a similar level of rationality, self-consciousness, awareness, capacity to feel and so on."[7]

Finally, Singer's extreme ethical universalism leads to an equally controversial argument regarding the moral obligation of what he terms the "absolute affluent" to reduce "absolute poverty." The absolutely (instead of relatively) affluent are those who have disposable income to spend on goods that are not necessary to maintaining their lives; the absolutely (instead of relatively) poor are those who do not even have enough to meet basic human needs for water, food, and shelter. In his argument, Singer first makes an empirical case that "rich people [in affluent countries] are allowing more than a billion people to continue to live in conditions of deprivation and to die prematurely." He then defends the consequentialist rejection of intrinsic differences between allowing people to die and killing them, especially when we have the means to prevent their death without significant sacrifice. His conclusion, defended against a suite of possible objections, is that "we [in affluent countries] are all murderers."[8]

As is demonstrated in Singer's work, more than any other of the three basic ethical theories consequentialism lends itself to science-ethics interactions. Singer regularly appeals to science in support of factual claims (e.g., with regard to fetal development) while also bringing ethical argument to bear on scientific practice (e.g., the treatment of animals in research). At the same time, Singer's uncompromising universalism with regard to such issues as the treatment of animals and humans in poverty points toward the third basic ethical theory, deontology.

[7] Singer 2011, pp. 135–136. [8] Singer 2011, p. 194.

Deontology

The term "deontology" derives from the Greek *deon* (duty) and *logos* (reason). This emphasis on the concept of reasoned duty harmonizes with a common understanding of ethics as critical reflection on inclinations or desires. For human beings, action not only manifests character traits (virtue ethics) and causes things to happen (emphasized in consequentialism) but emerges from willed intentions. Because human beings have multiple appetites (for water, food, power, sex, honor, and more) they must employ reason to decide which to pursue; a rationally endorsed appetite becomes the will, which is expressed in a command or imperative. In deontological ethics, right action is defined directly in terms of moral principles manifest in duties rather than in terms of virtues or good consequences. According to this ethical theory, the goal of moral action is not to perfect the character of an agent or produce a good state of affairs; it is to uphold the morality of action itself.

This approach to ethics is most commonly associated with the thought of Immanuel Kant. The first sentence of Kant's *Groundwork for the Metaphysics of Morals* (1785) proposes that the only "good without qualification [is] a *good will*" (393, his emphasis). Two arguments support this position. Character traits such as intelligence, courage, and perseverance may be laudable in many respects, but can be put to bad use when the will that animates them is not good. Even a brave person has to decide when it is proper to practice the virtue of courage. Additionally, with regard to ostensibly good states of affairs such as wealth, health, or happiness, an impartial spectator is normally uncomfortable when someone enjoys happiness without being "graced by any touch of a pure and good will" (393).[9] Only to the extent that people have good will do we think it is fair for them to be happy. It thus becomes the work of ethics to identify what more precisely constitutes the good will.

This begins by noting that just as scientific knowledge (which informs the mind) is typically expressed in declarative propositions, so ethical knowledge (which informs the will) takes the form of commands or imperatives. There are two kinds of imperatives: hypothetical and categorical.

[9] English quotations from Kant are from Kant 1993. Page references to the Akademie edition.

Appetite assessment is most commonly done hypothetically on the basis of appeals to external results (consequentialism). This yields imperatives of the form "If you want X, then do Y." If you want to earn good grades, then study hard; if you want to produce reliable knowledge, follow the scientific method. In such cases, however, the goodness of the will remains dependent on the goodness of whatever is being pursued. It is not good in itself. In order to escape this weakness, Kant argues for an assessment of intentions based in reason alone and the existence of a categorical imperative of the form "Do Y" (never mind the results). To appreciate Kant's concern and approach, imagine that we were trying to decide what 2 + 2 equals. We could decide this on the basis of appeals to external results. If I have just made two deposits of £200 in my bank account, then I might want to conclude that 2 + 2 equals 5 (since this would make me wealthier than if 2 + 2 equals only 4). But instead of deciding on the basis of external results, mathematics requires that the question of 2 + 2 be answered ignoring results in any particular context and on the basis of reasons internal to mathematics itself. Kant thinks something like this is required in ethics as well.

The categorical imperative states: "You ought to do such and such, *period*." This practical categorical imperative is analogous to the theoretical certainty of 2 + 2 = 4. The propositional certainty in mathematics is just another way of saying that if 2 + 2 equals anything but 4 then the system of mathematical propositions will contain a contradiction of the form "*A* and not-*A*." Something similar can be argued with regard to a categorical imperative to tell the truth: to speak is to attempt to communicate, but to tell a lie is not to communicate. To tell a lie involves the practical contradiction of communicating (*A*) and not communicating (not-*A*). Categorical imperatives are binding on the rational will because they derive from a principle that every rational person must accept on pain of contradiction.

Kant himself argued for the existence of one, overarching categorical imperative that includes such commands as do not lie, keep promises, and more. The fundamental, all-encompassing categorical imperative can nevertheless be stated in a number of different but equivalent forms. Of the two most prominent statements, the first is: "Act only according to that maxim by which you can at the same time will that it should become a universal law" (421). One must, in other words, be able to endorse the universal acceptability of a rule or plan of action. A maxim or rule that one should lie would be not only self-defeating (people would quickly stop relying on what others said) but also self-contradictory (people would be obliged to lie about lying). Related contradictions arise with maxims that endorsed stealing or cheating, especially insofar as such rules might be framed as personal exceptions. Persons who act according to such a rule would be acting irrationally, that is, according to rules they could not universalize. Insofar as science depends on truth-telling and related imperatives, such an argument can be used to support the practice of science.

A second formulation of the categorical imperative is: "Act in such a way that you treat humanity, whether in your own person or in the person of another, always at the same time as an end and never simply as a means" (A 429). This phrasing highlights the importance of personal autonomy, rights, and dignity for deontology. One cannot treat others as mere means, because such a maxim could not be universalized. This means that the experimental prescription of thalidomide prior to FDA approval was wrong, insofar as patients did not have sufficient information to grant their consent. The second formulation also explicitly constrains even action on oneself. One cannot intend self-destructive behavior, since this too would involve failing to respect oneself as an end. Moreover, it points up how Kantian moral autonomy is not the market utilitarian principle of respecting a person's preferences no matter what they are. Preferences must be rational – which opens the door to what libertarians might call paternalist limitations on the autonomy of those who would otherwise harm themselves.

The Kantian approach is complemented by another form of deontology known as contractarianism. Contractarianism, as initially developed in the thought of Thomas Hobbes, proposes to explain both the origins of political authority and, more pertinently here, moral obligation. According to Hobbes, when human beings enter into contracts they create (under certain conditions) categorical-like obligations. Such contracts can be both explicit and implicit. Hobbes, for instance, argues the existence of an implicit contract among individuals in society to place themselves under a sovereign authority in order to reduce the natural "war of everyone against everyone" (*Leviathan* 14) and enforce social peace. Such a contract establishes a more than hypothetical obligation (to obey the sovereign only *if* it produces peace) because only with the giving up of any right to exceptions on the part of subjects can the sovereign truly establish peace.

At a more explicit and legalistic level, whenever any business contract is freely agreed to, then the terms of the contract cease to be hypothetical and take on the character of categorical imperatives. Postulating a less explicit contract could also be used to explain the semicategorical imperatives manifest in the practice of science. At the level of ethics, other philosophers have argued that morality is constituted by those actions to which we would all agree insofar as we can think as unbiased agents – a view that could again be used to account for ethics in science. Such a version of contractarianism echoes the first of Kant's formulations of the categorical imperative.

One contemporary philosopher who has worked to articulate a multiple-command version of deontological ethics and relate this ethics to science is Bernard Gert. According to Gert, there are ten basic moral rules: do not kill, cause pain, disable, deprive of freedom, deprive of pleasure, deceive, or cheat; additionally persons should keep promises, obey the law, and do their duty. Toward each of these rules, Gert argues at length and from different perspectives that all impartial rational persons would take the following attitude:

> *Everyone (including myself) is always to obey the rule …, except when a fully informed, impartial rational person can publicly allow violating it. Anyone who violates the rule when a fully informed, impartial rational person cannot publicly allow such a violation may be punished.*[10]

For Gert this means that the multiple moral rules, although distinct, are not isolated from each other; they are part of a public moral system that applies to all moral agents. Gert makes an extended effort to clarify the sense in which moral agents are also impartial rational agents. Rationality, he argues, is best understood as an effort to avoid irrationality. Irrationality is "the more basic normative concept" because it delimits action.[11] Irrational actions should not be committed, whereas an action can be rational but still not be required. There are often multiple alternative rational responses to a given situation. In the end, irrationality is defined as what fully informed rational agents would avoid. Although Gert

[10] Gert 1998, p. 216. Italics in the original. [11] Gert 1998, p. 30.

admits the definition can appear circular, the circularity is more virtuous than vicious: through rationality we act in ways that are not "crazy," "idiotic," "stupid," or "silly."[12]

Gert's theory goes to great lengths to analyze how the moral rules, despite their rationality, can be rationally violated. Indeed, the potential for violation of the moral rules is built into the basic attitude toward them (see above the italicized statement of this attitude). Because "justifying violations of the moral rules is similar to justifying the moral rules themselves,"[13] Gert proposes a two-step procedure for justifying violations. The procedure involves asking, with regard to any potential violation or exception, a set of ten questions to discover the morally relevant facts, before proceeding to consider whether in light of the facts any particular exception would be publicly allowed by a fully informed, impartial rational person. The upshot may be described as an effort to distinguish essential from accidental or contingent features of any exception.

Gert has tested his qualified deontology against real-world issues in biomedical science.[14] More generally, applying his deontology to the question of science as a whole, Gert argues that science is inherently good even though it can sometimes have bad consequences. Science is a "social good" insofar as it "necessarily leads to an increase in the personal good of knowledge, whereas its bad effects are only contingent." Science is a prima facie good with reasons needing to be given for its delimitation. Nevertheless, "social goods like science, education, and medicine, may have sufficiently harmful contingent consequences that one can have adequate reasons for limiting them."[15] Even with a deontological-like justification of science it is possible to develop a consequentialist-like reason for regulating it.

Deontological ethics has faced numerous criticisms. Mill, for instance, argued that deontology always entails covert appeals to consequences. The categorical imperative demands that an action be morally prohibited if "the *consequences* of its universal adoption would be such as no one would choose to incur" (*Utilitarianism* I, para. 4). In response to such an objection, Kant would argue that it is not the consequences of universalization that make an act such as lying wrong. Rather, bad consequences arise because of a practical contradiction of the intention involved. A liar is essentially

[12] Gert 1998, p. 32. [13] Gert 1998, p. 222. [14] See, e.g, Gert et al. 1996, 1997.
[15] Gert et al. 1997, p. 96.

saying that "everyone else should tell the truth except for me." But insofar as we all are equal in dignity, liars have no good reasons for defending their special status. To lie, steal, or murder is to contradict oneself by doing something that one does not want others to do. The bad social consequences that result are just a material witness to a moral contradiction.

Kant has also been criticized for lack of clarity with regard the problematics of action description. Actions can often be described in more than one way. Is a lie always simply a lie or could it not be described in some circumstances as an effort to save life? For example, if Jon tells you he is intent on murdering Jane, then asks you Jane's whereabouts, must you really tell him the truth? On some interpretations of deontology, this would seem to be the case, since lying cannot be universalized. But this "lie" could be more adequately described as an action to save life.

Finally, deontologists have been criticized for holding that moral rules are absolute and cannot conflict. Consider the case of Dutch fishermen smuggling Jewish refugees to England during World War II. Their boats were occasionally stopped by Nazis, who inquired as to who was on board and where the boat was headed. The fishermen had two options: either lie or allow the passengers (and themselves) to be captured and killed. Here two absolute rules ("it is wrong to lie" and "it is wrong to facilitate the murder of innocent people") conflict. To account for this kind of difficulty, W.D. Ross argued that moral duties are not universal constraints. Rather, they are conditional (prima facie) obligations to act that arise out of situated relations. One must judge in a given case which duties apply and which duty trumps others.[16] Ross's deontology is more flexible than Kant's, but has been criticized for lacking unity and failing to specify how to handle conflicts beyond a vague appeal to the virtue of moral judgment. Gert describes his own position as "Ross with a theory," meaning that he develops a more carefully unified and nuanced account of how to qualify moral rules.[17]

Deontology has broad relevance to science. We have already indicated its centrality to the ethics of human subjects research and biomedical ethics. Its emphasis on obligation is also important in discussions about the duties and responsibilities of scientists as members of a profession. Furthermore, the concept of autonomy is widely invoked by those who argue that science

[16] Ross 1954. [17] Gert 1998, p. xi.

should remain independent of politics, religion, business, or other aspects of society. This appeal is often further justified by the beneficial social consequences that will occur as a result of protecting the autonomy of science. At the same time, noting that modern science and technology have created the power to radically change or destroy nature, Hans Jonas argues that there is now an internal contradiction in science. As a deontological guide for restraint of the destructive powers inherent in science, Jonas offers a new version of the categorical imperative: "Act so that the effects of your actions are compatible with the permanence of genuine human life."[18]

Strengths, weaknesses, and alternatives

When the three simplified overviews of virtue ethics, consequentialism, and deontology are approached using the map analogy suggested at the beginning of the chapter, it is appropriate to attempt some qualification of the strengths and weaknesses of each. Not all maps do the same things well. It is likewise important to note that despite their significant influence, these are not the only moral theories that might be considered.

Qualifications

As suggested, each basic theoretical framework has its distinctive strengths and weaknesses. Like different kinds of maps, each of which can call attention to, and help orient with regard to, some real aspect of the world being graphically represented, different theories highlight different aspects of moral experience. Moral experience truly does involve agents (as emphasized by virtue ethics), actions (as emphasized by deontology), and results (as emphasized by consequentialism). But neither agency, nor action, nor results constitute the whole of ethics. So typical questions for any ethical theory concern the best entry point for understanding relations between all three elements of moral life and, especially in the present context, which is most adequate for grappling with the manifold of issues related to science.

[18] Jonas 1984, p. 11.

Table 2.1 *Strengths and weaknesses of three major ethical theories*

Theory	Strengths	Weaknesses
Virtue ethics	Realistic guidance on how individuals become moral agents (through practice of virtues and character development). Relates ethics to human nature and practice.	Rationalizes elitist social orders and can turn nature into destiny. Sometimes appears circular.
Deontology	Firm moral principles support courageous conduct in the face of social pressures for compromise. In the form of human rights, protects human dignity.	Can seem to endorse moral rigidity if not fanaticism. Sometimes asks for rationality and will-power that only the few can practice.
Consequentialism	Practical results oriented, providing a basis for decision-making in business and public affairs. Compatible with pluralist democracy and has supported social justice.	Difficult to deal with unintended consequences and risks. Insofar as all suffering is to be treated equally, appears unrealistic.

Virtue ethics, for instance, provides realistic guidance on the processes by which agents acquire and develop moral character. It also grounds ethics in a notion of human nature and nature in general. Yet this theory is often associated with traditional, elitist cultures and can be interpreted in a way that makes biology into destiny. Although a revised version based on practices rather than nature can evade this charge, it then is open to charges of relativism: Which practices ought we to pursue? In some cases, to argue that virtues are what virtuous people do while virtuous individuals are those who practice the virtues can appear circular.

Deontology, by emphasizing firm moral principles, has a history of providing a basis for uncompromised adherence to right actions in the face of great pressures to the contrary. Many of those opposed to Nazi policies and practices acted and sacrificed their lives encouraged by the teachings of Kant and theories of human rights. Deontology has also supported refusals to cut corners in the practice of science, whether with regard to the treatment of human subjects or the fudging of data. Others, however, have argued the deontological approach is overly rational and encourages rigidity and obstreperousness, refusing to compromise or adapt when appropriate; in some cases fanaticism finds a justification in deontology.

Consequentialism is more practical, always (and perhaps sometimes too much so) willing to compromise. It functions well in a pluralistic democracy as a framework within which to reach public decisions and has promoted social justice by acknowledging diverse interest groups. But it can be difficult to know in advance all the consequences (intended or unintended) of actions or to fix a limit to the consideration of results, and can demand too much equality of consideration. When results are expressed in terms of probabilities and risks, things become even more complicated. By downplaying the significance of human rights in moral experience the door opens to mistreatment of some persons for the benefit of others.

One summary of these and related strengths and weaknesses is provided in Table 2.1.

Ethics of care

Both utilitarian and deontological moral reasoning adopt an impartial point of view. Bentham thinks in terms of aggregates of pleasures and pains; Mill, of moral agents as disinterested spectators. Kant thinks in terms of universalizable rules and inflexible duties. They all abstract from the details of a situation or particular relationship. But this demand for impartiality seems ill-suited to many aspects of human life. Friends and family, for example, are not just other members of the great crowd of humanity. They are special to us and it seems morally justified to treat them as such. Parenting is not a matter of cold duty, nor is friendship a calculation of pleasure and pain. These relationships have moral values that are not best discerned from the impartial point of view – especially when impartiality is monetized.[19]

This critique has its roots in a question that has been the subject of scientific research: Do women and men think differently about ethics? For instance, educational psychologist Lawrence Kohlberg in studies of moral development proposed a series of six progressive stages of ethical maturation. The fully mature person passes through a stage where rightness is conceived in terms of one's interpersonal relationships and reaches the highest stage, which is a Kantian view of rightness as conformity to universal principles. Kohlberg's colleague Carol Gilligan objected. She argued that fidelity to abstract principles applicable to all humanity is not a superior morality. Rather, it is a typically male way and is different from, but not in principle better than, a typically female emphasis on intimacy, caring, and personal relationships. In fact, caring and empathy may be better guides to what morality requires in many contexts than abstract rules or rational calculation.

Evolutionary psychology entered the debate by offering explanations for why women may more often adopt a different perspective in ethics. This scientific field interprets major features of human psychological life as the products of natural selection. A key difference between males and females is that men can father thousands of children, whereas women can have only a few children. This means that their optimal behavioral strategies will differ. Males will make only limited investments in many children, whereas women will invest heavily in a few and choose supporting partners. This is not to say that people do or should consciously calculate how to propagate their genes. It is just one allegedly scientific explanation for the general observation that women typically (but certainly not always) differ from men when it comes to moral thinking.

Feminist ethics has since become a multifaceted rethinking of traditional ethics and the ways it depreciates or devalues women's moral experience. Its proponents argue that traditional ethics overrates masculine traits such as autonomy while underrating interdependence and that it favors "male" ways of moral reasoning when emphasizing rules and universality over "female" ways of reasoning based in particularity and partiality. Furthermore, traditional ethics tends to ignore or trivialize moral

[19] Sandel 2012.

issues arising in the private realm typically associated with women and their role in caring for children, the infirm, and the elderly.

The ethics of care germinated from this insight in feminist ethics. It focuses on relationships rather than praiseworthy traits of persons or actions in the abstract. The ethics of care does not take duty as central or require the impartial promotion of everyone's interests alike. Furthermore, it does not picture ethics as a matter of choices made by autonomous agents. Rather, it begins with a view of agency as intrinsically relational and of ethics as a matter of cooperative negotiation in the pursuit of just and good relationships. The focus is often on small-scale, personal relationships. This perspective is relevant to science in at least two ways. First, it illuminates the moral motivation of many scientists who are driven into their career out of an urge to help care for loved ones who may benefit from their work. Second, it foregrounds the personal relationships in the daily life of scientists, including those between mentor and mentee and between researcher and test participants. These relationships often call for special, nuanced treatment that will differ from case to case.

This approach is limited, however, by the fact that personal relationships are not the whole of moral experience. If one does not have a personal relationship with a starving child, this fact alone does not mean that there is no obligation to help her or that her interests do not count. A sensible conclusion is that an ethical life includes both caring personal relationships and benevolent concern for people in general. Care ethics may not, then, be a stand-alone normative theory. Some claim it is best thought of as an additional principle of right action or a particular set of virtues. Others argue that the ethics of care can be extended into a full-fledged theory. No matter its status, it draws attention to important moral dimensions of human relationships that are often distorted or ignored in traditional normative theories.

Summary

One lesson from the thalidomide case is that the analysis of ethical issues entails thinking about a number of factors, including individual, professional, and institutional responsibility, rights, consequences, uncertainties, cultural norms, risks, expectations, and more. The facts of individual cases will often differ, and such differences matter for making sound moral judgments. Given this complexity, philosophical ethics is not likely to transform difficult questions into easy ones. In fact, ethical reflection often reveals just how nuanced and intricate the questions are. Nonetheless, the study of ethics can provide tools for thinking through such challenging issues. It helps promote critical analysis of intuitions, reasoned arguments, and defensible moral judgments. It encourages a move from unreflective hunches to principled and coherent positions, even though that stance will – as with any scientific position – remain open to modification in light of new evidence and further reflection.

Ethics is related to science in many ways, including ethical defenses and critiques of science. Most importantly, ethics pursues the knowledge necessary for distinguishing what people do value from what people should value. If such knowledge is possible, it is best grounded in the interpersonal process of reason-giving or justification. The three major normative theories surveyed each offer a different perspective on and approach to this process. Virtue ethics emphasizes the character of moral agents and the traits they must acquire in order to flourish. Utilitarian ethics focuses on the consequences of actions abstracted from agents, characterizing good outcomes in terms of the maximization of happiness. Deontological ethics emphasizes right action as conformity with a moral rule that is in accord with rationality. Finally, feminist ethics and the ethics of care, as potentially forming supplementary normative theories, focus on interpersonal relationships, justifying actions as right and outcomes as good insofar as they sustain those relationships.

Extending reflection: codes of conduct for computer scientists and software engineers

Professional codes of conduct affirm ethical principles that are based in one or more of the general ethical theories discussed above and are intended to guide the conduct of practitioners. For example, the first line of the Nuremberg Code, drafted shortly after revelation of the atrocious experiments conducted by Nazi physicians and scientists on concentration camp prisoners, reads: "The voluntary consent of the human subject is absolutely essential." In this way, it adapts the core of deontological theory – respect the dignity of all persons – into a concrete principle or imperative to guide professional conduct. In their work with human participants in experimental trials, scientists must honestly discuss the goals and risks of the trial and obtain free and informed consent from human subjects. As another example, one modern adaptation of the Hippocratic Oath appears to reference an ethics of care when it declares, "I will remember that there is art to medicine as well as science, and that warmth, sympathy, and understanding may outweigh the surgeon's knife or the chemist's drug" (see the Appendix, "Ethics Codes").

The function and status of codes is complex and debated.[20] They not only provide guidance for professionals but serve to define the field. For example, a physician who regularly violates a medical ethics code by doing harm to his or her patients is not just behaving unethically, but is no longer behaving *as a physician*. In this way, codes of ethics play a central role in defining the norms of a given scientific practice. In so doing, they shape scientific fields into professions, because part of what makes a profession (in addition to lengthy training in the service of socially valued goods) is standards of competence and conduct that govern activity and ensure quality and integrity. By listing the norms essential to professional conduct, codes serve as explicit statements of the rules of the game that is (metaphorically) being played by the practitioners of a field. Governing bodies, such as the American Anthropological Association or the American Chemical Society, take responsibility for ensuring the standards identified in the code are upheld by their members.

By the late twentieth century it was apparent that computers would play a crucial role in modern society. This meant that computer scientists and software engineers were acquiring significant power to do good or cause harm and to enable others to do good or cause harm. Just think, for example, of the influence that computing systems have on individual privacy, national security, media, democracy, and international finance. In 1973, in recognition of this power, the Association for Computing Machinery (ACM) adopted a first version of an ACM Code of Ethics and Professional Conduct (which was revised in the 1980s and 1990s). Subsequently, the ACM together with the Institute for Electrical and Electronic Engineers (IEEE) Computer Society adopted the ACM/IEEE-CS Software Engineering Code of Ethics and Professional Practice. A brief look at them shows that they draw from and interweave all of the ethical theories discussed

[20] See, e.g., Davis 2002 for a sensitive analysis of the issues.

above in seeking practical principles to guide the conduct of computing professionals.

For example, in its first moral imperative, the current ACM code (1992) affirms a deontological principle to "protect fundamental human rights." Yet in the very next sentence it adopts the consequentialist reasoning of utilitarianism to stress that computing professionals should "minimize negative consequences." What if these principles clash in a particular context? For example, if privacy is a "fundamental human right" designing a program that protects it might have negative consequences for a corporation that could make money from personal data or for a government that needs those data to ensure national security. What is the right thing to do? Which principle or whose interests trumps the others and why?

In its preamble, the ACM/ IEEE-CS code (1999) notes:

> The Code is not a simple ethical algorithm that generates ethical decisions. In some situations, standards may be in tension with each other or with standards from other sources. These situations require the software engineer to use ethical judgment to act in a manner which is most consistent with the spirit of the Code of Ethics and Professional Practice, given the circumstances.

In so recommeding, this code makes a direct appeal to the virtues of individual scientists and engineers. At the core of Aristotle's ethical theory is the insight that moral decision-making is not as simple as rule-following. One must have the requisite virtue to recognize the right course of action in a new context and follow through with it. For Aristotle, this central intellectual virtue is *phronesis* (practice wisdom), which the ACM/IEEE-CS code appeals to in the preamble and with its fourth principle of "judgment." In order for scientists to live up to the ideals "encoded" by their profession, they must cultivate the virtue of wise practical judgment so that they may answer: How to do things right? and What is the right thing to do?

Questions for research and discussion

1. Looking at these codes, what other virtues are defined as essential to the conduct of computer scientists and software engineers? How do these compare with the virtues found in other scientific and engineering codes of conduct?

2. Consider codes of conduct articulated by other professional scientific and technical societies. Could there be a science-wide code for all disciplines? If so, what principles or imperatives would it affirm? Or could it be, perhaps, that ethical norms are discipline-specific?
3. What is the hacker code of ethics and how does it compare with professional computing codes? What is open source software and why do some argue that all software should be free or open source?
4. The ACM code calls for computer scientists to contribute to human well-being and notes that this includes a "safe natural environment." Yet electronic waste from computers often contains contaminants such as lead, cadmium, mercury, and beryllium that cause health and pollution problems especially in the developing countries that import it. Do computer scientists and software engineers bear any moral responsibility for the environmental and human health problems caused by electronic waste?

Further reading about the cases

Bynum, Terrell Ward, and Simon Rogerson, eds. (2004) *Computer Ethics and Professional Responsibility*. Malden, MA: Blackwell.

Johnson, Deborah (2009) *Computer Ethics*, 4th edn. Upper Saddle River, NJ: Prentice Hall.

Mintz, Morton (1962) "'Heroine' of FDA Keeps Bad Drug Off of Market," *Washington Post*, July 15, front page.

Raymond, Eric S. (2001) *The Cathedral and the Bazaar: Musings on Linux and Open Source by an Accidental Revolutionary*. Cambridge, MA: O'Reilly Media.

Rigby, Kate (2007) *Thalidomide Kid*. Wigan, Lancs.: Bewrite Books.

Stephens, Trent, and Rock Brynner (2001) *Dark Remedy: The Impact of Thalidomide and Its Revival as a Vital Medicine*. New York: Basic Books.

Zimmer, Carl (2010) "Answers Begin to Emerge on How Thalidomide Caused Defects," *New York Times*, March 15.

3 Science and its norms

As indicated in Chapter 2, norms are forms of behavior expected by and constitutive of a group; ethics involves an effort at critical reflection on such norms. These norms can be implicit or explicit, the outgrowth of custom and tradition or the outcome of rational decision. This chapter gives a slightly more expansive account of the norms constitutive of science, in preparation for considerations of the complexities of their practical realization. It concerns the norms of science in a general sense - as these have developed historically and become implicitly constitutive of science as a knowledge-producing activity. It argues for a foundational distinction between myth (narrative) and science (nonnarrative rationality) and highlights the institutionalization of modern science that began shortly after Galileo Galilei's encounter with the church. The final sections survey epistemological and social norms intrinsic to the conduct of science.

Setting the stage: Galileo and the church

In the pantheon of science, Galileo Galilei (1564–1642), Isaac Newton (1643–1727), and Albert Einstein (1879–1955) are often taken to exemplify the ideal. But given his historical priority and conflict with church authority, it is Galileo who is commonly thought to be the most heroic figure - and thus to present in vivid form the general norms of science, even insofar as he was forced to betray them.

Two decades before Galileo's birth, in the year of his own death, the Polish astronomer Nicolaus Copernicus (1473–1543) published *De revolutionibus orbium coelestium* (On the revolution of celestial spheres), putting forth the first comprehensive heliocentric model for planetary motion. In 1596 Galileo's German contemporary Johannes Kepler (1571–1630) published *Mysterium cosmographicum* (Cosmographic mystery), a defense of Copernicus' model using mathematical arguments and appeals to theological symbolism; the relation between the Sun at the center, the outer stellar sphere, and the intermediate space of the planets was proposed as corresponding to the Father, Son, and Holy Spirit, respectively. Indeed, Kepler had a mystical sense of the relation between physical and spiritual such that with his formulation of the laws of planetary motion he was "thinking God's thoughts after him." One version of the *Mysterium cosmographicum* included an effort to reconcile biblical passages that imply geocentrism with the new heliocentric model.

Ten years later Galileo, using the newly invented telescope, began a series of observations that he thought provided empirical evidence for the same model. His observations, however, undermined common beliefs associated with the Ptolemaic, geocentric model. Among these observations, as reported in 1610 in his *Sidereus nuncius* (Starry messenger), were the existence of mountains on the Moon, the moons around the planet Jupiter, and the decomposition of cloudy masses in the night sky into dense collections of stars. In a letter to Kepler, he noted how some opponents rejected his observations by declining even to engage with the empirical evidence.

> My dear Kepler … What would you say of the learned here, who, replete with the pertinacity of an asp have steadfastly refused to cast a glance through the telescope? What shall we make of all this? Shall we laugh, or shall we cry?[1]

Against mathematical and empirical arguments were arguments from the Bible, common sense, and theology. In a famous letter of 1615 to Grand Duchess Christina, Galileo attempted to distinguish science from theology with the formula (quoted from Cardinal Baronius) that the Bible teaches "how one goes to heaven, not how heaven goes".[2] But the Catholic theologian Robert Cardinal Bellarmine argued against such an easy separation and for treating heliocentrism as no more than a model useful for some purposes but not representative of reality. First, since the plain sense of many passages in scripture presumes geocentrism, heliocentrism raises questions about the veracity of the Holy Spirit in regard to other, more central teachings. Second, our own common-sense experience is of the Earth as standing still rather than in rapid motion.

[1] De Santillana 1955, p. 9. [2] Drake 1957, p. 186.

Third, to date neither mathematical modeling nor empirical evidence had provided conclusive proof of heliocentrism. Fourth, others suggested that to trust in an instrumental enhancement of the senses such as that provided by the telescope constituted a kind of questioning of whether God had created humans with all necessary and appropriate perceptual abilities, and wondered whether instrumentation might distort rather than enhance perception. Fifth, in cases of doubt, it was not permissible to depart from traditional beliefs, especially when such departure might threaten something more important, namely faith and order. As far as Bellarmine was concerned, Galileo was permitted to undertake research on heliocentrism as a theory with instrumental value but not to advocate it as knowledge of reality.

For more than a decade, Bellarmine's position served as an intellectual *detente* between Galileo and the church. Then in 1632 Galileo published *Dialogo sopra i due massimi sistemi del mondo* (Dialogue on the two greatest world systems, written in Italian rather than Latin) comparing geocentrism and heliocentrism. In the text, not only were the better arguments given to the proponent of heliocentrism, named "Salviati," but the defender of geocentrism was named "Simplicio." In short order Galileo was called from his home in Florence to Rome, where he could stand trial "for holding as true the false doctrine taught by some that the Sun is the center of the world." In a white shirt of penitence, Galileo knelt and heard his sentence:

> This Holy Tribunal being therefore of intention to proceed against the disorder and mischief thence resulting . ...
>
> We say, pronounce, sentence, and declare that you ... have rendered yourself in the judgment of this Holy Office vehemently suspected of heresy, namely of having believed and held the doctrine – which is false and contrary to the sacred and divine Scriptures – that the Sun is the center of the world and does not move from east to west and that the Earth moves and is not the center of the world . ...
>
> And in order that this your grave and pernicious error and transgression may not remain altogether unpunished and that you may be more cautious in the future and an example to others ... we ordain that the book of the "Dialogues of Galileo Galilei" be prohibited by public edict.[3]

[3] De Santillana 1955, pp. 307 and 310.

The final pronouncement was signed by seven of the ten cardinals sitting in judgment. Following the sentence, Galileo spoke as follows:

> [D]esiring to remove from the minds of your Eminences, and of all faithful Christians, this vehement suspicion justly conceived against me, with sincere heart and unfeigned faith I abjure, curse, and detest the aforesaid errors and heresies and generally every other error, heresy, and sect whatsoever contrary to the Holy Church and I swear that in the future I will never say or assert, verbally or in writing, anything that might furnish occasion for a similar suspicion regarding me ....[4]

The legend that Galileo muttered under his breath, "E pur si muove" (Nevertheless it moves), has no contemporary warrant, although it may well express his ultimate belief. A few days later, Galileo was released into the custody of the Florentine ambassador, who described his charge as "extremely downcast." Later that year Galileo was granted permission to return under house arrest to his own home outside Florence, where he grew progressively blind and was to die nine years later, age 78.

The case of Galileo, which has more complexities than those recounted here, raises questions about the character of science. For present purposes it encourages considerations of modern science as a social institution structured by distinctive epistemological and social norms that could oppose both common sense and religion.

Emergence of natural philosophy

The idea of science as a disciplined or methodological inquiry into the nature of the world that should have implications for those who are not natural scientists – for example, religious believers or political leaders – has a distinctive history. This is also a controversial history, in part because of disagreements about precisely what constitutes the defining characteristics of science. The following selective observations detail some subtleties in the Galileo case and the rise of modern science as a novel knowledge-producing enterprise.

Prior to the period represented by Galileo there had, of course, been others who sought to understand the world in nonreligious or nonpolitical terms. But predecessors such as Aristotle or Lucretius saw themselves as

[4] De Santillana 1955, p. 312.

members of an elite community separate from the majority. Reflecting this separation, they understood the world differently than their fellow citizens, religious people, or political leaders. Indeed, according to Aristotle, the key distinction was this: for most people the world is explained by appeals to mythical religious narratives or what anthropologists call "just-so stories."

Mythical just-so stories in which superhuman beings or deities cause things to be the way they are can be found in all cultures. According to Hesiod's account of Greek myths, in the beginning Chaos gave birth to Gaea and Tartarus, and Gaea then brought forth Ouranous to cover herself, thus constituting the fundamental elements of the world: Earth, Underworld, and Sky. In like manner, according to an African myth, Unkulunkulu or the Great One emerged from the swamp of Uhlanga to create the Zulu people and their cattle and everything else, and to teach how to hunt, make fire, and grow food. Indigenous American myths explain such things as how the bear lost his tail, by getting it frozen in a river in the beginning time. More abstractly, the *Dao dejing* (a fourth-century-BCE Chinese text attributed to Laozi) says that originally there was a featureless something called the *Dao* or Way.

> The Way produces the One.
> The One produces two.
> Two produces three.
> Three produces the myriad beings.
> The myriad beings shoulder *yin* and embrace *yang*,
> and by blending these *qi* [energies] attain harmony.[5]

Such cosmogonic narratives share common themes of movement from disorder to order, the establishment of foundational distinctions, and the creation of cultural traditions.

During the sixth century BCE in the Greek diaspora, on the western coast of what is now Turkey, a few "natural philosophers" began to propose alternative explanations for the way things are, appealing not to mythical narratives but to *phusis* or nature, the inherent features of the things themselves, and to the *logos* or rational relationship between things. In Aristotle's articulation of this tradition, the physical world is composed

[5] Ivanhoe 2002, p. 45.

of earth, air, fire, and water and their interactions; in the generation before Aristotle the philosophers Leucippus and Democritus developed a proto-atomic theory of material reality. But in none of these cases – from Leucippus through Aristotle – was there any sense that the naturalistic explanation of things was one that should be exported from the few and taught to the many. Naturalistic explanation developed among an intellectual elite and existed alongside, without trying to transform or eliminate, religious or political narratives.

Narratives depend on imaginary characters with interests and motivations placed in dramatic situations that have to be worked out in unique interactions exhibiting a beginning, middle, and end. Narratives are one of the most basic forms of human speech which, when offered as explanations not just for individual human behaviors but for some fundamental aspects of reality (such as earth and sky) or the features of particular things (that bears lack tails), are said to take place in an aboriginal time that allows things to become archetypical. Because they resemble the pervasive human experience of competing interests, mythical narratives require little justification. The popularity of Homeric, biblical, and other stories can be taken as a given. With appeals to nature and logic, however, the situation is different. Not only are natural philosophical explanations not easily exported from the few to the many, even among the few, elaboration and justification are necessary. For example, Galileo must argue and demonstrate even to Kepler how his observations help confirm heliocentrism and/or falsify geocentrism. The conscious effort to elaborate and justify nonnarrative rationality gives rise to what are called scientific methods that embody the epistemological norms of science.

The first great effort to appeal to reason and nature to explain things can be found in the works of Aristotle, especially that collection of six books known as the *Organon* (Greek for "tool" or "instrument," in this case of natural philosophy). It is here that Aristotle tried to identify the unique structure of nonnarrative argument and explanation. The *Prior Analytics*, for instance, examines the deductive logic of the syllogism and the *Posterior Analytics* probes inductive inference, in an original effort to articulate a method for the empirical sciences. For more than a thousand years other natural philosophers adopted, modified, and extended in various elite traditions the elaboration and justification of nonnarrative, scientific explanation. This ongoing inquiry into the nature of scientific or systematic knowledge of the natural world included distinctions between empirical and theoretical knowledge, the methods (observational and mathematical) for acquiring such knowledge and assessing competing claims to knowledge, and the value of such knowledge once acquired. Discussions nevertheless remained within more or less closed intellectual communities that did not try to alter the ways other people thought about the world.

The Jewish, then the Christian, and finally the Islamic claims to divine revelation challenged this tradition of separation between natural philosophy and religion and politics. As the Christian revelation came into increasing contact with philosophical traditions of the Greek and Roman worlds, Christian intellectuals worked to bridge or harmonize natural knowledge and supernatural revelation. This bridge-building seemed to be required by two claims of revelation: that God created the world and that it was good (Genesis 1–2), and that the creator God was *logos* or rationality incarnate (see the opening text of the Gospel of John). If God created a good world, how could there be any conflict between different kinds of knowledge in creation (whether narrative or natural philosophical)? If God was the creator of nature and himself reason incarnate, how could his revelation be opposed to human reason about nature?

Early efforts to harmonize revelation and reason remained mostly within elite intellectual communities created by great philosophers and their students. Examples include the Jewish philosopher Philo in Alexandria, Egypt, and the Islamic philosopher Alfarabi in Baghdad and Damascus. Among these philosophers it was common to argue that revelation was reason given narrative form for the masses; in cases of conflict, reason simply trumped revelation. Since many religious leaders would find this view unacceptable, and such leaders often had the ear of political leaders who could make life difficult for dissenters, philosophers tended to write works that said one thing openly but another thing secretly.

In the Christian world of the northern Mediterranean that began to emerge following the Edict of Milan in 312, the revelation versus reason issue was different. There was less demand to harmonize revelation and reason, in part because of the more practical inclinations of Christian intellectuals; St. Augustine, for instance, was first and foremost a bishop, the pastor of a community. In addition, the natural scientific work of Aristotle was largely overshadowed by the more ethical and idealistic perspectives of Plato, which were more readily synthesized with Christian theology. With the recovery of Aristotle that began in twelfth-century Spain, however, the revelation–reason relationship became an issue of concern, but one that was approached with a commitment to avoid any subordination of revelation to reason. A corresponding effort ensued to inform public thinking with philosophical reasoning about nature.

St. Thomas Aquinas advanced the most influential synthesis of Aristotelian natural philosophy and Christian revelation. Thomas argued that the methods of science and its epistemological norms could simply be enclosed within revelation. In some rare cases natural scientific knowledge could correct statements of revelation, but only insofar as the statements at issue did not bear on questions of faith and morals. Galileo's belief that the Bible teaches "how to go to heaven not how the heavens go" thus echoed the Thomist harmonization of revelation with Aristotle. But the anti-Aristotelian science of Galileo did not yet exist as a social institution strong enough to enact this division of labor between the church and science.

The social institutionalization of science

The thousand-year emergence of natural philosophy was dramatically transformed beginning in the sixteenth century, especially in England and France, where science became a social institution. Two key figures in this transformation were the government official and philosopher Francis Bacon and the government adviser René Descartes, each of whom emphasized an aspect of Galileo's approach.

In his *Novum Organon*, Bacon undertook an extended criticism of Aristotelian aims and methods. Bacon argued for a radical repurposing of natural philosophy in which knowledge production would be more concerned with the development of power and control over nature than its contemplation. In support of this transformation, Bacon appealed to the Christian revelation of charity or love of neighbor as the highest good. To live out the divine commandment to practice charity and take care of others it was necessary, Bacon argued, to set aside fruitless disputation and get to work.

With regard to the method of such work, Bacon undertook to clear away false methods and propose new ones. Book 1, for instance, identified four "idols" that commonly divert scientific inquiry from its proper activity of creating new knowledge rather than simply preserving existing knowledge. "Idols of the tribe," or group preconceptions, lead people to see things in old ways. "Idols of the cave" are constituted by individual weaknesses and biases that distort experience. "Idols of the marketplace" are those that result from failures to use language carefully. "Idols of the theater" are manifested when people have too much respect for received philosophical systems and mistaken methods. While Bacon repeatedly castigates slavish followers of Aristotle, like Galileo he is more critical of those followers who have made an idol of the Stagirite (Aristotle) than of Aristotle himself. In book 2, Bacon proceeds in a positive manner to outline a new procedure of empirical induction for isolating form and cause in nature by what he calls the methods of agreement, difference, and variation. Bacon had little use for mathematical deduction and sought instead to reinvigorate observation and promote controlled, replicable experimentation as a key element in what would become the basic methods of science.

What is perhaps most significant in Bacon, however, is not so much his methodological proposals as his repurposing of natural philosophy for practical benefit and the "relief of man's estate." Although presented argumentatively in introductory material to the *Novum Organon* under the title "The Great Instauration," Bacon's argument took narrative form in *The New Atlantis* so as to appeal to a much larger audience. The story relates the discovery of a utopian society on an island in the Pacific Ocean dominated by a scientific research institution (Solomon's House) bridging theory and practice and funded by the state. A synthesis between theory and practice for the enhancement of practice promoted collaborations between natural philosophers and artisans, since it is artisans who know how to make things in ways that can be assisted by theoretical analysis (see Chapter 12 on engineering). The idea of a scientific research institution such as Solomon's House led to establishment of the Royal Society as the first social organization dedicated to the advancement of science and given official recognition by a government. Such a vision was further promulgated by the *philosophes* who created the *Encyclopédie* of the French Enlightenment.

The sociologist Joseph Ben-David argues that "the crucial difference in the place of science in England as compared with other countries about

1700 was that in England science was institutionalized."[6] When any activity becomes a social institution it means that society recognizes the activity as performing an important social function; there exist norms for the internal self-regulation of the activity; and there is some adaptation of norms in other areas of the social world to accommodate the newly institutionalized activity.

> In the case of science, institutionalization implies the recognition of exact and empirical research as a method of inquiry that leads to the discovery of important new knowledge. Such knowledge is distinct and independent of other ways of acquiring knowledge such as tradition, speculation, or revelation.[7]

The institutionalization of science also "imposes certain moral obligations on its practitioners," and social accommodations such as scientific freedom of speech and publication, including some measure of religious and political tolerance for scientists, and "a certain flexibility to make society and culture adaptable to constant change that results from the freedom of inquiry" (see Chapter 11 on science and culture).[8]

The "Royal Society of London for Improving Natural Knowledge" grew out of a mid-1640s "invisible college" of natural philosophers who met regularly to discuss Bacon's ideas for the institutionalization of science and the reform of its methods. Formal constitution took place in 1660 when twelve members of the group, after a public lecture at Gresham College, decided to found "a College for the Promoting of Physico-Mathematical Experimental Learning." This new group was then given monarchial recognition in 1662 as the Royal Society to "encourage philosophical studies, especially those which by actual experiments attempt either to shape out a new philosophy or to perfect the old" and thus became a self-governing organization with the right "to print such things, matters, and affairs touching and concerning" the Society – that is, to publish the results of its research.

In this the Royal Society became a prototype for subsequent formal scientific associations at both the governmental (national academy) and non-governmental organization levels, with its members becoming role models for scientists in society more generally. For instance, unlike continental

[6] Ben-David 1984, p. 75. [7] Ben-David 1984, p. 75. [8] Ben-David 1984, p. 76.

counterparts such as René Descartes or Gottfried Leibniz, members of the Royal Society did not subordinate their scientific work to some broader speculative philosophy, but instead focused piecemeal on well-defined technical investigations with a faith in the unlimited beneficial advancement of practical knowledge. From its beginnings, the Royal Society was also committed to informing the nonscientific public about science and its achievements through regular public lectures and demonstrations.

As one signal instance of its publication program, in 1665 the Royal Society initiated the *Philosophical Transactions*, which has become the oldest continuously published scientific periodical in the world. Henry Oldenburg, a native of Germany and first secretary of the society, who maintained an extensive network of scientific correspondence, became the *Transactions* editor. From the beginning Oldenburg drew on his network of associates to have manuscripts reviewed as part of the process of deciding whether or not to publish, thus establishing the practice of peer review. Peer review has ever since been a feature of the internal governance of science, albeit one that is facing major challenges as the information age continues to revolutionize the ways in which knowledge is produced and disseminated.

Scientific methods and epistemological norms

Beginning in the nineteenth century, natural philosophers turned with renewed interest to questions of what makes science a unique cognitive or knowledge-producing activity. What precisely was the scientific method and the epistemological norms on which it was based? In the English-speaking world, William Whewell and John Stuart Mill offered leading responses to this question. The first of these philosophers of science also coined the term "scientist" for one who advances science as systematic knowledge of the natural world. Whewell initially proposed "scientist" ironically, then a few years later in a more serious manner:

> We need very much a name to describe a cultivator of science in general. I should incline to call him a *Scientist*. Thus we might say, that as an Artist is a Musician, Painter, or Poet, a Scientist is a Mathematician, Physicist, or Naturalist.[9]

[9] Whewell 1840, p. cxiii.

In his 1840 *Philosophy of the Inductive Sciences* – the second volume of which in revised form was retitled, in explicit reference to Bacon, *Novum Organum Renovartum* (1858) – Whewell analyzed the methodology and epistemological norms of science. He steered a course between rationalism (which emphasized norms of intuition and deductive reasoning) and empiricism (which emphasized norms of observation and experimentation). Whewell called his method knowledge by "consilience." In contrast, Mill's *A System of Logic* (1843) sought to subordinate all scientific inference to norms of strict observation.

The difference between Mill and Whewell can be exemplified by their alternative interpretations of Kepler. For Mill, Kepler simply derived the elliptical orbits of the planets from clear data and careful work; the planetary ellipses were given by the astronomical observation plots; end of story. For Whewell, the data were incomplete and called for careful consideration of different possible orbital trajectories consistent with other facts already known about astronomical phenomena such as that planetary motion did not take place in zigzag forms; Kepler could not help but impose the idea of an ellipse on unclear data by means of creative hypothesizing.

Later philosophical analysis shifted from attempts to understand the norms of induction as the proper means for acquiring scientific knowledge, in part because the norms of experimental inference were becoming stabilized within the new social institution of science. Philosophical reflection in the mid-twentieth century turned instead to analyzing the normative structure of scientific knowledge once it had been acquired by whatever means. According to the model developed by German-American philosopher Carl Hempel, scientific explanations exhibit what is called a covering law or deductive-nomological structure. Scientific explanations work by identifying a general law that can be applied to or cover some specific fact, often by deducing a fact or observation from the law and some antecedent conditions (hence, deductive-nomological, *nomos* being the Greek word for "law"). One example would be using Newton's law of force equals mass times acceleration ($F = ma$) to deduce the impact of a speeding comet on the Earth. In such cases, the scientific law "covers" any number of particular events (from cannonballs to hockey pucks), and this covering by means of laws is the structure of scientific knowledge.

Hempel's contemporary, the Austrian-British philosopher Karl Popper, argued that for any deductive-nomological explanation to be scientific, it had to be falsifiable. After all, one could formulate a law statement such that "prayer makes people better" to explain the importance of prayer in the lives of many people. But if someone were to object that when sick person *X* prayed she was not cured of her illness a theologian might respond that she became better in a different sense by becoming more able to accept her sickness and pain. It is difficult to see how the prayer law statement could ever be falsified – a charge Popper also leveled against laws proposed in (scientific) Marxism and Freudian psychoanalysis. According to Popper, if an explanation is not sufficiently structured so that it could in principle be falsified by some empirical evidence, then it is not truly a scientific explanation.

Popper argued for distinguishing science from pseudo-science by means of a well-formulated demarcation criterion (i.e., falsifiability). Other criteria have been proposed, including testability, reproducibility, explanatory power, consistency, and simplicity – or some combination of these and still others. But whatever they are, it is argued that propositions must meet some epistemological standards in order to be accepted as scientific. They must be testable and the phenomena they reference reproducible; they need to have explanatory power, including some ability to predict phenomena; they need to be consistent with previously established propositions; and they should be as simple as possible. This problem of demarcating science from pseudo-science is further related to the problem of choosing between laws, models, or theories. In selecting between alternative theories, we can judge one to be scientifically superior to another if it explains a greater number of phenomena, is more consistent with already established theories, or is simpler. Of course all of these questions about what epistemic norms constitute science and what they mean in practice are the focus of ongoing philosophic debates.

Social norms in science

Science is a human activity as well as an epistemic method, a type of knowledge, and a set of laws and theories. But it was not until social scientists began to investigate the practices of science that the social or behavioral norms of science began to be explicitly articulated and examined. One of the early leaders in research on science as a social activity was Robert Merton.

As a sociologist, Merton argued that the appropriate way to provide something like covering law explanations for social phenomena was to analyze their functions using middle-level theories – theories situated somewhere between raw empirical data and high-level theories such as Newton's theory of gravity. In the 1930s and 1940s, partly in response to National Socialist and Soviet Communist efforts to subordinate science to the control of authoritarian political ideologies, Merton applied his middle-level functionalism to scientific behavior. Working from historical and empirical observations, Merton formulated a middle-level theory of the social norms that he saw operative in science as a social institution. It was, Merton argued, the gradual adoption of these norms that in fact constituted the creation of modern natural science as a social institution rather than simply the practices of isolated individuals such as Galileo or Newton. In his most commonly cited statement of these norms, he listed them as follows:

- Communalism, in which individuals cease to keep knowledge secret but systematically share it with others.
- Universalism, meaning that knowledge claims are evaluated in terms of universal or impersonal criteria, without reference to the nationality, religion, class, race, or gender of the scientists making them. (This norm also means that individual scientists rise through the professional ranks on the basis solely of their merit rather than personal or political ties.)
- Disinterestedness, in which scientists work to avoid letting personal interests influence the results of their knowledge-producing activities (although not necessarily the areas in which they work to produce knowledge). This also involves the institutionalization of self-policing that holds scientists accountable only to peer scientists rather than to other members of society and their interests.
- Organized skepticism, establishing a context in which all knowledge is tested and subject to rigorous, structured community scrutiny. This requires the temporary suspension of judgment and detached scrutiny of beliefs, even those deemed by some groups to be off limits for rational analysis.[10]

Ben-David, echoing Merton's CUDOS list ("communalism, universalism, disinterestedness, and organized skepticism"), calls attention to the

[10] Merton 1942.

"completely universalistic evaluation of contributions; the obligation to communicate one's discoveries to [others] for use and criticism; [and] the proper acknowledgment of the contributions of others."[11]

On the one hand, these social norms of science are clearly related to epistemological norms. They echo, for instance, the ideals Bacon develops in his criticisms of four idols that obstruct the development of science. This makes them special to the profession of science and its goal of producing knowledge. That is, a scientist acting as a scientist (rather than, say, a novelist) cannot simply invent a story that suits her interests or preferred worldview. On the other hand, the social norms are general norms of behavior necessary for any group. Any group, in order to function as a group, has to practice honesty among its members, the keeping of promises, and more. The Galileo case suggests, for instance, that courage may be a character virtue as valuable in science as in other aspects of life. It takes courage to endeavor to understand the world through reason and observations rather than by accepting the myths of a culture. Furthermore, if the findings of science contradict dominant religious or political beliefs, it may take courage to speak truth to power.

The operationalization of these social norms in science can also exhibit quite diverse forms. For instance, the practice of peer review, which is an operationalization of more than one Mertonian social norm, can be single or double blind, involve an indefinite number of reviewers, be applied to publications and/or grants, rest with senior or junior members of the scientific community, and more.

For some philosophers such as John Dewey and scientists such as Michael Polanyi these social norms are not limited to science but should be seen as the best example of social norms more generally. In *Democracy and Education* Dewey argues that because science is at once "the emancipation of mind from devotion to customary purposes" and "experience becoming rational" it is the basis for rational democracy and social progress.[12] Polanyi likewise argues that the "republic of science" depends on and operationalizes the ideals of democratic society and the free market: freedom of inquiry, individual initiative, and democratic decision-making. Polanyi even compares the production and circulation of knowledge in

[11] Ben-David 1984, pp. 75–76. [12] Dewey 1916, pp. 223 and 225.

science to that of methods for producing and circulating material goods as analyzed by Adam Smith.

In the last half of the twentieth century, historians and sociologists of science, along with scientists themselves, increasingly became interested in understanding how scientific knowledge advanced. According to the American physicist Thomas Kuhn, scientific knowledge production in a "normal" setting is constituted by the acceptance of some paradigm for scientific practice. In pre-paradigmatic form, scientists tend to flounder, performing first one experiment then another, proposing various theories, few of which lead to any cumulative knowledge production. A paradigm becomes established by a process that rests not only on cognitive achievements but on social influences. After that, scientific work takes on a focus that results in the accumulation of knowledge – until some point at which problems arise as a result of weaknesses in the ability of the paradigm or its theories to cover newly emerging observations. At this point, knowledge production becomes open to a scientific revolution and a new paradigm develops that can deal with the anomalies.

The marshaling of social influence to help establish a new paradigm will likely transcend Mertonian social norms and employ the manipulation of friendship networks, academic rewards, and even funding support. In some cases, as Kuhn notes, one generation of scientists with their paradigm commitments simply has to die off and be replaced by a new generation. At the same time, Kuhn claims that ultimately basic epistemological norms or values are manifested through paradigmatic change. For Kuhn, five criteria are controlling: accuracy, scope, fruitfulness, consistency, and simplicity.

In a nuanced extension of this argument, philosopher of science Helen Longino likewise grants the leading influence of "constitutive values" in science as "the source of the rules determining what constitutes scientific practice or scientific method." Constitutive values in this sense can include both epistemological and social norms of the Mertonian type. Beyond constitutive values, however, Longino also argues there exist contextual values that "belong to the social and cultural environment in which science is done."[13] Abstract constitutive values are in continuous dialogue

[13] Longino 1990, p. 4.

with such contextual values as, for instance, background assumptions about how authority and criticism should function as well as what kinds of problems deserve scientific attention. Indeed, without values arising from particular social contexts, constitutive values "are too impoverished to produce scientific theories of the beauty and power that characterize" existing theories.[14]

Summary

Myths explain the way things are through narratives that often involve the workings of deities and supernatural forces. They are not to be confirmed, verified, added to, or improved through observation or rational analysis. They are simply to be remembered and retold. By contrast, natural philosophy or science attempts to explain the way things are by appeal to the inherent features of the things themselves and the relation between things. Because science is a process of discovery (rather than the preservation of stories), it necessarily requires standards or norms that define legitimate methods for obtaining knowledge (how can we legitimately add to the stock of things we know?). From its beginnings, then, science has entailed attempts to elaborate and justify the norms that govern nonnarrative rationality.

In the contemporary world, communicating scientific knowledge to the larger nonscientific public continues to be problematic. As with the Galileo situation, there remain cases in which scientific theories such as evolution are rejected by significant segments of the population, so that scientists have to ask themselves how courageously to argue their beliefs. Even more demanding are questions about how much scientists should attempt to communicate by simplifying the theoretical complexities of their work in order to secure public funding – as when they colorize photographs from other planets in order to excite popular appreciation of space exploration. Last but not least are the dangers of sharing knowledge that can be used by enemy countries or nonstate actors to do harm. In the post-9/11 world, there have been numerous instances in which scientific knowledge has been removed from the public realm in ways that the creators of the French *Encyclopédie*, Dewey, Polanyi, and others would

[14] Longino 1990, p. 219.

have found incompatible with the normative ideals of a science and its potential to transform democratic intelligence.

Post-Galileo, recognizing that the transformation of popular social institutions could best be undertaken by other social institutions, scientists began to develop social formations for sheltering and promoting scientific knowledge production. The institutionalization of science requires the explicit articulation of certain epistemological and social norms in order to hold together the members of a larger social group. Among the epistemological norms, the most fundamental are reproducibility, explanatory power, scope, consistency, and simplicity. Complementing such epistemological norms are the Mertonian social norms of communalism, universalism, disinterestedness, and organized skepticism.

Extending reflection: anthropologists and the military

The German-American Franz Boas is considered the "father of modern anthropology." Boas believed that all social scientists have a responsibility to engage important social issues, but they must never employ deceitful methods. In 1919, he learned that four anthropologists conducting research in other countries were serving as informants for the US government. This prompted him to write an impassioned letter to *The Nation* where he articulated a fundamental norm for scientists. Soldiers, diplomats, politicians, and businessmen may be excused for deception and secretiveness, but

> Not so the scientist. The very essence of his life is the service of truth … A person … who uses science as a cover for political spying, who demeans himself to pose before a foreign government as an investigator and asks for assistance in his alleged researches in order to carry on, under this cloak, his political machinations, prostitutes science in an unpardonable way and forfeits the right to be classed as a scientist.[15]

Far from spurring self-scrutiny or apologies on the part of anthropologists, Boas' letter was met with disdain. The Anthropological Society of Washington passed a resolution condemning Boas for attacking the principles of American democracy and for endangering anthropologists abroad, who would now be suspected spies. The American Anthropological

[15] Boas 1919, p. 797.

Association (AAA), of which Boas was a founding member in 1902, voted to censure Boas.

Anthropologists performed extensive research for the US government during World War II in attempts to better understand Japanese and German cultures and identify weaknesses and means of persuasion to aid the war effort. In 1941, the AAA passed a resolution: "Be it resolved that the American Anthropological Association places itself and its resources and the specialized skills of its members at the disposal of the country for the successful prosecution of the war." American anthropologist Ruth Benedict wrote *The Chrysanthemum and the Sword* at the invitation of the US Office of War Information in order to better predict and understand Japanese behavior during the war.

In 1971, the AAA adopted its first code of ethics years after revelations that anthropologists had engaged in counterinsurgency research in Southeast Asia. In a striking reversal of its censure of Boas, the AAA code rejected any research conducted in secret and strongly advised anthropologists to avoid working for any government. (However, it was not until 2005 that the AAA rescinded its censure of Boas.) In 1998, in another turn of position, AAA eliminated the ban on government work and any reference to secret research.

In 2006, the US Army and Marine Corps published the *Counterinsurgency Field Manual*, which included tactics for mobilizing the cultural expertise of anthropologists to assist in military operations. That same year, the US Army deployed five Human Terrain Teams of social scientists with tactical military units in Iraq and Afghanistan to advise commanders about local sociocultural environments. This was the beginning of Human Terrain System, a program designed to supply sociocultural knowledge for the military. The program was justified by the claim that anthropologists can improve the military's understanding of foreign cultures, which can deter war, reduce violence, identify potential flashpoints, and promote peaceful development. As one Human Terrain Team member said, "One anthropologist can be much more effective than a B-2 bomber."[16]

The program prompted soul-searching in the anthropological community about its identity and norms of behavior. In 2008, the executive board

[16] Haddick 2009, n.p.

of the AAA asked anthropologists not to participate in Human Terrain System, because doing so contradicts the essence of anthropological methods that are based on building long-term relationships of trust. The anthropologist David Vine argues that supporting violent combat operations clearly violates the AAA code of ethics and its injunction to "avoid harm or wrong." Battlefield operations, he adds, often make it impossible to obtain informed, voluntary (i.e., free of coercion) consent from locals. By contrast, Marcus Griffin, the first Human Terrain System anthropologist to serve in Iraq, argues that the program is a vital tactic for reducing kinetic operations (those requiring direct military force) and misunderstandings. He concludes, "We can apply our specialized skills in the field to ameliorate the horrors of war, stem the loss of both American and Iraqi lives, and improve living conditions for Iraqis, or we can complain from the comfort and safety of the faculty lounge."[17]

Questions for research and discussion

1. Is the distinction between myth and science always clear-cut? Is it possible that science itself is another form of myth? Are myths, because they are nonscientific, somehow of less value than scientific explanations of the world? Might some forms of nonscientific (religious) narrative convey truths that are more substantive than anything science could offer?
2. Are different sets of epistemological and social norms present in different combinations or degrees in different sciences? If so, provide examples. If not, explain why not.
3. What epistemological or social norms might different types of researchers in the physical, biological, or social sciences, or in the humanities, experience as most important or as most problematic? Which might any researcher find most difficult to live up to or be most tempted to ignore?
4. Can you find examples where contemporary scientific practice deviates from the Mertonian norms? Are these deviations problematic or just an indication of changing times? If they are problematic, what reforms need to happen?

[17] Griffin 2007, p. B10.

Further reading about the cases

Finocchiaro, Maurice (2007) *Galileo on the World Systems: A New Abridged Translation and Guide*. Berkeley, CA: University of California Press.

Fluehr-Lobban, Carolyn (2008) "Anthropology and Ethics in America's Declining Imperial Age," *Anthropology Today*, vol. 24, no. 4, pp. 18–22.

Glenn, David (2007) "Anthropologists in a War Zone: Scholars Debate Their Role," *Chronicle of Higher Education*, vol. 54, no. 14, pp. A1–A12.

Griffin, Marcus (2007) "Research to Reduce Bloodshed," *Chronicle of Higher Education*, November 30, vol. 54, no. 14, p. B10.

Hofstadter, Dan (2010) *The Earth Moves: Galileo and the Roman Inquisition*. New York: W.W. Norton & Company.

Price, David (2008) *Anthropological Intelligence: The Deployment and Neglect of American Anthropology in the Second World War*. Durham, NC: Duke University Press.

4 Research ethics I

Responsible conduct

Chapter 3 introduced the epistemic and social or behavioral norms in science as a method of knowledge production and as a social institution. These norms were described in general terms by the sociologist Robert Merton as communalism, universalism, disinterestedness, and organized skepticism (known by the acronym CUDOS). In the last quarter of the twentieth century, questions arose in society and among a new generation of social scientists about the extent to which the normative ideals of science actually govern scientific practice. To what extent are scientists really living up to the normative ideals that science seems to espouse? Chapters 4, 5, and 6 examine various realities of science that pose challenges to its ideal normative structure. The present chapter digs into the details of operationalizing the norms of science and considers some of the scandals that have occurred as a result of their breach.

There are numerous ethical issues associated with scientific research, which presents a challenge for organizing them into a logical framework. Alphabetically they range from avoiding conflicts of interest and honesty in reporting results to protecting human subjects and recognizing intellectual property. Positively good scientific practices (GSP) or the responsible conduct of research (RCR) are often summarized under the rubric of scientific integrity or responsibility. Negatively, the official US governmental definition of scientific misconduct identifies FFP (fraud, falsification, and plagiarism) as the most egregious failures. Sometimes specifics are analyzed in terms of professional responsibilities to oneself as a scientist, to the scientific community, or to society as a whole. Another common organizer considers ethical issues in relation to the three overlapping, iterative moments of planning, conducting, and reporting research. This chapter adopts a version of the last organizer and distinguishes anticipating, doing, and disseminating research. But it should be recognized that any such framework is to some extent simply a matter of convenience rather than a natural kind. What is most important is to call attention to a number of specific possible experiences in which there will be ambiguities and dilemmas, temptations to cut corners, or opportunities to exercise strength of character. Critically analyzing these experiences helps to cultivate and reinforce appropriate institutional norms in the practice of science.

Setting the stage: a cloning scandal

The South Korean biomedical scientist Dr. Hwang Woo-Suk and his research team would begin work at 6 a.m. in their laboratories at Seoul National University (SNU) and often stay until midnight. The hard work appeared to pay dividends in 1999, when Hwang announced he had created two cloned cows. Though he offered media sessions and photo-ops, he did not provide scientifically verifiable data for the achievements. Despite the lack of data, Hwang gained tremendous popularity, because his work promised both economic gain and international recognition for South Korea. In 2004, Hwang and his team reported in the prestigious journal *Science* that they had derived an embryonic stem cell line from a cloned human blastocyst by using somatic cell nuclear transfer (SCNT). In 2005, *Science* published a second Hwang paper that reported further success in human cloning. Hwang's team claimed they had created eleven embryonic stem cell lines by using SCNT to inject skin cells from patients with disease or injury into enucleated oocytes (egg cells with their nuclei removed).

The papers drew international attention, because they were the first reported successes in human SCNT cloning. The 2005 paper was especially noteworthy, because the stem cells were derived from somatic cell donors that differed from the oocyte donor. (In the 2004 experiment, the eggs and somatic cells were from the same donor.) This seminal accomplishment in "therapeutic cloning" was a major step toward genetically tailored treatments for people suffering from Alzheimer's, Parkinson's, or spinal cord injuries. Due to the enormous medical and economic implications of his research, Hwang's celebrity status skyrocketed in South Korea. The Ministry of Science and Technology selected him as the first recipient of the title Supreme Scientist, which included a $15 million award, and he was appointed to head the new World Stem Cell Foundation at SNU. *Time* magazine named Hwang one of its "People Who Mattered 2004," claiming that "Hwang has already proved that human cloning is no longer science fiction, but a fact of life."[1]

That "fact," however, was soon challenged as questions surfaced about Hwang's research. In November 2005, Dr. Roh Sung-il, a coauthor on the 2004 paper, held a press conference in which he admitted that he had paid women for their eggs despite telling *Science* that all egg donors were unpaid volunteers.[2] Roh and Hwang both claimed that Hwang was unaware of the payments. It later emerged that eggs had also been used from two junior researchers. The South Korean Ministry of Health found that no commercial interests were involved and that no laws or ethical guidelines had been breached. Yet Hwang admitted to lying about the source of the eggs in order to protect the donor's privacy, and his team lied about the number of eggs used in the experiments. Furthermore, Roh had lied to *Science* about the payments, and it is a violation of international standards for scientists to conduct research on human subjects who are in a dependent relationship under them. Hwang resigned from his position as head of the Foundation, but vowed to continue his research, claiming that the experimental results were valid.

Public opinion of Hwang remained high. He was seen by most South Koreans as a hero driven by the noble desire to find cures. An investigative television show that accused Hwang of misconduct was forced off the air. Major sponsors of the show withdrew their support in the face of public outrage at such an "unpatriotic" program and in response to charges that producers of the show had used unethical tactics in obtaining information about Hwang's research. The editors of *Science* magazine also initially dismissed the program's claims as lacking credibility. Over a thousand sympathetic female supporters gathered outside Hwang's laboratory, all offering to donate their eggs for his research.

Then in December, 2005, allegations arose through posts on an online message board that both papers contained fabricated data. The allegations were picked up by the mainstream media. This initiated an investigation by SNU, which concluded that fraud had occurred, resulting from

[1] "The 2004 Time 100," *Time*, www.time.com/time/specials/packages/article/0,28804,1970858_1970909_1971678,00.html.

[2] Holden 2005.

serious misconduct. Hwang's team did not keep proper records and did not have proper evidence to support some of its most important claims. Furthermore, a significant amount of data presented in both papers was fabricated, including manipulated photos and DNA test results. The SNU investigation concluded that in fact no cloned stem cell lines existed. In light of these findings, *Science* retracted both papers, with the consent of Hwang and his coauthors. A now disgraced Hwang was dismissed from his position as professor at SNU.

In delivering the results of the SNU investigation, the dean of academic affairs noted that Hwang and other researchers failed to uphold standards of integrity and honesty. The editor-in-chief of *Science*, Donald Kennedy, issued a statement about the scandal: "Fraudulent research is a particularly disturbing event, because it threatens an enterprise built on trust."[3] *Science* conducted its own in-house investigation of its manuscript evaluation processes, including peer review. Its report concluded that operating in an atmosphere of trust is no longer sufficient and that "substantially stricter" requirements for reporting primary data would be institutionalized. Yet skilled researchers will always be able to perpetuate deceit, at least in the short term. There is no institutional or procedural substitute for virtuous scientists. As one group of bioethicists concluded, "The lesson to be learned is that we need to do a better job of holding research institutions accountable for setting up systems and mentorship that will produce integrity in its scientists."[4]

From norms to realities

In the preceding chapter, we argued against the idea that science is independent of ethics or "value-free." Certain principles and methods (emphasizing empirical evidence and logical consistency) derive from the goal of science to extend reliable knowledge. In the first instance, science could not function without epistemic norms structuring its practices. Complimenting these epistemic norms are moral ones such as those

[3] Statement available in "Science Editor-in-Chief Donald Kennedy's Statement on Latest Hwang Findings," AAAS website, www.aaas.org/news/releases/2006/0110stemstatement.shtml.

[4] Cho et al. 2006, p. 615.

identified by Merton as well as a more general commitment to honesty, integrity, and trustworthiness.

Thus, the very practice of science and its ideal of objectivity presuppose and require ethical norms. Scientists are responsible for upholding these norms. Doing so constitutes RCR (responsible conduct of research) or GSP (good scientific practice); failing to do so constitutes scientific misconduct. Such misconduct often amounts to the negation of science, because practices that violate the norms detract from the systematic pursuit of knowledge. This was clearly evident in the Hwang case: lies and fabricated data derailed the collective scientific endeavor to pursue knowledge. At the end of the ordeal, not only were reputations shattered, but there were no trustworthy findings on which to build further research.

The norms of science constitute an exacting ideal that is not always easy to implement. Science is an activity conducted by people who are, like all humans, susceptible to certain weaknesses of pride, ambition, greed, and vanity. The pleasure of being right and pain of being wrong can contribute to arrogance and defensiveness that might sway judgment to the point of making false claims or fabricating results. For much of its modern history, society trusted that scientists – as members of a community defined by impersonal rationality – were immune to imperfections and believed that their integrity could be assumed. In the wake of misconduct cases such as the Hwang affair, this assumption became difficult to defend. As a result, the scientific community has worked to make guiding norms more explicit while seeking improved mechanisms for instilling and enforcing these norms. In addition, governments have imposed greater oversight and regulation due to the perceived failures of science to act as an effective self-governing institution that nevertheless seeks public financial support.

This rethinking of assumptions has called a naive view of science into question. According to this view, scientists who deviate from the norms are anomalies. The vast majority of scientists properly internalize the norms and the resulting social institution constitutes a self-policing community of accountability between peers. In 1981, testifying before a US congressional subcommittee investigating fraud in science, then president of the National Academy of Sciences, Philip Handler, remarked that the rare instances of deviation from the norms can only be understood "as psychopathic behavior originating in minds that have made very bad judgments."[5] Handler recognized an element of human weakness in science, but it is an element that is methodically, automatically discarded by the system.

In the wake of scandals uncovered throughout the 1970s and 1980s, many now maintain that misconduct is in fact symptomatic of, rather than contrary to, the structure of science. This alternative view sees the structure of science not in terms of idealized norms but in terms of the concrete motivations and needs of scientists. The professionalization of science means that it is a career. Careerism sets the criteria for success, including quantity of publications, funding, tenure, and esteem. A system that rewards quantity creates incentives for mass production, which may come at the cost of dishonesty. Furthermore, with its emphasis on priority of discovery, science is a highly competitive race. Under the pressures of competition, some scientists yield to the temptation to cut corners, improve on or falsify data, or plagiarize the work of others.

As the Hwang case shows, the motive of scientists is not only to seek truth but to achieve recognition of their efforts. This explains why factors that often contribute to misconduct include the pursuit of fame, money, and reputation; the quest for promotion; and pressures to produce. According to this view, addressing misconduct is not a matter of automatic self-policing. Rather, it requires fundamental changes to the professional culture of science.

Part of this culture and another reality of contemporary research is what the physicist Alvin Weinberg and the historian Derek de Solla Price termed Big Science. Large and often multinational collaborative groups tend to diffuse accountability and inhibit communication. Research environments are so fast-paced and complex that mentors often do not have the time to explain decisions or instil norms of responsible conduct. Investigators cited this as a contributing factor in the Hwang misconduct case.

Another reality is the increasing commercialization of science. Privately funded research accounts for a growing percentage of the investments in science. Even publicly funded research conducted at universities is increasingly linked to private enterprise as governments seek to stimulate the transfer of knowledge from laboratories to markets. Such developments have multiplied scenarios in which scientists stand to gain financially as a

[5] In Rollin 2006, p. 261.

result of patenting, licensing, or otherwise marketing the results of their research. This in turn increases the potential for conflicts of interest in which a scientist's personal gain may compete with his or her professional obligation to pursue the truth.

But the issue is not always profits. Humanitarian interests can also lead researchers to cut and trim data. Consider, for instance, the testing of a new drug. A clinical trial might well yield a result that fails by some very small margin to reach the level of statistical significance in the technical sense but nevertheless seems to indicate some effectiveness. The researcher, aware of the vagaries of research results and of the good such a drug might do for desperately ill patients, and confident that more tests would yield statistical significance, might well alter or exclude some data. This would help bring the drug to market to help those who would otherwise suffer or die while further testing was being done. The distinction between bold determination and misconduct is not always a bright line.

Other factors that contribute to misconduct will vary in prominence between nations, cultures, scientific disciplines, and even between individual laboratories. For example, a contributing factor in the Hwang case was a strict South Korean lab culture that leaves junior researchers with little formal power to refuse unethical demands made by their superiors. (It should nevertheless be noted that junior scientists on Hwang's team acted as whistle-blowers by reporting their concerns to an investigative television program and posting allegations on an online message board.) Furthermore, South Korea has a research system that often distributes funding based on lobbying and personal ties rather than transparent, peer-reviewed competition. This system concentrates funding in the hands of the few well-connected researchers such as Hwang. It also prevents the development of multiple groups of experts to assess claims made by their peers.

Yet as Kennedy noted in the Hwang case, there are practical limits on the ability of peer reviewers to identify both unintentional error and intentional fraud. Teams of junior researchers often work tirelessly for lab chiefs who get most of the credit even though they are not involved directly in the day-to-day work. Replication is not as commonly performed as the ideal would indicate, because there are no prizes for second place.

In sum, there are several realities of science that can conflict with and undermine the normative ideal. Misconduct is not simply the anomalous workings of deranged minds or immoral characters. It is also endemic in contemporary science because it often results from the incentives and pressures established by the system itself.

Influential cases

In 1830, English mathematician Charles Babbage identified three malpractices in science: cooking, forging, and trimming of data. There have been several contemporary attempts to formulate a more precise definition. Definitions of misconduct are important for establishing the range of activities that should be investigated and that merit sanctions if guilt is determined. Before consulting these, however, it will be helpful to survey a small sampling of important cases from a wide variety of scientific fields.

Samuel G. Morton and physical anthropology

In the mid-nineteenth century, the American physician Samuel G. Morton used a collection of over 1,000 human skulls to rank various races in terms of intelligence, putting whites on the top, blacks on the bottom, and American Indians in between. The results were presented as inevitable conclusions, compelled by objective facts. But Morton's racial dogma shaped not only his theory but also the data from which it was derived. He juggled the numbers to get the results he wanted (e.g., by excluding subgroups and individuals with small skulls when he wanted to raise the group average). This data manipulation was done openly in scientific journals, so it was apparently performed unconsciously rather than deliberately.[6]

Piltdown man and human archeology

In the early twentieth century, an entire generation of British scientists was duped by a transparent hoax. The British Empire was at its peak and it seemed self-evident that Britain must have been the cradle of civilization. Yet Paleolithic cave paintings and tools were being discovered in France and Germany but not in Britain – until, that is, an amateur geologist named

[6] See Gould 1996.

Charles Dawson discovered the "Piltdown man" in a gravel pit in England. The skull and jaw bones had been salted in the pit by hoaxters, who even fashioned a "Paleolithic" cricket bat. The hoaxters hoped that their increasingly transparent and childish tricks would expose the gullibility of the British scientific community. But under the temptation to believe, the community long continued to accept the findings as legitimate.[7]

William Summerlin and immunology

In 1971, junior researcher William Summerlin began working for the highly regarded immunologist Robert Good at the Sloan-Kettering Institute for cancer research. Two years later, Summerlin reported a breakthrough in transplantation research to journalists, claiming that he had found a method for making human skin universally transplantable without rejection. Summerlin became a celebrity, but many scientists were skeptical because they could not replicate his work. Good reassured scientists, staking his reputation on his junior colleague's research. In October, 1973, one colleague suspected fraudulent research, but later remarked that he "lacked the moral courage" to suggest a hoax was being perpetrated. By March, 1974, however, Good had become convinced of the need to publish a report announcing failure to reproduce Summerlin's results. Summerlin requested a last-minute meeting with Good to argue that the negative report was unnecessary because his latest skin transplantation experiment with mice was going well. On his way to Good's lab to make the case, Summerlin used a felt-tip pen to ink black patches on white mice, supposedly just to make the transplanted black patches of skin stand out more clearly. Once this "improvement" of the data was noticed, Summerlin was immediately suspended from duty. Summerlin argued that his only error was succumbing to pressures created by Good to publish. Good denied creating unreasonable pressure, but an investigative committee did find that Good shared in the blame for allowing Summerlin to announce results to the press before they had been confirmed. Outside of this mild rebuke, the committee exonerated Good, arguing that the usual presumptions of trustworthiness in science would have made it difficult for Good to entertain the notion of fraud.[8]

[7] See Weiner 2003. [8] See Hixson 1976.

Mark Spector and oncology

In 1981, junior researcher Mark Spector and his mentor Efraim Racker at Cornell University published a paper in *Science* announcing a remarkable unified theory of cancer causation known as kinase cascade theory. The theory was so elegant and of such potential significance that it garnered headlines and attracted top researchers from around the world. Spector appeared to be both intellectually gifted for conceiving of the theory and uniquely talented as a technician, because he could often get experiments to work when everyone else failed. Indeed, rather than go through the laborious process of replicating his work, scientists from around the world would often send their samples to Spector so that he could run the analyses. They were convinced by the beauty of his theory and the cleanness of his results. But then a colleague tried to explain why his results were so erratic whereas Spector's were so clean. His work uncovered a cunning act of forgery. Spector denied any wrongdoing, claiming that someone else had spiked his test tubes.[9]

Retin A and aging research

Retin A is a cream product of Ortho Pharmaceutical, a subsidiary of the Johnson and Johnson Corporation. It had received FDA approval as an acne medication in 1971 and several older users reported a beneficial side effect: it made their skin smoother and younger looking. In the 1980s, Ortho began conducting the clinical trials necessary to market Retin A specifically as a wrinkle fighter. This promised to make an already lucrative drug even more profitable: at the time, the US cosmetic anti-aging business was roughly $3 billion. In January 1988, the *Journal of the American Medical Association* published an article claiming that Retin A could reverse the effects of aging on skin.[10] That issue also included an editorial titled "At Last! A Medical Treatment for Skin Aging." After the study was published, sales of Retin A quadrupled. While investigating this boom, a reporter for *Money Magazine* (*CNNMoney*) discovered that the author of the editorial and one of the authors of the research article received financial compensations

[9] See Wade 1981. [10] Weiss et al. 1988.

from Johnson and Johnson. The author of the editorial stated in an interview, "Yes, we have a financial relationship in this regard, and we have similar relationships with many, many groups ... This is a fact of life in American medicine today."[11] A dermatologist quoted in the same story conceded this fact, but feared that "in this case, science and marketing are becoming confused." A Congressional report noted that the *Journal of the American Medical Association* study was not well designed and the safety and effectiveness of Retin A were not established.[12] This heightened suspicions that financial incentives may have biased the clinical trial and the reporting of its results.

Bjørn Lomborg and environmental science

In 2001, the Danish political scientist Bjørn Lomborg published *The Skeptical Environmentalist: Measuring the Real State of the World*. Lomborg systematically attacked what he called the "Litany," or the worldview common in most environmental scientific publications, that global environmental systems are collapsing due to resource consumption, population growth, and pollution. In effect, he argued that those espousing this view are like Morton. They have dressed an environmentalist ideology in the garb of scientific facts, while ignoring or misrepresenting data contradicting their position. Anticipating the controversy this book would stir, Cambridge University Press subjected it to an unusually rigorous peer-review process. Despite this, many scientists and environmentalists argued that Cambridge should not publish the book. Once it was published, criticism intensified. *Scientific American* ran a series of essays against the book titled "Misleading Math about the Earth." The Union of Concerned Scientists argued that Lomborg consistently misused or misrepresented data and selectively cited only the literature that would support his conclusions. Several scientists brought formal charges of scientific dishonesty against Lomborg to the Danish Committees on Scientific Dishonesty (DCSD). Their findings were mixed, but did conclude that the book was scientifically dishonest. Lomborg filed a complaint, and a higher ranking ministry annulled the decision by DCSD, clearing Lomborg of all charges.[13]

[11] Vreeland 1989, n.p. [12] Stern 1994. [13] See Pielke 2004.

Yanomami blood samples and anthropology

The Yanomami are indigenous Amerindians residing in the Amazonian rain forest on the border between Brazil and Venezuela. In the late 1960s, anthropologists collected blood samples from several Yanomami villages. The Yanomami claim they were led to believe that those blood samples would be used only briefly for medical research and then destroyed. But thousands of frozen blood samples still existed forty years later in laboratories around the world. Many of the individuals who donated the blood samples are no longer alive and Yanomami funerary practices require that all body parts and social remains of the dead be ritually annihilated. It is unacceptable to the Yanomami people to think that parts of their ancestors are still in a lab. Some claim that failure to return the samples constitutes a callous disregard for the Yanomami's beliefs, while others argue that the issue distracts attention from the more serious threats to the Yanomami of malaria and extractive industries. In 2005, a Brazilian public prosecutor sent letters to fifteen institutions that he believed held blood samples. Yet it was not until 2010 that researchers agreed to return the blood samples.

The blood sample debate is only one of multiple controversies surrounding anthropological work with the Yanomami. Journalist Patrick Tierney accused the anthropologists Napoleon Chagnon and James Neel of research misconduct. Tierney accused them of exaggerating the degree of violence among the Yanomami, of fostering violence by distributing weapons, and of fabricating data in a 1988 paper. The debate over this book continues, with some turning the tables and accusing Tierney of shoddy scholarship and even outright misconduct in leveling unfounded accusations.[14]

The psychology of torture

In 1966, the US Air Force created a training program, SERE (Survival, Evasion, Resistance, and Escape), that included mock interrogations designed to train soldiers to resist enemy interrogations. SERE techniques were modeled from Chinese interrogations used against US soldiers in the Korean War and included slaps, sleep deprivation, stress positions, wall-

[14] See Glenn and Bartlett 2009.

slamming, and waterboarding. During the 1980s, the psychologists Jim Mitchell and Bruce Jessen supervised the SERE program. Jessen eventually switched from supervising the mock interrogations to playing the role of mock enemy interrogator. After the September 11, 2001, terrorist attacks, Mitchell and Jessen wrote a proposal for the CIA (US Central Intelligence Agency) to turn the SERE techniques into an American interrogation program to be used against captured alleged Al Qaeda operatives. In 2002, with the backing of the CIA, the two psychologists first tested their techniques on Abu Zubaydah, initially described as Al Qaeda's number three, in a CIA jail in Thailand. Zubaydah was confined in a box, slammed into the wall, stripped, exposed to the cold, blasted with rock music to prevent sleep, and waterboarded eighty-three times. The techniques continued until Jessen and Mitchell decided that no more information was forthcoming. During that interrogation, the US Justice Department completed a formal legal opinion authorizing the SERE methods. Jessen and Mitchell reportedly made between $1,000 and $2,000 a day apiece and they had permanent desks in the Counterterrorist Center. Their methods were used on at least twenty-seven more prisoners until, in 2009, the Obama administration discontinued the interrogation program calling it one of the CIA's "mistakes" and defining waterboarding as torture.[15]

Plagiarism in India and physics

In 2007, Indian prime minister Manmohan Singh doubled financing for research, claiming that newly industrializing nations such as China and South Korea have "leapfrogged ahead of us by their mastery of science and technology."[16] Additionally, new rules linked the number of published papers to promotions and pay increases. The resulting pressures to publish and a lack of awareness about misconduct have been associated with a rise in instances of plagiarism. This is compounded by the lack of professional or government institutions capable of detecting scientific misconduct. To fill this lacuna, some Indian scientists established the independent ethics watchdog group, the Society for Scientific Values.[17] The most high profile case of plagiarism in India comes from the field of theoretical physics. In

[15] See Shane and Mazzetti 2009. [16] Neelakantan 2008, n.p.

[17] See the website for the Society for Scientific Values, www.scientificvalues.org/.

2002, a research group at Kumaun University headed by the university's vice-chancellor, B.S. Rajput, was accused of plagiarism.[18] The main allegation centered on a paper published by Rajput and his student S.C. Joshi that was later found to copy significant portions of another paper published six years earlier by Stanford physicist Renata Kallosh.[19] Over forty Indian physicists endorsed a website that made several other charges of plagiarism against Rajput. Dr. Kavita Pandey, head of the Physics Department at Kumaun University, claimed that she was suspended for blowing the whistle on the vice-chancellor's plagiarism.[20] Rajput resigned after a formal inquiry found him guilty of plagiarism. In the wake of the scandal, attention turned to the peer-review process. Why had reviewers not detected the multiple acts of plagiarism committed by Rajput?

A spectrum of conduct

Research misconduct results when the norms of science are violated. Norms can pertain to defining and planning research, investigating and conducting research, and reporting and disseminating research. Breaches of norms can involve such egregious behaviors as outright fraud or less clear cases of misconduct such as trimming data. Defining misconduct in some cases seems straightforward (e.g., Summerlin, Hwang, and Rajput), but in other cases is less so (e.g., Did Lomborg inappropriately manipulate data? Was there an inappropriate conflict of interest in the Retin A study?). Scientific misconduct is, then, a broad and potentially vague term.

This is to be expected for two reasons. First, scientific conduct is not simply rule-following. Rather, it depends on intuition, judgment, and tacit knowledge. This means that identifying cases of misconduct is not usually as simple as identifying when someone did not stop at a stoplight or added two cups of sugar instead of one. Efforts to produce knowledge that is empirically based, community certified, and practically reliable involve multiple complex methods and sometimes depend on the "golden hands" of embodied expertise or insightful paradigm shifts. This means that in many instances the difference between boldness, mistakes, and misconduct can be debated. Second, the norms of science are generalized ideals – putting them into practice in particular contexts often

[18] See Ramachandran 2002. [19] See Joshi and Rajput 2002. [20] Kazmi 2002.

shows how fuzzy the boundaries are between creativity and bending or violating the norms.

Rather than paint it in stark terms, then, it is better to conceive of scientific conduct along a spectrum from the ideal behavior of RCR or GSP through questionable research practices (QRP) to the worst behavior of FFP (fabrication, falsification, and plagiarism). Articulations of the ideals and what counts as their violation can be found in codes of conduct, governmental regulations, institutional policies, and informal mentoring and education processes.[21] The vagueness of the term, lack of data, and biases toward either over- or underreporting have made estimating the prevalence of misconduct difficult. One influential survey of miscounduct reported roughly 2 percent of scientists admitting to FFP and nearly 34 percent admitting to QRP. But when asked about the behavior of their colleagues, admission rates were 14 percent for FFP and 72 percent for QRP. The study notes that these are likely conservative estimates of the actual prevalence of scientific misconduct.[22]

In Europe, there is not yet a widely instituted or universally accepted definition of misconduct. The UK, Denmark, Norway, and Germany tend to employ relatively broad definitions of misconduct (or "scientific dishonesty"). For example, the UK Wellcome Trust Fund includes FFP and "deviations from accepted practices."[23] In the US, broad definitions of misconduct have also been proposed. In 1986, for example, guidelines established by the US National Institutes of Health defined scientific misconduct as FFP or other acts that deviate from commonly accepted practices within the scientific community.

Subsequent reports by other US federal agencies, however, proposed narrowing the definition to just FFP. This was motivated in part out of concern that the clause about "other serious deviations" was too vague to be enforceable. Such a broad definition also invites an overexpansive

[21] For some important articulations of normative ideals in the sciences see Institute of Medicine and National Research Council 2002; National Academy of Sciences, National Academy of Engineering, and Institute of Medicine 1992; and National Academy of Sciences, National Academy of Engineering, and Institute of Medicine 2009.

[22] Fanelli 2009, n.p.

[23] Council of Science Editors, *White Paper on Promoting Integrity in Scientific Journal Publications*, 2012 update, n.p., Council of Science Editors website, www.councilscienceeditors.org/i4a/pages/index.cfm?pageid=3644.

use that might punish honest mistakes and stifle unorthodox approaches to research. Since 2000, the US federal-wide research misconduct policy states simply, "Research misconduct means fabrication, falsification, or plagiarism in proposing, performing, or reviewing research, or in reporting research results."[24] Fabrication is making up data or results that are then reported. Falsification includes manipulating, omitting, or changing data or results. Plagiarism is the appropriation of another's work without giving due credit, or the misappropriation of intellectual property. Other behaviors can also constitute misconduct that is legally sanctioned by some federal institutions, including failure to report misconduct, obstruction of investigations, abuse of confidentiality in peer review, and retaliation against whistle-blowers.

In addition to this narrow legal framing of the term, misconduct is still used more broadly to label actions that are ethically controversial or questionable. Such QRP include shingling of publications (duplicate or near-duplicate publications), self-plagiarism, citation amnesia (failing to cite important works in the field), careless data management, unacknowledged enhancing of digital images, honorary authorship, and excluding data from publication. The term could even apply to extreme instances of gullibility or credulousness as in the "Piltdown man" case. QRP and misconduct do not apply, however, to error (where there is no intent to deceive) or most differences in judgment regarding research design, statistical analyses, or data interpretation. What is important is to clearly acknowledge and explain as much as possible what procedures have been used for selecting and interpreting data. When this fails to happen, conduct can shade into unethical practices, as in the Morton case where relevant samples were excluded for no valid reason. The ideal of objectivity requires scientists to be as aware as possible of their biases and to take measures to counteract or at least disclose them.

Other instances of data management can make the determination of misconduct difficult and contentious. For example, the Lomborg case and other controversies in environmental science hinge not on intentional FFP, but the selection and interpretation of data. Depending on the methods and interpretations chosen by any given researcher, science paints a variety of

[24] "42 C.F.R. § 93.103 Research misconduct," *Justia.com*, http://law.justia.com/cfr/title42/42-1.0.1.8.71.1.29.4.html.

often conflicting pictures of the world. This can result from inappropriate biases. Yet it is not always the case that one party has true science on its side while another is misled or distorting the truth. For example, a data set may demonstrate that forest cover is increasing, but the reason for this may be an increase in forest plantations rather than recovery of more natural systems. Thus, the fact of more forest cover leaves room for interpretation about its meaning.

The flow 1: anticipating research

The term "scientific research" connotes the activities involved in creating and clearly formulating testable hypotheses, exploring hypotheses in laboratories, field studies, or simulations, and drawing and publishing conclusions that contribute to certified knowledge. This definition suggests a flow of research from planning projects through conducting research to reviewing and reporting results. Research flows from anticipating (in the office and in proposals), to doing (in the field, laboratory, or virtual environment), to disseminating (in conferences, publications, and popular media). Throughout this flow, researchers face questions about what constitutes responsible scientific practices. The categories of anticipating, doing, and disseminating are artificial constructs with fuzzy boundaries. Science often involves feedback in which disseminating influences anticipating and doing. But as a heuristic the distinctions are useful, although the topical categories that follow should be read with flexibility in mind.

Research begins with a question, an idea, or a hypothesis. From the very beginning ethical issues arise: Which hypothesis should be pursued? Are there questions that should not be asked? How can this idea be tested responsibly? Although they pertain to the entire flow of research, three issues are particularly important at the stage of planning and anticipation: (a) mentoring; (b) conflict of interest; and (c) judging the value of the research.

Mentoring

Mentors have responsibilities not only to transmit knowledge and skills, but also to initiate the next generation into the traditions and values of the scientific enterprise. Unlike an adviser, a mentor oversees not just the conduct of research, but the personal and professional development of his or her mentees. This special responsibility is crucial at the anticipation phase, because the mentor's experience and judgment are necessary for informing the conceptualization of a research project and the distribution of responsibilities for bringing it to fruition. From the inception of a project, mentors also play a leading role in ensuring the collegial atmosphere and accountability necessary for successful collaboration.

The mentor–mentee relationship is defined by its imbalance of power, knowledge, and experience. It is a fiduciary relationship, wherein the powerful party is entrusted with protecting the interests of the vulnerable party. Exploitation in such relationships is behind many instances of QRP and misconduct. Mentors may abuse their power by overworking their students, excluding them from the planning stages of grant proposals, failing to give them proper credit, discriminating against them, or failing to advance their careers. Yet those who strive to be good mentors often face obstacles such as lack of time and few incentives for effective mentoring.

The 1967 discovery of pulsars by Jocelyn Bell, then a twenty-four-year-old graduate student, is an important example of the difficulties associated with allocating credit between mentors and mentees. Under the supervision of her thesis adviser, Anthony Hewish, Bell was in charge of operating and analyzing data from a radio telescope. One day she detected "a bit of scruff" on the chart. She remembered seeing the same signal earlier, so she measured the period of its recurrence and determined it must be coming from an extraterrestrial source. Bell and Hewish later found more examples and together with three others published a paper announcing the discovery of what came to be known as "pulsars." Hewish was awarded the Nobel Prize; Bell did not share in the award. Some claimed that her recognition of the signal was the key act of discovery. But others, including Bell herself, said that she received ample recognition and was only doing what graduate students are expected to do.

Conflict of interest

Conflicting commitments – the need to divide limited time among various responsibilities – often pose dilemmas about prioritizing time, but they do not usually threaten the integrity of science. This is not the case with conflicts of interests. One good formulation of this concept comes from Michael Davis, who argues that

> a person has a confict of interest if, and only if, that person (a) is in a relationship with another requiring the exercise of judgment in the other's behalf and (b) has a (special) interest tending to interfere with the proper exercise of such judgment.[25]

All researchers have many interests that may at times conflict with one another. Scientists are responsible for thinking through potential conflicts in the anticipatory phase, before they become real and cause harm. Once a conflict of interest is in place, it can infect the entire flow of research.

Conflicts of interest can exist at both the individual and institutional levels. Those involving financial gain and personal relationships are the most important. Researchers are entitled to benefit financially from their work. But in some cases the prospect of financial gain may inappropriately influence the design of a project, the interpretation of data, or the dissemination of results. A clear example is the biased research conducted by the Center for Indoor Air Research funded by the tobacco industry. Similarly, funding agencies often require scientists to disclose personal relationships, because they may bias judgments about the worthiness of grant proposals. Even if a conflict of interest is only apparent, it can damage reputations and undermine trust.

Conflicts of interest can undermine scientific integrity and objectivity in two ways. First, they can affect a person's thought processes (judgment, perception, decision-making, or reasoning). The conflicting interest can bias or skew these processes. Second, a conflict of interest can affect motivation and behavior. That is, a scientist may be perfectly capable of sound thinking but might fail to carry it out due to temptations. Scientists need not be aware of conflicts of interest in order for them to impact thought and behavior, and even small gifts can exert subconscious influences. Many studies of articles published in biomedical journals show that a study sponsored by a pharmaceutical company is more likely to favor the company's products than a study funded by the government.[26] Conflicts of interest, both real and apparent, can undermine the trust placed by colleagues and by society in scientific research.

[25] Davis 2005, p. 402. [26] See, for example, Ridker and Torres 2006.

Judging the value of the research

When planning a project, researchers face difficult questions that should be confronted explicitly. Is the research really worth doing? Whose interests will it serve? Are there possible negative side effects? What are the justifications: making money, gaining notoriety, advancing theoretical understanding, developing applications, for military purposes, etc.? Researchers should consider if these reasons are morally justifiable and consistent with their obligations and integrity as scientists.

Scientists must make claims to private or public benefactors about the value of their proposed work. The scarcity of funds compared with the abundance of potential scientific pursuits pressures scientists to make exaggerated claims about the import of their work. This poses questions about what constitutes ethical promising and how to distinguish justifiable claims from unjustified hype. This issue has been especially acute with embryonic stem cell research where claims about the potential health benefits have occasionally stretched any reasonable assessment of likely outcomes. Irresponsible promising can not only raise hopes that are later dashed but may even constitute a type of dishonesty on a par with other acts of misconduct.

The flow 2: doing research

Once research has begun, new ethical issues are added to those discussed above. These include: (a) objectivity, inferences, and data management; (b) bias and self-deception; (c) trust; and (d) values embedded in research design.

Objectivity, inferences, and data management

Researchers draw conclusions based on their observations. They make inferences from data that are almost always incomplete and imperfect. How these data should be treated in the process of inference lies at the core of the ethics of doing research. What counts as a valid inference?

Even before a fact or data point is collected, scientists make decisions about where and what to investigate. Interpreting data entails yet further human acts of framing and meaning-making. The data a chemist sees, for example, is a line spiked high on a graph printed out from a gas chromatograph. When she points to this line and says "that is oxygen," she is drawing from a rich theoretical framework to interpret data as meaningful.

For the ideal of objectivity to guide practice it cannot mean that human perspectives are stripped from science. Rather, it means that in making the many unavoidable decisions and interpretations, scientists are guided by scientific norms as discussed in Chapter 3, especially behavioral norms of honesty, carefulness, open-mindedness, and skepticism. This ideal is compromised by dishonesty, carelessness, bias, and self-deception. Furthermore, the ideal means that the scientific community has structures to mitigate these corrupting influences such as peer review and experiment descriptions that allow replication.

Scientists may be tempted to inappropriately alter the data in order to present a case that is stronger than the data warrant. Such dishonesty amounts to clear-cut misconduct when the alterations include the outright fabrication or falsification of data. However, the issue is not often so simple. Disagreements often exist about when certain data may legitimately be considered outliers and thus appropriately ignored in reporting findings. Statistical tests and procedures can be used in questionable ways or ways that are not fully disclosed to the reader. Researchers may manipulate digital images in a variety of ways and to various extents. This was an issue in the Hwang case, as investigators discovered that his team had doctored photos of two authentic stem cell colonies to give the false impression that they had created eleven such colonies.

Misleading data can also result from carelessness in experimental design, measurements, or record-keeping. Responsible researchers must strive to avoid negligence, haste, and inattention in their work. The standards of data collection and management vary between disciplines, but it is widely acknowledged that researchers have an obligation to create an accurate and accessible record of their work sufficiently detailed to allow for checking and replication. This requires that researchers keep orderly and secure notebooks or electronic files. Beginning researchers often receive little or no formal training on these important topics.

Many misconduct investigations have raised questions about standards of care for recording, analyzing, and storing data. For example, in 1986 Nobel Prize-winning biologist and then professor at MIT, David Baltimore, coauthored a paper in the journal *Cell* with five others, including MIT colleague Tereza Imanishi-Kari. The paper reported a novel finding in the genetics of immune systems. Margot O'Toole, a postdoctoral fellow in Imanishi-Kari's lab, reported concerns about the paper after a year of unsuccessful attempts to replicate the study and after some of her own experiments produced contradictory results. When the US Congress subpoenaed Imanishi-Kari's notebooks, she admitted that she did not really have any. She only had disorganized sheets of paper. In the days before the hearing, she quickly bound them into a notebook. The investigators claimed they found clear signs of fraud: data were overwritten in different colors of ink, findings were erased, and dates were changed. At one point, Imanishi-Kari could not even make sense of the meaning of some of her numbers. She admitted to poor record-keeping but always maintained she was innocent of misconduct.[27]

Another example of carelessness is the practice of citing articles without actually reading them. One study found 391 biomedical articles over a ten-year period that cited retracted papers (the papers had often been retracted because of misconduct).[28] Scientists may often not take the time to study the growing reservoir of scientific knowledge. Instead, they may simply copy citations from secondary sources. Responsible conduct would seem to require that researchers actually read any articles that they cite. Otherwise, their own work may be contaminated by the errors or misconduct of others.

Bias and self-deception

Processes of inference can also be distorted by biases, which are systematic or nonrandom errors. For example, Morton's unconscious bias led to invalid inferences. Biases can also stem from consciously made false assumptions, such as the assumption of craniometrists that human head sizes and shapes determine personality traits and intelligence. This indicates why biases can be difficult to identify. They require an independent source of verification outside of a community of practitioners. If an entire field of science accepts the same bias, then it will not be identified. This

[27] See Kevles 1998. [28] See Howard 2011.

means that biases are not always best considered unethical. They may be more akin to hypotheses that are later proven wrong. Craniometrists, for example, may have conducted careful, honest, and responsible research and, as is the case with the progression of science, their biases or hypotheses were eventually discarded. Nonetheless, biases can stem from racial, patriarchal, or other assumptions, which again points out the importance of scientists' skepticism about the assumptions behind their research design and interpretation of data.

Self-deception is perhaps the greatest threat to the ethical ideal of scientific objectivity. It often stems from carelessness and wishful thinking. Hoping that his or her theory is true, a researcher may fall into the trap of experimenter expectancy, or seeing only what he or she wants to see. Self-deception is not intentional fraud – the researcher truly believes that he or she has not manipulated the data to accord with a preferred outcome. Yet there may be some self-awareness involved, as is the case, for example, when a researcher omits data that give the "wrong" answer.

Expectancy contributes to self-deception, which in turn leads to credulity. The Piltdown man hoax is one example of an entire community falling prey to a common delusion. Another example is the 1903 discovery of the N-Ray by the French physicist René Blondlot. Over the next three years over 100 scientists wrote more than 300 papers on N-Rays. Even after the American physicist R.W. Wood demonstrated that N-Rays were nothing more than an "observer effect," several French physicists continued to support Blondlot's work.

So self-deception is dangerous, because it can dupe entire communities into a set of false beliefs. But there is a danger in self-deception even when it leads to beliefs that later prove correct. For example, the English physicist Robert Hooke believed strongly in the Copernican heliocentric theory of the solar system. Proving the theory required observing a stellar parallax – a perceived difference in the position of a star due to the Earth's motion around the Sun. Hooke observed a star with a parallax of almost 30 seconds of arc. Yet, as it turns out he only observed what he wanted to see. There is a stellar parallax, but it is very small (about 1 second of arc); in fact, it is too small to be detected by Hooke's relatively crude telescope.[29]

[29] See Broad and Wade 1983 for more on the N-Ray and Hooke stories.

That heliocentrism later proved correct does not justify holding that belief as a result of credulousness or wishful thinking. For the ethical ideal of objectivity, getting the right answer is not most important. How that answer is derived is the key. It cannot be the result of blind faith or obedience, of expediency, or of deception, intentional or otherwise. As Jacob Bronowski exhorted his fellow scientists, "If we silence one scruple about our means, we infect ourselves and our ends together."[30] One landmark study reported that bias in science trends toward a pervasive over-reporting and over-selection of false positive results.[31] Another study in 2012 reported that researchers were only able to confirm six of fifty-three "landmark studies" in preclinical cancer research.[32]

Trust

Trust is essential to the conduct of science because understanding the world is a task that is far too big for any single individual to undertake successfully. Even describing the particulars of a small slice of reality – say, cellular metabolism or the marriage customs of a tribe – requires the collective efforts of several researchers. As Newton remarked in a 1676 letter to Hooke, "If I have seen a little further it is by standing on the shoulders of Giants." Because scientific knowledge is built up communally, its objectivity depends on the intersubjectivity of human communication. It follows that scientists must be able to rely on one another to be truthful. As Bronowski put the point: "We OUGHT to act in such a way that what IS true can be verified to be so."[33] In short, facts about what is the case rely on the values necessary for "objectivity."

If scientific predecessors conduct careless or dishonest work, then their shoulders will not be reliable perches for seeing further. Each member of an increasingly networked scientific community that relies on more and more specialized domains of expertise must trust in the work of all the others. Scientists have neither the time nor the expertise to independently verify every finding derived from the work of others; and in an endeavor that values priority of discovery, they certainly do not have the motivation.

[30] Bronowski 1956, p. 66. [31] Ioannidis 2005. [32] Begley, Glenn, and Ellis 2012.
[33] Bronowski 1956, p. 58.

Values embedded in research design

We have argued that the ideal of objectivity does not mean the absence of values or a view of the world somehow removed from human interests and perspectives. Rather, the ideal requires a critical awareness, explicit recognition, and rational defense of the values and perspectives that are unavoidable aspects of the human quest for knowledge. When scientists make decisions about equations, models, constants, and variables, they often must make certain assumptions that amount to the embedding of values in their experimental design. The ideal of objectivity demands self-awareness and an explicit justification of such choices.

The example of integrated assessment models (IAMs) to analyze climate change management strategies will illustrate the point.[34] IAMs are models of the global climate–society system. Environmental scientists and economists use IAMs to study various social responses to climate change and identify an economically optimal trajectory of investments in reducing greenhouse gas emissions. This requires choices about the criteria to define "optimality" (the objective function of the underlying optimization equation), and these choices are necessarily value-laden.

For example, some IAMs frame the goal of climate management strategies in terms of optimizing "utility" as a measure of time-aggregated societal wealth. These models sometimes assume a definition of utility that does not distinguish between situations of evenly distributed consumption and those where the wealthy consume a lot more than the poor. In other words, the scientific model makes a typical utilitarian value calculation where total utility matters, but the distribution of utility does not. The model may further assume that utility is a sufficient proxy metric for human happiness and that this can be adequately measured in terms of money and consumption. In other words, the model assumes that aggregated global utility is the ultimate social goal. These are all value judgments that are intrinsic to the model.

IAMs entail other value judgments as well, such as the choice of a utility discount rate (used to compare the value of future utility with that of present utility). Those who design the equations that govern the model must also make choices about how to quantify climate-related damages. Some,

[34] See Schienke et al. 2010.

for example, convert various climate change impacts such as droughts and floods into units of money and utility, and this conversion of course entails further assumptions about values. There are further value judgments to be made about the reliability of the model for guiding policy decisions.

For any scientific method or model that attempts to measure costs, risks, and benefits, these terms can be defined in a variety of ways and the chosen definition creates a certain way of framing the issue. In making one decision rather than another, a researcher creates and measures one reality rather than another. What counts as a cost, a benefit, a risk? Whose interests are included? The ideal of objectivity is not to avoid or eliminate these value judgments. Rather, it is to make them transparent and explicit and to justify them rationally while remaining open to the potential merits of alternative formulations. For example, perhaps a better way to structure IAMs is not with globally aggregated utility, but with utilities disaggregated by region or nation. African utility and consumption could be optimized separately and weighted equally with North American utility and consumption. This may be a more just or fair calculation given the high probability that damage from climate change will be borne primarily by poorer populations where people benefit little from the fossil fuel consumption by the wealthy that causes the damage.

The flow 3: disseminating research

As a communal enterprise, science depends on outlets (e.g., conferences, journals, and press releases) for disseminating information. As an activity governed by norms that define acceptable practices, science institutes the gate-keeping or quality control mechanism of peer review to ensure the work is sound. As a career, science requires ways to grant recognition for contributions to communal knowledge. As a commercial enterprise, research often generates intellectual property with restrictions on its dissemination. Thus, this section takes up the issues of: (a) peer review; (b) authorship and allocation of credit; and (c) intellectual property.

Peer review

In the seventeenth century, Newton and many other natural philosophers would keep new findings secret so that others could not claim the results as their own. Henry Oldenburg, secretary of the Royal Society, solved this problem by guaranteeing authors in the society's *Philosophical Transactions* both rapid publication and the support of the society if an author's claim to priority of discovery was questioned. Oldenburg also pioneered the practice of submitting manuscripts for review by experts prior to publication. These innovations evolved into the modern scientific journal and the practice of peer review. Together, they create a system that rapidly disseminates high-quality information and rewards authors with recognition through the practice of citation.

Since only scientific peers have the requisite knowledge, many important decisions about publication, hiring, promotion, tenure, the awarding of degrees, and funding depend on the peer-review system. Ideally, in terms of the dissemination of research results, this system eliminates errors, deceptions, and biases and prevents the publication of substandard research. In reality, however, many flaws slip through the system. This is partly because scientists rarely have sufficient time, incentive, or resources to approximate the ideal. The breakdown of peer review can also result from unethical behavior on the part of editors and reviewers. Most importantly, they may possess conflicts of interest that bias their findings, and they may violate the confidentiality of the work under review by stealing ideas, theories, or hypotheses.

New media technology has made peer review a contested domain in many professions. Mainstream journalism, with its fact-checking and gate-keeping practices, is under onslaught by blogs and other forms of new media. Under the influence of WebMD and other websites, physicians have lost their monopoly on the dissemination of health information to their patients. Similarly in science, not all pathways of scientific dissemination pass through the gate of peer review. New and emerging techniques for publishing research online often increase speed and access but at the cost of bypassing the quality control of peer review, although it could be argued that peer review happens in such cases as a postpublication process. One curious case study is the journal *Rejecta Mathematica*, which publishes papers that have been rejected by peer reviewers at other journals. The journal's website lists several ways in which previously rejected papers can be of value to the scientific community.

Furthermore, researchers have occasionally made premature announcements of their work to the press, as in the 1989 press conference about cold fusion at the University of Utah. In that case, scientists and a university eager to capitalize on a revolutionary development by staking priority of discovery disseminated their results at a press conference prior to publishing them in a peer-reviewed journal. The lesson from this case and others is that researchers should be very cautious in bypassing the peer-review system. If the preliminary results that are released to the public are later proven to be incorrect, then the effort of other researchers is wasted and public trust in science is undermined. Of course, given the flawed nature of peer review, these outcomes can never be avoided for certain, and in some cases urgency may rightfully preempt the peer-review process. In the 2009 swine flu pandemic, for example, scientists faced the difficult task of being responsive to the public's demand for knowledge while remaining honest about the knowledge gaps and uncertainties of a rapidly evolving situation.

Peer review is both epistemological *and* political – it is a matter of deciding who has the relevant knowledge *and* the power to make decisions. Accordingly, we will return to issues of peer review in Chapters 9 and 10, especially as we consider ways in which scientific peers are being asked to assess not only the intellectual quality of research but also its ethical and social implications. The "peer" category is currently a site of important flux and contestation. Who should count as a peer, that is, who ought to have the power to determine the value of research?

Authorship and allocation of credit

The practice of citing others' work reflects a core ethical principle of fairness and accountability in research: to give credit where credit is due. Failure to uphold this principle can amount to plagiarism. The principle also has a flip side: to not give credit where credit is not due. The practice of honorary authorship, listing undeserving authors (often because they provided financial support), violates this aspect of the principle. Responsibility and credit are closely related in this dual principle, because it states that a person should only receive credit to the extent that he or she can take responsibility (deserves praise for new knowledge or blame for errors) for the work.

Deciding the appropriate allocation of credit and responsibility is often made difficult by the communal nature of science. Mentors, for example, may insist on being listed as first author for any research issuing from their laboratory even if they have not been actively involved in that particular study. Is this fair because, without the mentor's support, the study would not have existed? Or is this unfair because only direct intellectual contributions should count in the determination of authorship? But what counts as an "intellectual contribution"?

Some scientific disciplines publish papers with dozens of authors because the study entailed the collaboration of multiple forms of expertise and even multiple laboratories. Does this mean that each author can legitimately be held responsible for the entirety of the publication? If a mistake or an instance of misconduct is discovered in just one element of the study, it is not obvious that all of the authors would be equally blameworthy. Some have proposed modifying the practice of authorship by assigning credit to individual authors only for the piece of the study that resulted from their direct contribution. This would clarify questions about responsibility but it would do so at the cost of further Balkanizing the research system. It would also introduce novel questions about how to weigh partial credit or credit for part of a publication. How would this compare with a single-author or a traditional multiauthor article?

A fundamentally important question bearing both on peer review and the allocation of credit is: What metrics should be used to determine a scientist's excellence, influence on the field, and value to society? The easiest metric is simply to count his or her number of publications, but this does not measure the quality of the work or the impact factor of the journals that print it. Incentivized by metrics that reward sheer quantity of publications, authors are often tempted to shingle their work or to divide it into the "least publishable unit" in order to inflate their numbers. Another strategy is to use a citation index that ranks scientists according to how often their work is cited. This may be a better metric, but it does not capture the reasons why the scientist is being cited or what qualitative influence their work has had on their field or beyond. Furthermore, there are biases built into the system such that established researchers and standard approaches are more likely to be cited than newer researchers or novel approaches. And citation search engines do not always cover all scholarly journals. Another metric is to count the patents that result from a scientist's work. But not all fields of science aim for applications, at least not in the short term.

The peer-review system and the allocation of credit revolve around the same vital questions: What constitutes excellent research? Who deserves praise and why? The metrics used to evaluate scientists are proxy answers to these questions and thus deserve careful ethical scrutiny.

Intellectual property

When scientific discoveries have profit potentials, oftentimes dissemination is restricted through the mechanisms of intellectual property. Intellectual property is a legal monopoly over creations of the mind that grant their owners certain exclusive rights to a variety of intangible assets such as discoveries, designs, and processes. Examples include patents, trademarks, copyright, and trade secrets.

Intellectual property rights create financial incentives to pursue new creations by granting their owners the right to profit from ideas, and they provide the wherewithal to recoup the costs of R&D. Indeed, this is the primary moral justification for intellectual property: it rewards the parties responsible for taking financial risks to create something of social value, by allowing them to profit from their work. Defenders of the practice argue that if the protections of intellectual property rights are not in place, then entrepreneurs will not invest in research and society will suffer. This is why the US Constitution permits federal patents intended to "promote the Progress of Science and useful Arts" (art. I, §8, clause 8).

Nonetheless, the role of intellectual property in science is controversial. The profit motive arguably inhibits the free flow of information and influences the kinds of research that are undertaken. For example, pharmaceutical research, which is overwhelmingly profit driven, is not surprisingly geared in the main toward the diseases that afflict wealthy nations. Might intellectual property skew science away from helping those who need it the most? Should scientists seek monetary gain through patents for their work? Or does this contradict the norms of science, which call on scientists to only seek the progress of knowledge and the recognition of their peers? Furthermore, controversies exist about what should be considered "intellectual property." Is a gene or an organism something that can or should be patented? Should indigenous or traditional forms of knowledge be considered intellectual property? Another contemporary issue with intellectual property in science is the enforcement challenges posed by digital technologies that can cheaply and quickly copy and distribute information.

Consider briefly just one of these controversial issues, namely, the patenting of human genes. The Human Genome Project (1989–2003) created a database with enormous medical and commercial potentials, which quickly raised the question of intellectual property: Who, if anyone, would own specific genes or even the entire human genome? Patents are exclusive rights granted by a government to an inventor that exclude others from making, using, and selling the invention. A gene patent is a patent on a specific gene sequence, its chemical composition, or the process of obtaining it. It is a subset of biological patents, which have existed since the 1906 US ruling that purified natural substances can be patented because they are more useful than their nonextracted, natural states (adrenaline was the first such substance to be patented). The 1970 US Supreme Court case of *Diamond v. Chakrabarty* clarified that an organism can be patented as long as it is truly "man-made," such as through genetic engineering – although this finding remains in flux as science and law coevolve.

By 2010, roughly 40,000 US patents existed relating to about 2,000 human genes. This does not mean that anyone owns genes that exist in any human body, as all genes in the human body (to date) are natural products (although genetic therapy muddies the issue). Rather, the patents cover isolated genes, methods of using them to manufacture products (e.g., drugs or consumer goods), and methods to use the genes to diagnose diseases.

In 2009, the American Civil Liberties Union together with several scientific and patient advocacy organizations filed a case against Myriad Genetics seeking to invalidate and discontinue all patents for naturally occurring genes.[35] A US District Court Judge ruled in favor of the American Civil Liberties Union, arguing that several of Myriad's patents, including some on the breast cancer genes *BRCA1* and *BRCA2*, had been improperly granted. The ruling hinged on the argument that DNA is fundamentally different than adrenaline or other chemicals found in the body. The ordering of nucleotides defines the construction of the human body, so merely isolating it in an unaltered state is not enough to change its status as a natural product. A later brief from the US Department of Justice upheld

[35] See Begley 2010; Schwartz and Pollack 2010.

the district court ruling that "genomic DNA that has merely been isolated from the human body, without further alteration or manipulation, is not patent-eligible."[36] This ongoing controversy about when a gene is "natural" (thus discovered) and when it is "man-made" (thus invented) has far-reaching implications for the biotechnology industry and the ethics of scientific research.

Research ethics in a global context

For much of the twentieth century, scientific research was concentrated in a small set of countries. Since the last decades of the twentieth century, science has become increasingly and genuinely global. In addition to South Korea, China and India are now often cited as emblematic of this new geography of science. China is in the midst of the most ambitious science-funding program since the US undertook its race to the moon in the 1960s. The Chinese government has set a target for investing 87 billion euros in research by the year 2020. Over a twenty-year period from the late 1980s to the early 2000s, India's investment in biotechnology quadrupled. The breakneck pace of globalizing science and the overwhelming emphasis on economic growth pose challenges for ensuring that emerging scientific powers conduct responsible research. Consider the following reports from India and China.

In *The Hindu*, a national Indian newspaper with a circulation approaching 1.5 million, the science journalist N. Gopal Raj began a 2002 opinion piece on "Scientific Misconduct" by noting how the practice of science depends on trust. Yet "reports keep surfacing from various countries about work being plagiarized, results which were doctored and data fabricated."[37] Raj mentioned four cases from India: fraudulent fossil discoveries (by V.J. Gupta of Punjab University in the 1980s), plagiarism (by R. Vijayaraghaven of the Tata Institute of Fundamental Research, 1995), questions of fraud (by B.K. Parida of the National Aerospace Laboratories, 2001), and charges of multiple plagiarism (as noted above, against B.S. Rajput, vice-chancellor of Kumaun University, 2002). Raj goes on to quote from an editorial in

[36] *Association for Molecular Pathology v. Myriad Genetics* (11–725, October 29, 2010), US Court of Appeals for the Federal Circuit, p. 10, *New York Times* website, http://graphics8.nytimes.com/packages/pdf/business/genepatents-USamicusbrief.pdf.

[37] Raj 2002, n.p.

Current Science (Bangalore, India), complaining that "scientific misconduct cases are rarely pursued and publicized in India." Precisely because as "the world leader in scientific research, the US has done the most to come to grips with scientific misconduct," Raj argues the need for India to better define scientific misconduct and establish clear procedures for addressing cases when they arise.

In 2010, sociologist Cong Cao made a related argument with regard to China. As he wrote, "China's path toward becoming an innovation-oriented nation by 2020 … will be significantly derailed if the nation does not make serious effort to eradicate misconduct in science."[38] After citing one case of charges that scientists from Jinggangshan University had fabricated as many as seventy papers, Cao went on to maintain that scientific misconduct was widespread and "likely more serious than any observer of Chinese science could imagine." Indeed, he noted that some estimates suggest that as much as "one-third of Chinese researchers have engaged in some sort of problematic practice." At the same time,

> The institutional watchdog responsible for investigating, exposing and punishing deviance exists on paper only, largely because of the lack of autonomy in the scientific community. And it is extremely difficult, if not impossible, to sanction high-profile scientists because of the interference from both the persons who commit the fraud and the political leadership who made them preeminent in the first place.

Cao suggests that "China's research community has adapted to an environment in which the influence of commercialism has been powerful and the bureaucracy has become seriously corrupt."

A few years later, a related report in *Science* quoted Xu Liangying, a Chinese historian of science, to the effect that the root cause of lack of both integrity and creativity in science is the declaration of Deng Xiaoping, in his post-Mao rehabilitation of science and technology as productive forces. As the reporter noted, "the Chinese words for "science" and "technology" have become fused into "scitech" … In China, science is expected to contribute directly to economic development and not to the pursuit of truth and knowledge."[39]

In China, a kind of crude pragmatism may thus aid and abet scientific misconduct. At the same time, and paradoxically, former Chinese Academy

[38] Cao 2010, n.p. [39] Hao 2008, p. 666.

of Sciences president Zhou Guangzhao, who criticizes the contemporary situation in which "success is often scored by quantity rather than quality," remembers with nostalgia the period during the 1950s and 1960s when scientists working on the Chinese atomic and hydrogen bombs worked collectively and creatively in pursuit of strengthening national military capabilities.

Such tales illustrate the cultural and values differences that can affect both formal governance frameworks and informal scientific practices. At an extreme, developing countries may serve as "ethics-free zones" where ethical oversight is simply nonexistent. In attempting to avoid such scenarios, the question arises as to whether scientific research must be governed by a universal ethical code.

In July, 2010, the Second World Conference on Research Integrity met in Singapore in order to craft such a code. The preamble of the "Singapore Statement on Research Integrity" asserts that there are "principles and professional responsibilities that are fundamental to the integrity of research wherever it is undertaken." Scientific research must adhere to a universal set of ethical principles. Yet even universal codes such as the UN Universal Declaration of Human Rights can be enacted and interpreted differently in different local contexts. So, as science globalizes, does it need a universal ethical code, what would such a code look like, and how much interpretive flexibility can be permitted for diverse local approaches?

Summary

Careerism, commercialization, Big Science, and human weaknesses are some of the major realities of science that can conflict with its ideal norms. When the norms are undermined, the result is misconduct and questionable research practices. Misconduct can be defined narrowly as fabrication, falsification, and plagiarism or more broadly to include other practices that seriously deviate from widely accepted standards. A broader definition may help to identify inappropriate behaviors, but it also may stifle novel approaches to science.

Throughout the flow of research – anticipating, doing, and disseminating – scientists face difficult choices about applying the norms, and powerful temptations to stray from the norms. Anticipating research raises issues about the appropriate roles of mentors, identifying potential conflicts of interest, and asking substantive questions about the value of the proposed work. Doing research involves upholding the standards of objectivity. This means upholding norms of honesty, carefulness, and open-mindedness in the interpretation and management of data and critically evaluating assumptions that might be built into research designs. Objectivity is threatened by bias and self-deception and is dependent on trust. Disseminating research poses questions about peer review and quality control, authorship and allocation of credit, and the appropriate role for intellectual property rights in scientific research. As a globalizing enterprise, scientific research is engaged in a dynamic tension between diverse local practices and standard, universal principles.

Extending reflection: Victor Ninov and Jan Hendrik Schön

It often seems like scientific misconduct is associated more with the socio- and biomedical sciences than with the physical sciences. In the 1988 Nova program "Do Scientists Cheat?" all eight cases of scientific misconduct involved anthropology, psychology, or medicine.[40] Since the post-World War II rise of concern for the ethics of science, the physical sciences largely escaped scrutiny. Any scrutiny was directed more toward physics-society relationships (think the atom bomb) than toward physics-physics relationships. When a physical science case did burst on the scene – such as that of the "cold fusion" claims of Fleischmann and Pons in 1989 – it was nipped in the bud by failures to replicate. Because of their theoretical and experimental rigor, the physical sciences seemed immune to the need for RCR education, which after all had originated in the National Institutes of Health.

Shortly after the turn of the millennium, however, the apparent purity of physics – as queen of the physical sciences – was subject to dramatic challenge. In 2001 and 2002 on both the west and east coasts of the US, it was revealed that physicists from two prestigious laboratories had practiced years of fraudulent research. As *Scientific American* reported at the time, "The physics community's collective jaw dropped this past summer when allegations of fraud were raised against two of their own [creating] a

[40] *Nova*, Public Broadcasting Service, Arlington, VA, October 25.

wake-up call for a field that has considered fraud within its ranks a freak occurrence."[41]

At Lawrence Berkeley, a world-class, federally funded US national laboratory in California, during 2001 it became clear that the nuclear chemist Victor Ninov had since the mid-1990s been fabricating evidence to support discoveries of new elements. Initial exposure centered on fabricated evidence for claims for a discovery of element 118. Although an internal investigation led to his being fired by the laboratory in 2001, Ninov maintained his innocence. Problems in replication were, he argued, caused by lack of skill on the part of other scientists or by faulty equipment. They were at most errors, not misconduct. Indeed, in many cases, scientific advances often appear to be dependent on the "golden hands" of experimentalists. Yet subsequent independent investigations also called into question earlier Ninov results from 1994 and 1996 related to the discoveries of elements 111 and 112 at the Centre for Heavy Ion Research in Darmstadt, Germany. By early 2002 the physics community concluded that Ninov had in reality perpetrated scientific fraud. The questions became why and how – for so long?

At Bell Labs, a world-class industrial laboratory in New Jersey, the case of Jan Hendrik Schön was equally if not more dramatic. Schön was an experimentalist wunderkind who, after earning his PhD in physics from the University of Konstanz in 1997, took a position at Bell Labs to continue work in condensed matter physics. In short order in 1999 he began publishing a series of papers with numerous coauthors in *Nature* and *Science*, the two most prominent scientific journals in the world. He published papers on plastic conductors and nano-scale transistors that promised to revolutionize electronics. Papers continued to multiply through 2000 and 2001, when in December his work was recognized in *Science* as the "Breakthrough of the Year."

Then in 2002 questions began to be raised by some physicists outside Schön's working group. The result was the formation of a special investigation committee from outside Bell Labs, leading, by December, to his work being described as "Breakdown of the Year." The journals *Nature* and *Science* withdrew a total of fifteen of the publications on which Schön had been first author. What was equally remarkable, however, was the quick

[41] Minkel 2002, p. 20.

exoneration of all nineteen coauthors (including his manager at Bell Labs), and his dissertation adviser – although two years later even Schön's doctorate was revoked on grounds that his dissertation exhibited fraudulent data.[42]

Questions for research and discussion

1. Does all the blame for misconduct lie with Ninov and Schön? For example, was it not possible that coauthors, mentors, and journal editors had been too ready to be associated with exciting if not flashy results? Would such an attitude contradict the norms of science? Why had peer review not detected weaknesses in the original submissions, with only outsiders having brought organized skepticism to bear? Why, in the middle of the Schön investigation, was the editor of *Science* so quick to reject the allegation that there was anything wrong with the peer-review process and to maintain "there is little journals can do about detecting research misconduct"?[43]
2. Is physics, as the paragon of the "hard" sciences, less susceptible to misconduct than other branches of science? Or are the same challenges to ideal conduct equally present in all disciplines?
3. Can you identify a principle for distinguishing legitimate from illegitimate instances of data omission? That is, when is it acceptable to ignore a specific observation?
4. Is there ever a legitimate role for the inclusion of nonexperts in peer-review processes? Should scientific peers evaluate the broader social impacts of an article or grant proposal in addition to its intellectual merit?[44]

Further reading about the cases

Altman, Lawrence, and William Broad (2005) "Global Trend: More Science, More Fraud," *New York Times*, December 20.
Goodstein, David (2010) *On Fact and Fraud: Cautionary Tales from the Front Lines of Science*. Princeton University Press.

[42] See Reich 2009. [43] Kennedy 2002, p. 13.
[44] For more on this topic see Chubin and Hackett 1990.

Reich, Eugenie Samuel (2009) *Plastic Fantastic: How the Biggest Fraud in Physics Shook the Scientific World*. New York: Palgrave Macmillan.

Vogel, Gretchen (2006) "Picking Up the Pieces after Hwang," *Science*, vol. 312, no. 5773, pp. 516–517.

Wade, Nicholas, and Choe Sang-Hun (2006) "Researcher Faked Evidence of Human Cloning, Koreans Report," *New York Times*, January 10.

Video and online resources for teaching about research misconduct

"Do Scientists Cheat?"

A Nova television program that originally aired October 25, 1988. Approximately 50 minutes run time. Through historical case studies and interviews with practicing scientists, this video examines cases of misconduct and various explanations for why it occurs. Available in seven segments on YouTube.

"The Lab"

A National Institutes of Health online interactive video that portrays a research misconduct case. It allows students to adopt the role of four different actors and make decisions about research integrity, mentoring responsibility, responsible authorship, handling of data, and questionable research practices. Includes a facilitator's guide. Available for free at http://ori.hhs.gov/TheLab/.

5 Research ethics II

Science involving humans

Following a review of some historical cases of fraud and misconduct in science, Chapter 4 considered key elements of GSP (good scientific practice) or RCR (responsible conduct of research). Yet well before public and professional attention was directed toward GSP or RCR in general the ethical practice of research had become an even more public and controversial issue in relation to two special types of scientific work, those having to do with the use of humans and animals in research. Interestingly, the issue of the ethical treatment of animals actually preceded that of the proper treatment of human beings, at least as a popular issue. Because of its greater salience today, however, it is appropriate to deal first with scientific research involving humans before turning, in the following chapter, to a discussion of research involving nonhuman animals.

Setting the stage: clinical trials in developing countries

One of the most human-intensive areas of science is that of experimental studies or trials of medical therapies. There are many more types of research with humans, including biological and genetic, psychological and social scientific, and even pedagogical research. But clinical trials research raises most issues in the most intensified form, and it is in the biomedical area that ethical standards have been developed and then extended to other types of research on human beings. The single most salient issue not raised in the biomedical area itself concerns the appropriateness of extending or adapting the standards of biomedical research to biological, genetic, psychological, and social scientific research involving human subjects.

Biomedical clinical experimental research studies divide into treatment trials (testing new drugs or combinations of drugs, surgical techniques, or radiation therapies), prevention trials (assessing ways to prevent illness or disease with medicines, vaccines, dietary supplements, or behavioral changes), diagnostic and screening trials (testing detection or identification procedures), and quality-of-life or supportive-care trials (exploring ways to improve palliative care for persons with chronic illnesses). The most prominent are treatment trials.

Each year in the developed countries of Europe and North America a large number of new pharmaceutical drugs and medical devices are made available to physicians as treatments for illness and disease. In some countries, such as the US, they may be marketed directly to the public (even when they require a prescription to be purchased). These drugs and devices are largely the products of biomedical research undertaken at private foundations such as the Institut Pasteur in France, government agencies such as the US National Institutes of Health, and corporate laboratories such as those of Novartis (Switzerland), Pfizer (US), Bayer (Germany), and GlaxoSmithKline (UK), to name four of the largest.

Before such products can be made available to physicians and the public, new pharmaceuticals must be discovered and developed. At one time the discovery process mainly involved isolating active agents from traditional remedies (as was the case with aspirin) or serendipitous identification (as with penicillin). Increasingly, however, discovery is based on research into molecular-level physiology and pathology, to identify the metabolic pathways of specific disease pathogens or counteractive chemicals. This shift is coordinate with the increasing dominance of a multinational, capital-intensive pharmaceutical industry over academic or government laboratories. While based in various countries, Novartis, Pfizer, Bayer, and GlaxoSmithKline are, in economic reality, transnational corporations, with profits derived from a global market. That market's center of gravity nevertheless remains in Europe and North America.

The center of gravity for clinical trials, however, has increasingly shifted toward developing countries. As one might expect, in highly developed countries, where illness and disease no longer figure prominently in everyday life and where people exercise a critically demanding attitude toward medical care in general, it has become increasingly difficult and time-consuming to secure sufficient numbers of clinical trials participants. This is the case not only because of the complexity of the bureaucratic monitoring required but also because free and informed consent requires that participants be able to resign from participation at any point if they become dissatisfied. Evidence from the early 2000s points to more than 60 percent of clinical trials in developed countries having to extend recruitment periods or proceed with fewer subjects than planned, and to more than 80 percent of trials being delayed a month or more because of low enrollment.[1]

The result, predictably, is that clinical trials are increasingly being outsourced to Africa, Asia, and South America. In 2008 the global clinical trial business was estimated to be $50 billion and growing at the rate of 10 percent each year. On the face of it, global outsourcing would seem to benefit at least three parties: for pharmaceutical companies, clinical trial costs are lowered; for patients in Europe and North America, new drugs are brought to market more quickly; and people in developing countries make money and/or receive medical treatments that would not otherwise be available.

But consider the following case. According to one investigative report of clinical trial practices in India, a fifty-five-year-old woman patient named Ramsakhi Devi from West Bengal had a cancerous tumor removed from her cheek. Then she was informed that in order to receive necessary follow-up chemotherapy and radiation treatment, she would need to sign up for a clinical trial. Although the consent forms were in English and Hindi, Devi was illiterate. Her son tried to help her, but even he misunderstood the forms, and told his mother there was only one available treatment option in the trial instead of three. Moreover, Devi never understood that she could drop out, but thought she had to finish the treatment regimen to be fully cured.[2]

Two other, more general cases: In a 1990 clinical trial in Thailand, 40,000 school children received either Havrix, an inactivated hepatitis A vaccine, or a hepatitis B vaccine. In a 1998 clinical trial in Bolivia, 650 infants who exhibited respiratory distress syndrome were treated with a new surfactant, Surfaxin, or a placebo, when the standard treatment for respiratory distress syndrome was one of four other surfactant drugs.[3] Although such clinical trials would not have been approved in Europe or the US, without these ethically deficient clinical trials none of the children involved would

[1] Watson and Torgerson 2006; Newsweek Online 2009.

[2] Hundley 2008. [3] See Hawkins and Emanuel 2008.

have received any treatments at all. As it was, at least half of the children in each case received some benefit.

The particular practice of outsourcing clinical trials to developing countries poses a spectrum of fundamental questions for research with human subjects, all of which raise broad questions such as

- What are the ethical protocols of clinical trials in Europe and North America?
- How did the existing protocols for clinical trials develop into their current form?
- What constitutes free and informed consent?
- Are clinical trial protocols for developed countries justly modified for that context?

How clinical trials work

Discovery of a new drug typically takes place in preclinical (*in vitro* or cell culture) and *in vivo* (animal) studies and leads to its patenting, that is, the filing for a state-recognized right to exclusive use for a limited time. Following discovery, a development clock starts ticking; a patent owner needs to develop and market the drug as rapidly as possible, in order to profit from its investment before the drug enters the public domain. Drug development involves determining formulation (drugs commonly need to be combined with other agents), dosage (how much for what period of time), delivery mechanism (injection, pill, inhalant, etc.), and safety (side effects, contraindications, risks, etc.). Research to determine how to apply a new discovery (focused on effectiveness) is subtly different from discovery (focused on truth or the conceptual adequacy of the model for some phenomenon), although the two are intertwined. There are more direct economic pressures in the development process, which typically involves more intensive *in vitro* and *in vivo* studies and a movement into clinical treatment trials. Ethical issues arise early in the relation between preclinical and clinical studies, especially how soon it is safe or ethically acceptable to move from one to the other.

Clinical treatment trials are required by governments in order to demonstrate both safety and effectiveness before a drug is approved for marketing. For instance, water is safe, but could not be marketed as a treatment for cancer because it lacks effectiveness. (This does not keep some naturopaths from recommending lots of water as a way to purge the body of toxins that cause cancer; they just cannot bottle, label, and sell water as a cure for cancer.) The most important and capital-intensive part of development is clinical trials.

Clinical trials regularly proceed through five stages. A controversial Phase 0 designates first-in-humans testing of new drugs at subtherapeutic dosages to make preliminary checks for drug target effects and assessment earlier in development. The goal is to expedite the clinical evaluation of new molecular substances without significant risk either to subject health or corporate economics. However, a 2006 Phase 0 testing of the immunomodulating drug TGN1412, despite being administered at a supposed subclinical dose, produced systemic organ failure in the subjects.

Phase I trials normally involve a small group (20–80) of healthy volunteers in an inpatient clinic where subjects can be observed full-time. The goal is to assess safety, tolerability, pharmacodynamics (how the body reacts to the drug), and pharmacokinetics (how the drug reacts to the body).

Phase II trials involve larger groups (100–300) and continue Phase I safety assessments while assessing how well the drug works. When new drug developments fail, it often happens in Phase II, when a drug does not work as expected or has toxic side effects.

Phase III trials are randomized and controlled studies on large patient groups (1,000–3,000) and aim to definitively assess drug safety and effectiveness. In some instances, regulatory agencies such as the European Medicines Agency or the US FDA (Food and Drug Administration) expect at least two successful Phase III trials to fully demonstrate safety and efficacy. As a control, subjects are treated with the drug to be tested or a placebo, ignorant of what they are receiving. In cases where some drug already exists as a standard treatment, ethical protocols require that it be used in place of a placebo, so that no subject is deprived of an existing standard of care. In such instances, the aim becomes one of demonstrating that the new drug is as safe and effective as the existing treatment or more so. Given their size and duration, Phase III trials are expensive, time-consuming, and difficult to design and implement, especially for therapies oriented toward chronic medical conditions for which existing treatment regimes are already in place or for therapies that might well interact with drugs widely available and in use for other conditions – both of which characterize an increasing percentage of the population from which clinical trial subjects may be enrolled.

Phase IV trials, known also as postmarketing surveillance studies, involve the safety surveillance and continuing technical support of a drug after it becomes publicly available. Controversies especially associated with Phase IV trials include the transparency and interpretation of results. The key characteristics of Phase 0–IV clinical trials are summarized in Table 5.1.

Consent is perhaps the most important ethical feature of clinical trials in Phases I–III, which further contributes to their complexity and cost. Any human subject involved must give his or her free and informed consent. This is the case even though, in part because of the placebo effect, in many instances it both would be easier and would yield more epistemologically sound results if subjects were enrolled in a trial without their knowledge. But given that there is often some risk to the health of human subjects, ethical guidelines require that they be appraised of the risks and then freely consent to participation. Indeed, freedom of consent is so important that, although subjects may be compensated for their participation, compensation itself must be limited to avoid becoming a coercive factor. So much is this the case, that human subjects are now more commonly called participants.

The use of placebos in the control group of Phase III trials also calls for special comment. Placebos (*placebo* in Latin means "I will please") was known from the 1700s as a treatment adapted more to please than benefit patients. For patients who demanded some form of treatment and nothing was available, either because the physician perceived their illness to be imaginary or because there was no known treatment, physicians often prescribed equally imaginary therapies. Remarkably, these simulated medical interventions often seem to have nonsimulated effects, appropriately termed placebo effects. Prior to the early twentieth century, placebos seem to have been widely and consciously employed in European and North American medicine. European and North American medical practitioners often attributed the apparent effectiveness of nonscientific medicine in underdeveloped countries to superstitious beliefs in traditional remedies and resulting placebo effects. Indeed, even in developed countries, the apparent therapeutic effectiveness of, for example, homeopathy, has

Table 5.1 *Summary of key characteristics of clinical trials*

Phase	Aim	Group size	Ethical issues
Preclinical	To identify potentially useful therapies	*In vitro* and *in vivo* studies	Extent of preclinical research to require before moving to clinical trials
Phase 0	First human testing to check for drug target effect	Small	Occasionally serious harm to participants
Phase I	To assess safety, tolerability, pharmacodynamics and kinetics	20–80 participants	Difficult to enroll healthy volunteers
Phase II	Continue to assess safety and begin to assess how well a drug works	100–200 participants	Often where clinical trials fail
Phase III	Randomized, controlled to assess safety and effectiveness	1,000–3,000 participants	Time-consuming and expensive; placebo ethics
Phase IV	Postmarketing surveillance studies	Total drug-taking population	Corporate resistance to transparency and difficult-to-interpret results

been attributed to the placebo effect which has been widely accepted as a real phenomenon.[4] In a subsequent study, the medical researcher Henry K. Beecher even provided empirical data to support the thesis that surgeons demonstrating a measurable degree of enthusiasm for a therapy had a higher success rate in treating chest pain and heart problems in patients than skeptical surgeons, thus pointing to another way in which attitude or belief appeared to have beneficial therapeutic consequences.[5] (The term "nocebo" was subsequently coined to designate this effect.) At the same time, the use of placebos by physicians in developed countries raised obvious ethical questions. Should physicians lie to their patients, even if it seemed to do their patients therapeutic good?

Then in 2001 the reality of the placebo effect came under serious challenge from a systematic study of clinical trials that concluded the phenomenon was itself spurious. When in Phase III clinical trials the control group placebo was replaced by no treatment at all, there was no statistically significant difference in control group outcomes.[6] Although this article created significant negative commentary, a subsequent metastudy by the same authors provided confirming data. The result is that placebo usage is now even more subject to ethical controversy. As with the move from preclinical to clinical trials, the placebo issue reveals that ethics and epistemology often mutually implicate each other.

How humans became research subjects

Science aspires to understand nature and human beings as part of nature. As long as science was primarily observational in its methods, and emphasized contemplative understanding rather than control, there were few reasons to separate physics from psychology. Astronomy observed the motions of the stars, psychology the motions of living entities. (Note: For Aristotle the soul, *psyche* in Greek, is simply the form of a living being, so that premodern psychology dealt not only with humans but with animals and even to some extent plants.) The emphasis on contemplation limited manipulative experiments of most any kind, including on humans.

[4] See Beecher 1955. [5] Beecher 1961.

[6] Hróbjartsson and Gøtzsche 2001; see also Rothman and Michels 1994.

With the emergence of modern natural science, however, the investigation of human beings became controversial. Much early scientific theory, along with theological beliefs and philosophical argument, conceived of humans as different from all other natural entities in ways that properly limited experimentation on them. Although medieval Muslim physician-philosophers such as Ibn Sina (or Avicenna) and others may have introduced some modest trial-and-error experimentation into individual case medical therapy, it was the Renaissance interest in nature in all its forms together with a determination to make medical treatments more effective that gave new impetus to anatomical and physiological research. But initially anatomical studies of human bodies were considered so objectionable that in some cities there were public riots when people found the dissection of corpses taking place in medical schools.

With regard to living human beings, however, there was general agreement even within the medical community that investigation should remain primarily observational. In the nineteenth century, Louis Pasteur agonized over treating the child, Joseph Meister, with a new rabies vaccine, even though it had proven effective in animal trials, and vaccinated the child only when it became clear he would die if left untreated. When modern medical scientists became imbued with enthusiasm for experimental investigations, they sometimes used not others but themselves as subjects. A few exemplary cases across the twentieth century:

- In 1900 Jesse Lazear infected himself with yellow fever and died as a result to prove that the disease was transmitted by mosquitos.
- In the 1930s Werner Forssmann practiced cardiac catheterization on himself and won a Nobel Prize in Physiology or Medicine (1956) for his work.
- In the 1940s J.B.S. Haldane subjected himself to various gases in decompression chamber experiments in order to learn how best to protect the welfare of sailors in submarines.
- In the 1980s Barry Marshall infected himself with *Helicobachter pylori* to prove the bacterium caused peptic ulcers and won a Nobel Prize in Physiology or Medicine (2005).
- In late 1990s Kevin Warwick did cybernetic implants on himself.

Scientists Seth Roberts and Allen Neuringer have even argued that self-experimentation is one way to address some of the difficulties of clinical trials.

The first studies of human beings that went beyond the observational and began to practice something like systematic experimentation on humans other than oneself took place on slaves or the poor. This coincided with the development of the new science of anthropology that Europeans used to study non-European peoples. Generally speaking, human experimentation was initially undertaken on humans who were often considered uncivilized if not less than human. As postcolonialist scholars have argued, colonial and imperial rule was often justified by anthropological research which, using the category of race, described the native peoples of Africa, the Americas, and Asia as of inferior intelligence or ability and thus in need of paternalistic rule by European powers or European immigrants. This was, of course, paradoxical: the experimentation was done on "less than humans," even though they were assumed to be human enough so that the results could be applied to "real humans." (Since the end of World War II such peoples are often just said to need development, and various economic development experiments have been undertaken in many countries.)

However, the most egregious experiments on humans were undertaken during World War II by Nazi doctors on the "racially inferior" Jews and other "deficient" groups and by Japanese doctors on those, especially Chinese, people that they determined were less than fully human.

From subjects to participants: free and informed consent

It is possible to identify among Roman, Islamic, medieval and early modern Christian physicians, discussions of what was and was not appropriate in treating people with various medical procedures that might today be deemed experimental. But as is evidenced by the Hippocratic tradition in European medicine, medical practice until the twentieth century cultivated a sense of physician paternalism at the expense of patient autonomy. Moreover, there is a clear difference between the issue of minimal patient consent to a medical treatment that might or might not be therapeutic and informed consent to medical research focused on identifying a treatment that might be of benefit to someone else. The degree to which a patient is informed about what will be taking place is also qualified by a limited Hippocratic commitment to truth-telling – limited, that is, by a larger commitment to beneficence – since the truth may on occasion make a patient worse.

According to the authoritative study of the history and theory of informed consent, "Formal requirements of informed consent have primarily emerged from two contexts: standards governing clinical medicine … and standards governing research involving human subjects." Although some level of research with human subjects may be coeval with the creation of medicine itself, "concern about its consequences and about the protection of human subjects is a recent phenomenon."[7] What raised this issue to the level of both political and scientific concern were the large numbers of experiments on human subjects, not only without consent but against their will, by German and Japanese biomedical researchers during the 1930s and 1940s.

Doctors' Trial and the Nuremberg Code

The famous "Doctors' Trial" in Nuremberg, Germany, immediately after World War II publicized the horrors of experimentation on concentration camp inmates. Jewish and other prisoners were forced to undergo medical experiments that commonly resulted in death, permanent disability, or disfigurement and as such would more accurately be described as medical torture. Examples included hypothermia experiments, freezing patients in attempts to discover new ways to protect them from or respond to severe cold that might be used to protect German troops on the Russian front during the winter; decompression chamber experiments to determine the effects of high altitude flight on airplane pilots; sterilization and abortion experiments, in which women were subjected to various attempts, from the vaginal injection of chemicals to heavy doses of x-rays, in search of quick and effective techniques; and studies of twins, who were treated with chemicals, forced infections, and dissections to determine the extent of similarities. Out of twenty-three defendants in the Doctors' Trial, seven were acquitted, seven sentenced to death, and the remainder given sentences ranging from ten years to life.

[7] Faden and Beauchamp 1986, p. 151.

One defense made by several of the accused was that medical experimentation on human beings was quite common. They argued that in fact there was little difference between experiments done with human subjects before and during the war, and that there were no legal restrictions on such experimentations. In fact, to some extent this was the case. In the early 1900s Dr. Albert Neisser had infected patients (mainly prostitutes) with syphilis, without their consent. While Neisser was publicly criticized, he enjoyed support from fellow researchers, and proposals to restrict such practices failed to be adopted into German law. In response to this situation, two advisers to the Doctors' Trial drafted a ten-point memorandum on "Permissible Medical Experiment" that became known as the "Nuremberg Code," and which calls for such standards as voluntary consent of patients, avoidance of unnecessary pain and suffering, and the reasonable belief that the experimentation will not end in death or disability.[8]

Although the code was not cited in any of the findings against the defendants and never itself became a formal part of law in Europe or North America, it has nevertheless had significant influence. Although there is no explicit reference to free and informed consent in the Universal Declaration of Human Rights (adopted a year later in 1948), at a number of points the Declaration makes claims closely associated with the Nuremberg Code. The Preamble of the Declaration speaks of the "disregard and contempt for human rights that have resulted in barbarous acts which have outraged the conscience of mankind." Article 5 states that "No one shall be subjected to torture or to cruel, inhuman or degrading treatment or punishment" and Article 27 that "Everyone has the right freely ... to share in scientific advancement and its benefits."[9] Taken together, the Nuremberg Code and the Declaration of Human Rights can be interpreted as providing a foundation for the principle of free and informed consent in scientific experimentation with human participants.

From the Declaration of Geneva to the Declaration of Helsinki

The year 1948 also witnessed adoption by the World Medical Association of the "Declaration of Geneva," meant to be an updated Hippocratic Oath for

[8] See the Appendix.

[9] Universal Declaration of Human Rights, United Nations, www.un.org/en/documents/udhr/.

physicians.[10] For the physician it states, "The health and life of my patient will be my first consideration" and "I will maintain the utmost respect for human life." Together these two points imply a commitment to free and informed consent, although there is no explicit articulation of this principle as such. The "International Code of Medical Ethics" adopted by the World Medical Association the following year, 1949, further states, "Any act, or advice which could weaken physical or mental resistance of a human being may be used only in his interest."

However, it was not until fifteen years later (in 1964), with the "World Medical Association Assembly" meeting in Helsinki, that what became known as the "Declaration of Helsinki" undertook to provide clear recommendations for "guiding physicians in biomedical research involving human subjects."[11] For the first time biomedical researchers were distinguished as a special class of physicians. The last paragraph of a four-paragraph introduction states,

> In the field of clinical research a fundamental distinction must be recognized between clinical research in which the aim is essentially therapeutic for a patient, and clinical research the essential object of which is purely scientific and without therapeutic value to the person subjected to the research.

The introduction was followed by a set of eleven principles organized into three parts: basic (five), for clinical research combined with professional care (two), and for nontherapeutic clinical research (four). The whole document was a spare fifteen paragraphs (two of which were broken into subsections). With regard to both experimental therapies and clinical research, the Declaration emphasized that "the doctor should obtain the patient's freely given consent" to an experimental treatment (paragraph II, 1) and that "clinical research on a human being cannot be undertaken without his free consent, after he has been fully informed" (paragraph III, 3a).

Since its original formulation, the Declaration of Helsinki has undergone multiple revisions, some more significant than others. The two most significant took place in 1975 and 2000. The 1975 revision was twice as long as its 1964 predecessor and pointedly strengthened the principle of free and informed consent:

> In any research on human beings, each potential subject must be adequately informed of the aims, methods, anticipated benefits and

[10] See the Appendix. [11] See the Appendix.

> potential hazards of the study and the discomfort it may entail. He or she should be informed that he or she is at liberty to abstain from participation in the study and that he or she is free to withdraw his or her consent to participation at any time. The doctor should then obtain the subject's freely given informed consent, preferably in writing. (Para. I, 9)[12]

Also introduced were the issues of concern for the environment, the welfare of animals used in preclinical studies, and the concept of experimental protocol oversight by some kind of "independent committee." In the United States these independent oversight committees came to be called institutional review boards. In Europe and other parts of the world they are called institutional ethics committees or ethical review boards.

Declaration of Helsinki controversy

The 2000 revision is much more controversial, especially as it relates to human subjects research in the form of clinical trials in developing countries.[13] These concerns grew out of experiences with drug trials to combat HIV/AIDS, especially in Africa. In the early 1990s a randomized, double-blind, placebo-controlled study in the US determined that the drug azidothymidine (AZT) reduced by nearly 70 percent the risk of maternal–infant HIV transmission. This meant that AZT treatment became the accepted standard of care that should replace placebos for any control groups in Phase III clinical trials of other drugs designed to address the same pathology. This immediately became the case in the US but not in developing countries, even when a clinical trial in the developing country was being funded and managed by the US government.

The World Health Organization justified the difference by arguing, essentially, that because an expensive drug such as AZT was not readily available in developing countries there was still a need to identify therapies that were better than nothing instead of therapies better than AZT.

[12] Declaration of Helsinki (1975), *Codes of Ethics Collection*, Center for the Study of Ethics in the Professions, Illinois Institute of Technology, http://ethics.iit.edu/ecodes/node/3931.

[13] This can be found, with footnotes added in 2002 and 2004, in Declaration of Helsinki, World Medical Association website, http://web.archive.org/web/20071027224123/www.wma.net/e/policy/pdf/17c.pdf.

Such trials nevertheless were in direct conflict with international research guidelines from the Council for International Organizations of Medical Sciences. Its International Ethical Guidelines for Biomedical Research involving Human Subjects stated clearly that when researchers from one country conducted clinical trials in another they were not allowed to lower their ethical standards. Already emerging in the later 1980s, a schism opened even wider between ethical universalists, who argued for applying the same standards in both developed and developing countries, and ethical pluralists, who argued this was both impossible and not morally required.

In an attempt to close this divide a 1996 revision of the Declaration of Helsinki proposed to allow placebos on some occasions when there existed a nonplacebo standard of care.[14] This created sufficient ethical controversy and reaction such that the 2000 revision was drafted to flatly deny such exceptions, requiring that "The benefits, risks, burdens and effectiveness of a new method should be tested against those of the best current prophylactic, diagnostic, and therapeutic methods" (para. 29). It further added that, "At the conclusion of the study, every patient entered into the study should be assured of access to the best proven prophylactic, diagnostic and therapeutic methods identified by the study" (para. 30).

The aftermath of these new, higher standards was perhaps not fully expected by those who promoted them. First the US Food and Drug Administration, which had previously justified its own guidelines by reference to the Helsinki Declaration, withdrew any reference to the Declaration. Then the European Commission, in its 2001 Clinical Trials Directive, simply ignored the 2000 revision and referred instead to the 1996 version.[15] Is it perhaps the case that sometimes the "perfect can be the enemy of the good"? But on what ethical basis does one decide when it is appropriate to retreat from higher standards instead of fighting for

[14] There is a draft comparison of 1996 and 2000 versions in "2000 Order – Side-by-Side Comparison of 1996 and 2000 Declaration of Helsinki," US Department of Health and Human Services website, www.hhs.gov/ohrp/archive/nhrpac/mtg12-00/h2000-1996.pdf; or for the 1996 version, see "World Medical Association Declaration of Helsinki," King's Health Partners Clinical Trials Office, King's College London, www.jcto.co.uk/Documents/Training/Declaration_of_Helsinki_1996_version.pdf.

[15] "Directive 2001/20/EC of the European Parliament and of the Council of 4 April 2001," European Organization for Research and Treatment of Cancer, www.eortc.be/services/doc/clinical-eu-directive-04-april-01.pdf.

them? Is this a case of consequentialism trumping deontology, or of there being failure of virtue in not knowing when to compromise? In the practice of human participants research, these kinds of questions are likely to be more prevalent and urgent – and to call for greater practical wisdom – than in other interactions between ethics and science.

The US case: autonomy, beneficence, and justice

In the US, it is well accepted that scientists who conduct research with human participants need to protect participant interests by complying with relevant state laws, governmental agency regulations, and professional codes of ethics. The aims, as summarized in an authoritative guide to RCR (responsible conduct of research) produced by a joint committee of the US National Academy of Sciences, National Academy of Engineering, and Institute of Medicine, are "to ensure that risks to human participants are minimized, that risks are reasonable given the expected benefits, that the participants or their authorized representatives provide informed consent, that the investigator has informed participants of key elements of the study protocol, and that the privacy of participants and the confidentiality of data are maintained."[16]

These five basic elements remain touchstones or central issues in ethics practiced with human participants:

- minimizing participant risks
- assuring that remaining risks are proportional to likely benefits
- informing participants about risks and experimental protocol
- requiring the free consent of participants
- respecting participant privacy through data confidentiality.

All five elements, it is important to note, call for continuing critical reflection by scientists and the public in dialogue.

Background

The key historical event that stimulated development of these guidelines in the US, however, was not the Doctors' Trial at Nuremberg. Indeed, in

[16] National Academy of Sciences, National Academy of Engineering, and Institute of Medicine 2009, p. 24.

the reflective view of one Shoah (Holocaust) survivor, immigrant, and biomedical researcher who participated in what he subsequently concluded were unethical protocols, there was until the late 1960s a kind of self-satisfaction or complacency in the US biomedical research establishment regarding ethics. It was assumed that Americans just could not behave like Germans.

To a large extent this attitude remained even after Beecher, in 1966, was able to get a "special article" exposé published in the *New England Journal of Medicine* documenting numerous failures in the practice of free and informed consent in US medical practice since World War II. Another even more devastating exposé, D.H. Pappworth's *Human Guinea Pigs*, appeared in England the following year. It focused primarily on unethical biomedical research practices in Great Britain and also had little effect. Things did not really begin to change until Peter Buxtun, a young social worker with the US Public Health Service, leaked information to an Associated Press reporter about unethical experiments on poor African-Americans in Tuskegee, Alabama, and the story became national news (Buxtun had made unsuccessful internal efforts to terminate the study, beginning the same year as Beecher's article).

The Tuskegee syphilis study and its aftermath

The Tuskegee experiments began in 1932 and continued until terminated as a result of the 1972 news stories and resultant US Congressional Hearings – thus beginning before and continuing long after the Nazi human experiments. The goal of the Tuskegee clinical study was to observe the natural progression of untreated syphilis. To this end, the Public Health Service, working with the Tuskegee Institute (a historically African-American entity) enrolled 399 poor African-American men infected with syphilis. In return for their participation they received free medical exams, some meals, and burial insurance. But they were never told they were part of an experiment or had syphilis, for which they were never treated. Instead, they were told they were being treated simply for "bad blood," which could refer to any number of illnesses, although in fact no treatment was offered for anything.

Most immorally, after penicillin became the recognized cure for syphilis in the 1940s, they were never given the antibiotic. The disease was simply allowed to continue its course. Indeed, not only were subjects not treated (for an illness they were not told they had), they were not told that a treatment existed, and in some cases subjects were prevented from receiving appropriate treatment elsewhere. Victims included not only the men themselves, many of whom died, but wives who contracted syphilis and children born with it.

As a result of public outcry, an ad hoc panel was quickly formed in August 1972, charged with determining whether the experiment was now or ever legitimate and what implications followed from a determination of illegitimacy. The "Final Report of the Tuskegee Syphilis Study" was issued in April 1973 – determining that the study was not ethically legitimate when initiated in 1932, became more unjust when penicillin became available, and should be terminated immediately with compensation being offered to the participants as well as the families of those who had died. Additionally, given what it determined were wholly inadequate governmental policies and procedures to protect the rights of human subjects, the report argued for creation of a standing national Human Investigations Board to formulate such policies and oversee appropriate procedures. In response to the worry that such bureaucratic regulation might slow down scientific progress the panel responded with a citation from German-American philosopher Hans Jonas, to the effect that "a slower progress in the conquest of disease would not threaten society, grievous as it is to those who have to deplore that their particular disease be not yet conquered, but that society would indeed be threatened by the erosion of those moral values whose loss, possibly caused by too ruthless a pursuit of scientific progress, would make its most dazzling triumphs not worth having."[17]

The government took the panel advice and in 1974 terminated the Tuskegee syphilis study. It nevertheless took more than another twenty years before President Bill Clinton in 1997 issued a formal governmental apology, declaring simply that

> The United States government did something that was wrong – deeply, profoundly, morally wrong. It was an outrage to our commitment to integrity and equality for all our citizens.[18]

[17] Jonas 1969, p. 245.

[18] "Remarks by the President in Apology for Experiment Done at Tuskegee," Office of the Press Secretary, May 16, 1997, http://clinton4.nara.gov/textonly/New/Remarks/Fri/19970516-898.html.

The same year the government terminated the Tuskegee experiment, however, it created a National Commission for the Protection of Human Subjects of Biomedical and Behavioral Research (1974–78) to undertake the task of addressing the inadequacy of policies and procedures to protect the rights of human subjects. In its four-year time span it produced eleven significant reports dealing with research on fetuses (1975), prisoners (1976), children (1977), and the mentally ill (1978), as well as on psychosurgery (1977), confidentiality (1977), institutional review boards (1978), and more general issues. But the most significant and influential was its last report, actually issued the year after it ceased to exist: "Ethical Principles and Guidelines for Protection of Human Subjects of Biomedical and Behavioral Research" (April 18, 1979), known more commonly as the "Belmont report," a name derived from the conference center where the Commission drafted it.[19]

The Belmont report

The key influence of the Belmont report was to identify three principles that should ground all particulars with regard to human participant research. Explicitly recognizing the immorality of the Tuskegee syphilis study and with supporting references to the Nuremberg Code and the Declaration of Helsinki, the Belmont report identifies the basic ethical principles of respect for persons (or personal autonomy), beneficence, and justice that should assist future ethical deliberations. Unlike all its other reports, the Belmont report of the National Commission makes no specific recommendations. Instead, it simply notes that respect for persons implies free and informed consent, beneficence implicates some kind of assessment of risks and benefits, and justice implies equity and fairness in the selection of participants.

As a critical ethical reflection that works more bottom-up than top-down, beginning with an experience of grappling with key ethical issues in practice rather than theoretical analysis, the Belmont report is a salutary contribution to ethics and philosophy as much as it is to scientific research. It serves as a case study demonstrating the point argued three years later by philosopher Stephen Toulmin, when he reflected on "How Medicine Saved the Life of Ethics." Analytic ethics had become so abstract that it was

[19] See Appendix.

losing its relevance to human affairs. Work in biomedical ethics revived philosophical ethics and made it once again relevant to life as much as it helped protect biomedical research from the dangers of inhumanity.

The Belmont report has become foundational for research with human participants, but note how it contains no mention of privacy or confidentiality. The very words are conspicuous today by their absence. In the later National Academies report, *On Being a Scientist*, protecting participant privacy and keeping data confidential are as important as autonomy, beneficence, and justice. Indeed, it might even be argued that protecting privacy is another aspect of respect for persons and their autonomy as well as justice if not beneficence. It was an aspect simply unrecognized in the later 1970s, one that perhaps could not have been recognized as of central importance before the advent of the Internet and the explosion of digital information with its ease of exchange and vulnerability to exploitation. Research involving human subjects via the Internet has now become an ethical issue in its own right.

And the advance of information technology will continue to pose new ethical questions surrounding, for example, digital data mining, tracking via GPS, mobile phone monitoring, bar code usage, RIFD technology, and electronic social networking. Such innovations and their uses for research raise a host of informed-consent and privacy issues in a world that has become a large-scale experiment in how humans are going to live amidst the blur of technoscientific change. Though the Internet may pose risks to research participant autonomy (in the form of privacy loss), it can also foster greater autonomy by empowering individuals to share information and form their own communities and research foundations. Patient-directed or patient-led research is likely to be a growing part of the scientific landscape.

Thus it is that biomedical ethics depends on ongoing discussion, education, and critical reflection. Philosopher Bernard Rollin appeals to reliance on what he terms "social consensus ethics" of common sense over professional ethics. He argues that without a possibility space that calls forth discussion, ethics degenerates into regulatory compliance. "Thinking in ethical terms [about human subjects research] must be made part of scientific thinking, and this can be achieved only by education."[20]

[20] Rollin 2006, p. 98.

The flow of human participants research: anticipating and practicing

As indicated in Chapter 4, the spectrum of particular issues resists any strong classification system. Sometimes specifics are analyzed in terms of responsibilities to oneself as a scientist, to a scientific community, and to society as a whole. In the case of human research, responsibilities to human participants have to be added. In applied or informal scientific research, there also exist responsibilities to employers or clients. As before, the present discussion adopts an organization that distinguishes anticipating, practicing, and disseminating research, but with a qualifier that any such framework is little more than a convenient heuristic. What is most important is to call attention to a number of specific possible experiences in which there will be temptations not to live up to sound moral standards – in order to cultivate moral courage and reinforce appropriate institutional norms in scientific practice.

Prominent issues include:

- the enrolling of human participants and respecting their free and informed consent;
- the continuous monitoring and assessing of the human participant research as it is taking place, together with a responsibility to communicate clearly with participants about how the research is proceeding; and
- the assessment of context-dependent variables.

Anticipating and practicing informed consent

There is no ethical thesis involved with anticipating and doing human participant research that has a stronger supporting consensus than that participants must give their free and informed consent. The thesis can be argued perhaps most strongly from a deontological perspective, on the basis that human beings must be respected as autonomous ends in themselves with an inherent right to make intelligent decisions about actions that will directly affect their lives. But there are sound consequentialist and virtue ethics arguments for informed consent as well. Without the practice of informed consent, historical evidence suggests that not only will patients be abused but the quality of biomedical research itself may suffer. Once compromised in one area, the virtue of biomedical researchers may also decline elsewhere. Cutting corners with regard to the treatment of participants can easily blend into cutting corners in data reporting and analysis.

In some cases, however, informed consent may be particularly difficult to practice or assess. Exactly how to treat children, adults with impaired mental abilities, persons who are critically ill, prisoners, those in serious pain, or those in a coma present special challenges. What happens if participants express a desire to abdicate becoming informed and instead want to turn decisions over to others?

Securing an "informed" consent and understanding what "informed" really means can be challenging. Because scientists are authority figures or may have a vested interest in enrolling participants in a research project, thus (intentionally or unintentionally) biasing any information they provide, it is sometimes argued that those who inform potential participants should be truly independent agents. Furthermore, it is increasingly artificial to specify a single purpose for collecting tissue samples or other specimens, insofar as such samples can easily and quite beneficially be repurposed for new research projects. The increasing complexity of genetic knowledge and molecular biology are also difficult to communicate. When simple causal relations are replaced by probabilities, or decision-making is practiced under conditions of uncertainty, it is often not clear what to communicate to participants.

With regard to what constitutes adequate information necessary for informed consent, there exist two models: the professional standard rule and the reasonable patient rule. In the first case, information must meet the standard of what the community of professional researchers thinks appropriate. In the second, the information must meet whatever standard is required by a community of reasonable patients or participants. The first tends to slight the nonprofessional's perspective; the second may do the same for individual concerns among professionals. A third model has proposed that the informing process is deficient if any information is not communicated that might materially affect the decision of a potential participant.

The individuality of the agent to whom information is given and from whom consent is sought is further challenged by genetic research. Genetic information is really "shared information" (with others in a family or ethnic group). The degree to which consent to do genetic research and create DNA databases can or should be given by individuals rather than groups becomes problematic.

Crossing cultures can present other communication challenges. How does one appropriately inform a person who understands health and disease from the perspective of Ayurvedic or traditional Chinese medicine about risks and benefits formulated in allopathic causal terms? In many nonmodern cultures the notion of consent often appears to be based much more in the family or community than in the individual. The practice of written consent, which is a requirement in European and North American contexts, may have quite different implications in an oral–aural culture, where the signing of papers has been historically experienced as closely linked to being cheated and exploited by foreigners. Confirming this point, a 2007 international conference on research ethics, including European scientists, ethicists, and partners from developing countries, concluded that

> In the developing countries, informed consent must be contextualized. Local tradition and cultural values must be respected and integrated into the process.[21]

The multiple complexities of new types of biomedical research have led to proposals to replace individual-based free and informed consent with other models, most prominently those of presumed consent and open consent. Illustrating the former, in 1999 the Icelandic Parliament, appealing to the principles of presumed consent, granted the private corporation deCODE Genetics an exclusive right to establish an Icelandic health sector database, based on the medical records, genealogical information, and genetic data of all Icelanders. The company would then be able to use the resultant knowledge to guide development of new pharmaceuticals. Protest led eventually to a 2003 Icelandic Supreme Court judgment that quashed the Icelandic database project, although the project was not fully terminated and the principle of presumed consent has become widely debated.

Illustrating the latter or open-consent model is the research of the Estonian Genome Project Foundation. The Foundation's project to collect

[21] European Commission 2007, p. 31.

DNA samples and related data from over 10,000 Estonian adults used a standard written informed-consent form but left open the particular research projects for which the data might be used. Signing the consent form authorized the Foundation to use the data for any open agenda. In an analysis of these Icelandic and Estonian genetic databank cases, one commentator concluded that

> the old notion of informed consent [has become] outdated and needs review. It is also not clear yet whether the two main alternatives – presumed consent and open consent – will fare any better. Old rules often cannot fit new situations, and the changing needs, knowledge and globalization in biomedical and genetic research may demand a new ethical and legal framework for consent.[22]

Monitoring and communication with participants

Once a research project has gotten under way, there arise complex ethical requirements for ongoing monitoring and communication with any consenting participants. In clinical trials this is obvious. Even before formal completion, clinical trials often yield actionable knowledge about the effectiveness or the dangers of the drug or device undergoing tests, in which case all participants need to be notified and the protocol altered appropriately. If an experimental therapy early on proves exceptionally effective, then ethics requires that participants in a control group be offered the therapy. If a therapy is determined to increase risk or cause harm, then participants receiving the therapy must be offered the opportunity to withdraw.

The widely accepted right to withdraw during a clinical trial or any other human participant research can also be quite problematic. To take just one extreme case: mechanical heart assist devices are tested on patients with advanced heart disease. If one were to suddenly decide to withdraw it would mean the death of the participant. Would accepting a participant's decision to withdraw be tantamount to assisting suicide?

In the monitoring and communicating process, privacy protection can also become an issue. To what extent do participants have the right to

[22] Kegley 2004, pp. 835–836.

keep their participation private, to not have other participants know who they are? To what extent do participants who would like to know others in the protocol pool have the right to do so? To what extent might such knowledge distort the results of the research project if participants begin to compare notes on their reactions and experiences during the project? To what degree would participants' interest in this group sharing override a possible scientific interest in inhibiting such sharing?

Complexities of context

One key problem concerns how to extend or adapt guidelines developed in the biomedical field to the social sciences, especially when there is little if any risk of physical harm to participants. However, it is not clear that the basic issues of respect for persons, beneficence, and justice simply wither away in social scientific human participants research. One need only think of the infamous "Stanford Prison Experiment," led by psychologist Philip Zimbardo to study the psychological effects of becoming a prisoner or a prison guard. The experiment spiraled out of control with some "guards" actually torturing some "prisoners."

The extent to which institutional rather than scientific context influences ethical practices also raises questions. In the US, all human participants research funded by the federal government must meet certain standards. Those same standards, however, are not obligatory in research supported with private funding. To some extent the scientific community promotes adherence to similar ethical guidelines through professional codes of practice and standards established by scientific journals. Many scientific journals will not publish human subjects research without clear documentation supporting the practice of informed consent. But proprietary research often does not seek dissemination by publication, in which case the ethical standards of journals have little or no purchase. Applied research in the fields of marketing, finance, and digital data mining, for instance, can be undertaken with little if any ethics oversight.

In many European countries, however, the situation is different: all human participant research is legally regulated. From a European perspective those areas of the world where such regulations are not in place are sometimes described as "ethics-free" zones.

The flow of human participants research: disseminating

One way to summarize ethical issues related especially to the dissemination of results from human participants research is as a tension between transparency and privacy. Researchers have an obligation to transparency in reporting results. Without full reporting of results, including negative results, it is difficult not just for other scientists to appreciate the research, but for the human participants as well to know the personal meaning of their participation. For example, participants in a clinical trial need to be informed after the trial is complete whether they received the drug being tested or a placebo. Not only can this information sometimes cause consternation in participants who received placebos but felt like they were responding positively (or negatively) to a drug, it can raise challenges to the protection of privacy and confidentiality, especially if there is any interaction among participants in a trial. The reporting of negative results can also be an occasion for consternation. The pharmaceutical firm funding the trials may have a vested interest in limiting negative results dissemination, even in ways that could adversely affect participants. What is the case for clinical trials is likely to exist *mutatis mutandis* (allowing for necessary changes) for any research protocol with human participants.

As an extension of informed consent, the protection of privacy can also create distinctive issues. To begin with, expectations regarding privacy can have quite different meanings in different contexts. For example, the social distance that North Americans think of as a necessary adjunct of respect for privacy is often experienced as lack of care by southern Europeans, while the kind of physical interactions experienced as normal among, for example, many Italians can be interpreted as invasions of privacy by even Nordic Europeans, not to mention Japanese people. Especially when clinical trials or other human participant research protocols are designed in one country and the cultural context for implementation is in another, it is easy to create practices which, against the best of intentions, undermine the practice of free and informed consent as well as privacy. When this occurs, further questions arise about the extent of moral blame which researchers should accept.

So much is privacy an issue in research involving human beings that the US Department of Homeland Security has developed privacy principles for its own science and technology security-related research projects, such as those that involve data mining. In 2008, at the direction of Congress, the Department's Privacy Office collaborated with the agency's director of science and technology to formulate what it called the "transparency principle," which requires the conducting of privacy impact assessments for all research projects using personally identifiable information. By creating these assessments from the inception of a project, researchers should be able to articulate and document the purpose of their research projects as required by what the Department also terms a "purpose specification principle."

The issue of privacy comes into play as well, sometimes in critical ways, in the practice and dissemination of historical research. Scientific historical research in law enforcement, intelligence, or other government agencies can reveal information about people, both deceased and living, that they or their relatives might prefer to keep private. To what extent do people have a right to privacy about the historically influential dimensions of their lives?

Summary

The use of humans and animals in scientific research has historically been the most important and controversial topic in the ethics of science. The last half of the twentieth century witnessed numerous declarations and codes that attempted to articulate principles to guide the conduct of such research. Foremost among them is the ideal of respecting persons and its operationalization through practices of gathering informed consent and protecting privacy. Other important ideals are beneficence and justice. In general, there is a historical trend from humans as research subjects (passive recipients) to humans as participants in research (active partners). How to interpret and apply guidelines throughout the flow of research, especially across different cultures, remains the subject of ongoing debate.

Extending reflection: using immorally acquired data

In early 1988, the US Environmental Protection Agency was developing human exposure standards as a basis for air pollution regulations for phosgene, a toxic gas that had been used during World War I as a chemical weapon of mass destruction, with threatened but unrealized uses during World War II. After the war, however, phosgene would be more often used in the production of pesticides and plastics. To determine dose-response ratios scientists often have to depend on animal models, but human data always have greater validity.

During World War II, in an effort to protect against potential use and/or to develop an advantage that would allow them to employ it again, German scientists in occupied France had actually conducted live phosgene experiments on prisoners with the aim of advancing knowledge and potentially creating an antidote. The question arose of whether the resulting and available research data should be incorporated into the EPA work. On the one side, those in favor of such reuse argued that data are data, and even if they have been acquired by immoral means it would be immoral not to use these data to help save lives. On the other, opponents argued that the data were not only tainted by their immoral origins, but were actually unreliable, since the physical conditions of the subjects were unknown and they were likely to have already been weak and malnourished. In response to the second argument, supporters of use countered that if similar data had become available from an industrial accident, they would certainly have been drawn on. In the end, however, in light of a letter signed by twenty-two agency scientists protesting any use of the German research, EPA Administrator Lee Thomas barred its consideration in phosgene risk standards.[23]

As it so happens, this was not the only controversy over use of scientific research based on immoral human experiments by German scientists. A large number of hypothermia experiments on concentration camp inmates, designed to support German military operations in extreme environmental conditions, has proved useful to post-World War II research in related areas. Despite a claim during the Doctors' Trial that there was no scientific value to any Nazi death camp research, in the early 1980s John S. Hayward of the University of Victoria, British Columbia, found the Nazi data on the rate of body cooling in cold water useful.[24] At the same time, as he confessed to Kristine Moe, an investigative science journalist concerned with the issue of reusing Nazi data,

[23] Shabecoff 1988; Sun 1988. [24] See Hayward and Erickson 1984.

> I don't want to have to use this data, but there is no other and will be no other in an ethical world. I've rationalized it a little bit. But to not use it would be equally bad. I'm trying to make something constructive out of it. I use it with my guard up, but it's useful.

In her article, Moe expressed surprise at discovering how more than forty-five research articles in the first four decades after World War II had made reference to Nazi experimental data, mostly in the area of hypothermia research, without raising any questions about the moral propriety of use or the scientific validity of the data.

In another case related to the same research, however, Robert Pozos at the Hypothermia Laboratory, University of Minnesota, also referenced hypothermia experiments on 300 prisoners at Dachau in a paper submitted to the *New England Journal of Medicine*. In this instance, the journal's editor, Arnold Relman, rejected the paper precisely because of these references. In Relman's words, the Nazi experiments "are such a gross violation of human standards that they are not to be trusted at all."[25] This principled stand no doubt reflected the conclusion of Beecher's article published two decades earlier that concluded, "It is debatable whether data obtained unethically should be published even with stern editorial comment."[26]

Any number of perspectives could be brought to bear on this question of the use of immorally acquired knowledge. In one of the most provocative and extended studies from a Jewish perspective – a perspective that is appropriate because of the dominance of Jews among those experimented on – Baruch Cohen suggests that words such as "knowledge," "information," and "data" are too abstract to reveal what is really present:

> Instead of the word "data," I suggest that we replace it with an Auschwitz bar of soap. This horrible bar of soap is the remains of murdered Jews. The image sensitizes and personalizes our dilemma. Imagine the extreme feeling of discomfort, and the mortified look of horror upon discovering that one just showered with the remains of murdered Jews.[27]

One might well rationalize the use of such a bar of soap, especially in a situation in which soap was required and nothing else available, on the basis that it does no harm to the murdered Jews. "No one will question the

[25] Moe 1984, p. 6. [26] Beecher 1966, p. 1359.
[27] Cohen 1990, p. 104.

fact that the bather's skin was cleansed by the soap." According to Cohen, however, "the bather's conscience ... was severely tarnished."[28]

Of course, the challenging analogy of a piece of knowledge with a piece of soap can itself be challenged. Information is not a physical object. Yet there are a manifold of other challenges that remain: What if clear references to the data were to function as another criticism against those who might deny the reality of the Holocaust? Would use of Nazi data set some kind of precedent for sanctioning human experimentation – or make others feel like the experiments were a little more acceptable than they had been because some good had been derived from them? Would it make any difference whether survivors of the Nazi experiments endorsed or opposed use of the data derived from their suffering? What if the experiments had been performed on your mother or father, sister or brother, or child?

What about the data on the etiology of syphilis derived from the immoral Tuskegee experiments? Or the radiation experiments on members of the US military?[29] Does the moral challenge of using data from immoral experiments not help explain the opposition to human embryonic stem cell research by those who sincerely believe that an embryo is already human?

Does the moral challenge of using data from immoral experiments not help explain some of the opposition to animal experimentation and environmental transformation expressed by people who sincerely believe that animals deserve respect and the environment care?

Questions for research and discussion

1. In some countries (such as the US), new drugs and therapies can be directly marketed to the public (even when they require a prescription for purchase). In the majority of developed countries, however, this is not the case. What might be the ethical arguments for and against such public marketing?
2. Does the Nuremberg Code (or its follow-on, the Code of Helsinki) appear to be founded on one or more ethical theories? If so, which one

[28] Cohen 1990, p. 122. [29] Moreno 2001.

or ones? If not, which theories might give the best reasons for why the behaviors described should be followed?

3. After World War II there was no Doctors' Trial for the medical researchers of the Japanese military Unit 731, which had performed human experiments and attempted to develop biological weapons of mass destruction. Instead, the commander of the Allied occupation, General Douglas MacArthur, pardoned the unit commander, microbiologist and Lieutenant General Shiro Ishii, and all his associates, in exchange for knowledge about the results of their experimental work.[30] To what extent was this morally justified?
4. Examine two or more ethics codes – such as the Helsinki Declaration, the Council for International Organizations of Medical Sciences' International Ethical Guidelines for Biomedical Research involving Human Subjects, some national guidelines, and the guidelines of a professional biomedical research association – to identify any apparent similarities and differences. What might an appropriate ethical response be to differences? How might ethical reflection help to harmonize differences or identify the superior code?

Further reading about the cases

Barenblatt, Daniel (2004) *A Plague upon Humanity: The Hidden History of Japan's Biological Warfare Program*. New York: Harper Collins Perennial.

McNeil, Donald (2010) "US Apologizes for Syphilis Tests in Guatemala," *New York Times*, October 1.

O'Meara, Alex (2009) *Chasing Medical Miracles: The Promise and Perils of Clinical Trials*. New York: Walker & Company.

Petryna, Adrianna (2009) *When Experiments Travel: Clinical Trials and the Global Search for Human Subjects*. Princeton University Press.

Sheldon, Mark, William P. Whitely, Brian Folker, Arthur W. Hafner, and Willard Gaylin (1989) "Nazi Data: Dissociation from Evil," *Hastings Center Report*, vol. 19, no. 4, p. 16.

[30] Barenblatt 2004.

6 Research ethics III

Science involving animals

In the previous chapter, we noted an emerging consensus in the scientific community that all human beings possess intrinsic moral worth, which means they cannot be used as mere resources in order to advance scientific knowledge. There is far less consensus about the moral status of nonhuman animals, which means that there is much greater disagreement about the principles that ought to guide research involving animals. The notion of free and informed consent that played such a central role in the previous chapter is of little use in this context as perhaps no other animal is capable of comprehending a proposed research project and communicating consent. Yet this fact alone does not mean that the perspective of animals merits no consideration in the conduct of scientific research. After all, human babies and those who are severely mentally handicapped are similarly incapable of understanding and communicating. Is there anything different about nonhuman animals that might justify treating them differently in the name of scientific progress?

Setting the stage: war over animal research

Animal research can take a variety of forms, from ethological studies of animal behavior and the paradox of scientific wildlife management to veterinary medical research and the genetic engineering of animals for specific forms of experimentation. Animals in research are not only used to test drugs but have been bred and engineered to do so. Other animals are used to test, not therapies, but cosmetics. Some animals live for the most part in the wild only to be, on occasion, tranquilized, trapped, tagged, and released. Still other animals are subjects of research in their own right, with electrodes implanted in their brains to learn more about the brains of animals and by extension humans.

The University of California, Los Angeles (UCLA) receives more than $1 billion annually in federal and private grants for work on 5,500 research projects. Of those, about 1,300 involve experiments on animals, including roughly 150,000 rodents. Twenty-one nonhuman primates are used in UCLA labs, fifteen of which are in the laboratory of the neuroscientist David Jentsch who uses them to study cognitive function, drug addiction, and psychiatric disorders. Due to its size, location, and well-known brand, UCLA has become the epicenter of the ongoing conflict between animal rights activists and research scientists. Due to his use of primates, Jentsch has found himself at the very heart of the war. And he is not backing down: "When the protestors come to my house, they chant, 'We will never give up,'" Jentsch says and then quickly adds, "But neither will I."[1]

Jentsch first knew he had become the target of animal rights protestors when he awoke one night in March, 2009, to see his car ablaze outside of his window. Several of his colleagues had already experienced such attacks. For example, in 2006 UCLA neurobiologist Dario Ringach quit his work on vision with monkeys after masked demonstrators repeatedly visited his home and pounded on his windows, terrifying his two young children. In 2007 activists from the Animal Liberation Front threw a hammer through a window at the home of Edythe London, a UCLA professor of pharmacology, then snaked a hose inside and flooded the house.

Jentsch has received letters stuffed with poisoned razor blades and death threats via voicemail and email. A spokesman for an underground animal rights group said, "If Jentsch won't stop when you ask nicely, when you picket in front of his house, or when you burn his car, maybe he'll stop when you hit him over the head with a two-by-four."[2] As a result of such threats, UCLA has aggressively defended its scientists through legal measures and by spending $1.4 million annually on security, including armed guards at some researchers' homes. On a national level, in 2006, the US government adopted the Animal Enterprise Terrorism Act, which prohibits persons from using force, violence, or threats "for the purpose of damaging or interfering with the operations of an animal enterprise." The Act does not "prohibit any expressive conduct (including peaceful picketing

[1] R. Wilson 2011, n.p. [2] R. Wilson 2011, n.p.

or other peaceful demonstration) protected from legal prohibition by the First Amendment of the Constitution."[3]

Animal rights groups such as the Animal Liberation Front, PETA (People for the Ethical Treatment of Animals), and the Humane Society of the United States often denounce research involving animals as both flawed and unethical. It is flawed, they claim, because results from animal research cannot be translated into cures for human diseases. The claim that it is unethical means that it is wrong to kill animals or cause them to suffer even if doing so would save human lives. Many animal rights groups do not endorse violence as a means for achieving the goal of eliminating animal research. Yet, as the UCLA attacks clearly show, some activists adopt an extremist position that the ends justify even violent means.

In the summer of 2009, Ringach and Jentsch published a call to arms for scientists in *The Journal of Neuroscience* titled "We Must Face the Threats."[4] They argued that scientists were losing a public relations battle with the anti-research lobby. It is no longer tenable, they argued, for scientists or universities to remain silent in hopes that extremists will not target them. Scientists must educate the public about the importance of animal research and their commitment to strict ethical guidelines: "individual investigators cannot delegate their responsibility any longer." If individual scientists do not speak out, Ringach and Jentsch worry, then society will lose out on the benefits of animal research.

Jacquie Calnan, president of the animal research advocacy group Americans for Medical Progress, shares their concern and argues that the best strategy is to put a human face on the issue. She uses herself as an example: as an epileptic she would not be able to work if it were not for Keppra, a drug that was developed and tested in animals. But even some scientists are not persuaded by this approach, which may exaggerate purported benefits from animal research. It could simply be, as one neuroscientist argued, that "scientists experiment on animals because that's what they have been trained to do. Custom will reconcile people to any atrocity. Once you do something long enough, you don't perceive the horror of it."[5]

[3] "18 USC §43 – Force, Violence, and Threats involving Animal Enterprises," Legal Information Institute, Cornell University Law School, www.law.cornell.edu/uscode/text/18/43.

[4] Ringach and Jentsch 2009. [5] R. Wilson 2011, n.p.

Jentsch disagrees: "Society has grappled with these issues and thinks using animals is legitimate. But we are constantly called upon to redefend it."[6] For him, "scientific community" must mean something more than custom or institutionalized habits. It must be more than a collection of individuals that publish in the same journals and attend the same conferences. "Scientific community" must also indicate solidarity in defense of those who are attacked and in defense of "the research we believe to be ethical and critical for our understanding of the brain in health and disease."[7] Jentsch put his own call to action into effect by founding the group Pro-Test for Science, which advocates for "science, reasoned discourse, and the belief that life-saving medical research must continue without violence and harassment from misguided activists."[8]

Ringach and Jentsch note, "We should also consider allowing members of the public access to research facilities so that they can observe, firsthand, the measures taken to ensure the well-being of the subjects involved in our scientific enterprise."[9] But, at least at UCLA, administrators will not allow such access, arguing that it puts researchers at even greater risk. This closed-door policy, however, creates an aura of secrecy and mistrust that may itself create risk for the researchers.

Farms, zoos, pets, wildlife preserves, and laboratories

Animal research takes two fundamentally different forms: informal and formal research on animals in order to increase scientific knowledge about animals and to provide better care for them; and mostly formal research using animals as a means to advance some not necessarily animal-related interest, as takes place when animal models are used in preclinical drug trials (the latter type, testing on animals for the purpose of scientific progress, is often referred to as vivisection). The former, especially in an

[6] R. Wilson 2011, n.p. [7] Ringach and Jentsch 2009, p. 11418.

[8] See the homepage of the Pro-Test for Science website, www.pro-test-for-science.org/#/homepage/. This group was inspired by Pro-Test, an organization founded in 2006 by sixteen-year-old Laurie Pycroft in Oxford, UK. She sought to provide a voice in favor of scientific research in the debate surrounding Oxford University's construction of a new biomedical research facility. Speaking of Research is a related organization advocating for animal research. See the Speaking of Research website, http://speakingofresearch.com/.

[9] Ringach and Jentsch 2009, p. 11418.

informal sense, has been around much longer than the latter, which in the most formal sense did not arrive on the historical scene until roughly the seventeenth century.

It is possible that as soon as humans began to domesticate animals humans also began to think in ethical terms about how animals should be treated. From the Axial Age in history, for instance, the Vedas, Upanishads, and the Buddhist sutras called for special recognition and respect for all sentient beings. In the Hebrew scriptures as well there are prohibitions against cruelty to animals and teachings of compassion for them. Israelites were forbidden to muzzle an ox that treads corn, so that it would be able to share in the grain it was making edible for its owners (Deuteronomy 25:4), or to yoke together an ox and an ass, who because they work in different rhythms would cause each other stress (Deuteronomy 22:10). "The righteous person pays attention to the life of his animals" (Proverbs 12:10).

Similarly, it is worth noting that shortly after initial articulation of the principle of free and informed consent guidelines for the treatment of humans involved with experiments, these same guidelines began to call attention to the treatment of animals as well. In preclinical experimentation, "special attention must be exercised in the conduct of research which may affect … the welfare of animals."[10]

As human beings began progressively to separate themselves from the agricultural world that was the characteristic background of the Axial Age and become increasingly urbanized as a result of the Industrial Revolution, they sought to preserve vestiges of the animal world in zoos, in wildlife preserves, and as household pets. At the same time that scientists undertook, during the scientific revolution, to open up the human body for scientific inspection, even more so did they begin to take animals into their laboratories.

The complexities and paradoxes of our attitudes toward animals in the laboratory reflect similar complexities and paradoxes of our attitudes in a nonlaboratory context toward what Donna Haraway has called our "companion species." The same laboratory that does crash tests on monkeys to study brain injuries might well have a bird feeder in the window and a pet

[10] Declaration of Helsinki, 1975, Introduction, para. 7, at the World Medical Association website, www.wma.net/en/30publications/10policies/b3/.

cat that receives the best veterinary care money can buy, even to the point of being cloned after its death because of a particular attachment. True, humans do not always live up to their ideals in regard to human experimentation. But with animals it is not even clear what the ideals are that humans might aspire to.

Imagine, for instance, the following situation. A farm family in rural America raises pigs for a living. Sows, which have been genetically engineered to produce more lean white meat than it would be possible to sustain outside the hog barn, are artificially inseminated and confined in gestation crates where they cannot so much as turn around. After the piglets are born they are raised only to the point at which they become succulent food, then slaughtered and sold as special, high-priced delicacies.

Yet the same family has a milk cow so that members can have fresh milk, and there are a number of semiferal cats living on the property that help keep the mouse population in check. The family also has a small flock of sheep that is protected from coyote attacks by putting out poison bait about every third or fourth year to keep the predator population down. The father, particularly, nevertheless loves the howl of the coyotes at night and the sense of wildness that such sounds lend to life in the country. The two children also have a pet dog, which is allowed to spend cold winter nights in the house where he is treated with great affection. The mother loves birdwatching and the oldest daughter is away at university majoring in molecular biology at the University of California Santa Barbara.

Meeting up for a vacation in San Diego, California, the family visits Sea World and marvels at the tricks the dolphins can perform, but the molecular biology major expresses some misgivings about how the dolphins are kept from the freedom of the ocean. In her first year at university, she happened to read about John Lily's work with dolphins and their apparent high intelligence, which leads her to question the way their behaviors are commodified in this commercial zoo. She also reads Haraway's study of the oncomouse, the patented knock-out organism, genetically engineered to get cancer so that it can be used in scientific research as an animal model for the testing of cancer therapy drugs. The oncomouse gives her both pause and hope, since her mother has had breast cancer for which the oncomouse may help find a cure.

At what point if any might members of this farm family want to harmonize or seek consistency in their plural attitudes toward animals? At what point might scientists who do research attempt to construct a more systematic, reflective equilibrium in their research interactions with animals? Or is this plethora not really an inconsistency that needs to be addressed but simply part of the diverse human condition?

Animal welfare and animal rights: a brief history

The question of how animals ought to be treated in scientific research could not truly arise until modern experimental science itself began to take shape in the 1500s. René Descartes in the early 1600s strengthened the new scientific approach to nature by characterizing animals as machines in a way that took hold of the newly secularized imagination to legitimate any kind of experimental treatment. One way of reading the post-Cartesian history of scientific attitudes toward animals is as an extended attempt to recover a less mechanistic appreciation of organic life. This is a slow history of twists and turns that has also consisted of a continuing dialogue of science with society. But for present purposes, consider the following miscellany of nodal points in this narrative:

1635: Ireland passes what Richard Ryder describes as the first legislation against animal cruelty in the English-speaking world. It prohibited pulling wool off sheep, attaching ploughs to horses' tails, and other "cruelty used to beasts."[11]

Late seventeenth century: John Locke argues against cruelty to animals, but only because cruelty might harm another human with property rights in the animal or because the person performing the action might develop the habit of being cruel to other people – not because of any harm to the animal as animal.[12]

1754: Jean-Jacques Rousseau argues that because animals are sentient "mankind is subjected to a kind of obligation even toward the brutes."[13]

1789 (year the French Revolution begins): Jeremy Bentham becomes the first philosopher to argue at length for inclusion of animals within the boundaries of the morally considerable:

[11] Ryder 2000, p. 49.

[12] *First Treatise of Government* (1689), chap. IX, §92; *Some Thoughts Concerning Education* (1693), pt. VII, §116.

[13] *Discours sur l'origine et les fondements de l'inégalité parmi les hommes* (1755), preface.

> The French have already discovered that the blackness of the skin is no reason a human being should be abandoned without redress to the caprice of a tormentor. It may one day come to be recognized that the number of the legs, the villosity of the skin, or the termination of the *os sacrum* are reasons equally insufficient for abandoning a sensitive being to the same fate. What else is it that should trace the insuperable line? Is it the faculty of reason or perhaps the faculty of discourse? But a full-grown horse or dog, is beyond comparison a more rational, as well as a more conversable animal, than an infant of a day or a week or even a month, old. But suppose the case were otherwise, what would it avail? The question is not, Can they *reason*?, nor Can they *talk*? but, Can they *suffer*?[14]

Early nineteenth century: In 1822, British MP Richard Martin (nicknamed "Humanity Dick"), after years of trying, finally succeeds in having Parliament pass the first laws protecting cattle, horses, and sheep from cruelty. (This legislation is strengthened in the Cruelty to Animals Acts of 1835, 1849, and 1876.) Two years later in 1824, Martin founds the Society for the Prevention of Cruelty to Animals, which establishes a network of inspectors to identify abusers and report them for prosecution. (In 1840, Queen Victoria endorses the organization, making it the Royal Society for the Prevention of Cruelty to Animals.)

1837: Arthur Schopenhauer praises the British for their attitude toward animals. In his words, Europeans are

> awakening more and more to a sense that beasts have rights, in proportion as the strange notion is being gradually overcome and outgrown, that the animal kingdom came into existence solely for the benefit and pleasure of man. ... To the honor, then, of the English be it said that they are the first people who have, in downright earnest, extended the protecting arm of the law to animals (*Über die Grundlage der Moral* [*On the Basis of Morality*] III, 8, 7, 3).

1859: Charles Darwin's *On the Origin of Species* and *Descent of Man and Selection in Relation to Sex* (1871) argue the continuity between animals and humans. "The main conclusion arrived at in this work, and now held by many naturalists who are well competent to form a sound judgment, is that man is descended from some less highly organised form" (*Descent of Man, and Selection in Relation to Sex* 21, 2).

[14] *Principles of Morals and Legislation* (1781), chap 17.

1933: In one of the great paradoxes with regard to the treatment of human beings and animals, the National Socialist Party passes the most comprehensive set of animal protection laws in Europe. In the *Tierschutzgesetz* (Animal protection law) Adolf Hitler announces (November 24) an end to animal cruelty: *Im neuen Reich darf es keine Tierquälerei mehr geben* (In the new Reich no more animal cruelty will be allowed). Followed by prohibitions of hunting (*Reichsjagdgesetz*, 1934), general environmental protection (*Naturschutzgesetz*, 1935), and more. Shortly before promulgation of the *Tierschutzgesetz*, vivisection was first banned, then restricted. Animal research was viewed as part of "Jewish science," and "internationalist" medicine, indicating a mechanistic mind that saw nature as something to be dominated, rather than respected.

1959: Publication of Russell and Burch's *The Principles of Humane Experimental Technique*, setting out the three Rs of animal experimentation: Replace, Reduce, and Refine.

Mid-1960s, in Great Britain: In response to Ruth Harrison's *Animal Machines* (1964), the British Parliament establishes a commission to investigate the welfare of industrially farmed animals. One outcome is establishment in 1967 of the Farm Animal Welfare Advisory Committee, subsequently (1979) renamed the Farm Animal Welfare Council. The Committee establishes animal care guidelines (sometimes referred to as the Brambell Report) since articulated as the "five freedoms" for animals:

1. Freedom from thirst and hunger – by ready access to fresh water and a diet to maintain full health and vigor
2. Freedom from discomfort – by providing an appropriate environment including shelter and a comfortable resting area
3. Freedom from pain, injury, and disease – by prevention or rapid diagnosis and treatment
4. Freedom to express normal behavior – by providing sufficient space, proper facilities and company of the animal's own kind
5. Freedom from fear and distress – by ensuring conditions and treatment which avoid mental suffering.

Further proposals are made to have the United Nations adopt a "Universal Declaration on Animal Welfare."

Mid-1960s, in United States: Institutional Animal Care and Use Committees are instituted. In 1961 a group of veterinarians created an Animal Care Panel, which in 1963 became an independent, nonprofit corporation (American Association for the Accreditation of Laboratory Animal Care – shortly renamed the Association for the Assessment and Accreditation of Laboratory Animal Care or AAALAC International) and published a first edition of *The Guide for the Care and Use of Laboratory Animals*. Subsequent editions of the *Guide*, which adopts the three Rs, are published by the US National Academy of Sciences and adopted by the US National Institutes of Health. In 1966 the US Animal Welfare Act, with its later revisions, requires creation of Institutional Animal Care and Use Committees to oversee compliance with procedures and principles outlined in the *Guide*.[15]

1975: Publication of Peter Singer's *Animal Liberation*, which develops in more analytic and extended detail Bentham's utilitarian argument of respect for animal interests and welfare because of their ability to feel pain and suffer. This was followed the next year by the founding of the Animal Liberation Front (ALF), which became active in protesting animal experimentation in science.

1980: Founding of PETA.

Early 2000s: An increasing number of directives are issued by the European Commission providing ethical guidelines for the use of animals in research.

2005: Nuffield Council on Bioethics issues a general report on *The Ethics of Research Involving Animals*. The report first states that there is "clear evidence" that specific types of animal research benefit society. It then argues that proper moral treatment of a being depends on the characteristics it possesses rather than the species to which it belongs. The report identifies five morally relevant characteristics or features to be weighed when considering whether a given research project is morally acceptable:

1. Sentience (the capacity to feel pleasure and pain)
2. Higher cognitive capacities (e.g., language)

[15] Committee for the Update of the Guide for the Care and Use of Laboratory Animals, National Research Council 2011.

3. The capacity to flourish (the ability to satisfy species-specific needs)
4. Sociability (being a member of a community)
5. Possession of a life (attributing value to life itself).

The report considers whether these features should be weighed against human benefit or if they should be considered absolute constraints.

2010: During a conference in Basel, Switzerland, roughly eighty life sciences researchers from across Europe create the "Basel Declaration." This two-page document notes ongoing opportunities and challenges, lists "fundamental principles" to guide the conduct of research with animals, and demands that "necessary research involving animals, including non-human primates, be allowed now and in the future."[16]

The animals issue: an analysis

Adapting a discussion by Arthur Caplan, one can identify three major areas of dispute with regard to animal research.[17] First, focusing mostly on product testing with animals, there is a disagreement about the need to conduct such research. On the one side are those who maintain that animal research is necessary to advance human health and safety. On the other are those willing to grant the goal while arguing that much animal testing is unnecessary or can be dramatically reduced if not eliminated with such techniques as computer simulations. The animal testing of cosmetics, for instance, is not justified, simply because cosmetics are not necessary or there are enough cosmetics that have already proved safe. Who really needs more high-tech cosmetics? More strongly, others go further and dispute that animal research can prove safety anyway, on the grounds that animal models do not advance relevant knowledge or are unreliable. Since all drugs and other products must ultimately be tested on humans at some point, it is not clear that human safety is ever significantly advanced. Furthermore, some argue that advances in computer modeling and non-invasive scanning technologies obviate the need for some kinds of animal testing. Of course, animal researchers like Jentsch maintain that animal models are often both beneficial and irreplaceable.

[16] "Basel Declaration," Basel Declaration website, www.basel-declaration.org/basel-declaration/.

[17] Caplan 1983.

Second, there is disagreement about the moral status of animals. On the one side are those to whom humans and animals appear as so different in kind as to demand quite different types of moral consideration. On the other are those to whom it appears that humans and at least some animals share such obvious similarities as to demand similar moral treatments. The arguments con and pro can be quite varied, with results having significant implications for all other possible disagreements as well.

Third, taking the issue of animal research as a whole, there is disagreement about the weight of this issue in relation to other moral questions. Some argue that in the larger scheme of things there is simply not that much animal suffering caused by humans. Animals and nature cause much more suffering to nonhuman animals than do humans. Additionally, any suffering caused by animal experimentation pales in comparison with the suffering caused by factory farming. Because of this, ethical discussions are largely beside the point. Those who are really opposed to human-caused animal pain would do better to devote themselves to organizing for political or cultural change than undertaking ethical analyses. Indeed, taking precisely this position, activist organizations such as PETA do engage in political agitation and, in some cases, even violent protest. Even short of joining PETA, there are many who think that comparisons between the amounts of pain caused in nature and in human-made environments are not at all beside the point, since the numbers of animals suffering in other contexts is much greater and with less oversight. In response it is argued that this is no excuse for ignoring the ethics of animal research, since animals cannot avoid the suffering they face in the laboratory and are in this context wholly dependent on humans to advocate for them.

Returning to the second dispute, the key issue becomes the degree to which sacrifices and concessions have to be made with regard to human goods in order to promote animal welfare and decrease animal suffering. That is, what degree of moral consideration should animals receive or what level of moral worth do they have? There are three basic criteria that have been proposed for moral worth: sentience, purposiveness, and shared narrative (Table 6.1).

With regard to sentience, it is argued by Bentham, Singer, and others (in a consequentialist manner) that the capacity to feel pain confers moral worth on organisms. Thus humans should not engage in any experiment where the degree of suffering produced in some sentient beings

Table 6.1 *Three ways to think about the moral status of animals*

	Singer	Regan	Diamond
General approach	Isolate morally salient property (capacity to suffer/sentience) prior to relation with humans	Isolate morally salient property (purposiveness) prior to any relation with humans	View animals as parts of relational webs and their properties as constituted by relations with humans
Reason to not use animals in research	Animals are capable of suffering	Animals are experiencing subjects of a life	Animals (e.g., pets) can be seen as involved in special relations with humans
Morally permissible to use animals if ...	They do not feel pain	Their welfare and inherent value is not diminished	They are not constituted as fellow creatures

outweighs the benefits produced in other sentient beings. Criticisms include arguments to the effect that if this were the case then it would appear to legitimate killing a few quickly and as painlessly as possible to reduce pain in others. Indeed, insofar as experiments could be rendered pain-free then there would seem to be no objection to them.

With regard to purposiveness, it is argued by Tom Regan and others (in a deontological manner) that possessing intentions or purposes confers moral worth on organisms. Beings that possess a will to survive have a right to survive; it is not permissible to interfere with the life plan of another. Human beings should not engage in any experiment that deprives other beings with purposes of the right to exercise those purposes or frustrates certain basic drives and intentions. One problem, however, concerns how to handle conflicting rights claims, as when the life plan of one being would be advanced by frustrating another's. Is there some way to establish a hierarchy such that, say, a human need for medicine could legitimate using animals in science to discover or invent it?

Finally, with regard to narrative- or life-sharing, Cora Diamond and others argue that both the sentience and purposiveness criteria attempt to isolate some property that can serve analytically to draw boundaries around those that belong to one group rather than another.[18] Diamond's position is more holistic and self-consciously anthropocentric (and virtue oriented). It begins with the experience of human life. Humans do not talk about themselves in terms of properties, but in terms of relationships as sons and daughters, parents, spouses, co-workers, neighbors, or citizens. The reason we do not eat fellow human beings is that these relational descriptions and associated shared narratives constitute us as not the sorts of things that eat each other. Consequentialists would have to admit that it is alright to eat humans as long as they did not suffer. Deontologists would say it is alright to eat humans as long as they agreed to it.

Diamond's argument is that consequentialist and deontological arguments miss the way we share bonds through descriptions and narratives, and that it is only insofar as humans can understand themselves as having positive relationships with nonhuman animals – as the two being companion species or fellow creatures – that humans will want to treat animals like themselves. Pets are illustrative of this point. Diamond notes

[18] See Diamond 1978.

that it could only be a cruel joke to call an animal a "pet" if it was being fattened-up for the dinner table. A pet, like a human, is simply not what one eats, by virtue of its place in a web of relations.

Antivivisectionists or vegetarians or those concerned with animal experimentation would do well to appeal to this deeply motivating narrative of being-in-relation rather than trying to abstract away from it to some bundle of shared properties. What is crucial is to recognize the ways animals are human-like, that is, are fellow creatures to whom we can relate in ways similar to our relationships with other humans. The criticism, of course, is that anthropocentrism will continue to deny limits to the treatment of animals who are not seen as human-like. Diamond seems to offer no culture-independent reason for determining which animals should be treated more like humans and which should not. Lingering in her analysis is the specter of relativism: Is it merely habit, dogma, convention, or prejudice that determines how animals are constituted? Is this also true of humans, such that the decision to constitute some humans as "slaves" is merely one culture's choice – a choice that can be neither right nor wrong?

Summary

This chapter first noted age-old complexities and paradoxes in human attitudes toward and relations with animals. It then undertook a historical survey of the question of how animals ought to be treated in scientific research, noting the many twists and turns in how animals are conceptualized and the resulting guidelines for action. The concluding section discussed three main facets of the debate concerning the use of animals in scientific research: (a) need; (b) moral status; and (c) relative weight of the issue. Finally, the chapter surveyed three ways to go about answering the question of moral status: (a) sentience; (b) purposiveness; and (c) shared narrative.

Extending reflection: Temple Grandin

At the outset of this chapter, we noted that the less common form of science involving animals includes research to increase knowledge about animals in order to provide better care for them. The story of Temple

Grandin illustrates this kind of animal research as well as its close association with design and engineering. Born in 1947, Grandin is a US professor of animal science at Colorado State University and a consultant to the livestock industry on animal behavior. Grandin has high-functioning autism and is also widely known for her autism advocacy, invention of the hug machine, designed to calm hypersensitive people, and defense of neurodiversity. Grandin has both an MS (Arizona State University, 1975) and a PhD (University of Illinois at Urbana-Champaign, 1989) in animal science. In 2004, she won the "Proggy" award from PETA in the "visionary" category. In 2009, she was named a fellow of the American Society of Agricultural and Biological Engineers. She has had a major impact on livestock operations around the globe. In North American meat plants, nearly half of all cattle are handled in the center track restrainer system that she designed.

To achieve her success, Grandin not only had to overcome now outdated medical stigmas associated with autism and the teasing of her classmates, but also the barriers associated with the male-dominated worlds of science and the livestock business. She often attributes her ideas for improved livestock-handling operations to her autism, which made her all too familiar with the feeling of being threatened by her environment. In addition, she has a remarkable visual memory, which allows her to recall details at will and to view her memories from different angles. As a graduate student in Arizona, Grandin first struck upon her ideas for designing more humane livestock facilities. Her designs depended on detailed observations concerning cattle behavior and interactions of cattle with human handlers. As just two examples, she designed a dip bath with steps and a sweeping, curved corral in order to reduce the stress experienced by the cattle.[19]

Grandin often justifies the humane treatment of animals on both pragmatic and moral grounds. As an example of the former, she noted when first proposing her designs for a stockyard that her facility would reduce the costs stemming from cattle breaking their legs, drowning, or becoming spooked and requiring more handling labor. From a moral perspective, Grandin argues in one of her most well-known essays titled "Animals Are Not Things" that, even though animals can be property, humans have certain moral responsibilities to treat them humanely. The extent of this

[19] See Temple Grandin's website, www.grandin.com/.

human responsibility is proportionate to the complexity of the animal's nervous system, because this determines their ability to feel fear and pain as well as their welfare needs: the development of the nervous system is a "major determinant of the welfare needs of the animal."[20] Humans can slaughter animals for their food and use them for research, Grandin maintains, but they must do so in a way that minimizes stress, fear, and pain.

Questions for research and discussion

1. Jentsch mused, "If a chimp had to suffer in miserable pain for five days, but then no one on earth would ever die of AIDS – would it be worth it? What if I could suffer for five days and then no one would die of AIDS?"[21] How would you go about thinking through these questions? Are they appropriate or relevant ways to frame the issue? How would Singer, Regan, and Diamond think through them?
2. Is the imaginary family on the farm described earlier full of moral contradictions when it comes to their views about animals? Do they need to adopt a more coherent approach to nonhuman animals or is this a defensible pluralism?
3. How would you weigh the five characteristics or features identified in the Nuffield report? Should human benefit be weighed as part of the mix or are there absolute limits, for example, should any use of animals capable of suffering (or capable of higher cognitive functioning) be prohibited even despite promising medical leads?
4. In reading through Temple Grandin's website, can you distill a core moral position when it comes to animal welfare and human responsibilities for animal welfare? Is it essentially the same as utilitarianism? How do her various practical designs for livestock operations and processing plants embody her moral position? How exactly does she think that her autism helps to "decode animal behavior"?

[20] See Grandin 2002, n.p. [21] In R. Wilson 2011, n.p.

Further reading about the cases

Blum, Deborah (1994) *The Monkey Wars*. Oxford University Press.

Grandin, Temple, and Catherine Johnson (2005) *Animals in Translation: Using the Mysteries of Autism to Decode Animal Behavior*. New York: Scribner.

Grandin, Temple, and Catherine Johnson (2010) *Animals Make Us Human: Creating the Best Life for Animals*. Boston: Houghton Mifflin Harcourt.

Sacks, Oliver (1995) *An Anthropologist on Mars: Seven Paradoxical Tales*. New York: Alfred A. Knopf.

7 The science of ethics

Ethical theories (as introduced in Chapter 2) begin with descriptions of behaviors that are considered moral and seek to explain *why* they are so considered. As such ethical theories also provide perspectives on the norms incorporated into science as a social institution, mapped out in the sociology of science (Chapter 3). Additionally, theories provide different frameworks for examining and promoting institutional norms in the practice of science (Chapters 4, 5, and 6). But the relationship between ethics and science can also be reversed. It is possible to ask not only what ethics has to say about science, but also what science has to say about ethics. Science can be used to try to respond to the "why" question about behavioral norms. The present chapter thus considers efforts to use, for example, decision science, evolution, and psychology to give scientific explanations for human behavior and some associated moral beliefs. Thus, whereas the previous three chapters focused on the ethical assessment of issues related to the practice of science, the present chapter turns to considerations of how science can be used to give an account of these practices.

Setting the stage: sexual harassment among scientists

In a 2009 issue of the peer-refereed scientific journal *PLoS ONE*, Min Tan (from the Guandong Entomological Institute, Guangzhou, China) and colleagues published a study of the practice of fellatio among fruit bats. According to the paper abstract:

> Oral sex is widely used in human foreplay, but rarely documented in other animals.... The short-nosed fruit bat *Cynopterus sphinx* exhibits resource defense polygyny and one sexually active male often roosts with groups of females.... Female bats often lick their mate's penis during dorsoventral copulation. The female lowers her head to lick the shaft or the base of

> the male's penis but does not lick the glans penis which has already penetrated the vagina. Males never withdrew their penis when it was licked by the mating partner. A positive relationship exists between the length of time that the female licked the male's penis during copulation and the duration of copulation. Furthermore, mating pairs spent significantly more time in copulation if the female licked her mate's penis than if fellatio was absent.[1]

Early the next year Dr. Dylan Evans at University College Cork (UCC) mentioned this paper to his colleague, Dr. Rossana Salerno Kennedy, in the course of what he considered a discussion about the uniqueness of human behaviors. After requesting a copy of the article - in order, she reported, to terminate an encounter that "shocked, insulted and humiliated" her - Kennedy initiated a sexual harassment complaint.[2] A subsequent UCC investigation asked whether Evans' action could "reasonably be regarded as sexually offensive, humiliating or intimidating" and concluded:

> We find that the action was a joke with sexual innuendo and it was reasonable for [Dr. Kennedy] to be offended. ... We therefore find the complaint on this action is upheld though it was not Dr. Evans' intention to cause [Dr. Kennedy] offence.[3]

As a result, the UCC president formally censured Dr. Evans, placed him on two years' probation, and required him to undergo sensitivity training and counseling - which led, he claimed, to a denial of tenure.

This event became a widely discussed issue of academic freedom and political correctness. The article "Fellatio by Fruit Bats Prolongs Copulation Time" turned into one of the most widely read publications of 2009. But among the numerous blogosphere and related commentaries, two kinds of response stand out. One emphasizes that male and female perceptions of human interactions often differ in fundamental ways. As one commentator remarked to defenders of Evans (with editing for grammar and clarity),

> Excuse the stereotyping, but you do come across as men who would not understand the disturbing nature of [this situation]. Let me remind you that inappropriate advances, physical, verbal and psychological are immensely disturbing for a woman.

[1] Tan et al. 2009, n.p. [2] See Walsh 2010. [3] In Reilly 2010, n.p.

Another response was to accept that Evans might well have been making advances on Kennedy but to justify it as "natural" on the basis of alleged historical, psychological, or biological reality. After all, aren't men always a little sexually aggressive in many mammalian species?[4]

The argument is that men and women have quite different attitudes toward sexual relationships, differences for which there are biological explanations. A few months after this discussion in the scientific community, a related exchange occurred in a syndicated personal advice column in the United States. A "Wandering Husband" wrote to "Ask Amy," arguing that it is as natural for men to "cheat" on their wives as it is for wives to object. "We love our wives, but [it's] not in our nature to be monogamous."[5]

In both the scientific and nonscientific communities, then, appeals are often made to science to justify a human behavior that is otherwise judged immoral. Scientific studies are cited to expose the illusion of some moral judgments. Such views are particularly common in the area of sexual behavior, with other examples occurring in debates about abortion and homosexuality. To what extent can such ethical arguments truly be grounded in science, either empirically or logically?

What can science tell us about ethics?

In many arguments about morality, distinctions need to be made between empirical facts and the quality of argumentation from those facts. If the facts are mistaken, the argument will usually fail. Yet sometimes the identification of relevant facts depends on clarification of the argument. The two – empirical facts and logical argument – cannot always be fully separated. Certainly this is the case with regard to efforts to define sexual harassment in the light of scientific knowledge about biological evolution and sexual behavior among animals. There is as much debate about the alleged biological facts as about their implication.

There are different types of harassment. In one type, often termed quid pro quo sexual harassment, a person with social power in the form of a teacher or laboratory director (usually a male) requests or demands sexually related interactions from a subordinate (often a female). Sometimes

[4] See Palmer and Thornhill 2000. [5] Ask Amy 2010, n.p.

this is done explicitly in exchange for favorable treatment in the form of grades, work assessments, coauthorship on a paper, or inclusion in a grant project. Other times the exchange is implicit. In a second type, sexually tinged behavior simply creates an environment that some persons experience as inhospitable. As a result, they find it more difficult to work than others and claim to be unfairly disadvantaged.

In the present context, the issue of sexual harassment has two distinct aspects. One is related to the responsible conduct of research. That is, since good-science guidelines commonly proscribe sexual harassment as a breach of the responsible planning, conducting, and disseminating of scientific research – in the same way that conflict of interest and data fudging are proscribed – this is simply another behavior to be highlighted in order to be more effectively limited. Much of Chapters 4, 5, and 6 took this approach to a diverse spectrum of practices. A second aspect of sexual harassment, however, concerns the reasons for the negative moral assessment. The interesting fact is that sexual harassment, perhaps more than any other commonly proscribed behavior, has often been defended, with some appeal to scientific knowledge used as a basis for criticizing a negative judgment of it.

Of course, since the word "harassment" has built-in negative connotations, to call a behavior sexual harassment implies that no justification is possible. To provisionally suspend such judgment, then, and thereby consider the ethical arguments bearing on the behavior, a more neutral description is needed. As a provisional substitute, such behavior may be described as "sexual interactions between individuals of differential authority or powers associated with other non-sexual interactions or exchanges."

Such sexual interactions are clearly not justified on the basis of standard behavioral protocols or ethical theories. An ethics of care, which is often but not always associated with feminism, is likely to be critical of such uses of power as well as of sexual promiscuity. Few if any virtue ethics theorists defend promiscuity; moreover, the use of power to realize narrow self-interests is easily considered a vice. Deontological moral theory would challenge the universalizability of any principle that appears to justify such personal relationships, especially because a strong argument can be made that they involve objectifying persons and treating them primarily as means rather than as ends in themselves. It is possible that an act-based consequentialism could in particular instances justify such behaviors, but a rule-based consequentialism would likely raise questions.

Underlying any such possible consequentialist justification of "sexual harassment" (in quotation marks to indicate a suspension of negative connotations), there would probably need to be a deontological qualifier: that the personal interactions, whatever they are, take place between freely consenting adults. An additional qualifier might need to be that any exchanges be transparent to and not unfairly disadvantage others.

As this preliminary analysis suggests, the use of science to ground ethical norms may be more complex than initially expected. Further complexities thus deserve to be considered in relation to appeals to biological evolution as well as to two other sciences: decision science and developmental psychology.

Evolutionary ethics

Justifications by reference to evolutionary biology of the commonly perceived negative behavior of sexual harassment go hand in hand with the development of biologically based explanations for behaviors that are perceived more positively. Altruism, for instance, is commonly praised in popular morality, and the effort to develop biologically based explanations for such behavior – that would seem at face value to be biologically counterproductive – has been a major theme in evolutionary theory. Both cases show the basic approach of many biological explanations. They begin by identifying certain behaviors as empirical givens (altruism or sexual harassment) and then seek to develop scientific explanations of what could cause them to be so prevalent as well as (perhaps) approved or disapproved.

The effort to base ethics on biological evolution is often called evolutionary ethics. Charles Darwin initiated this program when he argued that the moral sentiment of sympathy is an evolutionary development in humans, going so far as to maintain that Kant's concept of duty has an evolutionary base.[6] Other proponents of some form of evolutionary ethics have run the gamut from Herbert Spencer, a Victorian social scientist who coined the term "survival of the fittest" and developed a version known

[6] Darwin [1871] 1981, pt. I, chap. 5, para. 1.

as "social Darwinism," to such contemporary thinkers as E.O. Wilson, Richard Dawkins, Larry Arnhart, and Sam Harris.

Wilson's sociobiology and Dawkins' theory of the "selfish gene" share an appeal to gene reproduction as a way to explain cooperation. Wilson, for instance, defines sociobiology as the "extension of population biology and evolutionary theory to social organization."[7] Arguing that not just physical traits but also behaviors evolve over time, Wilson and other sociobiologists use genetic mutation and natural selection to explain such behaviors as hive interactions among "social insects," mating patterns in diverse animals, and pack hunting among some higher mammals. When applied to human behaviors like sexual interactions and the development of cooperation in social institutions such as armies, governments, and corporations – and even the emergence of religion, art, and the humanities[8] – sociobiological theory has been highly contested.

The same goes for Dawkins' theory of the selfish gene. In this gene-centered theory, genes have self-interest or are inherently programmed to reproduce themselves. Thus the more genes shared by any two individuals, the more sense it makes for them to cooperate or behave altruistically toward one another. The British biologist J.B.S. Haldane, for instance, is reported to have given this view dramatic formulation by saying he would lay down his life for two brothers or eight cousins. Yet as Dawkins himself admits, genetic reproduction in humans is at some level influenced by culture. Indeed, while Dawkins argues that cultural "memes" (another term he coined) also evolve through cultural selection (the study of which he calls "memetics"), the influence of culture on biological evolution poses complex questions. Contrary to Dawkins, the evolutionary biologist Stephen J. Gould, among others, argues that natural selection operates not on invisible genotypes, but on visible phenotype expressions, which are themselves influenced by the environment.

Although some social theorists have attempted to use evolutionary theory to support utopian political projects, political philosopher Arnhart appeals to Darwinian evolution in a provocative manner to support conservative political beliefs. According to Arnhart, some twenty natural desires constitute an evolved human nature. These include desires for sexual mating, familial bonding, property, social order, and knowledge. As he puts

[7] E. Wilson 1978, p. x. [8] See the last chapters of E. Wilson 1998.

it, "Even if evolution by natural selection is not purposeful, it produces organic beings that are purposeful."[9] For human beings to have purpose is natural, with some purposes being more natural than others.

John Dewey made a parallel argument in support of progressive politics. For Dewey, too, it is simply a fact of nature that human beings are organic entities that evaluate their experiences with an eye toward enhancing those experiences, and that the best means for realizing such enhancement looked like progressive politics.[10] Both Arnhart and Dewey have to include nonbiological selection when they identify some desires as more natural than others – as when, for instance, they both reject sexual predation, although arguably an evolved behavior, as less than natural for humans.

Such would probably have been the criticism of Thomas Henry Huxley, "Darwin's bulldog." In an 1893 essay, he wrote that he had no doubt about the evolutionary origin of sympathy and "the moral sentiments." At the same time, since "the immoral sentiments have no less been evolved, there is ... as much natural sanction for the one as the other."[11] The immoral sentiments of selfishness and anger are evolutionary developments as much as others. However, Arnhart and Dewey might well reply that the common description of selfishness and anger as being less than moral reveals a second-order sentiment with its own evolutionary foundations. Indeed, someone might even argue that the human interest in ethical theory and philosophy is an evolutionary development: we have evolved sentiments as well as the capacity to judge which ones are better and which ones are worse.

Extending Dewey, the neuroscientist Harris undertakes one of the most comprehensive contemporary efforts to ground ethics in evolutionary biology. He argues for a "science of morality." For Harris this science includes not only evolutionary biology and the emergence of human striving for biological and psychological flourishing, but the neuroscientific identification of peak brain functioning as an incontestable good and the use of science to critically assess various means for achieving human ends. Harris contends that science can derive "ought" conclusions from "is" premises, because science can show us what it *is* for humans to flourish and, thus, what we *ought* to do.

[9] Arnhart 2010, p. 29. [10] Dewey 1916. [11] Huxley 1893, para. 55.

Decision science

As Harris suggests, scientific ethics need not be limited to explaining behavior. It may also attempt to rationalize or improve it. Such is the case with decision science.

The elements of decision theory first emerged in the 1600s in efforts to analyze the best ways to invest money in merchant capitalism and in analyses of insurance risks and games of chance. The mathematical fields of statistics and probability grew out of and contributed to decision theory. During and after World War II, decision theory was used to analyze military strategy, particularly with regard to nuclear weapons.

An abstract case in decision theory that has been the subject of multiple interpretations and analyses is called the prisoner's dilemma. One version of this dilemma imagines two people, who are in reality guilty, arrested on suspicion of committing a serious crime for which there is sufficient evidence at present for only a less serious conviction. Suppose you are one of the prisoners. You and your partner in crime are separated and interrogated individually. You are offered the following deal: if you provide evidence that helps the state convict your partner and sentence him to prison for four years on the serious charge, you will be given the lenient sentence of only one year. Your partner is offered the same deal and you know this. If neither of you confess, you will both serve two years on the less serious charge; and if you both confess, you will each get three years. Confessing means a prisoner will serve at least one year and maybe three years; refusing to confess guarantees at least two years and risks four years in prison. Your decision will depend, first, on how likely you think it is that the other will confess.

The options, summarized in Table 7.1, can help prisoners (or others in similar circumstances) rationally assess their decision, given their particular interests. For instance, one relevant interest would be how much you wanted to avoid the maximum possible sentence. If the maximum sentence were the death penalty or life in prison, then it might be rational to confess, no matter what. Confession guarantees that no matter how your partner in crime might behave, you will not receive the maximum sentence, although you run the risk of the next most severe sentence.

The prisoner's dilemma analysis has also been extended into a game in which two competitors repeatedly play against each other, with payoffs

Table 7.1 *A prisoner's dilemma analysis*

Prisoner *A* Prisoner *B*	Refuses to confess	Confesses
Refuses to confess	*A* gets 2 years *B* gets 2 years	*A* gets 1 year *B* gets 4 years
Confesses	*A* gets 4 years *B* gets 1 year	*A* gets 3 years *B* gets 3 years

structured in a similar manner. Thus developed, it can be shown that a strategy of tit for tat, or responding in the same way as the competitor, will yield the best results for oneself.

This kind of decision-making analysis that seeks to identify optimal strategies is at the basis of many theories of economic behavior. However, empirical studies in behavioral economics have shown that so-called rational actors do not always act rationally.

Rational actor assumptions commonly inform decision science - i.e., that people possess unlimited time and computational power and a clearly defined utility function, and have indifference to logically equivalent descriptions of alternatives. Work in the analysis of economic decision-making has focused either on trying to extend the predictive power of rational actor assumptions or on articulating alternative and more behaviorally realistic assumptions. Herbert Simon, for instance, developed the notion of "satisficing" as a working substitution for the goal of optimizing. Amos Kahneman and Daniel Tversky explored the heuristics or shortcuts human beings take to satisfice under conditions of limited time or incomplete information. It could be argued that normative moral theories function as heuristics.

Psychology of moral development

Complementing evolutionary psychology (dealing with how human behaviors have evolved) and decision science (analyzing how human decisions can be improved) is the scientific study of moral development in individuals.

The Swiss child psychologist Jean Piaget created the field of cognitive development. For Piaget, the two fundamental phases of moral development are what he calls, echoing Kant, *heteronomous* and *autonomous* morality. In the heteronomous phase, children accept external laws precisely because they come from outside and appear to exhibit a kind of independence from their imaginations. In the autonomous phase, children seek to construct guidelines for their behavior more from within themselves. In the autonomous moral consciousness, however, an individual adopts inner guidelines because the person has rationally formulated them and not because they are innate. Inner guidelines reflect a basic human drive to think and reason about the world.

The heteronomous/autonomous distinction can be used to consider possible relationships between science and ethics. The former relation suggests that ethics or morality is best imposed on science from without - by social regulation. The latter supports guidelines for the practice of science developed from within - that is, by scientists themselves. This latter approach also supports the notion that science should be seen as an autonomous profession.

In studies that expanded Piaget's research program, the American developmental psychologist Lawrence Kohlberg argued that the movement from heteronomous to autonomous morality is more nuanced. It actually consists of six steps divided into three basic stages: preconventional, conventional, and postconventional (Table 7.2).[12]

Preconventional morality is self-centered and concerned with physical needs. This hedonistic morality is typical of preschool children. They aim to avoid physical pain by simple obedience or to pursue physical pleasure by means of instrumental exchanges: "I'll scratch your back if you scratch mine." Justice is making fair trades for mutual gain.

Conventional morality is social, concerned with what others think and getting along with others. This social morality is typical of teenagers and their cliques. The goal is either immediate social approval or action in accord with the laws that abstractly define the social order. Professional conformity in both personal and legalistic forms can further exemplify this stage of moral development. Justice is implicit or explicit rule-following.

Postconventional morality is idealistic, concerned with ideas and theories and their coherence and consistency. Here the focus becomes living in accord with an ideal social contract or understanding and living up to

[12] See Kohlberg et al. 1983.

Table 7.2 *Summary of Kohlberg's stages of moral development*

Preconventional morality
Pleasure-seeking and pain-avoiding.
Examples: The pragmatic ethics of the business people and scientists who do research simply to make money.
Conventional morality
Social-approval-seeking and law-abiding.
Examples: Members of a club, those in a military organization or corporate bureaucracy, and scientists who are guided by the ethos of the scientific community.
Postconventional morality
Seeking to live up to an implicit contract with all human beings or to abide by some universal moral principle.
Examples: Moral heroes and Nobel-Peace-Prize-winning scientists.

somewhat abstract principles of right and wrong independent of social approval or their articulation in any particular laws. Moral heroes such as Mohandas Gandhi, Martin Luther King Jr., or Aung San Suu Kyi perhaps best exemplify this level, in which justice becomes living in accord with universal principles that one discovers by oneself.

For both Piaget and Kohlberg, not all stages are equal. Subsequent stages are more comprehensively developed and include earlier stages. At Kohlberg's stage of conventional morality, for instance, people may continue in part to pursue physical pleasure as well as understand others who do so, but they are capable of recognizing limitations in this attitude and of criticizing its weaknesses in certain situations. Conventional moral consciousness will, however, find it difficult to understand those who operate at the postconventional level, often describing people such as Mahatma Gandhi as unrealistic or irrational. It is the ability of postconventional moral consciousness to encompass and criticize other stages, to make decisions about when it is most appropriate to use different moral frameworks, and to undertake self-criticism, that constitutes the superiority of this highest stage of moral development. As noted in Chapter 2, the feminist ethicist and psychologist Carol Gilligan critiques Kohlberg's levels as a male-centered account of morality. She argues that the levels fail to account for a more typical female approach to moral life, one that is less universalistic and more situated in particular bonds of caring relations.

The naturalistic fallacy

The most common objection to any attempt to create a science of ethics claims that to do so commits what is called the naturalistic fallacy, that is, attempts to identify the natural with the good. Usually traced back to the Scottish philosopher David Hume, the naturalistic fallacy occurs when empirical premises are used to support a normative conclusion. In Hume's words,

> In every system of morality, which I have hitherto met with, I have always remark'd, that the author proceeds for some time in the ordinary way of reasoning, [making] observations concerning human affairs; when of a sudden I am surpriz'd to find, that instead of the usual copulations of propositions, *is*, and *is not*, I meet with no proposition that is not connected with an *ought*, or an *ought not*. This change is imperceptible; but is, however, of the last consequence. For as this *ought*, or *ought not*, expresses some new relation or affirmation, 'tis necessary that it shou'd be observ'd and explain'd; and at the same time that a reason should be given, for what seems altogether inconceivable, how this new relation can be a deduction from others, which are entirely different from it.[13]

Thus does Hume point out a flaw in attempts to reason from the empirical *is* to the normative *ought*, from facts to values. Since the empirical truth of the premises does not guarantee the moral goodness or rightness of the conclusion, such an argument is invalid.

In the early 1900s the British philosopher G.E. Moore restated Hume's point when he maintained that any ethics which attempts to identify the good with the natural is always open to question. After one has identified some action as natural, like avoiding pain for example, one can still meaningfully ask whether it is good to avoid pain. Moore's "open question" argument shows that utilitarians cannot easily reduce goodness to the natural tendency to avoid physical pain.

Responses to the naturalistic fallacy and the open question argument come in two forms. One simply accepts the disjunction between nature

[13] Hume [1739] 2000, bk. III, pt. I, §I, para. 24.

and ethics. The scientific study of nature and the study of ethics are two different endeavors and, as such, should be kept separate. Among scientists, this has been vigorously argued by evolutionary biologist Stephen Jay Gould. According to Gould, science deals in empirical facts, discovering what *is* the case, while ethics deals in normative matters, uncovering what *ought* to be the case. Facts and norms constitute what Gould calls "non-overlapping magisteria" (or NOMA).[14] The political philosopher Leo Strauss holds a similar position, arguing that modern science can make humans clever in an instrumental sense of how best to achieve desired goals. But modern science cannot, Strauss maintains, tell us anything about which goals are best and most noble and thus most worthy of pursuit.[15] The philosopher of science Carl Hempel agrees: science can tell us which means are best for pursuing our ends, but it cannot tell us which ends we ought to pursue.

The other response seeks some accommodation between the two, even if it is only a hypothetical one. For example, biology reveals that in all organisms, from unicellular to the higher mammals, metabolism constitutes a dynamic interaction with the environment ordered toward maintaining structure in the midst of change, and that there likewise exists among organisms a tendency toward diversity and complexity. Given this fact about nature, *if* humans want to function in accord with this process *then* they will do so in appropriate ways, some of which they will describe as moral. This is in effect the core of Dewey's position, although he puts it less hypothetically, affirming that this is in fact what humans as purposive agents do – and should do, just more consciously, that is, with more scientific knowledge.

Options for a science of ethics

Whether or not there can be a science of ethics depends in part on two concepts: the concept of science and that of ethics. Different concepts will point toward different possible meanings for the notion of a science of ethics.

Simplifying, it is possible to distinguish three conceptions of science: weak, strong, and strongest. In its weakest sense, science is simply

[14] Gould 1999. [15] Strauss 1953.

systematic knowledge. When different pieces of information are organized in some way they constitute a science. In this weak sense, a cookbook can be described as a science of cooking.

In a second, stronger sense, science depends on some epistemological method to guide knowledge production, thus (as it were) organizing knowledge from the inside out. In one form this strong sense is constituted by methodological naturalism. The sciences of physics, chemistry, and biology all adopt methodological naturalism as a guide to knowledge production. This methodology commonly involves observation of the natural world, the construction of hypotheses about causal linkages, experimentation, iterative formation and improvement of laws and theories, and related activities.

The strongest form of science is ontological naturalism. Going beyond a methodological commitment to naturalism, ontological naturalism affirms the existence of only those phenomena and processes appealed to in naturalistic observation, hypothesis construction, experimentation, and theory formation. Ontological naturalism rejects the reality of nonnatural phenomena. The difficulty with ontological naturalism is that since it is impossible to prove a negative, the rejection of any nonnatural reality has to be something more like a commitment or a faith. Most scientists who practice methodological naturalism would not want to commit to ontological naturalism. Indeed, the commitment to ontological naturalism is sometimes described as scientism, an ideology that there is nothing that escapes the comprehension of science.

Ethics can also be distinguished into three types: descriptive ethics, normative ethics, and metaethics. By way of quick review: descriptive ethics gathers information and organizes it into empirical knowledge related to morality, such as how people think about norms, use norms in judgments and actions, or how the norms themselves evolve. Normative ethics attempts to argue for and against moral norms. Such classical moral theories as those of virtue ethics, utilitarianism, and deontology exemplify normative ethics. Finally, metaethics analyzes the scope and character of moral concepts and reasons, considering the extent to which terms such as good and bad refer to empirical phenomena. To some degree it asks the very question under review here, whether and to what extent there can be a science of ethics.

In the weak sense of science as systematic knowledge, there is no reason to deny a science of descriptive ethics. Insofar as descriptive ethics proceeds in some systematic manner it can be readily classified as scientific. Additionally, insofar as normative ethics makes and systematically analyzes arguments for and against various accepted or possible moral norms, it could be classified as science in the weak sense. Finally, as systematic conceptual and linguistic analysis of moral discourse, metaethics clearly satisfies the criteria for being a science in the weak sense. The real questions arise with regard to whether ethics in any of its three senses can be pursued as science in the strong or strongest senses.

Taking the case of science in the strong and strongest senses in relation to descriptive ethics, reasonable arguments can be made in their favor. Indeed, the science of ethics that applies methodological naturalism to descriptive ethics would seem to be the most common form of descriptive ethics. Examples include the history of morals, the psychology of moral development, and the sociology of morals. Any systematic study of morality that denied there was anything more to morality than human beliefs could also be counted as a science of ethics in the strongest sense of science as an ontological naturalism. For this position, "murder is wrong" is only a statement of belief and not a statement of *fact*. Insofar as metaethics focuses on the analysis of concepts and the language of morals, it can easily be compatible with both methodological and ontological naturalism.

From the perspective of this analysis, it should be clear that the most serious form of the question about whether there can be a science of ethics concerns normative ethics in relation to science as committed to methodological or ontological naturalism. The point can be summarized in Table 7.3.

In relation to this table, the question is whether evolutionary ethics, decision science, or developmental psychology can count as an ethics of science in the sense of methodological or ontological naturalism. Leaving aside the strongest case of ontological naturalism – since this is a claim which, as immune to proof, is commonly manifest as the ideology of scientism – the key question is whether there is some form of methodological naturalism that can escape the naturalistic fallacy and yield moral norms. Are there some naturalistic facts from which one can derive moral values? Stated more baldly: Can science tell us what to do? Can it discover knowledge not just about who we are and what we do in fact do but also about who we ought to be and what we ought to do?

Table 7.3 *Possibilities for a science of ethics*

	Forms of ethics		
Forms of science	Descriptive	Normative	Metaethics
Science as systematic body of knowledge	Systematic descriptions of what people claim or practice as moral behavior, e.g., history, psychology, and sociology of morals.	Systematic arguments for moral norms	Systematic analysis of moral concepts, language, and arguments, remaining neutral with regard to (but noting the character and implications of) methodological and ontological commitments.
Science as methodological naturalism		—	
Science as ontological naturalism	Systematic descriptions plus a denial that there is anything more.	—	

Note: —, unclear whether or how this would be possible without committing the naturalistic fallacy.

Why attempt a strong science of normative ethics?

Given the fact that there are weak forms of scientific ethics along with strong forms of descriptive ethics and metaethics, and in light of the difficult challenge faced by any attempt to construct a strong science of normative ethics, why try? There are at least three reasons.

First, there remain numerous disagreements among and within traditional ethical theories. Perhaps a science of ethics could overcome or resolve some or all of these disagreements and produce a stronger consensus within the field of ethics. To theorists such as E.O. Wilson, science offers the only real possibility for synthesizing knowledge not just in ethics but across all the sciences.[16]

Second, many more people accede to the arguments of science than to various types of ethical theory. Maybe a science of ethics could appeal to more people than, say, virtue theory, deontology, or even consequentialism. Indeed, in a modern, globalizing world the two common coins of the realm tend to be money and science. Since no one thinks ethics should be able to be bought, perhaps science offers the best possibility for reaching global agreement about moral values.

Third, and closely related to the other two, in a globalizing world science has a kind of intellectual influence that exceeds almost everything else. Karl Marx thought to make socialist politics scientific. Mary Baker Eddy wanted to restate Christianity in terms of science. When political and spiritual leaders see science as lending new prestige to their practices, why not attempt to make ethics into a science as well?

At the same time, there are reasons to be cautious. Appeals to science to justify ethical norms are not always benign. Darwinian evolution has been used repeatedly to justify various eugenics movements. This seems bad. But note how this judgment still presupposes some standard outside of Darwinian science by which to assess its conclusions. If we are to truly accept a science of ethics, then we may have to endorse conclusions that seemed morally wrong according to traditional ethical theories and common moral intuitions. Consider further the case of eugenics as a test for whether we can and should derive values and social policies from science.

[16] See E. Wilson 2000.

In *The Descent of Man*, Darwin observes how "the weak members of civilized societies propagate their kind," thus undermining processes of natural selection, as a result of their practices of caring for the sick, even suggesting the long-term deleterious influence of vaccination against smallpox. Only in the case of humans, he wrote, is anyone "so ignorant as to allow [the] worst animals to breed." At the same time, Darwin argues that it is not possible to use reason to check the sympathy which facilitates caring for the poor "without deterioration in the noblest part of our nature."[17] Darwin's contemporary, Spencer, did not so qualify his own appeal to evolutionary theory to criticize English Poor Laws:

> [T]here is an habitual neglect of the fact that the quality of a society is lowered morally and intellectually, by the artificial preservation of those who are least able to take care of themselves. ... [T]he effect is to produce, generation after generation, a greater unworthiness.[18]

Darwin's younger cousin, Francis Galton, went further still and argued for a program of eugenics for the planned improvement of the human race through the enforced sterilization of those deemed less fit to breed, a program that in fact became widely supported even by churches in the US.[19] Even more atrociously, Adolf Hitler and the National Socialists used the theory of evolution to justify a particularly heinous form of racial extermination.

To be fair, ethical theories have also been abused. Virtue theory, consequentialism, and deontology have all had exponents who used these theories to justify slavery. The point is simply that despite its prestige, there are also reasons to be cautious about the potential for moral abuse with appeals to science in ethics. Attempts to bring reason to bear in assessing human behavior must never be short-circuited by appeals to any kind of theory, whether scientific or ethical. Moral reasoning will always remain a complex dialogue between theory and experience, rational argument and emotional intuition (and science is showing these two functions of the mind aren't so separated), cultural tradition and abstract principle.

It must also be recognized that despite the greater reliability of scientific over nonscientific knowledge, science is not always so well established as

[17] Darwin [1871] 1981, pt. I, chap. 5, paras. 16 and 17.

[18] Spencer [1873] 1961, p. 313. [19] See Rosen 2004.

it may appear. The knowledge produced by methodological naturalism is only provisionally accepted and remains open to falsification. Under conditions of strong economic incentives to produce results, scientists often mine data for any statistically significant finding in a limited data set. One study of biomedical research goes so far as to argue that "most published research findings are false."[20] The evident prestige of science must not be allowed to obscure its limitations.

Methodological naturalism informing ethics: neuroscience

Although it is thus crucial to be cautious about any straightforward attempt to base normative ethics wholly in methodological naturalism, naturalistic scientific knowledge may nevertheless suggest boundaries on the possibility space of moral discourse. Philosopher Owen Flanagan, for instance, argues that any moral theory must meet what he terms "the principle of minimal psychological realism": "Make sure when constructing a moral theory or projecting a moral ideal that the character, decision processing, and behavior prescribed are possible … for creatures like us."[21] In this respect, methodological naturalism can be relevant to normative moral theory even if it fails to yield a normative ethics. This may even be true with regard to the ethics of science.

Philosopher and cognitive scientist William Casebeer, who defends a more robust position in the tradition of Dewey, has explored how science may circumscribe or argue for ethical theories even if it does not directly constitute such a theory.[22] He begins by outlining the differences among utilitarianism, deontology, and virtue theory, and the forms of moral cognition that each requires. Utilitarianism requires the ability to recognize and compute utility functions. Deontology requires abilities to "reason purely" and to be motivated by duty alone. Virtue ethics depends on persons being able to think about relations between character states and human flourishing. Somewhat oversimplified, utilitarianism emphasizes the prefrontal, limbic, and sensory portions of the brain; deontology, the frontal brain; and virtue ethics, a coordinated whole brain. After reviewing a collection of neuroscientific studies on brain functioning, Casebeer

[20] Ioannidis 2005. [21] Flanagan 1991, p. 32. [22] Casebeer 2003a.

concludes that "some version of pragmatic Aristotelian virtue theory is most compatible with the neurobiological sciences."[23]

Since the 1990s a variety of approaches to a naturalistic science of ethics has been pursued under a number of related rubrics: scientific ethics, empirical ethics, experimental ethics, and more. The social psychologist Jonathan Haidt, for instance, has done interviews with people thinking about ethical issues that call into question some of what philosophers have otherwise assumed are common ethical intuitions. He has also sought to build a bridge between a broad range of psychological and neuroscientific studies of human happiness. Other philosophers such as Kwame Anthony Appiah, while welcoming this new engagement of ethics with science, have also struck a cautionary note about the ability of experimental philosophy to resolve very many long-standing issues. The tensions between virtue ethics and consequentialism, for instance, may be perennial features of philosophy itself more than problems that will yield to empirical resolution.

Summary

This chapter surveyed work in evolutionary science, decision science, developmental psychology, and neuroscience in order to address the question: What can science tell us about ethics? There is widespread controversy on this score. Some maintain that science and ethics are two strictly separate domains: one tells us about facts, the other tells us about values. Others maintain a weak linkage between the two: science can provide a systematic description of people's moral beliefs and behaviors and a systematic analysis of moral concepts. Science can also explain the origins of morality and proscribe boundary conditions for any viable ethical theory, even if science does not constitute the substance of the theory. Still others argue for a stronger connection: science can ground normative ethics, because one can derive moral values from naturalistic facts. Any such project, however, is vulnerable to charges that it commits the naturalistic fallacy of illogically deriving "ought" conclusions from "is" premises. The idea of deriving moral norms from scientific claims is appealing because it promises to dissolve age-old disagreements in moral theory

[23] Casebeer 2003b, p. 845.

and command universal assent. Yet it is also a risky endeavor, because science has been marshaled in the name of causes, such as eugenics, that violate traditional ethical norms and common moral intuitions. But perhaps any truly scientific ethics would force us to abandon outdated and invalid beliefs.

Extending reflection: space colonization

It is likely that at some point in the future humans will attempt to establish a colony on Mars. Whether this should be called the "settling" or "peopling" rather than "colonizing" of Mars has been hotly debated. In any case, it will be a scientific and engineering project of historic proportions. However, the human beings who will attempt to do this will also be members of one or more states, societies, and cultures. Beyond the science and engineering work of planning and pursuing the development of a space settlement, the people involved will have to deal with such things as the language(s) to be spoken, economic and financial structures, laws and their enforcement – and morality. Since the project itself is so strongly scientific, it is also quite likely that appeals will be made to science to provide ethical guidance on such questions. What role can science play in decision-making regarding these more than scientific issues?

To some extent this question has been addressed in works of science fiction. Yet while space colonies are an established element in sci-fi stories, they often emphasize technical development and violence at the expense of ethical analysis and reflection. Kim Stanley Robinson's Mars Trilogy – *Red Mars*, *Green Mars*, and *Blue Mars* – is a case in point.[24] Characters in *Red Mars*, for instance, debate the ethics of terraforming the planet by introducing geological, chemical, and biological processes that would alter atmosphere and temperature to make it more Earthlike. One group argues that humans have no right to transform whole planets and that efforts should be made to preserve Mars in its prehuman state. Another maintains that the simple establishment of a colony means that terraforming has already begun and should continue. The opposition is resolved, however, through violence and revolution instead of ethical analysis and consensus-building.

[24] Robinson 1992, 1993, 1996.

The implication is that power and history will play out on other planets in much the same manner as on Earth.

Other discussions tend to emphasize the weakness or inadequacy of science. This is basically the argument of astrobiologist David Grinspoon, in commenting on a 1998 Mars Society panel on the "Ethics of Terraforming":

> But the future peopling of Mars is much more than a scientific endeavor. ... Any group that seeks to garner support for human journeys to Mars must reassure people that this goal is broadly humanistic and environmentally conscientious. ... I hope [discussants] succeed in burying the "pioneering the West" analogy before it does any more damage to the cause. While we're at it, let's retire the word "colonization," which carries a permanent stain, and talk instead about the "cultivation" or "animation" or "peopling" of Mars. I know that some of you Mars hounds will dismiss the above as a bunch of PC [political correctness] nonsense. Fine, but it's your movement that is not yet taking the world by storm.[25]

Questions for research and discussion

1. Returning to the issue of sexual harassment, could someone who rejects using science to rationalize such behavior, legitimately challenge science itself as a form of harassment?
2. To what extent can the naturalistic fallacy be overcome? Is it possible that science in the strong sense (methodological naturalism) both creates and depends on some version of the fact/value dichotomy that supports the naturalistic fallacy?
3. How might scientific studies of ethics be useful in promoting or reinforcing institutional norms in the practice of science, especially the practice of scientific research?
4. How might science actually contribute to reaching consensus on some of the key nonscientific questions related to space colonization? For instance, would the fact that English is the lingua franca for modern science have implications for a choice of language in a space colony? Could scientific arguments be made to support one language over another?

[25] Grinspoon 2004, n.p.

Further reading about the cases

Billings, Linda (2006) "How Shall We Live in Space? Culture, Law and Ethics in Spacefaring Society," *Space Policy*, vol. 22, no. 4, pp. 249–255.

Livingston, David M. (2000) "Lunar Ethics and Space Commercialization," Lunar Development Conference, Space Frontier Foundation, July.

Quirk, Joe (2006) *It's Not You It's Biology: The Real Reason Men and Women Are Different*. London: Running Press.

8 Transition

From ethics to politics and policy

Following the introduction to ethical theory (Chapter 2) and an analysis of how science as a social institution involves commitments to certain behavioral norms (Chapter 3), Chapters 4 through 6 surveyed attempts to cultivate these norms. Although some behavioral norms, such as those concerning the treatment of human subjects, reflect concerns from a larger, nonscientific society, even these were cast – as is typical – in distinctly science–science-relationship terms. Chapters 4, 5, and 6 thus surveyed leading issues related to ethics in the practice of science itself, more than in the maintenance of science–society relationships. Chapter 7 provided another take on science-science discourse, the efforts of scientists themselves to explain ethics. Are such considerations enough? Might something more be required? Consider the following scenario.

Setting the stage: developing a course

Two professors at a prominent research university – one a faculty member in science, the other in philosophy – happened to have read some equivalent of Chapters 4, 5, and 6. A number of such publications exist. One widely used example is the third edition of *On Being a Scientist: A Guide to Responsible Conduct in Research.*[1] Both faculty are intrigued and decide to collaborate to offer a course on science and ethics. The scientist thinks that ethics training would enhance the science curriculum, on top of which some GSP (good scientific practice) or RCR (responsible conduct of research) education is increasingly being required by funding agencies. The philosopher would like to step down from the ivory tower of abstract

[1] National Academy of Sciences, National Academy of Engineering, and Institute of Medicine 2009.

ideas and arguments and bring philosophy to bear in human affairs. What better way, in a society imbued with science, than to offer a course on ethics and science?

The two professors sit down to draft a syllabus. The scientist proposes to review the ethics codes of the relevant professional scientific associations, the legal obligations that scientists work under, and some prominent cases of fraud and misconduct that led to the destruction of scientific careers. The philosopher suggests introducing students to some basic ethical theory: to read Immanuel Kant's *Fundamental Principles of the Metaphysics of Morals* and John Stuart Mill's *Utilitarianism*, and to examine the strengths and weaknesses of deontology versus consequentialism.

The scientist responds by asking how such abstract theory would really benefit science students. Will this study of theory make the students more likely to be conscientious scientists? The philosopher counters by questioning whether simply learning about codes and cases will contribute any insight into ethical reasoning and how it is best pursued. How will students know the reasons for codes and be able to assess particular cases with morally sound argumentation? Is there not a danger that codes and cases will just function as boundary conditions that students learn to work within or around?

As they discuss their differing perspectives the two colleagues become aware of alternatives in the type of students to whom the course might be addressed. Will the students be mostly science students, philosophy students, nonscience and nonphilosophy students – or some mix of these options? Is this fundamentally going to be a science class or an ethics class? Thinking about this question raises further issues about how best to structure their course: with what assortment of readings, lectures, discussions, laboratory-like hands-on case studies, role playing, or more?

Then one day the scientist and the philosopher are reviewing their different perspectives over lunch in a local restaurant when they happen to be joined by a political scientist. After listening quietly for a few minutes, he asks, "How can you teach a class on science and ethics and leave out politics and policy?" For Aristotle, ethics is preparatory to politics, identifying the human ideal that political order should strive to cultivate. Today politicians concerned about the proper use of public funds to support scientific research have put pressure on the scientific community to pay more attention to issues of scientific fraud and misconduct.

And in the policy area, science is increasingly influential in the determination of regulatory standards as well as the ways governments fund and administer research agencies and projects. Surely a course on ethics and science should include some reference to the broader politics and policy contexts.

The questions that arise as the scientist, the philosopher, and their political science colleague begin to construct a syllabus are thus fourfold:

- What is the goal of this class?
- To whom is it addressed?
- What are the most effective ways to reach the goal with some particular set of participants?
- Is ethics itself enough?

The goals of teaching and learning

Parallel to the rise of the modern secular university there has been a debate about the *raison d'être* of higher education. At the primary-school level, learning to read and write and how to use numbers is simply an extension of learning to walk and talk. These are all skills that people need in order to function in a literate and numerate (as opposed to an oral–aural) culture.

The learning that takes place in secondary school is a continuation of primary-school learning. It enhances literacy and numeracy while imparting more of the information and knowledge that is woven into the fabric of culture, e.g., the history, politics, and science needed to function as a producer, consumer, and minimally informed citizen in an advanced technoscientific democracy.

At the tertiary or higher education level, however, a divide opens up. In the educational systems of many European countries some kind of divide actually occurs earlier between students assessed to have the intelligence and motivation sufficient to attend university and those who do not, and the two are tracked accordingly. In the US, with its more individualist ethos, tracking is more self-determined by personal success and failure than socially structured. Yet in both systems, at the university level itself, a divide ultimately emerges that has been well described by the British philosopher and historian Michael Oakeshott.

In an essay on the character of university education, Oakeshott begins by suggesting a distinction between training and learning. What happens at primary and secondary levels is more training than learning properly so-called. "Learning is the comprehensive activity in which we come to know ourselves and the world around us."[2] Education expands from meeting needs to addressing aspirations, from teaching practical skills to cultivating self-realization – not in an individualist sense, but as "historic, circumstantial personalities." According to Oakeshott, "there is no other way for [human beings] to make the most of [themselves] than by learning to recognize [themselves] in the mirror of [a historical] inheritance of human achievement."[3] At the university, teaching involves holding "up the mirror of human achievement before a pupil ... in such a manner that it reflects not merely what has caught the fancy of a current generation, but so that it reflects something which approximates more closely to the whole of that inheritance."[4]

Oakeshott goes on to contrast professional education, which takes place at the tertiary level – education into professions such as law, medicine, business, science, and engineering – with learning that raises students to a way of life that is, as it were, transprofessional. There is, he argues, "an important difference between learning which is concerned with the degree of understanding necessary to practice [a profession], and learning which is expressly focused upon an enterprise of understanding and explaining."[5] The goal of teaching from this perspective "is not imparting information; it is holding up the mirror of a civilization in such a manner that what is to be seen in it is [humans] thinking, [humans] engaged in the supremely intellectual activity of understanding the world and themselves."[6] Oakeshott admits, however, that "in a civilization which has sold itself to the plausible ethics of productivity and in doing so has given itself a narrow path upon which to tread, and in societies which have begun to think of themselves, more and more, in the exclusive terms of 'an economy,' it is only to be expected that universities should be pressed into the common pattern, and be made servants of the social purpose."[7]

Oakeshott's argument here is continuous with reflections on higher education that range from what John Henry Newman worked out during

[2] Oakeshott 2004, p. 374. [3] Oakeshott 2004, p. 376. [4] Oakeshott 2004, p. 378.
[5] Oakeshott 2004, p. 383. [6] Oakeshott 2004, p. 384. [7] Oakeshott 2004, p. 389.

the 1850s in *The Idea of a University* to Robert Paul Wolff's 1990s social-critical assessment in *The Ideal of the University*. Newman, for instance, defends the intrinsic goodness of knowledge and liberal education in the following words:

> Knowledge is capable of being its own end. Such is the constitution of the human mind, that any kind of knowledge, if it be really such, is its own reward.[8]

At the same time, the kind of general knowledge about what it means to be human that is present especially in ethics is also of benefit to the professions. The liberally educated person "can do what illiterate cannot; and the [person] who has learned to think and to reason and to compare and to discriminate and to analyze" will never be just a chemist or geologist but "will be placed in that state of intellect in which [it is possible to] take up any one of the sciences … with an ease, a grace, a versatility, and a success, to which another is a stranger."[9]

Wolff, by contrast, questions whether professional training of any kind – from law and medicine to science and engineering – is appropriate in the university. Wolff's basic position is that university education requires intellectual inquiry and critique while professional training, including (presumably) education to be a professional scientist, entails something more like indoctrination.

Science and ethics or ethics and science?

In choosing the goal for a course on ethics and science, then, there are two basic options. One would be an effort effectively to impart information about how best to practice science in a particular social context. This would fundamentally be a science class. Another would attempt to hold up the mirror of human achievement in ethics as a way to invite students to assess and reassess both science and who they are and want to be. This would fundamentally be an ethics or philosophy class.

Of course, the two need not be mutually exclusive. The differences in approach are nonetheless real. One has a tendency to emphasize a reflective examination of the history of ethics and the human condition, the

[8] Newman [1852] 1996, pt. 1, dis. 5, §2. [9] Newman [1852] 1996, pt. 1, dis. 7, §6.

other to focus more on indoctrination with regard to expected standards of behavior in various disciplinary, professional, or institutional contexts. One is more concerned with knowledge and understanding as goods in themselves, the other with their pragmatic utility for preserving or advancing a socially valued practice.

Those who teach ethics and science courses have made efforts to bridge the divide between the goals advocated by philosophers and the institutional needs of the scientific community. One influential construction was a report on *The Teaching of Ethics in Higher Education* that emerged from a research study by the Hastings Center. This report was more broadly focused on teaching ethics across the professions, but precisely for that reason can be read as applying to the ethics and science context. Beginning with a recognition of ethical dilemmas both internal to many scientific disciplines or professions and external to them in the form of relationships to society, the report set forth five goals for university-level ethics education:

(1) stimulating the moral imagination,
(2) recognizing ethical issues,
(3) developing analytic skills,
(4) eliciting a sense of moral obligation and personal responsibility, and
(5) tolerating as well as resisting disagreement and ambiguity.

Two qualifiers that deserve emphasis are, first, a further argument that ethics courses "ought not explicitly to seek behavioral change in students." Instead, ethics ought simply "to assist students in the formation of their personal values and moral ideals, to introduce them to the broad range of moral problems facing their society and the world, to provide them contact with important ethical theories and moral traditions, and to give them the opportunity to wrestle with problems of applied ethics, whether personal or professional."[10] Second,

> Courses in ethics should respect the pluralistic principles of our society, acknowledging the variety of moral perspectives that mark different religious and other groups. Indoctrination, whether political, theological, ideological, or philosophical, is wholly out of place. … Although students should be assisted in developing moral ideals and fashioning a coherent

[10] Hastings Center 1980, p. 81.

> way of approaching ethical theory and moral dilemmas, the task of the teacher is not to promote a special set of values, but only to promote those sensitivities and analytical skills necessary to help students reach their own moral judgments.[11]

This latter point may be at odds with itself. In the name of rejecting indoctrination, is not a commitment being advanced to indoctrinate ethical pluralism? Would it not be better simply to affirm and argue for ethical pluralism as a basic good?

For interdisciplinary ethics

Turning to the question of audience, there are multiple arguments for crafting the class for an interdisciplinary audience. Consider at least three: an argument from origins, from pedagogy, and from the inherently interdisciplinary character of ethics itself.

First, since the very idea of the class has multidisciplinary origins, the class itself would seem most appropriately constituted by a multi- or interdisciplinary group of students. In the imaginary stage-setting scenario, the course developers are a scientist and a philosopher. But even if this were not the case it is reasonable to suppose that some degree of interdisciplinary interest animates the project.

Interdisciplinarity originates in the recognition of limits to disciplinarity.[12] Disciplinarity itself developed in order to focus attention and effort, but as disciplinary formation proceeds over time its own narrowness can also inhibit applicability; many human concerns and problems are simply not adequately addressed by any single discipline. Interdisciplinarity then emerges in many forms in order to meet this challenge. An interdisciplinary class in science and ethics is simply a specific manifestation to address issues of ethics that are not naturally thematized in the practice of science as such – or to address issues of science that are not naturally at the forefront of ethics as such.

Second, a class composed of both science and philosophy students will enable students to learn from each other. Teachers are well complemented by students who contribute to each other's learning. Science students or

[11] Hastings Center 1980, p. 81.

[12] See, e.g., Frodeman 2010.

philosophy students alone would lack an ability to cross-fertilize each other's minds to the same extent.

Third, ethics itself is inherently interdisciplinary, much more so than any branch of science. Ethics emerged from philosophy as a kind of ur-disciplinary formation. Ethics took on the task of bridging differentiations in their broadest forms. Over the course of history ethics "has functioned as mediation and synthesis of: (1) human and cosmic reality, (2) individual and social orders, (3) reason and revelation, (4) science and human affairs, and (5) as a pathway to insight."[13] This means that any course that includes ethics introduces some level of interdisciplinarity.

Effective education

What is the most effective way or ways to conduct an interdisciplinary class in ethics and science? This is a widely debated topic. Indeed, some methods may also be judged more ethical but less effective than others, which raises further issues.

Before considering actual pedagogical methods it may be useful to note a divide in discussions of the topic. In the professional philosophical community, interest in the question of ethics education effectiveness has been vanishingly small. Despite some natural concern about this in the fields of applied, practical, or professional ethics, concern has tended to focus more on arguments regarding the ethics of teaching ethics than on research into the effectiveness of various methods. Even with regard to this issue, however, there exists no generally recognized code of ethics for those professional philosophers who teach ethics. With regard to methods, it has generally just been assumed that case studies are good vehicles for teaching especially nonphilosophy students. Yet there has been little empirical assessment of what works and what does not, in part because it is not even clear what "working" means. Reliance has rested more on first-person testimony and anecdote than systematic evidence. It is even revealing that in a world of multiple specialized journals, a journal dedicated to *Teaching Ethics* was not created until 2001.

Efforts to respond to the question of effectiveness are more commonly found among science educators and their collaborators than among

[13] Balsamo and Mitcham 2010, pp. 261–262.

philosophers alone. For instance, a report from a US National Academy of Engineering workshop on "Ethics Education and Scientific and Engineering Research" referencing the five goals from *The Teaching of Ethics in Higher Education* begins with a distinction between approaches that are decision oriented and those aiming to provide a basis for ethical conduct in science over the course of an entire scientific career. The former will naturally tend to stress professional codes and case studies, the latter to place some emphasis on theories and personal exemplars. However, even among scientists the actual assessment of differential effectiveness is minimal. Workshop participants tended to agree "that assessments of ethics instruction and mentoring were at an early stage of development" and that it is difficult to tell "if the right things are being measured or whether students can call on what they've learned afterwards, when needed."[14]

Thus, although scientists have perhaps been more explicitly concerned with issues of effectiveness, the result has been mostly to identify problems with assessment rather than actually doing so and thereby providing some guidance for best practice. One issue conspicuous by its absence in even these limited discussions, however, concerns effectiveness for nonscientists. What should be the goals of teaching and learning for nonscientists, especially philosophy students?

Ethics: from doing things right to doing the right things

Imagine, then, the following possibility: an interdisciplinary course on ethics and science directed toward a cohort of science and philosophy students being effectively taught via a variety of pedagogical methods. Assume as well that the course includes some discussion of ethical theory and professional codes of conduct. Is this enough?

From what may be called an internalist perspective - that is, internal to the practice of science - this may well be enough. What more does a scientist need to know than the behavioral norms for the practice of science and the alternative theoretical grounding for such norms? What more need a scientist do than produce "good science" (peer reviewed, not fabricated, falsified, or plagiarized)? The internalist focus so conceived is

[14] Hollander 2009, p. 31.

on how scientists, when doing science, should behave toward each other in the "republic of science." The internalist perspective concerns ethical questions that scientists themselves must ponder and attempt to implement if they are to do things right and be good scientists and how philosophy might help clarify and inform such methods and conduct.

Even from an internalist perspective, however, it is reasonable to argue the inadequacy of such a limited scope for the class. Scientists and their practices exist within a larger social order. They are funded by universities, public agencies, or corporations because of ideas about the public utility of science that are dominant in the nonscientific world. For scientists not to be aware of these and able to take them into account in their engagements with those outside the scientific community will constitute an ethical weakness if not outright failure. To focus an ethics and science course on the internalist ethics of how scientists relate to each other and ignore the ways scientists are also called on to relate to nonscientists would be to unnecessarily limit ethics. It would be as if ethics in general were to focus only on relations among friends without attending to the fact that human beings have many more nonfriends than friends – and that even friendship is modulated by the social institutions in which friends live. Relations among friends in a virtuous democracy are surely quite different than relations among friends in a vicious authoritarian state.

At the conclusion of the *Nicomachean Ethics* (X, 9, 1179a31–35), Aristotle asks simply, "If these issues and the virtues as well as friendship and pleasure have been considered, may we assume our investigation has reached its end?" His response is no, that to be complete, ethics must turn to politics and what kinds of laws or social structures are implicated by inquiries into the good.

From an externalist perspective it is even more obvious that a course on ethics and science requires something more than ethics alone in the strict sense. The fact that teaching and learning about ethics and science has now become a requirement often imposed by governments reinforces the case. Many courses take a minimalist approach – that is, focus simply on good practices in the conduct of scientific research. The present argument, however, is for a more robust approach that includes not just some theory and practice but history, politics, culture, economics, and other critical examinations of the relations between science and society.

More than codes, more than ethical theory, ethics and science must include reflection on how the good for science and the good of society are best related. The ethics–science relationship is driven by an internal logic to move from reflection on the right way to do science to what is the right thing for science to do.

This can only be addressed in a dialogue between science and society. Society needs to understand what science is, its interests, and how it works. But scientists likewise need to appreciate what society is, especially the spectrum of goods and interests in society that science may be used to address and that structure the context in which science operates. Additionally, both scientists and citizens are called by ethics to assess the legitimacy of these diverse goods and interests. Some goods may be less important than others and oftentimes goods conflict. Furthermore, an interest or need is not self-justifying and may in fact be frivolous, false, or corrosive when viewed in light of the whole.

Extending reflection: Einstein on ethics and science

Physicist Albert Einstein is often considered the greatest scientist since Isaac Newton. Like Newton, who was known in his own time as a natural philosopher, Einstein could also be described as a philosopher-scientist. For *Time* magazine, Einstein was even more; in its last issue of 1999 *Time* named Einstein "Person of the Century," edging out US president Franklin Delano Roosevelt, Indian independence leader Mohandas Gandhi, and UK prime minister Winston Churchill.

Among the reasons for its choice, *Time* included reference not only to Einstein's formulation of the theory of relativity and the fact that the twentieth century had become the most scientific and technological period in human history, but also his humanistic ethics. During World War I, even though a German citizen, Einstein was a pacifist and after the war supported proposals for multinational military disarmament. He further rejected the violence of Communism and worked with the League of Nations until determining that it had become ineffective, at which point he criticized it. In a presentation to science students at the California Institute of Technology in 1931 he said,

> It is not enough that you should understand about applied science in order that your work may increase man's blessings. Concern for the man

> himself and his fate must always form the chief interest of all technical endeavors. ... Never forget this in the midst of your diagrams and equations.[15]

In response to the rise of Nazi anti-Semitism Einstein became an advocate for Jewish immigration to Palestine but also expressed strong concern about the rights of Arabs in any potential Jewish state.

He was not, however, wholly lacking in political realism. Having himself immigrated to the US, in 1939 he signed a letter to President Roosevelt calling attention to the danger of an atomic bomb and thereby stimulated development of this weapon of mass destruction in the face of its potential acquisition by Hitler. Yet after World War II and the use of the bomb on Japan, Einstein became an outspoken advocate for nuclear nonproliferation and disarmament. In 1946, in an article published in the *New York Times* he argued that with regard to nuclear weapons "everything has changed, save our modes of thinking"[16] and that "the bomb [is] a problem not to physics but of ethics."[17] A few days before his death, with British philosopher Bertrand Russell he issued a manifesto calling on scientists of the world to "assemble in conference to appraise the perils that have arisen as a result of the development of weapons of mass destruction" – a manifesto that led to establishment two years later of the Pugwash Conferences on Science and World Affairs, which have worked ever since to limit military scientific research, development, and deployment. (The name "Pugwash" is drawn from the fishing village in Nova Scotia, Canada, where the first conference took place.)

As *Time* magazine concluded in its cover story, justifying its selection of Einstein as "Person of the Century",

> Coming as they did at the height of the cold war, the haloed professor's pronouncements seemed well meaning if naive; *Life* magazine listed Einstein as one of [the US's 50 prominent "dupes and fellow travelers." [But according to historian of science David Cassidy,] "He had a straight moral sense that others could not always see, even other moral people." Harvard physicist and historian Gerald Holton adds, "If Einstein's ideas are really naive, the world is really in pretty bad shape." Rather, it seems to him that Einstein's humane and democratic instincts are "an ideal political model

[15] *New York Times* 1931, p. 6. [16] Einstein 1988, p. 376.

[17] Quoted in Loring 1955, citing Einstein 1946.

for the 21st century," embodying the very best of [the twentieth] century as well as our highest hopes for the next. What more could we ask of a man to personify the past 100 years?[18]

Questions for research and discussion

1. What kinds of ethical issues might have been prominent in Einstein's scientific work, as that of a theoretical more than a laboratory or experimental scientist? Was he naive or idealistic? Is there a place for ethical idealism in science (or in ethics)?
2. Bertrand Russell, Einstein's collaborator on the Pugwash manifesto, could be argued to be almost as important to philosophy, at least English-language philosophy, as Einstein was to science. What were Russell's views on the relation between ethics and science?
3. Recalling the stage-setting case of a scientist and a philosopher working to develop an interdisciplinary course on ethics and science, how might the example of Einstein influence course structure?
4. As complementary or alternative to the views and practices of Einstein, some other leading physicists whose personal perspectives on ethics and science might be considered are Niels Bohr, Patrick Blackett, J. Robert Oppenheimer, Hans Bethe, Joseph Rotblat, Edward Teller, Andrei Sakharov, and Freeman Dyson.

Further reading about the cases

Bok, Derek (2004) *Universities in the Marketplace: The Commercialization of Higher Education*. Princeton University Press.

Elliot, Deni (2006) *Ethics in the First Person: A Guide to Teaching and Learning Practical Ethics*. Lanham, MD: Rowman & Littlefield.

Oakeshott, Michael (2010) *The Voice of Liberal Learning*. Indianapolis, IN: Liberty Fund.

Rowe, David, and Robert Schulman, eds. (2007) *Einstein on Politics: His Private Thoughts and Public Stands on Nationalism, Zionism, War, Peace, and the Bomb*. Princeton University Press.

Schweber, Silvan (2000) *In the Shadow of the Bomb: Oppenheimer, Bethe, and the Moral Responsibility of the Scientist*. Princeton University Press.

[18] Golden 1999, n.p.

9 Science and politics I

Policy for science

Chapter 8 made the case that a book on ethics and science should include considerations of science–society relationships. Thinking must extend beyond doing things right to doing the right things. Thus the remaining chapters explore the social contexts of scientific research. Chapters 9 and 10 form a natural pair: the former covers the making of policies to guide the conduct of science, the latter deals with the use of science to guide policymaking. Notice how in the political context concern for "good science" and "certified knowledge" tends now to be discussed in terms of "sound science" (science that is good for society) and "responsible knowledge." The final two chapters broaden the perspective beyond politics to consider the place of science in ideational culture (the world of ideas and beliefs) and material culture (technologies and their human significance).

Setting the stage: government funding of embryonic stem cell research

Early in his administration, US President George W. Bush gave a nationally televised address about government funding of research on human embryonic stem cells (ESCs). He announced a policy that would restrict federal funding of research involving ESCs. This policy for science can be used as a case study in the political governance of science, which includes state regulation and promotion of scientific research.

ESCs are undifferentiated cells derived by technological means from embryos. The first reported isolation of ESCs occurred in 1998. Because of their origins, research involving ESCs have the capacity for prolonged self-renewal and the potential to become many specialized cell types. These properties created interest in ESCs for two reasons. First, they could provide scientific insights into cellular and developmental processes. Second, they held out the promise of medical treatments for diabetes, spinal cord injuries, Parkinson's disease, and other degenerative disorders.

For years, ESCs had been a source of public contention. Indeed, the ethics of research on human embryos had sparked debate since the 1970s advent of *in vitro* fertilization, which yields more embryos than are used for reproduction. Should such "spare" embryos be used for research if they are going to be discarded anyway? In the public debate, few disapproved of the goals of scientific understanding and medical cures, but many objected to the means of destroying human embryos in order to obtain ESCs. The debate hinged on the moral status of human embryos. Are embryos just clumps of cells, potential persons, or something in between? Many people are torn by ethical tensions between such values as respect for nascent human life, the relief of suffering, and freedom of scientific inquiry. President Bush wrestled with this dilemma in his speech: "As the genius of science extends the horizons of what we can do, we increasingly confront complex questions about what we should do."[1]

Since 1996, the United States had prohibited national government funding of human embryo research. State support could greatly accelerate research, but it would promote practices that many tax-paying citizens judge immoral. Bush sought counsel from scientists and noted that, worldwide, researchers had developed roughly sixty stem cell lines as of the time of his speech. This figure later became a source of contention, with some claiming it to be an exaggeration. But Bush decided to limit government support for ESC research to those cell lines already in existence as of August 9, 2001, because "the life-and-death decision has already been made." He hoped this policy would promote the science without encouraging the further destruction of embryos – and, in fact, it did appear to spur alternative lines of research and the search for stem cells in various forms of adult tissue as well as the possibility of deriving stem cells from embryo development without directly harming embryos.[2] But to what extent and how should ethical concerns be applied through political means to influence the direction of scientific research?

[1] "President George W. Bush's Address on Stem Cell Research," *Inside Politics*, CNN TV website, http://edition.cnn.com/2001/ALLPOLITICS/08/09/bush.transcript/index.html.

[2] See President's Council on Bioethics 2005.

Bush vetoed subsequent legislation that would have supported the use of government funds for research on "surplus" human embryos created in fertility clinics. Part of the motivation behind the opposed legislation was concern that US biomedical research was falling behind other countries. Indeed, Singapore had announced a doubling of its research budget, with an emphasis on stem cell science. Much of this work was carried out in a giant research center known as "Biopolis," funded in part by Singapore's Stem Cell Consortium. Some prominent ESC scientists relocated from the US to Singapore to take advantage of the favorable research climate.

In 2009, newly elected US President Barack Obama signed an executive order that expanded the use of federal funds for ESC research. He cited global competitive advantage in his remarks: "When government fails to make these investments, opportunities are missed. Promising avenues go unexplored. Some of our best scientists leave for other countries that will sponsor their work. And those countries may surge ahead of ours in the advances that transform our lives." President Obama noted that he was siding with the "majority of Americans" and that the Bush administration had forced a "false choice between sound science and moral values." "In this case," he remarked, "I believe the two are not inconsistent."[3] This policy was central to Obama's promise, made in his inaugural address, to "restore science to its rightful place."[4] What is the rightful place of science?

Science in context

The ESC case shows that there is no bright line between science and its many social contexts. ESCs are derived using equipment and machines and researchers intend to employ them through therapeutic technologies, and so they are intertwined with the development of artifacts and systems and markets of production and consumption. ESCs also pose profound moral questions beyond the issues of how to conduct good science,

[3] See Obama's "Remarks of President Barack Obama – As Prepared for Delivery," Office of the Press Secretary, White House website, www.whitehouse.gov/the_press_office/Remarks-of-the-President-As-Prepared-for-Delivery-Signing-of-Stem-Cell-Executive-Order-and-Scientific-Integrity-Presidential-Memorandum.

[4] "President Barack Obama's Inaugural Address," *The Whitehouse Blog*, www.whitehouse.gov/blog/inaugural-address.

and so they are intertwined with religious, moral, and political debate. These are questions about the limits of science and its appropriate place in the natural world and the constellation of human endeavors. Looking at this case, it is hard to say where "science" ends and "society" begins. Since science is so deeply implicated with its social contexts, it stands to reason that the ethical dimensions of science extend beyond laboratory doors. Indeed, whereas previous chapters focused primarily on the question of how to conduct good science, the ESC case and the following chapters pose broader questions about which science to pursue.

Such questions are economic, moral, and political in nature. For example, it takes money to do science, which poses questions such as: How much money should be invested in which kinds of science? Who should pay for what kind of research? Who should benefit from the results? These are not scientific questions, although scientists may think they have a privileged vantage point for responding. So, who should make these decisions on the basis of what criteria? Like any economic activity, science must face the fact of finite resources. Investments in scientific research projects come at the cost of alternative uses of those funds, either within science or outside it. Investments in science are also uncertain, as governments and corporations make many decisions about research not knowing whether or to what extent they will yield benefits. Some opponents to ESC research, for example, claimed prospects for medical benefits were overstated.

Science not only confronts finite resources and incomplete knowledge. In multicultural democracies it also exists in contexts of ethical pluralism. In a globalized world, no single state can determine the research trajectory of science. Some would push forward with a particular line of research while others call for restraint. Some claimed Bush's embryonic stem cell policy was arbitrary, while others defended it. Still others argued it did not go far enough to protect embryos, while many scientists claimed it was a severe blow to research. The policy did not apply to ESC research funded by the private sector, which raised further controversies. Can it be morally legitimate for the private sector to conduct research that would be illegal if funded by public resources? How much power can and should governments exercise over research conducted in the private sector? Should foreign relations be affected when other states adopt contrasting or competing policies for science?

Science and politics are thus intertwined because of needs for knowledge and money and competing ethical claims. On one hand, many nevertheless argue that the freedom of scientific inquiry must be protected, which requires scientific independence or "keeping politics out of science." The ability of scientists to freely pursue the truth is sometimes claimed to distinguish democracy from authoritarian government. Freedom of science is treated like freedom of the press, a source of information that can help guide the state and thus should not be constrained or manipulated by the state, even when the truths discovered by science are inconvenient or untimely.

On the other hand, others argue that science often raises issues that are not themselves scientific in nature, and there are many instances in which science deserves to be restrained by ethical principles. Scientific experimentation on human subjects, for example, is limited by principles of free and informed consent. Even the press is limited by national security concerns and moral values that reject acquiring information under false pretenses or knowingly presenting false information as if it were factual. Those who argue that research must be assessed within the context of other goods (rather than elevated as an overriding moral imperative) argue that politics is a necessary and healthy part of science.

These conflicting responses mean that science must be simultaneously separated from and placed within its political context. We must strike a balance somewhere between "value-free science" and science as just "politics by other means." This is a major challenge for science policy. Policy, as distinct from politics, constitutes a settled guideline for action that occupies a conceptual space in between general principle and statutory law. Policies are more specific than ethical principles but not as subject to enforcement as law. Policies are often based on both scientific knowledge and political debate. Science policy can refer to either "science for policy," which denotes the use of scientific knowledge as an aid to decision-making (Chapter 10), or "policy for science," which denotes guidelines for influencing and managing the shape, scale, and speed of scientific research agendas (the present chapter). Bush's stem cell decision exemplifies both instances of science policy. First, scientific information about the nature of ESCs, their potential uses, and the number of existing stem cell lines all influenced a science for policy. Second, Bush's decision was a policy for science, because it established a guideline for action when it comes to federal funding of ESC research.

The key point in both cases is that the way science is used and the magnitude and type of scientific research that is performed - research that holds increasingly important implications for society - are the result of choices. These choices raise some basic ethical questions.

The next two sections explore the general theme of science and the social order. The following three sections look at policies for science from the different perspectives of budgets (input driven), demands (outcome driven), and commercialization (market driven). The concluding two sections explore issues of responsibility raised by broadening the ethics of science beyond the production of good, peer-reviewed knowledge: What additional responsibilities do scientists have and what responsibilities can be delegated to other parties?

The social contract for science: the linear model

Writing during World War II, the sociologist Robert K. Merton argued that the goal of science is a distinctive form of knowledge production. To achieve its goal, science depends on the four institutional norms discussed in Chapter 3. This normative structure is susceptible to attack from other social institutions. Religious traditions may decry scientific skepticism for undermining their convictions. Capitalist economies and military establishments may stunt the communal pursuit of knowledge by imposing restrictions on intellectual property or mandating secrecy. Most importantly for Merton, rabid nationalism and authoritarian regimes violate universalism and disinterestedness by substituting their own criteria for what counts as knowledge in place of the impersonal criteria employed by scientific peers. In Nazi Germany, for example, a claim to knowledge would be accepted because it was espoused by someone who is *echt deutsch* or a "true German," whereas another claim would be rejected because it was espoused by a Jew or did not comport with the ruling political ideology. When politicians define the criteria for knowledge, it is no longer science; it is politics.

Watching this corruption of science unfold in Nazi Germany, Merton argued that politicians and the public must respect the boundaries of science, allowing it to perform as a self-policing community of free thought in the pursuit of knowledge. The lesson of the German experience during World War II, Merton argued, is simple: if a society values the knowledge science can produce, then it must protect the autonomy of science and shield it from external social influences.

This is also the lesson that Vannevar Bush derived from American science during World War II. A research engineer, Bush directed the US Office of Scientific Research and Development to advance such scientific technologies as the submarine, radar, and atomic weapons. Because Bush convinced President Franklin Roosevelt that war success hinged on superior military science and technology, the war years witnessed a monumental increase in national support of R&D. As the war neared its end, Bush argued for the peacetime extension of public investments in science.

His proposal for a postwar policy for science was titled *Science: The Endless Frontier*, and it equated scientific progress with social progress.[5] What is good for science (as defined by scientists) is good for society. This means that good science as defined by a self-policing community of peers will result in social improvements as defined by such external criteria as health, economic prosperity, and national security. Scientific inquiry, not motivated by needs or specifically directed toward any social goal, would serve as a major source of public benefit. The paradox is that research performed without any thought of social benefit is nonetheless justified by resulting benefits. Bush navigated this paradox by replacing the term "pure" with "basic" research, suggesting that undirected inquiry is foundational to social progress. In this way, the widely held ideal of pure science – that science for science's sake is superior to the application of discoveries made by others – was justified by its ultimate social utility. Michael Polanyi would later use Adam Smith's "invisible hand" for the same purpose. Just as in economics, the free pursuit of self-interest increases material production for public benefit, so in science freedom to do research increases knowledge production for beneficial application.

The resulting "social contract" for science holds that scientists should be held accountable only to their peers, not to any external standards imposed by politics or other social institutions. Scientists are responsible for producing good science. Society is responsible for putting the science to good use. This is why scientists have emphasized the intrinsic norms of science in their ethics training while downplaying the social dimensions of science: young researchers must learn how to produce good science

[5] Bush 1945.

(i.e., that is not the result of falsification, fabrication, or other misconduct), but they do not need to consider how that science relates to society. That relationship is presumed to be straightforward or linear: more (good) science brings more social intelligence and progress. Indeed, for this reason this social contract for science has often been called the "linear model."

Questioning the social contract: governing science

The linear model social contract offers a rationale for investing in science while protecting its autonomy: as long as science is free to produce certified knowledge, then society will benefit. But as Daniel Sarewitz points out, the societal consequences of science are not inherent in the natural laws sought by researchers. Those consequences occur at the interface of the laboratory and society – where knowledge and innovation interact with the cultural, economic, and political institutions of society. So, the rationale for more good science is founded on a particular view of the science–society relationship: "that the transition from the controlled, idealized, context-independent world of the laboratory to the intricate, context-saturated world of society will create social benefit."[6]

But this view of the science–society relation is open to several objections. For example, science can and does contribute not just to intended benefits but to unintended problems as well. Consider how the R&D of plastics is implicated in both enhanced medical care and environmental pollution. Scientists can produce plenty of knowledge certified as good by peers, but that knowledge may be trivial (e.g., treatments for balding), dangerous (e.g., weaponized infectious agents), or controversial (e.g., ESCs). This suggests a distinction between good or certified knowledge (peer reviewed and free from misconduct) on one hand and sound, responsible, or reliable knowledge on the other. In short, it may be that more good science is not linearly or automatically good for society.

The linear model would have us erect a strong barrier between science and politics. The reasons for such a barrier are clear: it prevents the substitution of political claims for scientific claims and keeps out fraud, false claims, and junk science that cannot stand the test of peer review. But the solution of walling off an internal community of peer accountability

[6] Sarewitz 1996, p. 10.

creates a new problem. Now scientists are motivated to produce knowledge that is valid and important in the eyes of their peers; they are seldom motivated to consider the relevance or implications of their work for society at large. Indeed, according to Bush's social contract, scientists do not have responsibility for considering these implications, even as they continue to grow in importance through the discovery of powerful new knowledge that transforms society.

Scientific autonomy may work if science is little more than the activity of a small and marginal group of thinkers. But Merton and Bush were writing at a pivotal moment in the emergence of what the nuclear physicist Alvin Weinberg termed "Big Science." Scientific progress increasingly relies on big budgets, big machines, and big laboratories, and has big impacts on society. It thus necessarily raises issues that call for political support, direction, and control. Contemporary science cannot be understood apart from the social, political, technological, and economic contexts that allow it to work. Monetary and political support as well as economic returns and consumption would seem to have become institutional imperatives added to Merton's list of requirements for scientific success. Science is inextricably a part of politics and society.

The view that *somehow* more science translates into a better world points to an accountability gap: the system of internal scientific accountability includes no mechanisms to guide that translation or measures to indicate its success. Since science is presumed to be valuable, the ethics of science and responsibilities of scientists are limited to questions of how to conduct good science. But the accountability gap adds another dimension to the ethics of science and perhaps to the responsibility of scientists. Scientists need to consider not just how to conduct good science but also why: What is the value of the research? Which knowledge should be pursued? Which scientific pursuits should be banned or regulated? How can we ensure the transformations brought about by science are for the good – and who defines the "good"?

In short, since science cannot be divorced from society, the challenge is to expand the notion of "good" or "certified" knowledge from what peers accept to some broader notion of social accountability – yet a notion that still respects the essential need of science for independence in assessing truth claims. In laying the groundwork for the predominant social contract for science (the linear model), Merton, Bush, and Polanyi did not specify which research is most likely to lead to benefits nor how research can be planned, justified, or assessed in terms of benefits. They left this to the marketplace. So, the adequacy of the linear model crucially depends on the links between knowledge production, free markets, and social well-being. The linear model assumes that science is the basis of practical benefits. But those benefits should not be used as the standard for evaluating science or as mechanisms to explicitly manage research, because that would steer science away from its goal of pursuing more certified knowledge. Increasingly, society is challenging this contract. It is demanding not just good science or certified knowledge, but science that is good for society (sound) and responsible knowledge.

Policies for science budgets

Although the linear model for investing in science described above (i.e., what is good for science is good for society) has been long criticized, it is still a dominant force in political rhetoric. If more science means a better society, then the emphasis will be on securing and increasing monetary inputs into the R&D system. As Daniel Greenberg wryly noted, "More money for more science is the commanding passion of the politics of science."[7]

Science policy should not and cannot be reduced to budgets. Nonetheless, science budgets remain important foci of analysis. They provide a synoptic view of who is funding what kind of research at what levels. And they stimulate ethical questions about the distribution of investments in research and the resulting benefits. The main ethical theme highlighted by science budget policy is the just allocation of limited resources. Although the linear model suggests we never need to worry about doing too much research, policymakers face the reality of trade-offs. Which science is most important to fund? Given the fact that investments in science come at the expense of other activities, how should research be weighed against other goods?

This section adopts the definitions for R&D of the AAAS (American Association for the Advancement of Science). Research is a "systematic study directed toward more complete scientific knowledge or understanding

[7] Greenberg 2001, p. 3.

of the subject studied." It can be either "basic" or "applied" depending on whether or not the knowledge is being sought with a specific need in mind. "Development" is then defined as the "systematic use of the knowledge gained from research for the production of materials, devices, systems, or methods."[8]

Industrialized nations tend to invest similar amounts of money into R&D. However, the types of investments and the structures of R&D enterprises and innovation systems differ significantly, posing ethical questions. This section canvasses the normative dimensions of five topics pertinent to policies for science budgets.

The first topic is the ratios of public to private funding of scientific research. In the early twenty-first century, these ratios varied from 1:5 in Japan to 1:2 in the US to 2:3 in France. Due to its profit-driven nature, the private sector tends to focus on development rather than research. This has led many, including V. Bush, to argue for the importance of publicly funding basic research, which is pictured as the "wellspring" of innovation. As Bush put it, during World War II, scientists had been living off the "fat" of earlier basic research and were in danger of depleting the stores of new knowledge. Others support publicly funded applied research to provide public goods that are not well expressed in the market. The threats of pandemic flu outbreaks and biological terrorist attacks are cases where the private sector would not act without public inducement. Such low-probability, one-time events do not sustain a continuous market demand. Many contend that the state is obligated to prepare for such events by developing drugs and vaccines. Others are concerned about a corrosive effect of corporations on academic freedom of inquiry. The "academic–industrial complex" raises questions about whether the profit motive might distort the public good or pose conflicts of interests that inhibit the reporting of negative results.

In sum, market dynamics may jeopardize scientific progress, intellectual integrity, the exchange of knowledge, the responsible conduct of research, social justice, and noncommercial or public goods. By contrast, free-market libertarians promote the elimination of much public funding

[8] "Definitions of Key Terms," AAAS website, www.aaas.org/spp/rd/define.htm. For data and statistics related to R&D, consult the RAND Corporation website, www.rand.org/, the AAAS Directorate for Science and Policy Programs website, www.aaas.org/spp/, and the NSF Division of Science Resource Statistics website, www.nsf.gov/statistics/.

of science, by citing government corruption and inefficiencies. From this standpoint, the market – including charitable organizations funded by wealthy philanthropists – is a better vehicle for directing funds to promising research even in basic areas.

A second topic is the distribution of public funds by sector. The US government spends roughly half of its R&D budget on defense, and its military R&D intensity (proportion of defense spending to nondefense spending) is more than two and a half times that of the UK or France, which are second and third on the list. The US devotes roughly 50 percent of nonmilitary R&D to biomedical science, whereas this number in Japan and Germany is just 4 percent. By contrast, Japan devotes roughly 20 percent of its civilian R&D to energy, whereas the US spends just 3 percent on energy. Such differences ought to prompt reflection on whether some R&D portfolios could be considered ethically superior or more just than others.

Third, similar ethical questions pertain to the organization of national R&D investments. For example, in the US there is no such thing as a national R&D budget. Rather, R&D outlays are distributed across more than twenty national agencies. This buffers science from suffering a major cut that could result if there were a centralized R&D agency. At the same time, the distributed pattern of investments makes it difficult to set strategic priorities. Indeed, scientists often express their own concerns about imbalances in funding different branches of science. The biomedical research community, for instance, has even been known to argue for greater funding for other sciences on the ground that too much money for medicine comes at the expense of other fields such as chemistry and computer science on which biomedicine increasingly depends. As one former director of the US National Institutes of Health once argued in an op-ed article in the *Washington Post*, a major diagnostic tool such as magnetic resonance imaging is the interdisciplinary "producer of atomic, nuclear and high-energy physics, quantum chemistry, computer science, cryogenics, solid state physics, and applied medicine."[9]

Fourth, it is important to consider the procedures behind science budgets. On the macro and meso (mid) levels the national budget process involves deliberations among elected representatives. At these levels, "external" criteria are used to decide which science will be

[9] Varmus 2000, p. A33.

done – its direction and scale. In the political realm, science is far from an autonomous activity. From a policy perspective, funds are spent according to what R&D mix policymakers think will most benefit society and, from the perspective of politics, funds are spent according to the bargaining power of various interest groups and the aspirations of politicians. This culminates in appropriations to various government agencies. Those agencies, in line with their missions, then distribute funds to individual researchers and research institutions. These micro-level allocations are primarily made by peer review, the main "internal" mechanism for determining scientific merit. But micro-level allocations can also be driven by politics. External politics intervenes when legislators make decisions about funding special science projects that benefit their constituents ("earmarking" of science projects is the term used in the US context). This practice is controversial because it bypasses peer review. Those who support it, however, argue that peer review has several biases that favor the already scientifically established. Without some "earmarking," an institution like MIT and the state of Massachusetts would receive a disproportionate share of federal funds in comparison, say, with the state of Arkansas.

Finally, since World War II, the scientific enterprise has been extremely successful in securing more government money. Yet, as Greenberg notes, this political triumph has come at a cost to the ethical integrity of science: scientists have been successful in securing funds in part through far-fetched promises about cures, solutions, or industrial spin-offs, baseless warnings about the threat of foreign scientific supremacy, contrived allegations of public hostility toward science, false assertions that funding for research is declining, and flimsy predictions about imminent shortages of scientific personnel. Scientists tread morally fraught terrain by claiming among themselves that their primary interest is in the conceptual aspects of their subject, but publicly justifying their work by claiming that it always leads to useful results. Such tactics have helped secure scientific autonomy with little external scrutiny and public accountability. But more extensive review and evaluation of science is necessary if it is to better serve societal needs. Indeed, such scrutiny is a growing aspect of the politics of science, as investors in research seek ways to improve returns on investment and ensure that inputs into science bring desired outcomes.

Science outcomes

To focus solely on budgets or monetary inputs in policies for science is to trust that the internal peer-review mechanisms of science will generate the best return on investment. Governments, corporations, philanthropists, and other investors in scientific research, however, naturally have an interest in trying to assure beneficial outcomes from their investment. Thus, they are interested in measuring outcomes and instituting mechanisms for more effectively linking investments to goals.

V. Bush argued that "Statistically it is certain that important and highly useful discoveries will result from some fraction of the work undertaken [by basic scientists]; but the results of any one particular investigation cannot be predicted with accuracy."[10] This justifies an emphasis on budgetary inputs. If any line of research is as likely as any other to bear fruit, then the R&D system should simply maximize the opportunities for scientists to pursue their work along whichever paths they choose. This prioritizes scientific autonomy above social control or steering of research. But political and social contexts do and should strongly influence the course of science by setting research priorities, which determine the paths that scientists will travel according to socially valuable goals. The US government, for example, heavily funds biomedical research, because politicians want economic growth and increased public health and presume that this kind of research will yield those outcomes. The government funds herpetology to a much smaller extent, because its likely outputs (e.g., knowledge about reptiles) are not as highly valued.

Another reason to question scientific autonomy is grounded in a theory of social justice. According to John Rawls, the just distribution of resources in society is best determined not by a fair competition among interest groups but by imagining oneself in what he calls an "original position" behind a "veil of ignorance." In the original position one does not know what kind of person one might be or what place one might occupy in a social order. In the present instance it would be important to imagine oneself as not being a scientist but entering into society as a person of low intelligence or a member of some disadvantaged group. If one did not know in advance whether one was going to become a scientist or a

[10] "The Importance of Basic Research," chap. 3, in Bush 1945, n.p.

nonscientist (and scientists in fact compose only a small fraction of the population), would one then still be in favor of an arrangement in which scientists are supported with tax funds to do what they think best in place of more targeted social investments?

A third reason to question a focus on the autonomous allocation of budgetary inputs is fueled in part by breakdowns in the view that more science equals social progress. Despite enormous public and private investments in science, old problems persist and new ones have arisen. Some infectious diseases have rebounded through resistance to antibiotics and new diseases have emerged. Healthcare costs tend to increase as science and technology advance. Global environmental challenges persist. Terrorist attacks demonstrate the dangers inherent in research systems capable of producing weapons of mass destruction. To take a more specific example, ten years after completion of the $3 billion Human Genome Project, its primary rationale and goal – discovering the genetic roots of common diseases and generating cures – remains elusive. In 2000, US president Bill Clinton said that the research would "revolutionize the diagnosis, prevention and treatment of most, if not all, human diseases." Yet, as one influential science journalist argues, despite the massive monetary inputs, the value in terms of achieving these medical goals and health outcomes has not been realized.[11]

Furthermore, scientific activity has itself grown and outstripped the available research funding. Indeed, bigger research budgets mean the training of more scientists who in turn demand more money to support their research. As competition for funding increases and as funding agencies demand greater levels of demonstrable social value from research, scientists are tempted to make overblown claims about the likely benefits of any given research project.

For all of these reasons, investors in science are increasingly devising metrics for evaluating science policies in terms of outcomes. In applying these metrics, the connection between science budgets and desired social outcomes is often unclear. For example, in 1969, the US Department of Defense commissioned "Project Hindsight," a retrospective survey of the contribution of scientific research to the development of existing weapons systems. According to policy analyst Donald Stokes, this report "undercut any simple belief that scientific discoveries were the immediate source of

[11] See Wade 2010.

continuing improvements in military technology."[12] Other analysts have generalized this insight to question the contribution of research investments to health, well-being, security, and economic growth. Many health indicators are independent of the state of scientific knowledge. In the industrialized world happiness has actually decreased over the past half century.[13] Advanced security systems are often brittle and easily breached at the same time they threaten privacy. And there is little empirical research on the connection between R&D and the economy. Indeed, prima facie arguments can be drawn from the examples of economic development in Japan and the four Asian Tigers (Hong Kong, Singapore, South Korea, and Taiwan) that there may actually be a "followers' advantage" in not funding the most advanced scientific research.

This is not to deny some role for science in achieving social progress. It is simply to point out the limits of any belief that benefits will easily or automatically result from investments in research. There is a need to understand and manage the relationship between scientific research and social goods. Governments have experimented with several outcomes-based performance measures designed to address this problem. Most prevalent are attempts to stimulate and manage the laboratory-to-marketplace relationship in order to maximize economic benefits from research. In the US, this kind of accountability is mandated by the Government Performance and Results Act (1993), which requires research agencies to quantitatively measure progress against established goals.

Indeed, quantitative economic indicators are primarily used to track and manage the contribution of science to society. But these indicators in turn rely on their own assumption. Whereas an emphasis on inputs assumes that more science automatically contributes to a better society, an emphasis on economic outputs assumes that a growing economy fueled by rapid innovation is equivalent to a better society capable of fostering a higher quality of life for its citizens.

R&D, the market, and well-being

As noted earlier, the linear model depends crucially on the market. Scientific research produces certified knowledge that entrepreneurs

[12] Stokes 1997, p. 55. [13] Lane 2000; Easterbrook 2003.

rely on to develop commercially viable innovations. In the marketplace consumers then practice an economic democracy to determine which innovations succeed in being profitable and which fail. To an extent, economists acknowledge capitalist markets as realms of "creative destruction," as reliance on the market necessarily entails acceptance of many mistakes and bad choices, both at the level of entrepreneurial creativity and in consumer choice. But the acceptance of mistakes and failures of intelligence seems to be one of the costs of democracy.

Science and technology thus enter and influence society primarily through the market, which is governed by the quest for profit and consumer choice. Investments in R&D are widely believed to be a major engine of economic growth, spurring job creation, new industries, more consumption, and greater productivity. Governments often invest in R&D with the understanding that doing so will enhance their position in a competitive international economy. Corporations and industries invest in R&D because it leads to the innovation of new goods and services that can generate profits. In their role as catalysts for economic growth, science and technology have contributed to a steady rise in the standard of living in developed nations over the past century. "Standard of living" refers to the purchasing power available to an individual, quantified by measures such as per capita gross national product. It is a way to quantify the affluence or material well-being widely presumed to indicate progress.

But what is the relationship between economic growth and a rising standard of living, on one hand, and societal welfare and quality of life, on the other hand? Does more (quantity) mean better (quality)? A higher standard of living affords greater chances to pursue personal aspirations. These aspirations will include the use and consumption of science-based technologies such as automobiles, microwaves, computers, and the Internet. So, do more of these things mean people are leading better lives? In some sense, the answer would seem to be "yes" as technologies respond to long-standing human desires to, for example, fly or to have more ready access to information. But consider also that no matter how wealthy they were, people in the eighteenth century could not fly in an airplane, those in the 1940s could not use a microwave oven, those in the 1950s could not use a personal computer, and those in the 1970s could not use the Internet. Yet they were not miserable as a result of this.

The capacity to fulfill current aspirations gives "standard of living" its meaning, and since aspirations are tied to one's material environment, the absence of a technology not yet invented is not experienced as a source of deprivation. The fact that a modern urbanite would be miserable living in a cave does not mean a well-fed Paleolithic hunter was miserable too. Hunters had aspirations suited to their times, just as urbanites do.[14]

If life is in any sense better as a result of technoscientific innovation, it is not because of a direct contribution of any particular artifact – say, the mobile phone – to personal happiness. Rather, it is the more general contribution of science to an economic system that satisfies elemental needs and provides opportunities for self-fulfillment. Yet this economic system – free-market capitalism and R&D – poses two ethical challenges. First, it does not always satisfy needs and provide opportunities in an equitable fashion. Second, it generates new problems and an intensification of needs and dependencies.

To illustrate the first point, consider the fact that only 10 percent of global health research is devoted toward 90 percent of the total disease burden. This "90/10 gap" stems from the proprietary nature of the products of R&D. Incentives such as patent laws and intellectual property rights allow innovations to contribute to profit and wealth-creation. They direct the R&D system toward the needs of those who can afford those products and away from the needs of the global poor. The current R&D system is not designed to improve the quality of life in poor regions. For example, US government spending on space and defense constitutes nearly 70 percent of the R&D budget, but this has little connection to the developmental needs of the South. Similarly with the 90/10 gap: a biomedical research agenda aligned with the needs of the industrialized world diverges from the needs of the South for malaria, tuberculosis, and other vaccines. The R&D system is skewed away from these urgent problems to the less compelling needs of those who have already achieved a high standard of living.

Second, consider what happens once a nation becomes "developed" through the market-based application of science and technology. Now its citizens drive automobiles and consume electricity contributing to environmental pollution, they live in sprawling suburbs contributing to

[14] See Sarewitz 1996, chap. 7 for this argument.

a decline in community, and they demand high-tech medical interventions contributing to more expensive healthcare. These "externalities" accompany the development process as millions of individuals seeking personal gain contribute to processes that undermine societal and environmental welfare. Science-based technologies come to comprise the very fabric of society and could not be abandoned without terrible disruption. Imagine the prospects of eliminating cars, airplanes, or computers. But this means that science and technology do not just satisfy needs; they often create new needs and dependencies with their attendant social and environmental challenges. For all of this, there is scant evidence that ever greater levels of consumption contribute to happier lives. Indeed, life in highly developed societies is often stressful, frantic, and disorienting even for the wealthiest.

Scientists' responsibilities for knowledge and its consequences

The scientific community has already accepted a broadening of its definition of "good science" in the context of research involving human participants. Respect for persons, justice, and beneficence are in these situations intrinsic criteria in the definition of good science (see Chapter 5). Yet, violating these principles does not necessarily lead to uncertified knowledge in the same way that falsification or fabrication do. Indeed, one could gain much certified knowledge as judged by one's peers through research that harms human subjects or does not allow their informed consent. Thus, methods for the treatment of human subjects are derived from broader societal values.

To what extent can societal values inform or modify notions of good science and scientific responsibility? As an example, consider the above remarks about the indirect contributions of science to social and environmental problems. To some degree scientists are justified in responding that these problems are far afield from their specific lines of research, which may in fact be more directly connected to other first-order beneficial outcomes. Are scientists somehow supposed to know in advance the second-order consequences of their work and determine whether these are, on balance, good or bad? There surely are some limits to the expansion of scientific responsibility.

In the case of research with human subjects, the expansion is justifiable both because (a) the principles are widely shared and (b) the research participants are directly impacted. Yet these conditions are not often in place. It could be considered irresponsible to research the incorporation of toxic chemicals into paint intended solely for toys. But consider research on toxic chemicals intended for military purposes. Whether this constitutes responsible conduct depends on prior value judgments about war and contextual considerations about the legitimacy of any given use of force. The same point pertains to ESC research – some will consider it responsible research, whereas others disagree. Next, consider basic chemical or physical research where the values implications for society are far in the future and unclear. Can Albert Einstein be held responsible for all the consequences made possible from his basic discoveries about the nature of the universe, such as $E = mc^2$? We cannot label all basic research irresponsible simply because its practical value is not apparent or it has some indeterminable probability of contributing to social problems.

The concept of responsible science can be stretched too far, setting the bar impossibly high for scientists. Individual scientists and scientific institutions cannot reasonably be expected to resolve fundamental values disputes or foresee, let alone control, all of the potential implications of their work. Yet the traditional social contract for science, the linear model, sets the bar too low. It holds that scientists are considered to have no general moral responsibility for considering the potential consequences of their work beyond the realm of science, that is, beyond their role responsibility for advancing certified knowledge. But as the history of research with human subjects shows, it is in the self-interest of scientists to consider the social impacts of research. If they do not shoulder this responsibility, then external regulators will, which in turn diminishes scientific freedom and autonomy.

Philosopher of science Heather Douglas has argued that scientists' role responsibility for advancing knowledge does not exempt them from the general moral responsibility of considering the unintended consequences of such action. This means that scientists are responsible for not acting with recklessness (knowingly creating an unreasonable risk to self or others) or negligence (unknowingly but faultily creating an unreasonable risk). In practice, this would require scientists to weigh potential goods and harms of their research and to uphold the reasonable person standard in terms of foresight. According to this argument, if scientists foresee a scenario in which apparent risks outweigh apparent benefits, but proceed anyway, then they can be held responsible for the consequences. This amounts to a responsibility not to do certain types of research, such as aboveground nuclear tests, which harm public health, welfare, or the environment with no comparable level of benefits.

René von Schomberg and others at the European Commission's Directorate General for Research, Governance and Ethics have similarly developed the concept of responsible research and innovation. The basic idea is to assess proposed research from a broader perspective capable of taking social, ethical, environmental, and cultural dimensions into account. Responsible research and innovation adopts a participatory and deliberative approach to this assessment and is defined as:

> a transparent, interactive process by which societal actors and innovators become mutually responsive to each other with a view to the (ethical) acceptability, sustainability and societal desirability of the innovation process and its marketable products (in order to allow a proper embedding of scientific and technological advances in our society).[15]

Of course, the ongoing challenge in pluralist societies is to determine what is ethically acceptable and what constitutes a "proper embedding" of science in society.

Distributing responsibility

Part of the reason scientists cannot legitimately be expected to shoulder full responsibility for the consequences of their work is that they do not have the expertise. They are trained to conduct science, not to consider its ethical, legal, economic, political, social, and environmental implications. Closing the accountability gap between good science and a good society requires a different kind of knowledge. In the 1970s the interdisciplinary field of STS (science, technology, and society) studies began to seek this knowledge. The field of STS exhibits affinities with socialist efforts from the 1930s to develop a "science of science" as well as early twenty-first

[15] René von Schomberg, "Definition," *What Is Responsible Research and Innovation?*, European Commission website, n.p., http://ec.europa.eu/bepa/european-group-ethics/docs/activities/schomberg.pdf.

century efforts to promote "research on research" for understanding how science influences society and how it can be directed in a manner most consistent with worthy social goals and cultural norms. This science of science is necessarily interdisciplinary, because the challenge is not to further advance a narrowly defined field of science but to comprehend, evaluate, and influence science as it interfaces with other spheres of society.

In this interdisciplinary field numerous new questions arise: Who should be involved? Does the nonscientific public have a participatory role to play in setting policies for science? How does interdisciplinary STS research best interface with the R&D system and the market? Is it through scholarship, practical policy analysis and advice to governments, or public activism? Finally, what are the ends toward which science should be steered?

Considering only the question of means of engagement, nonscientific actors can influence the R&D system "upstream" (prior to the funding of scientific research), "midstream" (during the conduct of research) or "downstream" (during the development and commercialization of research). Upstream engagements include the use by governments of offices of technology assessment and general bioethics commissions to provide advice and facilitate public dialogue about new and emerging sciences and technologies. Oftentimes, these bodies are comprised of an interdisciplinary team of scientists, engineers, philosophers, and stakeholders. The Danish Board of Technology and the Dutch Rathenau Instituut are world leaders in the practice of upstream social and ethical assessment of science and technology. A related practice is "extended peer review," such as citizen panels and consensus conferences, which engage user communities in the review of funding applications. "Community-initiated research" or "community-based research" occurs when scientists take suggestions from local citizens on which research to perform. This practice is commonly carried out through "science shops," which mediate between citizen groups and research institutions.

Another example of upstream engagement of the social dimensions of science can be found at the US NSF (National Science Foundation). In 1997, NSF adopted an additional criterion in the review of proposals for funding.[16] In addition to the intellectual merit of the proposed project

[16] See Holbrook 2005, 2009.

(i.e., its excellence as judged by disciplinary peers according to their own internal standards), NSF now asks reviewers of research proposals to evaluate their "broader impacts" for science and society. This is a case where an "external" ethical and social criterion has become part of the "internal" peer-review process. It is especially interesting because NSF primarily funds basic research, unlike more mission-oriented agencies that are motivated to produce relatively near-term social benefits.

"Midstream" integration of science and society can be seen in the ELSI (ethical, legal, and social implications) projects as part of both the US Human Genome Project and the National Nanotechnology Initiative. The funding agencies administering these projects devoted roughly 4 percent of the project budget to an interdisciplinary science of science designed to understand, evaluate, and manage the societal implications of the biomedical and nanotechnology R&D. The STS scholar Erik Fisher has further advanced this model through his research program "Socio-Technical Integration Research."[17] Other midstream integration includes regulatory bodies such as institutional review boards or, more commonly in Europe, independent ethics committees and ethical review boards, which review research proposals and evaluate, not only their scientific merit, but also their ethical implications (see Chapter 5).

Midstream engagement with the ethics of science is often presented as a solution to the Collingridge dilemma. First described by STS scholar David Collingridge, this dilemma is a double-bind problem.[18] Upstream attempts to integrate science and society face an "information problem" as impacts cannot easily be predicted in the early stages of research. But downstream efforts at integration face a "power problem" as the trajectories of technoscientific developments are already entrenched and thus difficult to change. In short, steering science is difficult in the early stages of research because of uncertainty, but it is difficult later on because the science has become an integral part of society. Solely relying on the upstream model could lead to extreme precaution such that the pursuit of knowledge is unnecessarily constrained. Relying solely on the downstream model, however, would license a determinism in which society would be forced to

[17] "About Stir," Center for Nanotechnology in Society, University of Arizona website, http://cns.asu.edu/stir/.

[18] See Collingridge 1980.

adapt to emerging technological systems but not proactively modulate their development.

In sum, focusing on the magnitude of scientific and economic growth sets aside qualitative questions about which direction we ought to take. In truth, such questions are unavoidable. It is just that neither the linear model of scientific autonomy nor the market model of science for economic growth subjects qualitative questions to explicit consideration. Bush would leave such questions in the hands of scientists, and the market model leaves them up to unreflective consumer preferences and corporate profits. The ELSI projects and similar initiatives can be seen as ways to create a more inclusive and self-conscious dialogue about the kind of world we want to create and the kind of science we will need to get there.

Summary

Following World War II, scientists advanced a social contract model for the funding of an autonomous community of researchers. The contract involved a moral division of labor between scientists and society: scientists produce knowledge and society determines how the knowledge will be used. If the knowledge is misused, then that is the responsibility of politicians or business leaders, but not scientists. Scientists are charged only with producing good science (certified knowledge), which requires upholding norms of objectivity in research. Society gives money and autonomy to science in return for the knowledge and the benefits that will naturally emerge. This formed the core of what has come to be known as the linear model of science policy.

But the moral division of labor between science and society was being proposed at just the moment in history when science became "big" and ever more tightly coupled with society, both because it required more money to operate and because the products of its labors were profoundly altering society. The new reality of Big Science meant that the ethics of science does not stop at laboratory doors and scientists would have to partner with others to consider which direction research should take and whether some directions should be prohibited or severely curtailed. Scientific responsibility now increasingly pertains not just to the question of how best to do science, but to questions of what science is for and which science should be done. According to the post-World War II social contract, the scientific community promised to expand certified knowledge in exchange for an unusual lack of oversight. This contract has now shifted toward collaboration between scientists and other sectors of society in both defining and pursuing responsible science.

Extending reflection: dual use and publishing a deadly blueprint

Is knowledge an unqualified good and is the right to pursue knowledge absolute? These questions were raised by an episode that began in 1951 when Johan Hultin, a doctoral student in microbiology, dug through six feet of tundra and permafrost in Alaska and discovered the well-preserved bodies of four victims of the 1918 Spanish Flu pandemic. Hoping to recover live flu virus, he transported tissue samples to his lab and exposed ferrets to them. The animals did not get sick and Hultin abandoned the project. But in 1995, scientists at the US Armed Forces Institute of Pathology set about the task of resurrecting the flu virus from their collection of dried and fixed tissue from victims of the pandemic. With Hultin's assistance and advanced genetic sequencing techniques, the attempt succeeded this time. In 2005, the complete genetic sequence of the 1918 influenza A (H1N1) virus was published in *Science*.[19]

The decision to publish the flu genome was approved by a US governmental advisory board, which concluded that the scientific benefit of the research outweighed its potential risk of misuse. This knowledge could help scientists identify and combat the next pandemic. But it could also be used to *cause* the next pandemic. This is an example of the dual-use dilemma, which arises when the same research project has the potential to be used for harm as well as for good. This dilemma often occurs. For example, scientists have published an article describing how to render the mousepox virus more virulent and immune to vaccination. They have synthesized the polio virus from scratch in order to warn society that terrorists could do the same. They have built and tested bacteria-laden weapons for "threat assessment" purposes. And in 2011 scientists in the US and the Netherlands created a highly transmissible form of a deadly flu virus, A (H5N1), that does not normally spread from person to person. In the latter

[19] Tumpey et al. 2005.

case, a US government advisory panel requested that the journals *Nature* and *Science* keep certain experimental details out of the published results so that terrorists are not able to replicate the experiment.

Emerging research in synthetic biology raises similar dual-use concerns. The ability to render DNA into digital information that can be manipulated and reassembled as DNA in a novel living organism poses the threat of pathogens that have never before existed in nature.

The dilemma is about trade-offs: knowledge and freedom of inquiry exist within a broader ecology of goods, including security and human health. Sometimes these interact synergistically, but at other times they clash. When values collide, decisions must be made. Several policy options exist regarding the imposition of limits on dual-use research and the censorship of potentially dangerous knowledge. Some options are less intrusive or restrictive, granting the scientific community (e.g., individual scientists, journal editors, and scientific societies) the authority to make decisions. Other options are more restrictive, granting governments overriding decision-making authority.

Questions for research and discussion

1. Should the viral genome have been published? What criteria or standards should have been used in making this decision? Who should make such decisions?
2. Is the concept of an implicit social contract unique for science as a social institution? Are there other implicit social contracts, e.g., for medicine, education, engineering, or business? What is the relation between an implicit social contract and an explicit business or legal contract? What limitations exist, if any (and why), on any type of contract?
3. How might discussions and disagreements about policies for science be compared and contrasted with discussions and disagreements about policies for education, for business, for the military, for healthcare, for families, and more? Are questions about who should formulate, for instance, policies for business (and whether the business community should have the final say) analogous to questions about who should formulate policies for science? To what extent or under what circumstances should a government ensure that any of its

policies for science (or education, business, etc.) be adopted by the private sector?

4. What research projects other than embryonic stem cell research have raised public challenges to the linear model social contract for science?
5. As noted in the opening paragraph and then illustrated throughout the chapter, there are two sets of terms that spar with each other in different contexts: "good science" versus "sound science" and "certified knowledge" versus "responsible knowledge." What is the significance of these rhetorical shifts in different contexts? Is it reasonable to make connections with the distinction in logic between a "valid" and a "sound" argument?

Further reading about the cases

Briggle, Adam (2005) "Double Effect and Dual Use," in Carl Mitcham, ed., *Encyclopedia of Science, Technology, and Ethics*. Detroit, MI: Macmillan Reference USA, vol. 2, pp. 543–546.

Cohen, Cynthia (2007) *Renewing the Stuff of Life: Stem Cells, Ethics, and Public Policy*. Oxford University Press.

Cohen, Eric (2004) "Science, Democracy, and Stem Cells." *Philosophy Today*, vol. 48, no. 5, pp. 23–29.

Miller, Seumas, and Michael Selgelid (2008) *Ethical and Philosophical Considerations of the Dual-Use Dilemma in the Biological Sciences*. London: Springer.

President's Council on Bioethics (2004) *Monitoring Stem Cell Research*. Washington, DC: US Government Printing Office.

10 Science and politics II

Science for policy

The previous chapter explored the ethical dimensions of policies that guide the conduct of science and raised questions about scientists' responsibilities for the broader outcomes of their work. This chapter continues to focus on science in its social context, with emphasis shifted to the role of science and scientists in informing public policy. Considering how scientists ought to contribute to political decision-making and policy formation raises ethical issues about relationships scientists have with the military, courts of law, and the media. This in turn prompts further questions about science and culture, which will be explored in the next chapter.

Setting the stage: climate change and an inconvenient heretic

No policy issue has been more dependent on input from science and more contested than that of global climate change. Global climate change refers to the ways average planetary weather patterns alter over time. For example, evidence of ancient climates shows that in the last 800,000 years the planet has seen a series of oscillations between ice ages and warmer interglacial periods. Because of the long timescales involved, climate change is not subject to direct individual experience; humans experience weather, not climate. Science is needed to identify climate change. The scientific study of climate or climatology depends in turn on interdisciplinary analysis of the atmosphere, including circulation patterns and interactions with ocean and land masses; the global monitoring of weather patterns along with human historical records; measurements of ancient atmospheric compositions from small samples of air trapped for thousands of years in glacial ice cores and dendrochronological reconstructions of changes in plant growth; and more. This scientific dependence has encouraged the assumption that defining and responding to climate change are scientific and technological in nature.

In 1896, the Swedish chemist Svante Arrhenius, who would eventually win the 1903 Nobel Prize in Chemistry, first suggested the possibility of human-induced climate change through the burning of fossil fuels. But it was not until the 1980s that large numbers of scientists became convinced of the dangers of a "greenhouse effect" caused by carbon dioxide and other heat-trapping gases. Increased concern about climate change has led to an unprecedented, worldwide scientific effort to understand its causes and consequences. In 1990, the US Congress created the US Global Change Research Program with a roughly $2 billion annual budget that is spent on satellites, data systems, ecology, oceanography, atmospheric chemistry, and global climate models used to generate predictions about the climate.

At the international level, in 1988 the United Nations and the World Meteorological Association founded the Intergovernmental Panel on Climate Change (IPCC) "to assess scientific, technical and socio-economic information relevant for the understanding of climate change."[1] On a roughly five-year basis, the IPCC issues assessment reports that synthesize enormous amounts of scientific data and distill a "summary for policymakers." These reports inform the United Nations Framework Convention on Climate Change, which seeks a global political response to climate change.[2] In 1997, the Convention launched the "Kyoto Protocol," which set binding limitations on greenhouse gas emissions by signatory states. Citing concerns about costs and uncertainty regarding the magnitude and consequences of climate change, the US refused to adopt the protocol. At the beginning of 2011, altogether 191 countries had signed and ratified the protocol, but China, India, and Brazil also had not committed to lowering their greenhouse gas emissions. At the end of that same year Canada withdrew from the treaty.

Former US vice-president Al Gore's 2006 documentary film *An Inconvenient Truth* argued that scientific research had painted a clear picture for policymakers: swift and bold action is needed to ward off a planetary disaster.

[1] "Working Group II: Impacts, Adaptation, and Vulnerability," Intergovernmental Panel on Climate Change, www.ipcc-wg2.gov/.

[2] See the United Nations Framework Convention on Climate Change website, http://unfccc.int/2860.php.

For this film Gore, together with the IPCC, won the 2007 Nobel Peace Prize. In 2009, an international scientific conference on climate change in Copenhagen gave voice to a growing scientific consensus that "inaction is inexcusable." The science had spoken a clear truth to power; all that was needed was the political willpower to overcome the "inconvenience" of overhauling the world economy in order to ward off a global disaster.

For Freeman Dyson, a world-renowned Princeton physicist and recipient of the 2000 Templeton Prize, the picture is not so clear. Dyson does not deny the existence of anthropogenic global climate change caused by greenhouse gas emissions. Rather, he accuses Gore and many scientists of relying too heavily on global climate models, which he argues do not adequately model the actual world. So many assumptions are built into the models that their predictions are unreliable. To make the bold statements of certainty found in Gore's documentary or many scientific reports, Dyson argues, is dishonest and irresponsible. Climate change has become the primary article of faith in a new "secular religion," which, in its moral urgency, is exaggerating the dangers, zealously sweeping uncertainty aside, and unfairly branding skeptics as ignorant or biased. For Dyson, heretics who question the scientific consensus are crucial for scientific progress. Experts comprising the orthodoxy often manifest a "know it all" hubris when in fact there are gaps in their knowledge.

More important than evidence and factual claims is what Dyson calls a "deeper disagreement about values." On one hand, environmentalists who think "nature knows best" decry any major anthropogenic disruption of nature. On the other, "humanists" contend that protecting the existing biosphere is not as important as helping fellow human beings. Dyson, who self-identifies as a humanist, argues that "humans have a duty to restructure nature for their survival" and suggests that humans can control the amount of carbon dioxide in the atmosphere through the use of a "carbon bank" comprised of genetically engineered fast-growing trees. He also favors coal as an energy source because it is affordable and offers millions of people the chance to increase their standards of living. Similarly, he opposes most policy responses to climate change because they will increase costs, thereby harming the poor. Critics of Dyson note that he has no expertise in climate science and contend that his so-called "humanism" is actually a foolish belief that technoscience can control nature to a degree that constitutes its own hubris.

For Dyson, the orthodoxy has captured left-leaning political support and public attention by communicating a false sense of certainty. This is not only misleading, he argues, but it has the effect of drawing attention and resources away from problems that are more serious and certain, such as poverty, war, and disease. Because scientists wield an authority that is a kind of power, they need to make claims carefully, with adequate justification and sufficient evidence. If they are wrong (convey a false certainty), those who trust their authority will be harmed.

In reply to Dyson's call for more evidence and greater certainty, many leading climate scientists respond that if we wait for sufficient proof it may be too late. Moreover, "certainty" is more a feature of mathematics than of empirical science, where strong consensus and contingent failure to falsify function as the primary warrants for confirmation and reliable knowledge. The demand for certainty has been used more than once by vested interests to avoid taking action on such dangers as cigarette smoking and worker exposure to toxic industrial chemicals. Then again, climatologists are neither politicians nor economists, and taking major action will be costly, with the burdens unevenly distributed. After decades of scientific research, the core policy question remains unanswered: What should be done and who is responsible for doing it? Behind this question and the impotent public response is another: When and how should scientists contribute to public policy formation?

Science and decision-making

Ideas about policy for science developed initially within science among scientists. By contrast, arguments for bringing science into policy and decision-making originated outside science, with politicians and philosophers.

Mathematician and philosopher W.K. Clifford, in an 1877 essay on "The Ethics of Belief," begins with a thought experiment in which a ship owner thinks that his ship may require repairs. Before his ship departs, however, he talks himself out of his doubts by recalling that the ship has sailed safely many times before. He also believes in providence, and so trusts God would not allow his ship to sink. Nevertheless, in mid-ocean the ship sinks; all aboard perish. Clifford argues that the ship owner is morally responsible because he allowed his beliefs to be guided by wishful thinking rather than by evidence. Evidence in this context has distinctly scientific connotations. Clifford further insists that the owner would have been just as culpable if the ship had not sunk, because "it is wrong always, everywhere, and for anyone, to believe anything upon insufficient evidence."[3]

The ship owner is a metaphor for captains of both industry and the "ship of state." Clifford's argument implies that in forming policies, whether industrial or political, people have a moral responsibility to make decisions in the light of empirical evidence about the way things are. Insofar as science offers privileged insight into the unseen dimensions of the way things are, policymakers have a responsibility to seek out scientific knowledge.

Public philosopher Walter Lippmann makes a similar argument from practical necessity. A society that has "grown furiously and to colossal dimensions by the application of technical knowledge [can only] be brought under control" by the use of scientific intelligence. Both industry and politics now depend on knowledge of the environment that cannot be had except through science. Modern industry depends on "physical laws and chemical combinations that no eye [can] see, and only a trained mind [can] conceive"; it is not possible to administer "without scientific aid a world complicated by scientists." Political reality too is so complex as to require social scientific input. Lippmann concludes, "the more enlightened directing minds have called in experts" of all kinds, from statisticians to engineers and scientists.

Remarkably, however, Lippman also argues for a wall to separate scientists from decision-makers. The legitimate "power of the expert depends upon separating himself from those who make the decisions, upon not caring, in his expert self, what decision is made." In Lippmann's example, a Secretary of State who seeks intelligence from social scientists about some foreign country "will not tolerate … the suspicion that they have [their own] 'policy.'"[4] In other words, science for policy is crucial but scientists should not become policymakers. The separation is equally beneficial to scientists in that it keeps politicians and policymakers from trying to create "science" that will justify *ex post facto* their policy decisions.

[3] Clifford 1999, p. 77.

[4] For all quotes, see Lippmann 1922, pp. 376–381.

At the same time, scientists have often felt a moral obligation to bring their expertise to bear on and become involved in the shaping of public policies. For example, many scientists involved with nuclear weapons felt that, having discovered their potential in nature, they had a responsibility to create a R&D project that would make them available to the Allies fighting Nazi totalitarianism. After World War II some of these same scientists felt they should be the authors of nuclear weapons policy, because of their knowledge of the dangers of nuclear weapons – a knowledge greater than that of politicians or the public. Additionally, biologists and medical scientists have for hundreds of years felt obligated to influence healthcare and educational policies.

In like manner, many scientists have claimed knowledge pertinent to core policy questions related to climate change: Is the climate warming? If so, how much, why, and what are the likely consequences? Faced with such questions, governments call on scientists for intelligence and scientists communicate their knowledge. Ideally, it might seem, the reliable voice of science would be translated into wise policy actions as soon as politicians accept the *scientific* truth over mere public opinion.

Yet climatologists regularly fail to see the information they provide translate into what they imagine to be rational policy. One explanation is that in a democracy, politicians and interest groups ignore "inconvenient" truths in favor of more politically palatable beliefs. Two muck-raking science historians have gone further, arguing that a tiny minority of scientists with tight connections to vested industrial and political interests manipulate public opinion by shamelessly denying well-established scientific facts and spreading unwarranted doubt about topics ranging from smoking to climate change.[5] Another explanation favored by scientists is public ignorance. The public simply has an insufficient scientific literacy and is thus easily duped into believing something that is not supported by science. What is needed is a more robust science education for the public.

Such explanations undoubtedly have some merit. But the opening case study suggests something else may also be at play. The ideal of authoritative science producing intelligence that leads directly to sound political action rests on an assumption that deserves further scrutiny: that scientific knowledge means the same thing to scientists and various publics.

[5] Oreskes and Conway 2010.

Consider again the issue of climate change. Billions of dollars have been invested in climate science through the US Global Change Research Program and IPCC while political gridlock and controversy remain. Furthermore, Dyson's argument indicates the lingering existence of scientific controversy about the magnitude of climate change, the likely consequences, and the right policy responses. In the absence of exceptionally strong scientific consensus, there will always be expertise available to support both sides in any conflict. It can be difficult for politicians and the public to determine whose expertise to trust and which experts may be most morally compromised in what ways. The vested interests of scientists themselves in preserving their own authoritative image should not be discounted.

Indeed, in a 2009 "climate-gate" scandal, hackers exposed thousands of private emails among several prominent scientists in the Climate Research Unit at the University of East Anglia, a few of which appeared to reveal efforts to manipulate data in order to buttress the case for anthropogenic climate change. One infamous exchange had scientists discussing a need to "hide the decline" in some temperature records. Climate skeptics used this as an opportunity to show that "expert knowledge" may be just opinion or even deception masquerading as the neutral, authoritative voice of science. Media reports had difficulty interpreting the nuances of internal exchanges among scientists. Subsequent analysis of the communications argued that "hide the decline" referred to attempts by scientists to balance tree-ring data (that showed temperatures decreasing since the 1960s) with measured temperature data (which showed temperature increasing since the 1960s). The "hiding" in question was simply the replacement of less reliable proxy dendrochronology data with more reliable recorded temperature data, an acceptable and even preferred practice in paleoclimatology. Although the emails clearly revealed scientists occasionally being rude and dismissive of some colleagues, institutional investigations of the allegations found no evidence of fraud or scientific misconduct.

The implication that science means different things to scientists and various publics is not intended to discount the value of science for policymaking. Rather, it suggests that the link between science and policy is more complex than simply plugging science into politics and deriving the right answer. What counts as "the science" and the authoritative experts are often contested. This may be in part because morally compromised "merchants of doubt" shamelessly deny and obfuscate well-founded scientific claims. But it is also because nature is sufficiently complex to produce what Daniel Sarewitz calls "an excess of objectivity" – different scientific studies will often legitimately produce different results. This contributes to "postnormal science" where scientific results become ammunition used within political debates rather than objective, universal, and authoritative statements that can transcend and settle debates.[6] If you want to believe that a certain chemical or industrial process is safe (or harmful), then just choose the scientific study that bolsters your foregone conclusion. Whereas Lippmann and Gore argue for the importance of "speaking truth to power," Dyson and Sarewitz raise a confounding question: Who does and who should have the power to claim they represent the truth?

Even when a strong scientific consensus exists, determining the right response is an ethical and political issue rather than a strictly logical consequence of scientific knowledge. To illustrate with an extreme example: Imagine astronomers had determined that headed for the Earth was a large asteroid which would crash into it and certainly destroy all human life. Imagine as well that engineers had determined the asteroid was too large to be deflected or destroyed by existing rocket and explosive technologies, and that there was insufficient time to develop anything approaching the required capabilities. The human response would vary wildly. Some Christians might welcome the forthcoming destruction as the end times and second coming and hold revival services. Some hedonists might respond with pleasure orgies and stoics with quiet resignation. Hindus could see Shiva in the sky and Buddhists a confirmation of kalpa-length, transterrestrial cosmological cycles worthy of intensified meditation. One could even imagine scientists, despite their own forecasts of impending doom, arguing for intensified research to see if their predictions were right; and of engineers, despite their own diagnoses of technological impossibility, prescribing the design and construction of a wide array of devices and structures anyway. Of course, politicians would inveigh against scientific fear mongering and corporations would go out making as much money off the disaster as possible. The only certainty is that responses would differ greatly, depending on and reflecting vast differences in culture, ethics, and worldviews.

[6] See Funtowicz and Ravetz 1993.

The present chapter explores the implications and complexities conveyed dramatically by the example. First, it revisits and requestions the social contract for science. Second, it highlights key issues involved in the uses of science by the military, the courts, and media.

The social contract for science revisited

Chapter 9 discussed the "social contract" for science that emerged in conjunction with World War II. That contract maintained that investments in science will inevitably bring about a healthier, wealthier, and more secure society. Good science was assumed to be of social value, so the policy model should be: invest more money into more science. That chapter then proceeded to reconsider the assumptions and implications of this contract. Similarly, this chapter identifies and critiques a predominant social contract pertaining to science for policy (the use of scientific knowledge in decision-making). The contract examined here can be seen as another version of the linear model, one that states roughly that value-free and autonomous science will deliver knowledge capable of compelling rational political action.

In the sixteenth and seventeenth centuries, Europe was divided by religious and political factions that often clashed violently. Each was certain that it knew the will of God and the proper structure of political authority and communal order. Multiple truths legitimated multiple forms of power. Of course, what was "true" for one faction was heresy or mere opinion for another. Conflicting claims to authority were founded on incommensurable certainties, which left little room for compromise. As a result, warfare often became the default strategy for resolving conflicts, which made life uncertain and social stability fragile. The defining question, then, was how to secure universal consent that could guarantee peaceful social order. Is there a source of truth that all could agree on and that would thereby legitimate a common authority?

In the midst of this conflict-filled situation there emerged the scientific revolution and a new vision of the physical world that gave human beings unprecedented powers. Modern science is a complex phenomenon that sees the knowledge it produces as both truth and power. Galileo Galilei's new physics of falling bodies, for instance, not only corrected Aristotle's views but enabled the design of more effective military artillery. This new science easily became allied with arguments by such philosophers as Niccolò Machiavelli and Thomas Hobbes for a shift in political affairs from the pursuit of spiritual goods to material ones, which could then be achieved through the means offered by technoscience. Science could not, of course, answer the question of what the ideal end of a political order should be. But it did offer a tool for the effective realization of political ends in the context of a "lowering of the standards" to this-worldly rather than other-worldly ideals. As such, science became an indirect support for the rise of a new political consensus expressed through democracy that placed material welfare and security above spiritual welfare and virtue. This new political order then turned to science to provide the means to achieve its mundane ends.

Science became the legitimating knowledge for ways of communal life. It was seen as extra- or nonpolitical because it spoke simply of the world as it is and not of a world as interpreted through values or religious narratives. As political scientist Yaron Ezrahi notes, "the role of knowledge and technique in directing and justifying action has become central to modern Western liberal-democratic notions of authority, accountability, and order."[7] Because it is neutral or objective, science can secure the assent of all of the opposing worldviews that comprise a pluralist society.

For the early moderns, politics increasingly became a human enterprise exposed to the disruption of *fortuna*, or contingent forces. The political order was understood as a human construction designed to secure pleasure and minimize pain. The principle constraint on realizing such goals was not a supernatural will or lack of virtue, but rather nature, particularly our limited capacity for understanding, predicting, and controlling nature, including the nature of individual humans and societies. Early modern theorists argued that science could increase understanding and control and should therefore be established as a guide for political action. Modern democracy thus uses science as a source of instrumental knowledge to enhance effectiveness in achieving goals.

This has inspired various proposals for technocracy, or rule by those experts possessing the knowledge necessary for organizing society for greater and more efficient productivity (see Chapter 12). Technocracy is also sometimes spoken of as an attempt to "scientize politics." Indeed,

[7] Ezrahi 1990, p. 3.

the nineteenth century witnessed the rise of utopian visions of science rationalizing democracy, carrying politics on its wings above scarcity, conflict, and chance. Scientific discourses from physics to physiology were extended from nature to society. They would replace myths, ideology, or authority with knowledge as the basis of social action. One apotheosis of the replacement of politics with technical rationality came in the early twentieth century. The "scientific management" of Frederick Winslow Taylor spread to matters of policy, for example, in the notion that forestry science could provide the "one best way" to manage public forests. Policymaking is simply the identification and application of the most effective means to achieve given ends. Thus, the word "policy" came to connote an instrumentalist process of isolating problems and applying expert tools to solve them.

Paradoxically, the very notion of scientizing politics requires, as Lippmann argued, a measure of separation between science and politics. The intrusion of politics into science is often referred to as the "politicization of science" and can take the form of mischaracterizing, distorting, or censoring scientific knowledge. "Misused" science would be less able to fulfill its instrumental role of helping society meet its goals. Even if the truths that it speaks are inconvenient - as in the case of global climate change - science must be heard for the good of society. Altering or ignoring the facts does not make them disappear; it only delays rational political action. Even worse, the politicization of science undermines its authoritative role in policymaking.

Recall again but modify the case of a scientific prediction of the catastrophic asteroid impact. Imagine that the prediction were of an asteroid encounter that were in fact capable of deflection by rockets and nuclear explosives. Surely in this situation an almost global political will would form to fund any necessary research, then design, construct, and launch the needed rockets and explosives. Dual and back-up systems would be built as well, to ensure world-saving outcomes in case one system failed.

Consider, however, one more modification. What if the astronomers were fundamentalist end-time-believing Christians? Would the prediction have the same unifying and galvanizing effect? What if the prediction were not that the asteroid would wipe out all human life on the planet but only that depending on where it hit it might produce different degrees of catastrophe? What if the nuclear rocket strategy had a high probability of backfiring and perhaps causing more damage than some of the predicted asteroid-caused catastrophes? What if scientists disagreed about the prediction, with a minority claiming the asteroid would not hit the Earth at all? Finally, what might the impact of the prediction be on Mongolian nomads, even if they heard about it? Such a spectrum of possibilities suggests that when science influences policy its ability to do so will depend to a large extent on context – and on how scientists themselves approach the exercise of their influence. The options thus deserve a critical analysis.

Questioning the social contract again: science governing

The social contract vision of science for policy, or governing through (rather than of) science, has been criticized on descriptive, epistemological, and normative grounds. These criticisms of the received model for science informing policy can be briefly stated and then further explored. First, the model does not provide a sufficiently nuanced account of the relationship between science and politics or policy. Second, the contractually produced knowledge from science is not always of a kind useful to governance. Third, the contract model can on occasion actually obscure if not oppose the kind of ethical reflection required in political decision-making, especially in a democracy.

Descriptive inadequacies

With regard to the descriptive lack of nuance: if the contract is right, then faced with a common body of scientific information, different nations would produce the same policy decisions. Clearly this does not always happen. In numerous areas of governance that depend on input from scientific expertise, from drug and food regulation to economic and military affairs, dialogue with the same communities of scientific knowledge often yields divergent policies. For instance, despite drawing on a common science of genetically modifying crops, the EU and the US have adopted different policies regarding the planting, importation, and labeling of genetically modified foods.

One complication is an often-invoked myth (especially among scientists) that the presentation of scientific knowledge is not itself a vector for inserting policy preferences into the public realm. Challenging the myth, political scientist Roger Pielke Jr. describes how science actually influences policy formation by distinguishing four idealized roles for the scientist who engages with politics: pure knowledge exponent, advocate, arbiter, and honest broker.[8] To illustrate the distinctions, he imagines someone such as a politician, policy analyst, or citizen asking for help in finalizing dinner plans. The pure knowledge exponent scientist responds like a detached bystander lost in his own world by describing the physiology of digestion and chemistry of nutrition, which may be interesting but probably not immediately helpful. The issue advocate scientist, by contrast, acts like a salesperson and immediately argues for Joe's Steak House right down the street, but with a peculiarly scientific rhetoric that deploys information about the number of meters distant and the special nutritional qualities of bovine muscle tissue heated sufficiently to unwind the molecular protein bonds in a process known as denaturing.

The arbiter scientist would, Pielke suggests, behave more like a hotel concierge. She would question the inquirer about what he wants from dinner: healthy nutrition, good economic value, quiet and safe ambience, or what? Once informed that he was primarily interested in affordable quiet and safety, she would inform him about the most acoustically well-designed restaurants under good management in the neighborhood within his price range. The arbiter scientist engages with the public and communicates knowledge guided strongly by publicly expressed needs or interests. The honest broker scientist, by contrast, distances herself somewhat from the immediate needs or interests of any inquirer and, without asking for any details about his needs or interests, offers a matrix of information about restaurants in the area covering, for instance, nutritional value, price range, ambience, distance, and more. The effect will often be to stimulate rethinking on the part of an inquirer, maybe a reconsideration of the needs or interests with which he may have been operating even if he did not take the opportunity to express them.

Pielke's spectrum of alternative engagements between science and policy is certainly more adequate than any simply conceived, one-way, univocal science-to-policy model. Although promoting the honest broker role, he is also pluralist in admitting that each ideal type may be appropriate

[8] Pielke 2007; see also Pielke 2006.

in the right context. Whatever it is, it just needs to be adopted with conscious recognition and transparent admission to any interlocutors. The advocate scientist, for instance, should say up front, "Let me tell you the scientific support for adopting course of action X," making it clear that other scientists might well marshal knowledge in support of action Y. What is illegitimate, Pielke argues strongly, is stealth issue advocacy, which occurs when the advocate scientist fails to recognize or to admit advocacy. It is even more illegitimate when advocates consciously hide or deny their advocacy.

Pielke and other researchers such as Sarewitz argue that a better path is to recognize the limits of science and distance it from politics while more robustly connecting it to specific policy alternatives.[9] Research will not settle political and ethical disputes about what kind of world we wish to live in. But scientists can connect their research to specific policies, once citizens or politicians have decided which outcomes to pursue. In this way, scientists provide an array of options that are clearly related to policy goals. Rather than simply report findings from pure research or advocate, either openly or stealthily, a particular course of action, scientists should work to help policymakers and the public understand which courses of action are consistent with our current – always fallible – knowledge about the world.

But there are inadequacies as well in Pielke's account of the science–policy–politics nexus. Although he characterizes his four possible ways for science to inform policy as ideal types, that of the so-called honest broker is impossibly ideal. One of the strongest findings in STS (science, technology, and society) studies is that all knowledge production has what may be termed an engagement coefficient, simply because scientists are embodied, historical, and culturally situated beings. To think otherwise is to imagine science as a neutral "mirror of nature" or a "view from nowhere." Modern natural science is constituted by a unique reduction of the human lifeworld (as argued in Chapter 2) and a particular set of moral norms (see Chapter 3). To propose any scientific input to policy is, at a minimum, effectively to affirm and promote the value of science itself – it is to cast the issue in scientific terms, which lends it a particular, nonneutral valence.

[9] See, e.g., Sarewitz 2004.

The vicious interpretation of such unavoidable commitments is that all science is culturally biased or captive of special interests and no better than any other opinion or worldview, a position that promotes skepticism if not relativism and cynicism about appeals to science. But one need not go this far, and in fact there are strong arguments for a modest realist interpretation that grants "well-ordered science" an appropriately qualified but nevertheless privileged position in the political realm.[10] No matter how high the wall separating science and politics, the relation between the two will involve dialogue. It may not be possible to transcend the arbiter or concierge model.

Epistemological issues

This points toward a second concern regarding the science–policy interface, focused on the character of scientific knowledge. The most general statement of this concern is whether science can produce knowledge directly useful to governance. Clearly on some occasions and to some extent it does, otherwise science would not have become so well ensconced in public affairs. Not only politicians, but citizens of all stripes rely on scientific expertise in making decisions about everything from child-bearing and rearing to diet, exercise, healthcare, and the determination of death. At the same time, scientific knowledge is sometimes thought to be able to deliver more than it can, a mistake arising from what has been described as a mythical quest for certainty.

In a popular view, unfortunately sometimes accepted by scientists themselves, science produces cognitive certainty. Thus when science revises its knowledge base – especially in regard to immediately useful knowledge, as when nutritionists revise assessments of what constitutes a healthy diet or medical researchers alter their recommendations regarding therapies for different illnesses – nonscientists become dismissive. ("Why should we believe scientists who can't make up their minds?") The idea that science should produce certainty is, however, a misunderstanding influenced by Christian theology and the notion of the certainty of faith conflated with logical and mathematical concepts of certainty. In science, knowledge is better described as certified by a consensus among

[10] See Kitcher 2001.

experts even while it remains subject to future falsifiability or other qualification.

In religion and politics, especially as these forms of life have developed in European and related cultures, certainty is understood as the basis for decisive action. Religious faith and national patriotism, both of which suspend doubt, get results. Introducing patriotic certainty ("My country right or wrong") into an encounter between nation states readily, without further debate, turns words into deeds. This univocal implication is too often taken to be the model for how science should inform politics or policy. Together with the difficulty that the public experiences appreciating the character of scientific knowledge, science is regularly misunderstood and expected to provide a level of determination that is unrealistic.

Another version of the epistemological problem was developed by Hobbes who criticized the modern empirical sciences because the knowledge they produced was restricted to an elite and lacked the kind of certainty required to constitute a political order. In order to overcome competing claims to the certainty of faith (and thus to short-circuit the resulting conflicts), Hobbes sought a kind of deductive knowledge from indubitable assumptions that would guarantee universal consent. He thus began with the description of a materially unacceptable state of nature (a "war of every man against every man" producing a life that is "solitary, poor, nasty, brutish, and short") (*Leviathan* I, 13) that humans would, without doubt, seek to escape; from there he deduced the necessity of submission to an absolute sovereign.

As he also observed, the inductive sciences of laboratory work were unable to yield anything close to this level of certainty. The laboratory is a bounded space: although anyone could gawk curiously, only the few are qualified to make authoritative interpretations of the events that unfold there. It is a private or secret space, not a civil or public space, and indeed managing the private/public distinction is essential to the credibility of the experimental sciences. Not everyone is qualified to produce or even assess expert knowledge. As Hobbes noted, experimental science is based on the fallible senses, its inductive methods are prone to all sorts of errors and inaccuracies, and its methods require interpretations and manipulations that could take a variety of forms while nonetheless remaining consistent with observations.

Normative questions

The epistemological problem thus merges with a third issue, in which reliance on scientific expertise shuts down ethical reflection appropriate to the public realm. The problem of scientific knowledge in this sense is a subset of the problem of expertise, which often conflicts with personal autonomy and democratic participation. Experts routinely serve in privileged capacities on government advisory panels, regulatory committees, and more. As Robert Crease and Evan Selinger note, "the authority so conferred on experts seems to collide with the democratic and antielitist urge to accord equality to all opinions; it also risks elitism, ideology, and partisanship sneaking in under the guise of value-neutral expertise."[11] Modern society is increasingly dependent on expertise. Can such dependence be compatible with democracy?[12]

One dimension of this tension concerns how to identify expertise or the kind of expertise that is needed. Pielke's four ideal types are constructed from the point of view of the scientific experts themselves. Another typology may be constructed from the perspective of those seeking scientific expertise, with such nonscientific principals distinguished into those seeking agents, debate coaches, teachers, or proxies. Again imagine someone trying to finalize a dinner decision. Principals seeking scientists to act as agents (sometimes called "hired guns") want someone to scout out and/or help run a gauntlet of ignorance to realize their own goals. They do not want those goals questioned. Expert witnesses in court cases play this kind of role. In like manner, principals seeking scientific debate coaches want help in responding to anyone who might offer intellectual objections to a decision. Scientific assistants to politicians and corporate leaders often function in this manner. ("Tell me what science I can cite if objection X comes up.")

Principals seeking science teachers want to learn the science. Students place themselves under the tutelage of scientists in order not only to become scientists themselves but sometimes to become, for instance, scientific journalists or simply better informed citizens. Finally, at the opposite extreme are principals who want scientist proxies to whom they can delegate decision-making, trusting they share or will respect the

[11] Crease and Selinger 2006, p. 3. [12] See Schattschneider 1960.

principal's basic values and commitments. This readily occurs when medical patients are so overwhelmed with information about an illness that they feel unable to decide between alternative treatments offered by the attending physician. ("Doctor, you decide. You know better than me. I cannot think about it anymore.")

This makes obvious what Pielke's taxonomy does not: principals have needs and interests that can bias their use of science just as much as scientists have needs and interests that can bias their inputs to policy. In any science for policy, both deserve to be acknowledged and should enter the dialogue.

Further fruitful complications to dialogue occur through a distinction between what has been called contributory and interactional expertise. Contributory experts are those who do science and therefore contribute to a scientific discipline. This is the normal connotation of scientific expertise. But another kind of expert emerges when someone interacts in an intense way with a contributory expert. Over a period of time, journalists, historians, or activist citizens may become so well versed in the science that they acquire a second-order expertise or authority.

Finally, the concept of representation in science and in democracy forms another point of fruitful dialogue. Because representation is a complex and imperfect phenomenon in democracy (where both delegate and trustee models vie with direct participation) and in science (where data, laws, and theories can be interpreted in both realist and antirealist terms) the two forms of representation can occasionally complement and correct each other. As Lippmann noted, science can "give representation to persons, ideas, and objects which would never automatically find themselves represented ... by an election."[13] But lest scientific representation become a dictatorship of the invisible, it deserves to be modulated by the visible. From such abstractions, however, it is appropriate to turn to particulars.

Science in the military

The issue of science in the military is fraught for three reasons. First, military defense is an area that politicians from both right and left agree is a fundamental responsibility of the state. Second, scientific knowledge

[13] Lippmann 1922, pp. 379–380.

(in the form of military intelligence) and technological development (weapons systems) have increasingly transformed the character of warfare. Third, in scientifically advanced countries military R&D is typically a large component of the budget; in the US, for instance, just over half of the federal R&D budget flows through the Department of Defense. When military and national intelligence research is included the figure goes even higher. Although the US is by far the largest spender on scientific research in support of national defense policymaking, other countries invest significant resources as well. This poses an ethical challenge to scientists: What justifies the contributions of science to enhance military policy decision-making?

Philosopher Kenneth Kemp, who has taught at the US Air Force Academy, is among the few to have actually contributed to military intelligence and made an explicit argument in defense of integrating science into military affairs. For Kemp scientific research for the military is a civic duty. He begins with two assumptions: (a) war, or at least preparedness for war, is a legitimate means of pursuing just policy objectives; and (b) it is the duty of government to protect society from certain kinds of aggression, including by means of warfare when this is the only effective means. Given these assumptions, there are three reasons to think scientists have a duty to participate in military research. First, scientific expertise can improve a government's ability to wage and deter war. Second, scientists can minimize risks to military personnel by making available intelligence and technological advantages that increase their prospects of survival. Third, smarter weapons and military medical research can minimize the destructiveness of war for combatants and noncombatants alike. Kemp nevertheless admits that scientists have no duty to conduct military research in nations that pursue unjust foreign policies. Presumably, individual scientists must make their own judgments with regard to the just or unjust character of their nation's *casus belli*.

While sensitive and measured, Kemp's argument assumes a typical image of science as neutral and tame. Science is neutral, because it is simply the instrumental means by which the nation achieves its military objectives. It is tame, because it is confined to the context of a particular military conflict. Both views can be challenged.

First, science and technology are not only means to preestablished objectives. They also occasionally alter objectives and create new ones. Prior to the scientific discoveries and inventions leading to the development of the atomic bomb, for example, government leaders could not conceive of the deterrence policy of mutually assured destruction. Technoscience created new policy options and goals. The more recent use of unmanned aerial vehicles ("drones") for surveillance and targeted killings illustrates the same point. Drones make new kinds of missions possible. This changes the strategies and tactics of political leaders, who may formulate policies that would have otherwise not been considered. Science is transformative, not neutral, insofar as it alters the conditions and conceivable objectives of military action.

Second, scientific knowledge and science-based technologies are not tame in the sense that they cannot be confined only to causes that are just. Even if nuclear weapons were created in submission to a just cause, they are not easily contained and used only in the service of justice. Terrorists and nations with unjust foreign policies can acquire and use them. In this way, science is feral, not tame, because it opens possibilities that escalate the stakes of any future conflict. The transformative and feral nature of science calls into question Kemp's defense of military research as a civic duty. It suggests that introducing science into military affairs may burden future generations with more costly and deadly wars. At the very least, it suggests that scientists must take much more into account than any single military objective or cause, because their work will transform future objectives and outlive the current cause.

Science in the courtroom

Courts of law play an essential role in applying and interpreting legislation in order to resolve disputes. They also enable society to adapt to changing conditions, which are often precipitated by scientific discoveries and technological innovation. For example, the judicial system has been instrumental in defining the legal and ethical dimensions of product liability, toxic chemicals, biomedical technologies, electronic eavesdropping, genetic engineering, and more. Courts are sites of adjudication where society works out responses to scientific and technological risks to public health, the environment, privacy, and community. This process might be thought of as primarily one involved with determining policy for science, but this activity depends at the same time on drawing science and scientists into courtrooms to provide expert testimony.

The challenge for the legal system is to digest the technical information and to recognize "good science" or "legitimate expertise." According to the social contract of science for policy, the relationship between science and the courts might initially appear straightforward: legal institutions should seek out the findings of science and incorporate them into their judicial decisions. But as the analysis of alternative science for policy relationships argued, the situation is seldom so simple.

Scientists, as purveyors of the truth, are empowered with the trust of the relatively unsophisticated judges and juries and may be tempted to skew facts or suppress evidence in order to sway the legal process toward a preferred conclusion. This temptation would be especially strong in situations where a conflict of interest exists. For example, if a corporation is being sued for marketing some allegedly harmful product, then an expert scientific witness might be paid quite well for testimony for the defense that questions the certainty of evidence from the plaintiff. This seems to have repeatedly been true in law suits against tobacco companies.[14]

Such personal ethical issues are nevertheless subordinate to larger considerations. As lawyer and STS scholar Sheila Jasanoff argues, scientific claims are contested, contingent on circumstances, intertwined with values and interests, and actually co-constructed within courtroom settings. Courts, like regulatory agencies, conduct most of their scientific inquiries at the frontiers of scientific knowledge where claims are fluid and uncertain. This means that the challenge is more complex than allowing "good" science in while keeping the "bad" science out; part of the process is defining what will count as good, legitimate, or authoritative science. The intertwined nature of science and ethics also means that proposals for creating special "science courts" separate from the normal judicial system threaten to shift moral and legal questions into the hands of experts.

The legal system is not a passive recipient of science, but an active player in defining legitimate knowledge and determining who is entitled to speak authoritatively. For example, attorneys cross-examine expert witnesses and recruit their own scientists to contradict the claims made by

[14] See Proctor 2012.

other scientists. The facts presented in a legal case depend on the skills and intentions of the lawyers eliciting expert presentations. Furthermore, because of a 1993 Supreme Court decision in *Daubert v. Merrell Dow Pharmaceuticals, Inc.*, US federal courts are required to determine prior to its submission that scientific evidence or testimony is reliable and relevant. In the resulting collaborative process, courts create and structure the "credibility market" for certain scientific applications such as DNA typing for identifying criminals or, more recently, neuroimaging or brain scan techniques for detecting lies. This suggests that a successful interaction between science and the legal system involves not simply identifying sound science but co-constructing the legitimacy or social acceptability of scientific expertise.

The courts thus serve as stages on which scientists acting as exponents, advocates, arbiters, and honest brokers can dramatically interact with principals seeking agents, debate coaches, teachers, and proxies. The improvised script deconstructs expert authority by making transparent the values, biases, and assumptions embedded in many expert claims. Exposing these preconceptions is just as important as "getting the facts right." The credibility of science can be challenged on many levels: a specific claim, a particular scientist, the methods used, and the institutions that certify those methods. Courts similarly expose the interpretive flexibility in the meanings scientific facts have for different social actors. The legal theater is an important site of civic education about science, technology, and policy. Although the adversarial features of the courtroom can become indiscriminately deconstructive and unduly acrimonious, the decentralized, small-scale character of judicial proceedings allows for the emergence of multiple perspectives on the ethics of science for policy.

Science in the media

The media – newspapers, magazines, radio, film, television, and the Internet – comprises another important channel through which science informs policy.[15] With the specialization of science and the invention of communities of scientific peers in the modern era, scientific practice withdrew from the public realm and a knowledge gap solidified between

[15] See Nelkin 1995.

experts and nonexperts. The specialization and increasing complexity of science created opportunities and needs for the "popularization" of science. In the mid-nineteenth century, communication of science began to address the general public through the daily press, general interest magazines, fairs, and museum exhibitions. The communication of science to the public consolidated itself into a specific media genre with its own rules and norms. Journalists came to dominate this genre, providing the mediation necessary to make scientific work more suitable and accessible to the public and thereby to influence policy.

The social contract of science for policy again presumes that media communication begins where the real scientific discourse ends. Once scientific knowledge has been certified it can be offered in a simplified form to nonexperts. Because the knowledge is both complex and stabilized prior to being publicized for popular consumption, it will inevitably be distorted and diluted by the translational work of journalists. In contrast to the more pure pursuit of knowledge practiced in science, the media is portrayed as a realm of simplification and sensationalism driven by the pursuit of profit. According to this model the flow of information is also unidirectional, from scientists to the public but not vice versa. It constitutes what has been termed the deficit model for the public understanding of science. The public is deficient in its understanding because it lacks knowledge that it needs and which must be imparted to it by scientists through the media. The hypothesis was that this could create a virtuous circle: once the public became sufficiently appreciative of the value of science it would be motivated to demand greater reliance on science which would in turn advance the value of science.

The 1980s witnessed the first challenges to the deficit model of the public understanding of science. As already noted, scientific knowledge is rarely as settled and certain as the deficit model presumes. In addition, with roots that can be traced back to John Dewey's response to Lippmann, many critics have argued that the "public" is not as passive, monolithic, or ignorant as the model presumes. Indeed, in the case of genetically modified organisms, greater understanding of biotechnology often correlates with more negative opinions about genetically modified organisms. Science journalist Daniel Greenberg has argued more generally that there is no relationship, either positive or negative, between scientific literacy and support for science.

Defining the public as deficient is a way for scientists to reinforce their status as experts and their authority to produce the only legitimate knowledge, which in turn marginalizes other groups and robs them of the power to set agendas and influence public decisions. In an influential study of Cumbrian sheep farmers, Brian Wynne showed that laypeople were capable of extensive reflection on their relationships with scientific experts. He also defended the epistemological status of their own "local knowledge" in relation to the "universal knowledge" of scientists. Several studies have since argued that scientific institutions should adopt a model of public engagement that stresses dialogue over the one-way communication of knowledge. For example, in communicating the risks associated with a nuclear power plant or the outbreak of an infectious disease, it is important for scientists to understand and respect the nature of a public's concerns. This information is vital for clearly communicating knowledge and uncertainties.

Another ethical issue stemming from the relationship between science and the media is hype. Media outlets need to sell stories in a competitive market and scientists are increasingly asked to demonstrate the social relevance of their work. These twin pressures drive coverage of science toward sensationalist claims of "breakthroughs" that are always on the verge of curing diseases or solving crises. Scientists need to emphasize the benefits of their work in order to ensure continued support and funding, which creates incentives to frame the potential of their work in misleading ways, to call press conferences prematurely, or even to manufacture good news or issue irresponsible promises. Media representatives need to sell stories, but this need too often replaces critical and honest appraisals of science with hyperbolic cheerleading. Greenberg portrays the deficit model of public understanding of science as itself an irresponsible hype; it is used to generate more funding for science under the false pretense that greater scientific literacy is necessary for economic or social progress. Others have called on scientists and science journalists to replace hubristic metaphors (e.g., the human genome as the "blueprint" of human nature or the "key" to curing diseases) with a humbler framing that is truer to the complex and uncertain fate of a given line of scientific research.[16]

[16] See Nerlich et al. 2009.

Finally, new media such as science blogs have created expanded coverage of scientific developments – which, of course, has to compete with expanded blog coverage of everything else. As with all forms of new media journalism, old standards for quality assurance (e.g., editorial review, vetting sources for credibility, and institutional fact-checking) are being eroded and new standards (e.g., wiki-style communities of peer review and open source records for fact-checking) are being innovated. Perhaps ironically, as the Internet has opened more channels for the communication of science, scientific literacy has not improved. Individuals can choose the information sources that are tailored to their interests and confirm their values and biases. At its extreme, the new media age may create a world in which all can choose their own reality and their own truths. As more sources of information clamor for attention and allegiance, Balkanization may ensue, and there may no longer be a recognizable scientific community that stands as the legitimate guardian of certified knowledge.

Summary

The idea that science should play a primary role in government decision-making has roots in the formulation of the distinctly modern understanding of the state. In contrast to premodern political theory, which understood the state as constituted to pursue virtue, justice, or religious ideals, modern political theory conceives the state as oriented toward the pursuit of security and progressive achievements in material welfare. Because it provides reliable and allegedly neutral knowledge about the interactions of matter and energy, science enables political decision-making and government action to achieve material welfare more effectively. Additionally, as society has become larger and more complex through the promotion of modern science and technology, political decision-making has come increasingly to rely on inputs from science. Such inputs include scientific surveys of lands, waters, and resources; population censuses and data collection on economic activity; determination of standards for health, safety, and environmental regulation; meteorological and epidemiological projections and predictions; diplomatic and military intelligence research; opinion polls and social scientific analysis of human behavior; and more. Indeed, the use of science across the board to formulate policies as guidelines for action constitutes a distinctly new dimension of government.

But as scientists have become increasingly influential advisers to politicians and the public in order to enhance the intelligence and effectiveness of public policy, questions have arisen with regard to the previously assumed neutrality of science and the congruence of interests between the scientific community and society as a whole. Descriptive, epistemological, and normative criticisms have been raised against any naive model of science and scientists always playing noncontroversially beneficial roles in policy formation. Scientists often have their own interests which, like those of any social class, can influence (consciously or not) their behavior. Any adequate description of the role scientists play in politics and policy needs to acknowledge distinctions between scientists as exponents, advocates, arbiters, and honest brokers – although the honest broker role may well be an impossible ideal, since science advice necessarily advocates to some extent for the value of science. Epistemologically, it is not clear that the fallibilistic character of scientific knowledge is as useful or as easily assimilated into political affairs as has sometimes been thought. Normatively, it must be recognized that appeals to science can short-circuit debates about political ideals and that citizens can approach science with multiple interests; among these interests are those of principals seeking agents, debate coaches, teachers, and decision-making proxies.

Any more adequate view of the insertion of science into politics and policy that would emerge from such criticisms will have implications in a variety of societal contexts. The ideal image of science in the military is that it can instrumentally serve the objectives of just nations. But science and technology may actively shape those objectives in ways that escape the boundaries of any single conflict or the control of any single nation. Ideally, science would help dispel courtroom controversies by delivering the truth, but in reality courts must judge between dueling experts and make decisions in the midst of uncertainty and controversy. In so doing, they actively construct scientific claims and public realities. Similarly, the idea that the media should popularize preestablished scientific knowledge for a receptive public fails to appreciate the complexities of both the knowledge and the public's interests. The communication of science through the media often simplifies or sensationalizes at the same time that it fails to appreciate the true interests and distinctive cognitive resources animating both citizens and politicians – not to mention the transformations in communication that are taking place through the Internet and other interactive media.

Extending reflection: premature science? Predicting earthquakes and linking autism with vaccinations

Communicating scientific research to the public may create a tension between scientists' responsibility to inform the public about their results and their responsibility not to cause unwarranted social disturbance by communicating results prematurely. The cases of earthquake prediction and the supposed autism–vaccination linkage illustrate this tension. They also put in context two central lessons from this chapter: scientists speak with a great deal of authority to influence society and science does not obtain certainty. Thus, when scientists speak, they need to be sensitive to the potential consequences of errors.

Brian Brady, an American geophysicist, began to research earthquakes in the early 1970s. He formulated a theory that earthquakes are preceded by characteristic, identifiable patterns of microfractures and other seismic activity. This meant that if the patterns and activity were observed, the occurrence of an earthquake could be predicted with a high degree of accuracy. As geophysicist Susan Hough later noted, Brady's conclusions were based on limited data with no rigorous statistical analysis. But this was common for papers published during the early to mid-1970s when the seismological community was optimistic about the possibility of predicting earthquakes.

In 1974, a magnitude 8.1 earthquake struck southwest of Lima, Peru, killing 78 people and causing major damage. Using observations from this area and his theory, Brady argued that the preparation phase for an even larger earthquake had begun. By August, 1977, he formulated his first specific prediction, namely that a magnitude 8.4 earthquake would strike near Lima in late 1980. In June 1978, he refined the prediction, stating that the earthquake would occur in late October to November of 1981 with a magnitude of 9.2 ± 0.2.[17] Brady began to communicate his results to scientists in Peru, at the US Geological Survey, and to the US Office of Foreign Disaster Assistance. Many were skeptical, pointing to a lack of published papers explaining, let alone validating, Brady's theory. Others, however, championed Brady's cause, arguing that he was a brilliant maverick whose theory was poorly understood. Convinced of his theory, Brady, along with

[17] See Olson et al. 1989.

the Office of Foreign Disaster Assistance science adviser Paul Krumpe, promulgated the prediction widely.

An official hearing of the National Earthquake Prediction Evaluation Council in January, 1981, concluded that Brady's theory was full of holes and not clearly related to observations. In short, the Council could find no merit in Brady's prediction. But in Peru, this verdict did not squelch the growing anxiety among the public. Word of the prediction had already reached the Peruvian public – especially alarming was a request made by the Peruvian Red Cross to the Office of Foreign Disaster Assistance for preparedness items, including 100,000 body bags. In April 1981, Brady adjusted his prediction, saying that the earthquake would occur on June 28 of that year. As that day approached, the prediction garnered headlines in Lima, residents who could afford to do so left town, and property values and tourism revenues plunged. The city became a virtual ghost town, but nothing happened – June 28 came and went with no earthquake.

A similar story about the communication of scientific results began in 1998 when the Royal Free Hospital in London called a press conference to unveil the results of a new study published in *The Lancet* and conducted in the lab of gastroenterologist Andrew Wakefield. With flashbulbs popping, Wakefield announced that he had discovered a new syndrome that he believed was triggered by the MMR (measles, mumps, rubella) vaccine. Nine of the twelve children involved in the study had developed autism between one and fourteen days after the MMR vaccination. Though the paper noted that "we did not prove an association" between MMR and autism, Wakefield said in the press conference that "it's a moral issue for me, and I can't support the continued use of [the MMR vaccine] until the issue has been resolved."[18]

The press conference and the study triggered a massive panic and a continuing controversy about the safety of vaccinations. Sharon Begley, science writer for *Newsweek*, argued that the ensuing panic was inevitable because many legitimate scientists went on to produce evidence of a link between vaccinations and autism and the press and public health agencies stoked the mounting fears. But, she added, the panic is also inexplicable, because by the early 2000s scientific support for the link had evaporated. Indeed, the first cracks in the theory linking vaccines and autism

[18] Deer 2004, n.p.

pertained to Wakefield's study. One of his graduate students attempted to confirm a key step in Wakefield's hypothesis, but continually obtained negative results. But according to the graduate student, Wakefield would not listen to contrary evidence. Furthermore, the editor of *The Lancet* later found that there were "fatal conflicts of interest" in the study and twelve coauthors formally retracted the paper's suggestion that MMR and autism were linked.

Wakefield was charged with professional misconduct, but this was only one development that undermined the vaccine theory of autism. Begley argued that an "overwhelming body of evidence" showed that childhood vaccines do not increase the risk of autism. In the US, three test cases were tried in a special "vaccine court." The cases resulted in the finding that there is no evidence that the MMR vaccination is associated with autism and that the evidence "falls far short" of showing a connection between autism and thiomersal, a mercury-containing preservative used in many vaccines.

Nonetheless, confusion, controversy, and fear persist about the safety of vaccinations. This is in part because it is impossible to prove a negative such as "vaccines do not cause autism." It may also be due to a lack of public understanding of science or even the manipulation of parental fears by advocacy groups. Begley and many physicians worry about websites that advise parents not to vaccinate their children, because this advice is based on false or misleading information in the guise of established science. But continued debate is also due to the existence of legitimate scientific disagreements. Indeed, L.G. Goes, a parent of an autistic child, argued on the website for the advocacy group "Age of Autism" that Begley had misrepresented the scientific record. Goes claimed that Begley could only reach her conclusions by omitting several studies that support the vaccine theory of autism. Furthermore, according to Goes, Begley failed to mention that one key detractor of the theory holds a vaccine patent, which implies a conflict of interest.

Questions for research and discussion

1. It is widely maintained that scientific progress requires freedom of communication within the scientific community. Should the same freedom apply to communication between scientists and the public? Does the public have the right to hear any and every scientific

hypothesis, result, and prediction, no matter how unwarranted it may be? Might the avoidance of social disturbances be more important than such a right? After all, in the social sphere false beliefs can lead to harmful action.

2. Consider again the different role options that scientists can assume when seeking to influence policy, along with the role options that citizens can ask that scientists play. In what ways might these two sets of options mesh with each other? How might they be used to further reflect on the particular issues discussed in relation to the military, law, and media?
3. The communication process within the scientific community is filtered by the peer-review process, which ideally eliminates unwarranted claims and results. Do or should the media serve the same function in the communication process between scientists and the public? How should the media handle the communication of scientific results? When and how should research results be communicated to the public? In the information age, who should count as a "peer" and a member of "the media"?
4. The principal–agent problem highlights difficulties that arise under conditions of asymmetric information when any principal engages an agent. The principal needs an agent because the agent knows more about something than the principal; furthermore, the principal wants the agent to use that knowledge to advance the principal's interest. But precisely because the agent has knowledge or skills that the principal lacks, it is difficult for the principal to check whether the agent is indeed acting in the principal's interest. How might the principal–agent problem be manifest in science for policy practices?
5. Using some of the conceptual and analytic tools explored in this chapter, develop a case study analysis of the IPCC (Intergovernmental Panel on Climate Change). Does the case study confirm or challenge the broad argument of the chapter? What adaptations, if any, might be proposed for the IPCC?

Further reading about the cases

Allen, C.R. (1976) "Responsibilities in Earthquake Prediction," *Bulletin of the Seismological Society of America*, vol. 66, pp. 2069–2074.

Dawidoff, Nicholas (2009) "The Civil Heretic," *New York Times*, March 25.
Dessler, Andrew, and Edward Parson (2010) *The Science and Politics of Global Climate Change: A Guide to the Debate*, 2nd edn. Cambridge University Press.
Gardiner, Stephen, Simon Caney, Dale Jamieson, and Henry Shue, eds. (2010) *Climate Ethics: Essential Readings*. Oxford University Press.
Hough, Susan (2009) *Predicting the Unpredictable: The Tumultuous Science of Earthquake Prediction*. Princeton University Press.
Offit, Paul (2010) *Autism's False Prophets: Bad Science, Risky Medicine, and the Search for a Cure*. New York: Columbia University Press.
Wakefield, Andrew (2010) *Callous Disregard: Autism and Vaccines: The Truth Behind a Tragedy*. New York: Skyhorse.

11 Science and ideational culture

As we saw in the previous two chapters, science is more than the practice of scientists, and ethics is an issue not only within the scientific community but also for the larger society within which modern science exists. Those chapters, however, were largely limited to politics. This chapter highlights interactions between science and culture. The term "ideational culture" denotes something much broader than politics and policies, namely, the attitudes, values, goals, practices, and beliefs that comprise a way of life and a way of ordering and making sense of experience. Science entails certain methods and practices for obtaining knowledge, as well as a set of theories or ideas. Yet these are not the only methods or theories to be found in human cultures, and science finds itself constantly interacting with the other methods and theories prominent in the contemporary world. The story of the Templeton Foundation illustrates the issues that arise when we adopt this wider perspective on science and its relationship to other spheres of society. This chapter then goes on to map four modes of interaction between science and culture. The final chapter considers the professional ethics of engineers, which is an important bridge between scientists and material culture.

Setting the stage: the Templeton Foundation

John Marks Templeton was born in 1912 in Winchester, Tennessee, not far from where John Scopes in 1925 was tried for teaching evolution in the public schools. A lifelong member of the Presbyterian Church, Templeton thus grew up in a culture in which the relation between science and religion took dramatic form as a conflict between biblical theology and the theory of evolution. He attended Yale University, earned a degree in economics (1934), and was awarded a Rhodes Scholarship to Oxford University.

An extremely successful career in financial investment led to the creation of Templeton Growth Ltd. (1954).

In 1972 he established as a complement to the Nobel Prizes in science, literature, and peace, the Templeton Prize for Progress in Religion (in 2001 renamed the Templeton Prize for Progress toward Research or Discoveries about Spiritual Realities), with the first award going the next year to Mother Teresa of Calcutta. Subsequent prizes have been given to such figures as the Indian philosopher Sarvepalli Radhakrishnan (1975), evangelist Billy Graham (1982), historians of science and religion Stanley Jaki (1987) and Ian Barbour (1999), and physicists and cosmologists Paul Davies (1995), Freeman Dyson (2000), George F.R. Ellis (2004), Charles Townes (2005), and John D. Barrow (2006).

In 1987 Templeton was knighted and established the John Templeton Foundation "to serve as a philanthropic catalyst for discovery in areas engaging life's biggest questions [ranging] from explorations into the laws of nature and the universe to questions on the nature of love, gratitude, forgiveness, and creativity."[1] By 2007 the Templeton Foundation had distributed more than $60 million in grants to support a vision that included collaboration rather than conflict between religion and science.

But the activities of the Templeton Foundation have not been without controversies of their own. For instance, the Foundation has been accused somewhat speciously of supporting intelligent design research. More substantively, people within the scientific community have questioned the appropriateness of accepting funds from a foundation that to some extent promotes research in support of religious claims. For instance, when in the late 1990s Templeton sought to make a grant to the AAAS to help support a program on science and religion, the evolutionary biologist and incoming AAAS President Stephen J. Gould questioned its propriety. A prominent physicist argued that "there is a conflict between the values and goals of the Templeton Foundation and those of the AAAS."[2] One result was a broadening of the AAAS program to a "Dialogue on Science, Ethics, and Religion."

More strongly, the cosmologist Sean Carroll once declined to participate in a Templeton conference, arguing that "the entire purpose of the

[1] See the Mission statement, Templeton Foundation website, www.templeton.org/who-we-are/about-the-foundation/mission.

[2] Macilwain 2000, p. 819.

Templeton Foundation is to blur the line between straightforward science and explicitly religious activity, making it seem like the two enterprises are part of one big undertaking."[3] In *The God Delusion,* biologist Richard Dawkins suggested that Templeton money can corrupt scientists if not science. But Al Teich, head of the AAAS science policy program, advised a more accommodating approach: "Religious leaders are listened to. Their views are very important and we need to talk to them if science is going to be influential and take a role in shaping our lives."[4]

This whole debate raises questions of an ethical character about the epistemology of science. Indeed, knowledge and ethics are deeply intertwined – our beliefs inform our actions, so might we have a duty to pursue the truth? But what is the truth and how do we go about pursuing it? Is science the only reliable path toward knowledge or are there other viable paths? More specifically, what could be wrong with following Templeton and using science to investigate religious ideas or using religion or ethics to investigate scientific ideas?

This chapter explores the interactions of modern science and the cultural world of experience and ideas. The first section discusses the ways in which science directly impacts the beliefs, values, and identities of individuals. The second introduces four ways of conceiving of the relationship between science and other aspects of ideational culture.

Science and personal experience

What are the ethical implications of modern science for individual nonscientists? It is clear that science poses ethical questions to scientists and policymakers. But what about everyone else? Is science sufficiently removed from their lives as not to warrant reflection? Of course, individuals constantly encounter science-based technologies in everyday life and these encounters are ethically charged. But does science – as methods and theories rather than artifacts – have a similar influence on individuals in their everyday lives? On first inspection, it seems that science is an esoteric affair, confined to laboratories or field stations. If this is the case, then the sciences, as philosopher Jürgen Habermas argues, impact the human lifeworld only through the technological applications of their theories.

[3] Carroll 2005, n.p. [4] Macilwain 2000, p. 819.

But the Templeton case helps us see that science influences individuals directly in ways that go beyond its contributions to technology. To gain a sense of this influence, consider, first, science as a body of knowledge. Individuals regularly encounter science in this sense. It can take the form of medical advice from a doctor or dietary information from a nutritionist. Science in this sense often is conveyed through the media in reports about, for example, environmental pollution or global climate change. The pertinent ethical question for individuals pertains to how they should interpret and use science. Should they change their beliefs and behaviors?

This question is made complex by the fact that science often outstrips common-sense experience. Scientific studies report a connection between smoking and lung cancer, but for the individual smoker this correlation is not part of the immediate, lived experience. In her groundbreaking book *Silent Spring,* the scientist Rachel Carson claimed that pesticide use by homeowners and farmers was contributing to the decline of songbirds and other wildlife. This, however, was not part of the experience of people using pesticides. Indeed, science is often essential for identifying phenomena that are not immediately perceptible to people, such as CFCs and their role in ozone depletion and greenhouse gases and their role in global climate change.

As physicist Werner Heisenberg remarked, progress in science involves sacrifices of "the possibility of making the phenomena of nature immediately and directly comprehensible to our way of thought."[5] Individuals do not experience what scientists claim to be a reality, so why should they change their beliefs and habits? This helps explain why many smokers do not quit until the negative impacts become "real" to them through illness or pain. It also explains why "global warming" becomes important to many individuals only when it is – perhaps inappropriately – linked to specific severe weather events such as hurricanes and droughts.

So, one ethical dimension to the nonscientist's experience of science pertains to the interpretation and use of scientific knowledge. Which scientific findings, experts, and theories should be believed and what do they imply for the way one lives? Just as technological artifacts are not simply neutral instruments, neither is science just a collection of knowledge

[5] In Ezrahi 1990, p. 270.

claims to be used appropriately or inappropriately. Science also shapes mental lives by permeating beliefs, modes of thinking, perceiving, and acting. It structures social institutions and cultural practices, presents a framework for thinking, and influences our sense of self. It does so both in terms of form (methods and practices) and content (theories, attitudes, and ideas). We are immersed in scientific beliefs like fish in water – they are so pervasive that we hardly notice them.

Indeed, Templeton started his foundation because he was acutely aware of science, not just as knowledge to be used or ignored by pregiven subjects, but as a profound shaper of subjectivity. Science configures human ideas and, thus, personal experience. Think for a moment about some of your basic beliefs: what is the earth composed of, what is water, why does a rock fall to the ground, what causes illness, why are plants green, what is the Sun, how does the human body function? You can begin to see how your worldview is profoundly influenced by modern science.

To get a better sense of this deeper structuring of individual experience by science, consider some implications of evolutionary theories. In *The Laws* (X), Plato has the Athenian stranger attack those natural philosophers who teach that the heavenly bodies were brought into being not by divine intelligence but by natural necessity and chance. Such evolutionary theorists teach that the gods and their moral laws are human inventions. Thus, according to the Athenian, this scientific naturalism subverts religious and moral order by teaching atheism and relativism. He responds to this threat by arguing for intelligent design as the ultimate source of order. In contemporary society, similar claims have been made by proponents of biblical creationism against the theory of biological evolution by natural selection. Many defenders of creationism argue that Darwinian evolution promotes a materialistic view of the world that undermines the dignity of human beings. On the other side, proponents of evolutionary theory often claim that creationism reinforces dogmatic and fundamentalist beliefs.

The debate between evolution and creationism is often characterized as a matter of public policy – for example, regarding school funding and curricula. But these public policy questions are significant in large part because of the implications for individuals. Parents are concerned about what their children learn in school, because it will shape their identities and values. As it is conveyed through school systems, science is a major enculturating force that configures human conceptions of self and world.

Biological evolution tells of the history of life and the human place therein. Physics and chemistry tell of the nature of the universe, energy, and matter. The social sciences similarly inform a certain way of categorizing and understanding political, economic, and cultural life.

As the case of evolution demonstrates, the influence of science is in no way value neutral. Indeed, modern societies often promote and teach various sciences out of convictions that doing so is instrumentally valuable because it creates individuals capable of contributing to knowledge economies. Society also supports science because of its intrinsic value in fostering critical thinking and rationality. Of course, these claims are themselves controversial as the case of biblical creationism demonstrates.

Other criticisms of science stem from the phenomenological tradition. Here, the argument is not that science undermines traditional values structures, but that it estranges individuals from direct experience with a primordial lifeworld. Science tends to abstract and generalize. It treats the human body or nature, for example, as objects characterized by systems and processes. This detracts from an engagement with the human body as the felt and lived-through center of subjective experience and an engagement with nature as a vital source of meaning, surprise, and otherness. Many individuals reject modern Western scientific medicine for this reason, turning instead to alternative or Eastern models that encode different body images (e.g., body functions as regulated by the flow of *qi* in traditional Chinese medicine).

In summary, when one considers all of the ongoing revolutionary theories and methods of the modern sciences, it becomes apparent that they influence human lives just as profoundly as modern technology does. Individuals living in an age of automobiles and computers encounter opportunities and situations unknown to those prior to that age. Similarly, individuals living in an era after Newton and Darwin inhabit a new world of beliefs, experiences, practices, and values.

Science and culture

From its beginnings in the Western world, modern science was often seen as an opaque sphere that may conflict with and transform other spheres of life. Where once there had been a more seamless integration of culture, many felt that there was now a disruption that called for an ethical response. The question was how to reconcile these new understandings of self and world with older and more familiar accounts. It is this ambiguous, disorienting legacy of the Enlightenment that Gould, Dawkins, Templeton, and countless others have attempted to understand and come to terms with.

Adopting the work of Ian Barbour, we can identify four basic attempts, which amount to four ways of conceiving and evaluating the relationship between modern science and other aspects of culture: independence, conflict, dialogue, and integration. Each perspective can house diverse and even contradictory conceptual and normative claims. Nonetheless each can be briefly and simply introduced.

The first maintains that science is and should be an *independent* realm. Many holding this view argue, with Habermas, that science only impacts individual lives indirectly through science-based technologies. One important ethical implication of this view is that it justifies autonomy for the scientific community. If science only impacts society through technological applications then scientists can be granted autonomy, as social regulation and oversight need only occur at the later stage of application. Another implication is that society can effectively be cordoned off into separate spheres of practices and beliefs.

By contrast, the other three perspectives maintain that science directly impacts ideational culture and individual lives in ways that go beyond its contribution to material culture. Some of these direct influences were discussed above. But there is disagreement about how to conceive of the impacts of science. The *conflict* view tends to treat (modern or Western) science in abstract and monistic terms and place it in contrast to all or certain aspects of culture. This establishes a general debate between utopian and dystopian views of the impacts of science – that is, polar opposite hopes about whether science should win or lose the conflict. The utopian view stems from early modern thinkers who saw in science the promise of certainty, liberation, and power. The dystopian view has roots in eighteenth-century Romantic criticisms of science as an overbearing rationality that threatens diversity and human meaningfulness.

By contrast, the analytic approach views sciences in the plural and emphasizes the many impacts they have on culture. Historian of science Richard Olson summarized this view:

> there is no monolithic "scientific rationality" that shapes our views about a myriad of topics. Instead, there are many different sciences and many

> different scientific practices, or rationalities, each of which functions in our culture to affect the views of different groups of people for different purposes.[6]

This view holds that the relationships between science, culture, and individual life are far more complex than simple independence or conflict. It is this complexity that invites proposals, such as Templeton's, for *dialogue*, where various sciences and scientists engage the methods and theories of other social groups in hopes of advancing mutual understanding. Many argue that this engagement can or should go so far as to blur the distinctions between science and other social endeavors, leading to a true *integration*.

Before proceeding, it should be noted that all four kinds of interaction stem from cultures heavily influenced by the revealed Abrahamic religions (Judaism, Christianity, and Islam). Abrahamic religions, despite providing a cultural climate hospitable to the emergence of modern science, also made claims to knowledge fundamentally opposed to science. For example, by presenting the natural world as created by a God who is rational, and humans as created in the image of God, Christian theology provides a ready justification for humans to use their own rationality to understand the rationality God has infused into nature. At the same time, Christianity also claims to have special and distinctive knowledge from revelation about reality. The relations between these two forms of knowledge – reason and revelation – is an ongoing issue of inquiry and debate.

By contrast, in cultures influenced by dharma–dao religions such as Hinduism, Buddhism, Daoism, and Confucianism there appear to be much fewer instances of the tensions between alternative science–culture relationships. The Dalai Lama, for example, often recognizes Buddhism and modern science as similar both in terms of theory (emphasizing complex interrelations) and method (empiricism). He sees no problem in rejecting traditional cosmology in ancient Buddhist texts on the basis of new insights from modern science.

Independence: separating science from culture

The separation of science from other facets of society has been repeatedly defended. One kind of defense posits a strict division between facts

[6] Olson 2008, p. 5.

and values, or between questions of *what* and questions of *why*. Science offers empirical descriptions of physical reality, while religion and ethics interpret the meaning of human existence and determine right conduct, including the appropriate uses of scientific knowledge. Gould, for example, argued that science and religion constitute "non-overlapping magisteria." A magisterium is a domain where one form of teaching holds the appropriate tools for discourse. Science covers the empirical world, and religion covers the world of meaning and value. Ethics defends a strict and proper division between the magisteria. Similarly, the theologian Karl Barth insisted that history rather than nature is the domain of God's activities. Evolutionary biology, for example, poses no threat to religion, because God is revealed in the historical category of human culture rather than in the natural category of biology.

The independence of science has also been argued on the grounds of its specialness. Science policy scholar David Guston identified four reasons why science is often defended as special, each of which requires a degree of autonomy or independence for its protection. First, science is epistemologically special because it searches for objective truth. Second, sociological specialness is the claim that science has a unique normative order that provides for self-governance. Third, Platonic specialness refers to its esoteric, technical nature far removed from the knowledge of common citizens. Finally, science is defended as economically special, both because investments in research are crucial for productivity and because such investments need not be directly guided by a concern with application.

Often invoking these kinds of scientific specialness, the physical chemist and philosopher Michael Polanyi put forward the normative argument for the autonomy of science in "The Republic of Science." Science, he argues, is driven by a concern for truth or a unified picture of reality, which benefits society. Society acts as an external force that can either facilitate (by defending the autonomy of science) or inhibit (by interfering with science) this quest.

Conflict: science and culture in opposition

Many Enlightenment thinkers understood modern science not primarily as a fount of technological innovation – a useful byproduct – but as a new way of understanding nature and the human condition. They were introducing a revolutionary break with history. Such momentous change was bound to conflict with established ways of thinking, perceiving, and acting. Thus, in addition to scientific methods and theories, contestations between scientific, religious, and other cultural worldviews are an enduring legacy of the Enlightenment.

The historical break of the Enlightenment is captured in a fundamentally ethical ideal of *progress*. Thomas Paine's 1795 *Age of Reason*, for example, argued that without kings, history, or God, the exercise of reason alone could create better societies than have ever existed in which people will be healthier, happier, freer, wealthier, longer lived, and more productive. In 1784, Immanuel Kant similarly answered the question "What Is Enlightenment?" with the simple command: "Dare to know!" Humanity will transcend limitations and awaken from the dogmatic slumbers of tradition, irrationality, superstition, and tyranny. The mathematician and biologist Jacob Bronowski argued, "science has humanized our values. Men have asked for freedom, justice and respect precisely as the scientific spirit has spread among them."[7]

For such thinkers, science is a liberating and rationalizing influence on ideational culture. Its methodological ideal of objectivity promises consensus and peace, whereas religious belief delivers division and war. And its theories promise to transcend the outmoded ideas of the ancients and deliver the certain knowledge necessary for rationally ordering society and mastering nature. Some philosophers known as logical positivists went so far as to claim that scientific discourse provides the norm for all meaningful statements. Statements in ethics, metaphysics, and religion cannot be true or false, because they are meaningless expressions of emotion devoid of cognitive significance.

But modern science has been questioned and attacked from several perspectives concerned that progress in scientific rationality actually generates novel problems and may undermine rather than advance genuine human progress. First, many objected to the methods of the new natural sciences, particularly as they rely on technological instrumentation. How could we be certain that the telescope or the microscope did not distort our senses rather than extend them? This question was especially acute for those who believed that God has fitted humans with just the right sensory

[7] Bronowski 1956, p. 70.

apparatuses to perceive the world accurately. Skepticism about scientific methods takes other forms as well. Why, for example, should we trust or consent to a community of experts who legitimate knowledge claims in the secretive space of the laboratory?

The second type of resistance takes aim at scientific theories. From the moment Galileo gazed at the heavens, modern science began arriving at conclusions that were at odds, not only with common sense as noted above, but also with traditional authorities and received wisdom. These covered the entire range of fundamental questions, such as the movements of heavenly bodies, the origin of the earth, the nature of living organisms and disease, the basis of mind, and the nature and origins of humanity. Historian Bruce Mazlish argued that modern scientific theories challenge "four discontinuities."[8] These discontinuities have long served to inform and orient human experience, and therefore challenges to them naturally elicit backlash. The theories of Nicolaus Copernicus, Charles Darwin, and Sigmund Freud each respectively overturned illusions of human specialness derived from humans' supposed separation from and domination over the cosmos (heliocentrism), the animal world (biological evolution), and the passions (the unconscious mind). The fourth discontinuity in need of reexamination is the notion that humans are discontinuous and distinct from the machines they make.

One could argue that both forms of resistance to the Enlightenment (based on methods and theories) have been overcome. The scientific method is now largely used by philosophers and educators to defend science against superstitions or irrational methods of acquiring knowledge. Additionally, religious and cultural traditions have reinterpreted their worldviews in light of scientific evidence, the explanatory and predictive powers of science, and the practical successes of science-based technologies.

But as the Templeton Foundation illustrates, the questioning in fact continues to run both ways. Indeed, it often reaches a fevered pitch such as during the so-called "science wars" and "culture wars" at the end of the twentieth and beginning of the twenty-first centuries. The former pertained primarily to matters of method, whereas the latter principally involved theoretical debates. First, in terms of method, in the 1960s and 1970s many intellectuals began to investigate science as inherently

[8] Mazlish 1995.

a historical and social activity rather than a method for transcending society. These scholars eventually formed the interdisciplinary field of STS (science, technology, and society) studies. Their approach to science paralleled the Enlightenment approach to the study of religion, which began with the assumption that religion is a human cultural creation just like poetry, kinship, or dining. So too, STS scholars understand science as a social and human activity. They therefore look to contextual features to help explain scientific changes, rather than appealing solely to noncontextual standards of rationality and validity.

Thomas Kuhn inspired the contextual approach to science with *The Structure of Scientific Revolutions*, which pictured science not as the linear accumulation of truths leading to a mirroring of nature, but rather as a social process that undergoes periodic "paradigm shifts" as communities define and redefine problems and acceptable solutions. The antirealism latent in Kuhn was more forcefully advanced by David Bloor, who founded the "strong programme" in the sociology of science. This approach adopts the symmetry principle, which maintains that all knowledge claims – both "true" and "false" beliefs in science – must be explained by the same social, nonrational reasons. Scientific "reality" is not acceptable as a belief explanation over "erroneous," irrational ideas that are subsequently discarded. Although most STS scholars are not so radically antirealist, they found themselves pulled into the so-called science wars as scientists sought to defend their claims to objective knowledge.

Sandra Harding, Donna Haraway, and other feminists also critique the axiom that knowledge can be obtained only by using methods that strip away contextual values and interests. They argue that interests, often amounting to systematic gender bias, are always embedded in science. There is a need to uncover these hidden influences. All knowledge is necessarily "situated" in particular contexts such that the goal should be, not to strip away bias, but to assess the impacts of values and interests on knowledge claims. If values are allowed to masquerade as "objective," then they command authority without ever being explicitly investigated. The idea of situated knowledge is also used in feminist studies of the connection between Western science and colonial and postcolonial domination of developing nations. These studies deconstruct the notion that Western science is superior because it is "generic" and not itself "local," just like the methods of knowledge acquisition in other cultures.

In terms of theories, there are many who continue to resist scientific accounts, especially those pertaining to human nature and the origin of the universe. Such resistance spans the political spectrum from extreme liberal defenders of nature against the risks posed by industrial science to extreme conservative defenders of traditional values threatened by scientific theories.

The first group has historical roots in Romantic attacks against a scientific hegemony of reason in human affairs, a narrowly utilitarian conception of progress, and a mechanical image of life and the universe. In an 1802 letter, the English poet William Blake summarized these sentiments: "Pray God us keep/ From Single vision and Newton's sleep!"[9] Modern scientific theories are abstracted from the human lifeworld. Insofar as the authority of science becomes insinuated as a pervasive common-sense view of the world, it threatens to diminish the human capacity to understand and appreciate the inherent mysteries of the human condition.

This Romantic confrontation with science was portrayed by physicist and novelist C.P. Snow as a clash of "the two cultures." It first arose in the nineteenth century in intellectual battles such as the one between Thomas Huxley, the biologist known as "Darwin's bulldog," and the poet and cultural critic Matthew Arnold. Snow recommended greater mutual awareness, but ultimately argued that social problems require science and technology. Scientists have "the future in their bones," whereas the literati, heirs of Blake and the Romantics, are "natural Luddites" who have been left behind by progress.

The second, conservative, resistance to science is not necessarily rooted in religion. Secular conservatives, for example, can consider scientific progress a threat to traditional virtues and cultural and family values. But this kind of conflict takes its most strident form between scientific materialists such as Dawkins and religious fundamentalists. The former contend that science offers the only reliable route to knowledge, that matter and energy are the fundamental realities of the universe, and that religious beliefs should be dismissed as meaningless statements that do more harm than good. To appropriate Gould's term, there is and should be no "magisterium" left for religion, because even human nature can be explicated

[9] Letter to Thomas Butt, November 22, 1802, in Geoffrey Keynes, ed., *The Letters of William Blake* (1956).

in naturalistic terms. Dawkins and others such as astronomer Carl Sagan even argue that adopting the scientific worldview actually increases one's sense of beauty, meaning, and wonder – science discovers a reality so intricate, immense, and complex that it cannot help but inspire awe. By contrast, religious fundamentalists use religion to dictate the purview and course of scientific investigation. Biblical literalists, for example, hold that scripture reveals the fundamental truth of the universe; therefore any contrary scientific evidence is false and threatens to lead humans astray. They believe the impoverished worldview of modern science – which provides knowledge of means, but not ends – leads to anomie, hedonism, and moral decline and must be checked by rigorous moral standards.

Dialogue: science and culture in conversation

Just as we must recognize some measure of scientific independence from society, there is no doubting the persistence of such conflicts. Yet dialogue too has been a central dynamic between science and other aspects of culture. In 1632, Galileo Galilei published his *Dialogue on the Great World Systems*. Galileo used three interlocutors to debate the new Copernican system (Earth and other planets orbit the Sun) versus the traditional Ptolemaic system (Earth as the center of the universe). Galileo set up a straw man defense of the traditional system and the Catholic Church put his dialogue on the Index of Forbidden Books. From its beginnings, then, dialogue between modern science and society can actually be a mask for more conflict. But, as the Templeton Foundation shows, dialogue can also be genuine. Inspired by Galileo's dialogue, Bronowski authored a searching dialogue between a literary scholar and a scientist. Yet unlike Galileo, Bronowski gives both interlocutors strong arguments that culminate in an appreciation of the deep similarities between art and science.

The need for such dialogue stems from the fact that there is far more complexity than can be captured with a simple dichotomy between "Science," on one hand, and "Religion," "Art," "Humanities," or "Society," on the other hand. After all, there is no single religious or Christian or even Protestant or Catholic response to modern science. There is also no single ethical assessment of science. This is in large part because there is no single "science" to assess, but rather a variety of sciences. Indeed, modern science was not born wholly formed at a single, revolutionary stroke.

Rather, many sciences have emerged and continue to arise from within a diversity of historical and social contexts through processes of mutual interpretation and co-shaping. These processes occasionally take antagonistic forms, but more often they involve dialogue and integration.

We can briefly illustrate this point by revisiting some of the relationships characterized above in terms of conflict. Most STS scholars, for example, are not combatants against science, but are bridging divides, creating new scientific methods and theories along the way. Indeed, Snow quickly revisited his "two cultures" thesis in order to recognize a "third culture" of social scientists and ethicists who study the human dimensions of the sciences and create dialogue between science and society. Many Romantic-inspired and feminist criticisms of science have similarly resulted in new or alternative scientific and medical practices. Furthermore, since Thomas Aquinas integrated Aristotelian philosophy with Christian dogma, theologians and scientists have formulated a variety of alternatives to the science–religion relationship that are far more subtle than straightforward opposition.

The Templeton Foundation continues this tradition insofar as it consists of dialogue between various scientific and nonscientific perspectives. This dialogue has been especially fruitful at the intersections of theological and scientific methods and theories. In terms of method, for example, some argue that theological doctrines are equivalent to scientific hypotheses. Others argue that both scientists and theologians use theory-laden models, methods, and metaphors to investigate and describe experience. Both kinds of methods, then, may be assessed in terms of coherence, comprehensiveness, and fruitfulness.

In terms of theories, the Roman Catholic author Ernan McMullin contended that the big bang theory may not prove the Christian doctrine of creation, but does suggest that the universe is dependent on God (although others use the big bang to disprove the existence of God). Another Catholic author, Karl Rahner, argued that Christian anthropology is compatible with evolutionary theory. Hinduism accords a central place to consciousness in its approach to reality, and thus finds ample room for dialogue with quantum physicists, systems biologists, and others seeking a role for observers in science and critical of mechanistic accounts of nature and mind. In Islamic theology, knowledge is the key to human happiness and salvation. Though science in this religion is not the most important form of knowledge, it is also the case that the line between reason and revelation is blurred, because reason is a minor revelation given to everyone in their quest for God, the source of all knowledge.

Integration: bringing science and culture together

Relationships among the sciences and between the sciences and other aspects of culture go beyond indirect interactions to actual integration of methods and theories. As the sociobiologist E.O. Wilson noted, "consilience" or the unification of knowledge is a long-standing human quest. Consilience stands in opposition to the fragmentation of knowledge first into science and the humanities and then further into many specialized scientific and humanistic disciplines. Wilson argues for the need to reclaim a unified worldview in order to manage contemporary problems. For Wilson, the unification of knowledge requires that all phenomena be reduced to those consistent with scientific materialism. Consciousness and emotion, for example, are reduced to neurons and brain chemistry. Many see this kind of integration as in reality a colonization or elimination of other ways of knowing.

Science and religion have also witnessed periods of intense integration. For example, Victorian Britain was a context in which science and religion were widely seen as mutually supportive. The Royal Society of London partnered with the Archbishop of Canterbury and the Bishop of London to commission several works of natural theology collectively known as the Bridgewater Treatises. Natural theology is based on the premise that the order and intelligibility of the universe suggests an underlying purpose or design. The emergence of life in particular implies a natural teleology and that the universe is oriented toward an emergent intelligence. Thus, natural theology (as opposed to revealed theology) begins with reason and observation to construct and confirm subsequent religious claims. Alternatively, the Jesuit priest, philosopher, and scientist Pierre Teilhard de Chardin began with traditional religious claims and reformulated them in light of contemporary science. He reinterpreted Christian eschatology in terms of evolution toward an "Omega Point" of universal consciousness, an idea that prompted the Catholic Church to censure his work. The philosopher Alfred North Whitehead went even further, rejecting traditional doctrines and formulating a systematic synthesis of science and religion.

Olson developed the concept of "scientism" as a tool for investigating such integrations of sciences and other aspects of culture. The term "scientism" indicates "the transfer of ideas, practices, attitudes, and methodologies from the context of the study of the natural world ... into the study of humans and their social institutions."[10] Olson stressed that there are numerous scientisms, which means that the natural sciences have shaped values and become integrated into understandings of self and society in diverse and even contradictory ways.

Since the Enlightenment, social theorists and humanists have borrowed heavily from the natural sciences in their understandings of humans and their societies. Indeed, many held that it is just such appropriations of the natural sciences (i.e., scientisms) that would lead to social and moral progress. But the meaning of "progress" hinges on which natural science one has in mind. There has always been disagreement about which models, methods, and theories from the physical sciences to integrate into humanistic, religious, and other endeavors. The sciences are a kaleidoscope through which to view the human condition, leading to vastly different understandings and proposals for social reform. We can briefly illustrate this with a look at three very different thinkers and their attempts to integrate scientific knowledge with society: Isaac Newton, Johann Wolfgang von Goethe, and Charles Darwin.

David Hume announced his intention to become the Newton of the moral and social sciences and developed an associationist psychology (the idea that mental processes operate by the association of one state with its successor states) that was openly modeled on the patterns set by Newtonian natural philosophy. Importantly, Hume adopted Newton's more cautious, less speculative *Principia* rather than the *Optics* as his model. This entailed a commitment to reducing explanations to the greatest possible simplicity. Complex phenomena must be analyzed into their component simple parts. One can then recompose the complex situation by combining the parts, now understood in isolation, much as a mechanic can take apart and reassemble a clock. This analytic reductivism was adopted by Bentham and other utilitarian moral and social theorists. The happiness of each individual could be ascertained by adding up experiences that individually produce pleasure and subtracting those that produce pain.

[10] Olson 2008, p. 1.

The happiness of the whole would then be the sum of these individual calculations.

Social theorists who appropriated the biological and physiological sciences attacked this mechanical view derived from the physical sciences. Henri de Saint-Simon, for example, argued that society, like a complex organism, cannot be reduced to its component parts. The emergent hierarchical arrangement of the parts is also essential. Thus, Saint-Simon argued that social and economic progress requires management by an elite class just as a complex organism has a coordinating central nervous system.

Goethe and F.W.J. Schelling developed a form of natural science, *Naturphilosophie*, that was radically opposed to the reductive and objective aspects of Newtonian physics. Goethe is best known as a poet, novelist, and playwright, but he devoted much of his time to observing and theorizing about the natural world. He and Schelling were deeply influenced by the Kantian insight that subjective elements - features of human mental faculties - structure human experiences and knowledge. *Naturphilosophie* thus placed subjective considerations at the center of science. Goethe's 1810 study in color theory, *Zur Farbenlehre*, dismissed the dispassionate quantitative approach of Newton as wrongheaded as well as deadening and alienating. He argued that colors must be understood in terms of the experiences of observers, which means that psychological and physiological phenomena are at least as important as physical phenomena.

Through such examples, Olson argues that the Romantics were not anti-science, just anti-Newtonian-science. Indeed, Romanticism was itself partly a scientistic extension of *Naturphilosophie* into art and politics. This version of natural science informed a culture that celebrated the imaginary, the unreal, the organic, the exotic, and the intense passions resulting from the conflict and resolution of opposed elements. Schelling's emphasis on nature as purposefully expressing an ultimate "World Soul" was appropriated by Hegel, who understood history as a teleological process of "Spirit" gradually coming to disclose itself in self-consciousness and creativity. This organicist historicism in turn informed diverse political movements.

Darwin's theory of evolution by natural selection was also appropriated into a wide range of political outlooks and social theories. "Social

Darwinism" has been used to support everything from individualistic laissez-faire economic policies to various socialisms and communisms to European supremacy and domination via imperialism to race-based nationalism and state-managed eugenics policies. Some of this diversity of scientisms is explicable by the differences between Darwin's *On the Origin of Species* and *The Descent of Man*. The former emphasized individual competition and struggle, whereas the latter stressed in-group cooperation and sexual selection. As a result, those who use the former as a model for their theories of society and human nature focus on competition for wealth and power, while those who draw from the latter focus on intra-group cooperation and the search for approval or intergroup competition and war.

Summary

Science affects nonscientists both because they need to interpret and manage scientific information and because their cultures – beliefs, values, and practices – are shaped by scientific methods and theories. Science deeply shapes not only modern material culture, but also the social mindscapes, political programs, moral vocabularies, beliefs, and conceptual schemes that comprise ideational culture. Becoming more aware of the ways in which this occurs is itself an ethical endeavor. The interactions between science and other facets of culture can be loosely grouped into four categories. Stated as claims about what science is or should be, these four categories are: (a) science is and ought to be an independent sphere; (b) science is fundamentally in conflict with religion, art, the humanities, and other aspects of culture; (c) science can and should enter into dialogue with other spheres; (d) science can and should become integrated with other theories and methods.

Extending reflection: intelligent design in public schools

According to the Discovery Institute, "The theory of intelligent design holds that certain features of the universe and of living things are best explained by an intelligent cause, not an undirected process such as natural selection."[11] In 2005, a US District Court in Pennsylvania tried the case of *Tammy Kitzmiller et al. v. Dover Area School District*. At issue was a simple question: Is it permissible to teach intelligent design in public high school biology classes as an alternative to evolution? The plaintiffs successfully argued that intelligent design is a form of creationism. Thus any public school policy requiring the teaching of intelligent design violates the Establishment Clause to the First Amendment to the US Constitution. This clause states that "Congress shall make no law respecting an establishment of religion."[12] The judge argued that intelligent design "is not science" in part because it "violates the centuries-old ground rules of science by invoking and permitting supernatural causation."[13]

This decision has not, however, laid to rest the controversies surrounding intelligent design, its relation to science, and its role in public education. We can briefly cast some of these controversies into the fourfold taxonomy used above. For the judge in the Dover case and nearly all scientists, this is clearly a place where independence must be protected. Intelligent design is not a science and therefore has no place in a scientific classroom. To include it in a scientific curriculum is to compromise the integrity and autonomy of science. For many proponents of creationism, the issue is clearly one of conflict: the whole point is to wage and win a battle to ensure that the biblical truth triumphs over godless evolution. For these individuals, intelligent design is a useful ploy for undermining evolutionary science. Others see the issue as a perfect opportunity to create dialogue by teaching the controversy so that students can explore the borders between science and religion.

Intelligent design can also be seen as an integration of religion and science. It is a contemporary version of natural theology, which holds that the existence of God can be inferred from the evidence of design in nature, of which science has made us more aware. Its arguments for the existence of God are based entirely on human reason (i.e., science)

[11] "Questions about Intelligent Design," Question1, The Center for Science and Culture, Discovery.org, www.discovery.org/csc/topQuestions.php.

[12] *Tammy Kitzmiller et al. v. Dover Area School District* (04cv2688, December 20, 2005), US District Court for the Middle District of Pennsylvania, p. 9, www.pamd.uscourts.gov/kitzmiller/kitzmiller_342.pdf.

[13] *Tammy Kitzmiller et al. v. Dover Area School District*, p. 64.

rather than historical revelation or religious experience. Proponents of intelligent design can claim that they are following in the footsteps of the founders of modern science in seeing God's handiwork in nature. After all, Newton claimed that the eye could not have been contrived without skill in optics and Boyle extolled the evidence of benevolent design throughout the natural order.

But science would later mature to assert its independence from religion. Hume began the process by arguing that the organizing principle responsible for patterns in nature might be within organisms, not external to them. Darwin culminated the project by showing that adaptation can be explained by random variation and natural selection; that is, automatic and impersonal process in nature can account for the appearance of design. Of course, it is just this point that proponents of intelligent design now debate, but is this a scientific debate?

Questions for research and discussion

1. What could be wrong with teaching the controversy over evolution versus intelligent design or teaching both theories in a science class and letting the students make up their own minds? Should students have the right to opt out of learning about evolution if this theory contradicts their religious beliefs? Who should have the authority to establish school science curricula?
2. Why are public schools in liberal democracies allowed to teach science but not religion? After all, science and religion are both ways (methods) of knowing that generate certain beliefs (theories). What is it about religious ways and beliefs that violate state neutrality that is not true about science?
3. The philosopher Karl Popper argued for "falsification" as central to demarcating science from nonscience. What did he mean by this and how does it apply to the intelligent design controversy? What other philosophic conceptions of science exist and can they be fitted into the fourfold taxonomy of relations above?
4. Are there any scientific theories - or aspects of the current scientific worldview - that you find difficult to accept? If so, can you give an account as to why that is and any justification for your beliefs? If not, how do you handle disagreements with those who do refuse certain aspects of the scientific worldview?

Further reading about the cases

Behe, Michael (1996) *Darwin's Black Box: The Biochemical Challenge to Evolution*. New York: Simon & Schuster.

Stewart, Robert, ed. (2007) *Intelligent Design: William A. Dembski and Michael Ruse in Dialogue*. Minneapolis, MN: Fortress.

Templeton, John Marks, and Robert Herrmann (1994) *Is God the Only Reality? Science Points to a Deeper Meaning of the Universe*. New York: Continuum.

12 Science applied

Ethics and engineering

The final chapter once again expands appreciation of the ethical dimensions of science, this time into the domain of engineering.[1] Expansion is justified insofar as engineering is a kind of applied science - although that is not all it is. Additionally, all scientific research is increasingly dependent on engineered instrumentation to form the interactive technoscience that founds the contemporary human-built world. Scientific engineers who have been at the forefront of constructing this world have also been leaders in ethical reflection on professional responsibilities. Codes of ethics for engineers, for instance, anticipated codes of ethics for scientists by more than half a century. Considering the ethics–engineering relationship is thus useful both to help place the ethics–science relationship in perspective and to stimulate further reflection on that relationship.

Setting the stage: the *Challenger* and *Columbia* disasters

After the Manhattan Project, one of the most iconic and important fusions of science and engineering was the US Apollo program, launched in a 1961 speech by President John F. Kennedy when he announced the goal of "landing a man on the moon" by the end of the decade. Scientists and engineers worked together to design a vehicle and sociotechnical system capable of accomplishing a politically defined goal. The Cold War successor to the Apollo program was created in 1972 when President Richard Nixon announced that NASA (the US National Aeronautics and Space Administration) would develop a permanent space station and reusable shuttle to provide regular service between it and Earth. The original vision

[1] More than other chapters, this one draws heavily on previous work. See in general Mitcham 1994; Downey et al. 2007; and Mitcham and Muñoz 2010.

was of a shuttle that would be, not just politically but also commercially, beneficial and provide regular service by the mid-1980s.

On the night of January 27, 1986, engineers and managers at NASA were preparing to launch the space shuttle *Challenger* as only the twenty-fifth launch in a series that began in 1981, but which had been projected by now to be taking place multiple times each month. A program that was supposed to save money and turn space travel into a regularized activity was over budget and seriously behind schedule. In 1985 NASA had managed only nine launches and was determined to do better, with *Challenger* scheduled as a first launch of the new year. But because the December launch of the space shuttle *Columbia* had been delayed a record seven times, *Challenger* had already been pushed forward and then suffered its own delays. There was extreme pressure not to let the launch slip into February; January had to see a launch.

As a result, consternation ensued when in a flight-readiness teleconference Roger Boisjoly and other engineers questioned the safety of the o-ring seals on the solid rocket booster because of record low temperatures at the Cape Canaveral launch site. The engineers were told, however, that people had to make a management decision and one in particular was asked to "take off his engineering hat and put on his management hat."[2] The decision to launch and resulting disaster, where seven astronauts died in an explosion 73 seconds after liftoff, had a devastating impact on NASA and became a prominent feature in subsequent discussions concerning the focus and scope of ethics in the engineering profession. (One can only wonder why it did not have an equally significant impact on ethics in the management profession.)

The night prior to the launch Boisjoly and other engineers explicitly opposed continuing the countdown, only to have their recommendation overridden by senior management. As a result of their testimony before the Presidential Commission during its postdisaster investigation, these engineers came under severe pressure from their employers. The commission, led by former secretary of state William P. Rogers and astronaut Neil Armstrong, concluded that NASA, its Marshall Space Flight Center, and the contractor Morton Thiokol (manufacturer of the booster) were guilty

[2] *Presidential Commission on the Space Shuttle Challenger Disaster*, vol. 1 (Washington, DC: US Government Printing Office, 1986), vol. 1, p. 94.

of faulty management and poor engineering. The commission concluded that the ambitious launch schedule of NASA had outstripped its resources and overridden warnings from engineers.

In many respects, however, the findings produced as many questions as answers. For example, the shuttle crew never knew of the safety concerns of some engineers. Was no one morally responsible for notifying those most directly affected by such issues? One social scientist, in an extended examination of the case, argued that NASA and the shuttle project had become victim to a process she termed the "normalization of deviance," as a series of risks were taken without any apparent failure, thereby creating progressively more dangerous operating assumptions.[3] Is no one responsible for monitoring such a standards-shifting process? Finally, might politicians and others be demanding more safety than is reasonable in an inherently risk-filled project?

Boisjoly, who ultimately resigned to become an engineering ethics consultant, turned into an outspoken advocate for both greater autonomy in the engineering profession and the inclusion of ethics in engineering curricula. Indeed, his repeated presentations at engineering schools and professional engineering association meetings played a significant role in persuading ABET (an acronym-based name for what was formerly known as the Accreditation Board for Engineering and Technology) to institute in 2000 a stronger than previous requirement for the teaching of engineering ethics. Among eleven outcomes that ABET specifies must be part of any accredited engineering degree program, number six is "an understanding of ethical and professional responsibility."[4]

The successful launch of the space shuttle *Discovery* on September 29, 1988, marked a return to US human space flight. The *Challenger* explosion had prompted hundreds of design and procedural changes and cost $2.4 billion. But fifteen years later, on February 1, 2003, the space program experienced another devastating accident when the shuttle *Columbia* disintegrated on reentry into the atmosphere, killing all seven crew members. An investigation concluded the catastrophe was the result of damage sustained during launch, when a piece of foam insulation broke off of the external tank and struck the leading edge of the left wing. Obviously prone to such disasters and lacking a convincing mission in the absence

[3] Vaughan 1996. [4] See Lattuca et al. 2006, p. 18.

of a Cold War space race, the shuttle began to lose public support, and in 2008 President George W. Bush signed a law that scheduled the program for mandatory retirement in four years. President Barack Obama later endorsed a shift toward reliance on the private sector as the optimal strategy for furthering manned space flight and NASA ended the shuttle program with mission number 135, completed by *Atlantis* in July 2011.

Overview, definitions, and contrasts

The need for engineering ethics is not subject to debate, although its focus and scope are. The powers available to engineers as a function of their technical expertise, like those of scientists, surely call for complementary special obligations. As in the professional ethics of science, however, precisely how to articulate or to apply these responsibilities are topics of debate. Certainly engineers have a responsibility to act with technical competence. But should engineering ethics emphasize "doing things right" - at the expense of concern for "doing the right thing" and the development of substantive moral decision-making? To what extent do engineers need be conversant with ethical theory? Should engineering ethics, like the ethics of computer professionals, focus on protecting certain existing legal rights? Or does its scope extend, after the manner of environmental ethics, to new dimensions of the morally considerable? Given that engineers even more than scientists conduct work that is value-laden throughout, engineering ethics must cover far more than disasters such as the *Challenger*. What role, then, should case studies of disasters and moral exemplars play? Is there not even a case to be made that engineering ethics, in our engineered world, should be taken up by everyone, not simply engineers?

Most textbooks agree, for instance, that engineering ethics is broader than research ethics and bears on three distinct relationships:

- among engineers and their professional colleagues,
- between engineers and their employers or clients, and
- between engineers and society in general.

Some authors also argue for consideration of the natural environment. But exactly how to conceive and weigh these diverse relationships will influence more particular judgments about, for instance, the proper content of ethics codes, tensions between company loyalty and professional autonomy, and support for whistle-blowers. In all such cases it is helpful to begin by situating engineering and engineering ethics in broad historical and social contexts.

Defining engineering

The classic definition of modern or scientific engineering is that formulated in conjunction with establishment of the British Institution of Civil Engineers (ICE). In 1818, at the first meeting of the Institution, H.R. Palmer proposed a preliminary description of the engineer as "a mediator between the Philosopher and the working Mechanic," that is, one who learns the principles of nature from natural philosophy "and adapts them to [human] circumstances" while the "working mechanic ... brings [the engineer's] ideas into reality."[5] Ten years later, in conjunction with the application for a royal charter, the Institution of Civil Engineers president Thomas Tredgold more carefully defined engineering as the "art of directing the great sources of power in nature for the use and convenience of [human beings]."[6]

It is noteworthy what this definition leaves out as well as what it includes. Tredgold leaves out any explicit reference to science, although this had been present in Palmer's recognition that the engineer learns from natural philosophy or science the principles of nature. But then Tredgold strengthens Palmer's notion of adaptation to human circumstances by referencing human "use and convenience" as the ethical end. "Use and convenience" is a technical term associated with the development of utilitarian philosophy during the same period. David Hume, for instance, observed that all art or well-designed making is oriented toward human "use and convenience" (*An Enquiry Concerning the Principles of Morals* II, 2).

This affirmation of the primacy of use and convenience in relation to making is another aspect of a historical shift in the ordering of human affairs from other-worldly to this-world interests (see Chapters 2 and 10). At the same time, even within the framework of modern human

[5] Minutes of the Proceedings of the Institution of Civil Engineers, vol. 1 (1818–1823), January 2, 1818, ICE archives, London.

[6] Tredgold, 1828, ICE archives, London.

commitments to this world and material progress, use and convenience are subject to divergent interpretations. The social context in which this-worldly ends are to be pursued remains open and debatable. Although Tredgold and the Institution of Civil Engineers viewed use and convenience as the nonproblematic purpose for engineering, no subsequent engineering ethics code reaffirmed this end. Use and convenience appears to operate at such a high level of generality as to require interpretation and application.

Ethics will necessarily come into play in any related discussion of the particular meaning of use and convenience or the contexts in which use and convenience are to be pursued. Useful to whom (factory owners, investors, consumers)? Convenient for whom (workers, sellers, purchasers)? Can science, especially the social sciences, help respond to such questions? Could answers be engineered (or managed)?

Engineering versus science

Science is taken to depend on a disinterested pursuit of knowledge, an activity especially manifested in research that leads to scientific publication. Unlike engineering, there is no explicit commitment to practical value – although it is common to argue that science does have indirect application value for engineering and technology, and thereby for economic development and societal welfare. By contrast, research in the engineering sciences and design practice is explicitly oriented toward the creation of something useful that is often patented or protected by trade secrecy.

Because science is slightly more remote from applicability, the rules of behavior for scientists can be left out of sight and in the hands of scientists; because engineering (like medicine) is immediately useful to the public, guidelines for behavior need to be front and center. In popular image, moreover, the scientist tends to be thought of as university based, whereas the typical engineer works for or owns a business. Finally, the most widely assessed ethical issue in science is that of fraud or misconduct in the reporting of results to fellow scientists, whereas in engineering it is whistle-blowing: the public disclosure of otherwise private information about unsafe products, processes, or systems. Such contrasts are summarized in Table 12.1.

Table 12.1 *Ethics related to science and engineering*

Ethics related to:	Science	Engineering
Goals	Knowledge or truth and publication	Practical effectiveness and patents
Codes of conduct	More implicit	More explicit
Institutional base	University or governmental–corporate research laboratory	Development or manufacturing divisions of business corporations
Public issues	Fraud or misconduct in reporting results	Whistle-blowing or exposing unsafe products, processes, or systems

Such distinctions are, of course, breaking down as scientists become increasingly interested in translating discoveries into marketable products. Technoscience transgresses multiple science/engineering boundaries. Nevertheless, such contrasts provide a preliminary orientation for consideration of historical developments in engineering ethics.

A history of ideals in engineering ethics

Human beings have since antiquity undertaken projects that might, from a modern vantage point, be interpreted as engineering – witness, for example, Egyptian pyramids, Roman aqueducts, the Great Wall and Grand Canal in China, the Brihadishwara Temple in India – just as it has been claimed that science has a history reaching back to the Greeks. Nonetheless, the first engineers as such did not appear until the Renaissance. It was at this time that a systematic or scientific approach to questions of what works and why in both structures and machines began to displace the earlier trial-and-error practices of artisans and architects. Indeed, Galileo Galilei's 1638 treatise *Two New Sciences*, which adopts a scientific approach to practical problems and structural analysis, is widely regarded as a landmark text in the history of engineering.

Since its modern emergence, there have developed three distinct theoretical ideals in engineering ethics.

First ideal: obedience to authority and company loyalty

The first theory of engineering ethics is that engineers have a fundamental obligation to obey or to be loyal to institutional authorities in which they are embedded. Engineering as a profession initially took shape within the military. An "engineer" was originally a soldier who designed military fortifications and/or operated engines of war such as catapults. What is often taken as the archetypical engineering school is the École Polytechnique founded at Paris in 1794, which became a military institution under Napoleon Bonaparte. In the US the first school to offer engineering degrees was the Military Academy at West Point founded in 1802. Within such contexts, the overarching duty of engineers, as with other soldiers, was to obey orders.

During the same period as the founding of professional engineering schools a few designers of "public works" began to call themselves "civil engineers" - a term which continues in some languages to denote all nonmilitary engineering. The creation of this civilian counterpart to armed forces engineering initially gave little reason to alter the basic sense of engineering obligation. Civil engineering was simply peacetime military engineering, with use and convenience replacing offensive and defensive utilities, and engineers remained duty-bound to obey those for whom they worked, whether some branch of the government or a private corporation.

The late eighteenth and early nineteenth centuries also witnessed formation of the first professional engineering societies as organizations. However, none of the original associations - which today would be called nongovernmental organizations - included any formal code of ethics. Formal ethics statements had to wait until the early twentieth century. On analogy with physicians and lawyers, whose codes prescribe a fundamental obligation to patients and clients, the early codes of conduct in professional engineering - such as those formulated in 1912 by the American Institute of Electrical Engineers (later to become the Institute of Electrical and Electronic Engineers) and in 1914 by the American Society of Civil Engineers - defined the primary duty of the engineer to serve as a "faithful agent or trustee" of an employing company.

There is undoubtedly some moral legitimacy in the related principles of obedience and loyalty. Loyalty, especially, is a widely recognized virtue under many circumstances. But the problem with any ethics code emphasizing obedience is that it leaves adherents subject to manipulation by external powers that may well be unjust. Even in the military, for instance, it is now acknowledged that a soldier is obligated to carry out only legitimate or just orders. Physicians and lawyers, too, are obligated to be loyal to their patients and clients, only to the extent that patients and clients pursue health and justice, respectively. Attempts to address this weakness in the principles of obedience and loyalty, and to articulate an ideal for engineering comparable to those of health in medicine and justice in law, gave rise to a second theory of engineering ethics.

Second ideal: technocratic leadership and efficiency

Slightly at odds with both the implicit code of obedience and the explicit code of company loyalty is the ideology of leadership in technological progress through pursuit of the ideals of technical perfection and efficiency. During the first third of the twentieth century in the US this vision of engineering activity spawned the technocracy movement or the idea that engineers should be given political and economic power. Although never explicitly articulated in the form of a code of conduct, it has influenced how engineers and the public think about the profession. Economist Thorstein Veblen, for example, argued that if engineers were freed from subservience to business interests their own standards of good and bad, right and wrong, would lead to the creation of a sounder economy and better consumer products.

The technocracy concept was formulated during the same historical period in which governments were establishing independent agencies to regulate transport, construction, communications, foods, pharmaceuticals, banking, and more. In all such cases technical experts from science and engineering were given governing responsibilities to oversee the operations of public and private activities with the aim of increasing perfection, efficiency, and safety. The pursuit of efficiency also spilled over from industrial to social life. Engineering efficiency became a model for enhancing personal use and convenience in managing one's health, finances, education, and general comportment.

Again there are good reasons to practice some degree of technocratic leadership and the pursuit of efficiency. Certainly the subordination of production to short-term money-making with little concern for the good of products being produced is not desirable in the long run, and inefficiency or waste readily seems to be another form of badness. Moreover, in a highly complex technical world it is often difficult for average citizens to know what would be in their own best interests. It remains an open question whether efficiency can be adequately promoted by consumer pull in imperfect markets or requires a push from technical professionals.

Nevertheless, when technical decision-making becomes an end, it is easily decoupled from general human welfare. Not only can regulatory agencies be captured by the industries or activities they are supposed to regulate but the pursuit of efficiency is not always compatible with personal happiness. The pursuit of technical perfection for its own sake is not always the best use of limited societal resources – as when, for example, cars are designed to go faster than the speed limits engineered into roadbeds. The concepts of technical perfection and efficiency virtually require the assumption of clearly defined boundary conditions that perforce can exclude important and relevant factors, including legitimate psychological, environmental, and human concerns. Think of how perfected mining machines can wreak havoc on mountain ecosystems or imagine how a perfected "happiness pill" that is safe and effective might diminish and flatten human life.

Technical efficiency entails minimizing inputs to achieve desired outputs or maximizing outputs from given inputs – or both. It therefore hinges completely on how inputs and outputs are framed, which is itself not a purely technical matter. From the examples above, should the integrity of mountain ecosystems be taken into account and what shall count as "happiness"? Technocracy shifts value decisions into the hands of technical experts away from the realm of democratic deliberation. In recognition of such objections there has developed a third theory of engineering ethics, that of social responsibility.

Third ideal: public safety, health, and welfare

The anti-nuclear weapons movement of the 1950s and 1960s and the consumer and environmental movements of the 1960s and 1970s provoked some engineers to challenge political and corporate direction. In conjunction with a renewed concern for democratic values and civil rights this led to new ideas about engineering ethics.

In the US the seeds of transformation were planted immediately after World War II when in 1947 the Engineers' Council for Professional Development (which later became ABET) drew up the first transdisciplinary engineering ethics code, committing the engineer "to interest himself [or herself] in public welfare." Revisions in 1963 and 1974 strengthened this commitment to the point where the first of four "fundamental principles" required engineers to use "their knowledge and skill for the enhancement of human welfare," and the first of seven "fundamental canons" stated that "Engineers shall hold paramount the safety, health and welfare of the public."

This third theory addresses many problems with the other two, and has been widely adopted by the professional engineering community. It also allows for the retention of desirable elements from prior theories. Obedience or loyalty remain, but within a larger framework where the primary loyalty is not to a corporation but to the public as a whole. Leadership in technical perfection and efficiency likewise remain, but are explicitly subordinated to the public welfare. There are nevertheless two issues that can be raised with regard to engineering responsibility for public safety, health, and welfare. One concerns whether engineers qua engineers really have any privileged knowledge with regard to safety, health, and welfare. The other concerns the relationship between engineers and the public they are ostensibly called on to protect.

Perspectives from various countries

The question of a social contract for engineering naturally raises further questions about the roles played by engineering in various social contexts. Issues of engineering ethics, for instance, often exhibit distinctive features across cultural and political geographies. Consider, for example, the character of engineering ethics discourse in four representative countries from Europe, Latin America, and Asia.

Germany: engineers and philosophers

The development of engineering ethics in Germany exhibits a more theoretical base than elsewhere. Immediately after World War II, because some members had been compromised by involvement with National Socialism, the Verein Deutscher Ingenieure (VDI or Association of German Engineers) undertook to promote philosophical reflection and self-criticism within the technical community. This led to a sustained dialogue between engineers and philosophers.

In the early 1950s, the VDI sponsored a series of conferences on "The Responsibility of Engineers," "Humanity and Work in the Technological Era," "Changes in Humanity through Technology," and "Humanity in the Force Field of Technology." Out of the first conference came "The Engineer's Confession," a Hippocratic-like oath for VDI members, and later the formation of a special *Mensch und Technik* (Humanity and Technology) committee composed of engineers and philosophers. Broken down into a number of working groups on "Pedagogy and Technology," "Sociology and Technology," "Religion and Technology," "Philosophy and Technology," etc., the *Mensch und Technik* groups produced by the mid-1970s a number of important studies focusing on technology and values.

This work in turn led to replacement of the "Engineer's Confession" and to further interdisciplinary engineering-philosophy research, especially on the theoretical framework of technology assessment. With regard to professional ethics, one 1980 *Mensch und Technik* report titled *VDI: Zukunftige Aufgaben* (VDI: Future Tasks) proposed simply: "The aim of all engineers is the improvement of the possibilities of life for all humanity by the development and appropriate application of technical means." Echoes of the Tredgold definition are obvious, but arguments in support of this thesis were made with philosophical reference to the ideas of Immanuel Kant, G.W.F. Hegel, and other German philosophers. As for technology assessment, a second working group in 1986 identified eight fields of value (environmental quality, health, safety, functionality, economics, living standards, personal development, and social quality), mapped out their interrelations, and developed a set of recommendations for implementation in the design of technical products and projects.[7] (See Figure 12.1.)

Such broad interests can also be found reflected in efforts to develop a Europe-wide approach to engineering ethics. For instance, at the beginning of the new millennium a multinational team of European engineering

[7] The previous three paragraphs are condensed from Huning and Mitcham 1993.

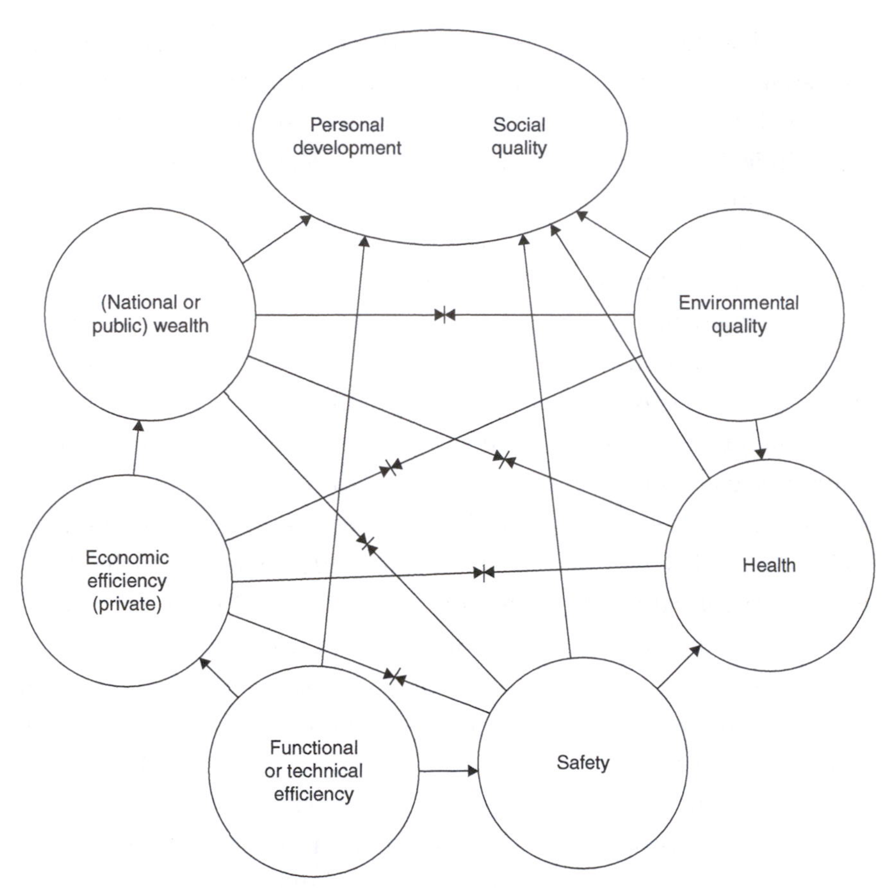

Figure 12.1 *Eight values for engineering.* Adapted from VDI-Richtlinien 3780, Technikbewertung: begriffe und Grundlagen (1991).

educators published a framework text which examined technical systems and decision-making, and introduced reflection on technological development as a whole as a social issue.[8] This last question, especially, tends to go well beyond the more standard forms of engineering ethics and to merge with the ethics and policy of technology.

Chile: codes with legal force

In another distinctive approach, the "Code of Professional Ethics of the Engineers of the Colegio de Ingenieros de Chile" (Association of Engineers

[8] Goujon and Dubreuil 2001.

of Chile) actually has the force of law, having been formulated in response to legislation calling for such codes in all professional organizations. Although the Colegio was founded in 1958, ironically the code was not formulated until it was required by the authoritarian regime of Augusto Pinochet in the early 1980s.

The Chilean code, like many in developing countries, does not mention any responsibility to public safety, health, and welfare. Instead, the code consists primarily of an extended list of actions deemed contrary to sound professional conduct, and thus punishable by professional censure. Among many unremarkable canons against conflict of interest, graft, etc., however, is one rejecting "actions or failures to act that favor or permit the unnecessary use of foreign engineering for objectives and work for which Chilean engineering is sufficient and adequate." Such a canon, emphasizing national interests, can also be found in other codes throughout Latin America, from Argentina to Venezuela.

Such a canon need not have simply nationalistic implications. Many countries experience a serious difficulty in addressing their own problems. Driven by mimetic desire, engineers and scientists in developing countries often devote themselves to high-tech pursuits that yield international prestige rather than to less glamorous but more useful tasks.

In promulgating its professional code, the Colegio of Chile also published a pamphlet that included the Code of Professional Ethics of the Unión Panaméricana de Asociaciones de Ingenieros (Pan American Union of Associations of Engineers). This transnational code is one of only three in existence, the other two being those of the Fédération Européenne d'Associations Nationales d'Ingénieurs (European Federation of National Engineering Associations) and the World Federation of Engineering Organizations. All three transnational codes, appropriately enough, place great stress on the public good or social responsibility – and especially on protection of the environment.

Japan: merging science and engineering

Japanese engineering has not always been separated from science as much as it has in Europe or the US. This is exemplified in one of the first and most influential code-like documents, a 1954 "Statement on Atomic

Research in Japan" issued by the Japanese Science Council (JSC), which includes both scientists and engineers. This statement set forth what have become known as the "Three Principles for the Peaceful Use of Atomic Energy": all research shall be conducted with full openness to the public, democratically administered, and carried out under the autonomous control of the Japanese themselves.

These principles reflected a desire among the Japanese during the 1950s to distance themselves from US interests and policy (the Allied occupation ended in 1952). Immediately after World War II, the US had prohibited all Japanese research in aviation, atomic energy, and any other war-related area. But in the mid-1950s, following a Communist victory in China and the outbreak of war in Korea, US policy shifted toward encouraging certain kinds of military-related science and engineering and the incorporation of Japan into the Western alliance. Indeed, Japanese scientists and engineers recognized that the Three Principles were at odds with, for example, the US policy of secrecy in atomic research. Perhaps in order to avoid publicity and the possible development of opposition, the JSC statement was not initially translated into English. It also stated a policy which, although formulated by scientists and engineers, was readily adopted by the government, thus reflecting the greater political influence of the Japanese technical community in comparison with other countries.

However, in the 1990s this prestige was called into question by some well-publicized incidents associated with nuclear power generation – a sodium leak at the Monju fast-breeder reactor (1995) and a criticality accident at the Tokaimura reactor (1999). Public reaction influenced the Japanese Accreditation Board for Engineering Education (JABEE) to introduce in 2000 new requirements that accredited engineering degree programs include cultivating an understanding of engineering ethics and the social responsibilities of engineers. But unlike the related ABET criterion, the JABEE ethics criterion is listed up front, even before scientific and technical knowledge. For Japanese engineers, reflecting a strong sense of communal responsibility in their culture as a whole, ethics is high on the educational agenda. This is likely to become even more pronounced as a result of the Fukushima Daiichi nuclear disaster following the Tohoku earthquake and tsunami in March 2011.

China: tradition and modernity

As the most populous and rapidly developing country in world history, the People's Republic of China (PRC) – which across the twentieth century arguably experienced more wrenching social change than any other – is home to large-scale engineering achievements and sobering disasters. Just consider the Great Wall and Grand Canal or the Three Gorges Dam and a system of high-speed trains more extensive than in the rest of the world combined. At the same time, in 1975 the Banqiao Reservoir Dam collapse caused more casualties than any other dam failure in history; in 2009 a twelve-story apartment building on the outskirts of Shanghai toppled over due to a foundation failure; and in 2011 two high-speed trains collided in Zhejiang Province, causing the second-deadliest such accident in the world. Environmental pollution is as bad as in any developing country and has impacts far beyond China's borders.

Additionally, in China remarkably large numbers of engineers occupy political leadership positions in the Chinese Communist Party and PRC. There is also more discourse on the ethics of science and engineering than in any other developing country or in any other country at a historically comparable stage of technological development. During the 1990s, the Graduate University of the Chinese Academy of Sciences established a program on the philosophy of technology and engineering, and subsequently founded the Chinese journal, *Engineering Studies* (2004–present).

Engineering ethics discourse in these contexts struggles with tensions inherited from pre-Communist China (efforts to overthrow feudalism and colonialism), years of dominance by Mao Zedong (red versus expert), and opening up under engineer Deng Xiaoping (rapid economic development and globalization). As one young scholar has described the situation, "engineering and engineering ethics studies in China [are drawing] on resources from China's long cultural history, reconstructing the Marxist social criticism of technology, and learning from European and North American intellectuals" to ask

> How can science, technology, and engineering best contribute to enhancing Chinese ways of life? What is the most ethical way to deal with the social and environmental problems that often arise from

technological and engineering change? How can we avoid engineering mistakes while promoting Chinese economic development?

Working with such questions, Chinese scholars have "a responsibility to think globally and to rethink locally in order to redefine the significance of 'made in China.'"[9]

Confidence and doubt in engineering

Despite many differences across various countries, one common denominator is a confidence with regard to engineering action as inherently policy relevant. Doubts can nevertheless be raised about any unqualified commitment to engineering for policy. One question concerns the public bias in favor of action. At the level of personal morality, our intuition is to distinguish between action that produces harm and inaction that allows harm to occur. For pushing a person in front of a car, someone is culpable; for failing to grab a person who is running in front of a car, people are not. For the former commission of an action that produces harm, we hold ourselves responsible and punish others; for the latter omission of actions that allow harm to occur, we feel regret or express apology and commiserate with others. The intuition has in fact been codified in the motto, *Primum non nocere*, Latin for "First, do no harm," which plays a major role in biomedical ethics. It also underlies what is known as the precautionary principle: that any action or policy, especially those affecting the environment, must be shown not harmful before being implemented.[10]

There are, however, multiple problems with the nonmaleficence principle. One is the *reductio ad absurdum* that taken literally it biases inaction over action to such an extent that one might well argue it implies quietism as the most moral behavior. ("Don't do something, just stand there.") Furthermore, is there not something naive about such a principle, insofar as it presumes there could be actions to achieve benefits that would never have any negative side effects or unintended consequences? The idea that one could have a deontological obligation not to harm, to which any consequentialist obligation to do good must remain hostage, seems especially unreasonable in the public policy realm. Is it not better to approach policy

[9] Qin 2010, pp. 101 and 104. [10] Harremoës 2002.

implementations in terms of costs, benefits, and trade-offs? Engineers especially find it difficult simply to stand by and not act.

Braden Allenby and Daniel Sarewitz distinguish three levels of cause-and-effect relationships in engineering. Level I occurs when a specific device is engineered to achieve a clearly defined social goal: "a vaccine prevents a particular disease, or a ... manufacturing process eliminates the use of toxic chemicals." Here one can be confident of the results because the policy goal and engineered means to the goal are simple and direct. At Level II, engineering becomes part of "a networked social and cultural phenomenon [functioning] in a broader context that can be complicated, messy, and far less predictable or understandable." Examples include transport and communication systems. At Level II, "acting to achieve a particular intended outcome is often difficult because the internal system behavior is too complicated to predict." Confidence wanes, but without being wholly overwhelmed by doubt.

The first two levels are familiar and engineers can make reasonable efforts to assess the outcomes, intended and unintended, of their actions into systems. At Level III, however, the system has become so large and complex that its boundaries are difficult to determine; it has become a "complex, constantly changing and adapting system in which human, built, and natural elements interact in ways that produce emergent behaviors which may be difficult to perceive, much less understand and manage." At this level, it is reasonable for doubt to trump confidence. The experience of the techno-lifeworld, according to Allenby and Sarewitz, is that "We inhabit Level III, but we act as if we live on Level II, and we work with Level I tools."[11]

What does this recognition imply? The authors appear to recommend simply the practice of greater caution. Despite confidence in the analysis itself, doubts arise about the practical adequacy of the recommendation.

Toward a duty *plus respicere* in engineering - and in science

Across multiple issues considered in this volume, we have proposed that the most general ethical obligation of those engaged with science - whether

[11] Allenby and Sarewitz 2011, pp. 63 and 161.

scientists, engineers, or all of us living in and depending on the techno-lifeworld – is a duty to take more into account, to enlarge the scope of reflection. Let us call this a duty *plus respicere*, from the Latin *plus*, more + *respicere*, to be concerned about. In different contexts this duty can involve movement across disciplines of expertise, going out from communities of expertise into the larger techno-lifeworld, and reaching from the techno-lifeworld into the realms of expertise. As a fitting conclusion to the final chapter, let us sketch an argument to this effect.

One unifier of various engineering activities throughout its disciplinary branches and cultural contexts is design. The research engineer investigates new principles and processes, which a development engineer can use for designing the prototype of a new product, process, or system. Prototype design will then be modified by the production engineer so that it is more easily manufactured, while operational and maintenance engineers have input from the perspectives of their engagements. But the central activity is that of designing, which must take into account production, marketing, maintenance, and use. As such engineering design aims at creating systems, devices, and processes that are desirable and socially valuable. The design activity is one "in which engineers translate certain functions or aims into a working product or system."[12]

For design to become more than dreaming, for it to become serious, it must involve making, the introduction of something new into the world. This making begins in miniature and moves toward making at an intended use scale. But as making, at all levels it has impact on the world, however small. Science may plausibly claim that the outcome of its research activity is a nonphysical reality, namely knowledge, which can only have an indirect influence. By contrast, the outcome of engineering design research is often a physical object that becomes part of the physical world. If it is successful it may even become an exceptionally significant part of the world.

Engineering design is further motivated by a restlessness that imparts to it a profoundly active and transformative character. The method of "testing to destruction," in which devices or materials are intentionally loaded until they fail, in order to discover their limits and thus improve a design, is in this sense a revealing aspect of engineering.

[12] Van de Poel and Royakkers 2011, p. 165.

External impact of engineering

Testing to destruction readily leaves the engineering laboratory and becomes part of general engineering practice. According to Henry Petroski, "To understand what engineering is and what engineers do is to understand how failures can happen and how they can contribute more than successes to advance technology."[13] This normalacy of using to failure is what leads Martin and Schinzinger to argue for conceiving of engineering as social experimentation.

It is precisely this turning of the world into a laboratory that produces the unique ethical challenges of a technoscientific society. According to the German philosopher Hans Lenk, a member of the VDI *Mensch und Technik* committee, the expanding impact of modern engineering can be summarized as follows. In contrast to premodern technics, modern engineering influences more people, natural systems, and future generations than ever before. Moreover, not only have human beings become research subjects, so has their genetic structure and behavior, with personal privacy also increasingly at risk. Finally, engineering design research introduces a new dynamism into all human action by investing more and more of its dimensions with that restlessness that is the hallmark of engineering.[14]

In short, engineering now has an impact across space and through time greater than any other human action; think nuclear weapons and global atmospheric CO_2 concentrations. It also extends more deeply into human nature, both psychologically and physiologically; think information technology and genetic engineering. Finally, the opening of such technical possibilities through engineering tends to draw human action into its dynamic vortex. As the atomic scientist J. Robert Oppenheimer remarked about the design for a hydrogen bomb, which he opposed developing, the possibility was so "technically sweet" it could not fail to be tried. The question of the wisdom of engaging in promoting such restlessness must be an ultimate issue of the ethics of engineering.

The internal character of engineering

This "external" feature of engineering design is complemented by an "internal" feature of modeling. Modeling is not only a miniature making

[13] Petroski 1985, p. xii. [14] Lenk 1983, pp. 196–197.

but also an idealization or a simplification. Because it is simplification oriented toward making, it is not particularly concerned with truth. Conceptually shallow models can be technoscientifically powerful.

Engineering models the world by simplifying it, by focusing on only some one aspect of what is. Free-body diagrams, for instance, treat an object *as if* all forces were acting directly on its center of gravity, in order to model matter–force interactions. But this "as if" denotes also something that *is not*. The simplified model is not the complex reality. All forces do not act on the center of gravity of some object; many act on its surface, which may alter the effect in complex ways. To concentrate on gross problems it is not only permissible to ignore such complexities, but better. Otherwise action can be held up indefinitely.

The paradox is that precisely from not reflecting the complexity of reality comes power to change what is into something that is not yet. The modeling of terrestrial gravity, for instance, as independent of Sun, Moon, planets, and all variations in geology makes possible the calculation of the trajectories of military projectiles. The carefully defined boundary conditions within which the mechanical engineer determines efficiency – taking into account only mechanical energy and heat, but not social dislocation or pollution or biological destruction – is what makes possible improvements in the strictly mechanical functioning of engines.

More generally, looking at the world as a whole as if it were a clock, or the brain as if it were a computer, or thought as if it were an electrochemical process, brings with it tremendous power to transform the thing modeled precisely by overlooking the rich complexity of its reality, by abstracting from the lifeworld within which we actually live. It is thus no accident that engineering design, given its inner demands for idealization, should readily abstract from and refuse to consider one of the most subtle dimensions of the lifeworld – that is, ethics.

Dangers of idealization

With the overlooking of many aspects of reality that is an inner feature of engineering comes not only power but danger – the danger of overlooking something important. Indeed, what failure points up is precisely that something has been overlooked. Since simplification is an inner methodological feature of engineering, and there will always be occasions when it is not possible to anticipate what particular idealization parameters are fully appropriate, important aspects of things can regularly be expected to be overlooked – thus creating failures small and large, risks minimal and great.

When dealing with progressively more complex projects, and their risks, engineers attempt to develop more complex models. Inherent within engineering design methods is not only a movement toward simplification but also a countermovement toward "complexification." Systems engineering, interdisciplinary engineering, the transformation of civil into environmental engineering, and multifactor technology assessments all illustrate this latter tendency.

Yet a general modeling conundrum may be stated as follows: the use of a simplifying model in a technical design process also complicates the process, since it introduces a new factor to be considered, namely the relation between the model and the phenomenon modeled. To attempt to model this new relationship will only further complicate the situation. More simply put: there is no way to model a model. One can only attend to the modeled (real-world) phenomenon, attempt to take into account all relevant factors, and then pay attention to see if in reality things work the way the model projects.

While implicit in interdisciplinary design, environmental engineering, and approaches that envision engineering as part of larger sociotechnical systems, the principle involved here is seldom formulated as such, and thus deserves explicit articulation. From the perspective of engineering design, the fundamental imperative in the face of failure amid complexity can be phrased as "Take more factors into account."

The obligation to take more into account, as a general counterbalance to model simplification, has a moral dimension, not just because it can on occasion avoid some specific harm. The moral dimension of taking more into account is realized when it links engineering design research into more general considerations of and reflections on the good. In this sense the duty *plus respicere* may be thought of as the engineering equivalent of the motto "Think globally, act locally."

Stating the issue even more pointedly: to take more into account in engineering will include taking ethics into account. The problem of the remoteness and subtlety of ethical factors in engineering research and design is obvious. Indeed, this itself might even be said to constitute a distinct ethical problem. Thus an imperative to seek to reduce such remoteness becomes part of the duty *plus respicere*.

Summary

As science increasingly becomes commercialized and technological, the ethics of science must expand to include issues and themes that have characterized ethical reflection on engineering. Engineering as a distinct profession emerged as an effort to extend appropriate aspects of science into practical affairs for human use and convenience. The profession has historically held three theories about its primary functional obligations: obedience to authority and company loyalty; technocratic leadership in efficiency and perfection; responsibility to protect public safety, health, and welfare.

The engineering for policy aspect of the contract argues that the integration of engineering into public policy formation is even more important for enhancing public intelligence than is the case with science. A survey of engineering and ethics in the context of Germany, Chile, Japan, and China confirms the practice of policy-relevant engineering in multiple forms. At the same time, there also exists a dialectic of confidence and doubt in the ability of engineering to function effectively in the policy context.

The best hope for a more effective integration of engineering into public affairs lies with the practice of a duty *plus respicere*, to take more into account. An argument for such a duty makes the following points. Engineering is characterized by a restless dissatisfaction with the current state of the world and the drive to design a better world. It exercises power over the world by overlooking its rich complexity. This introduces the danger that something important may be overlooked, which in turn has given rise to movements such as systems engineering and participatory and values-sensitive design to introduce more complexity into engineering models. The fundamental imperative for engineers operating in a complex, interdependent world thus becomes: take more things into account. This imperative also increasingly pertains to scientists who now conduct their research in an age of accountability: scientists are being asked to take the broader impacts of their work into account.

Extending reflection: sustainability and geoengineering

Among some engineers the sense of ethical responsibility to protect public safety, health, and welfare has been reframed as a concern for sustainability. As a concept, sustainable development is subject to two quite different interpretations. In one the focus on sustainability implies some form of protection of the environment; in the other what is to be sustained is the process of development. Although the concept of sustainability is thus fraught with difficulties, it has arguably become a new name for the good and thus deserving of extended ethical attention.

Professor of Technology, Policy, and Management Karel Mulder at the Delft University of Technology (Netherlands) puts the case for engineering attention to issues of sustainability in the following terms:

> Engineers are future builders. They shape the world through their product and process designs, their management of technical systems and their innovations. It is the task of the engineer – in co-operation with other disciplines – to meet the needs of our society.

Because science teaches us that industrial society is no longer sustainable, this society must undergo a fundamental transformation in which engineers will "play an essential role." But engineers are not being "trained to undertake this important task." In order to encourage "scientifically trained engineers [to] focus on questions of sustainability" Mulder promotes the teaching of "sustainable development for engineers." Although engineers are embedded in a society that does not always appreciate the need for sustainable approaches, "engineers should [still] learn to think strategically about the sustainability challenges."[15]

Mulder concludes with an important qualifier. Although engineering "can and will have a major role to play in sustainable development," it will never

> relieve us of our problems at no cost and without requiring any further adaptation. Solutions will always be "socio-technical."[16]

Indeed, without this recognition, improved technologies can actually become enemies of truly sustainable development. Equally important, a

[15] Mulder 2006, p. 9. [16] Mulder 2006, p. 273.

demand for fully sustainable technologies can undermine taking meliorating action now.

The former point alludes to what is known as the Jevons paradox. In 1865 the British economist and philosopher William Stanley Jevons investigated industrial efforts to improve efficiency in order to cut down the use of coal, a limited resource. His discovery was that rather than reducing consumption, increases in efficiency actually increased it. In more general terms, the Jevons paradox argues that improvements in sustainability at the level of engineering will not necessarily produce sustainable development at the societal level. This highlights the centrality of human desires and character to any consideration of sustainability. Without self-control, any savings made from efficiency measures may simply be diverted into more resource use – especially as a consumerist image of the good life remains ascendant.

The latter point echoes an equally important counsel in ethics: do not let the perfect become an enemy of the good. Because of the dangers of the pursuit of moral perfectionism, philosophers as different as Buddha, Confucius, and Aristotle have argued that action should aim at a mean between extremes of excess and defect. In the early twentieth century, research by the Italian engineer and philosopher Vilfredo Pareto led to formulation of a related 80–20 rule: that it takes 20 percent of the work to complete the first 80 percent of a task; the last 20 percent of the task takes 80 percent of the work. The American philosopher of design Herbert Simon argued that because of limits to knowledge and time, the better response to tasks by real-world engineers and decision-makers is not to seek optimum or perfect solutions but simply adequate ones. Optimizing strategies are trumped by what Simon termed "satisficing" (from satisfy + suffice) strategies.

However, there may be dangers in being content with satisficing. One of the most ambitious attempts to pursue sustainability in the grand manner, to some extent without worrying overly much about perfection, is called earth systems engineering and management (ESEM). ESEM is an emerging field of research that seeks to analyze, design, and manage coupled human-natural systems on large, even planetary, scales.[17] The basic impulse behind ESEM is recognition of what Allenby and Sarewitz describe

[17] See Allenby 2005.

as the complexities of Level III technology. Environmental problems and ecological systems are too complex and integrated to be treated in a piecemeal fashion.

One prominent type of ESEM research is "geoengineering" or proposals for the deliberate manipulation of the Earth's climate in order to counteract the unsustainable effects of greenhouse gas emissions. It is, thus, a third type of response to anthropogenic climate change: mitigation seeks to reduce greenhouse gas emissions; adaptation seeks to reduce the vulnerability of human and natural systems to climate change effects; and geoengineering seeks to alter the climate in order to effectively neutralize the effects of greenhouse gas emissions.

Geoengineering has garnered increasingly serious attention in light of continued political failures to accomplish mitigation and adaptation objectives. There are two main kinds of geoengineering strategies, those that would reduce the amount of solar radiation entering the Earth's atmosphere (solar radiation management) and those that would scrub carbon dioxide from the atmosphere. Examples of the former include the lacing of the upper atmosphere with particles of sulfur to make it more reflective and the deployment of giant mirrors into low Earth orbit to reflect incoming solar radiation. An example of the latter is iron fertilization, the introduction of iron into the upper ocean to stimulate a phytoplankton bloom that would draw carbon dioxide from the atmosphere. Many of the strategies are so inexpensive that they could be undertaken by a single research team, not to mention a nation acting on its own.

Geoengineering clearly illustrates the external impacts of engineering since the entire planet would become a laboratory for studying the efficacy of various climate management strategies. It also demonstrates the problems of idealization. Any geoengineering project would rely on models that simplify the complex systems to be manipulated. This introduces the possibility that something important will be overlooked. What will be the fate of the carbon sequestered by the phytoplankton and what ecological effects will the massive bloom cause? What are the long-term consequences of continually lacing the atmosphere with sulfur? How would the climate react if the mirrors suddenly stopped functioning? Might the resulting climate shifts benefit different parts of the planet unevenly? What unintended consequences might result from planetary-scale engineering projects?

The danger of overlooking something important has prompted many to contend that geoengineering should not be conducted. It is, they argue, hubris to pretend that human beings can "design" or "manage" the Earth. This may indicate how, if we really attempt to take more into account, action might be paralysed by all the thinking that must be done. It also raises a peculiar twist that could be given to the notion of taking more into account. Perhaps the goal should be to lead lives and create societies where there is less that needs to be taken into account. In this case, for example, perhaps humans should relinquish lifeways that have such broad-ranging and long-lasting planetary impacts.

Others see geoengineering as a last-ditch effort that should only be implemented if, in the words of the US presidential science adviser John Holdren, "we get desperate enough." What nearly everyone now agrees, however, "is that the technology necessary to reshape the climate is so powerful, and so easily implemented, that the world must decide how to govern its use before the wrong nation - or even the wrong individual - starts to change the climate all on its own."[18]

In 2010 a group of scientists and engineers convened the Asilomar International Conference on Climate Intervention Technologies, modeled on the 1975 Asilomar Conference on Recombinant DNA to develop guidelines for bioengineering. As a result of its deliberations, the conference formulated five principles to guide the responsible pursuit of geoengineering:

1. Promoting the collective benefit of humankind and the environment must be the primary purpose.
2. Governments must clarify responsibilities, and, when necessary, create new mechanisms for the governance and oversight of large-scale climate engineering research activities.
3. Climate-engineering research should be conducted openly and cooperatively, preferably within a framework that has broad international support.
4. Assessing potential intended and unintended consequences, impacts, and risks will be critical to providing policymakers and the public with the information needed to evaluate the potential for climate

[18] Wood 2009, n.p.

engineering to be implemented as a complement to mitigation and adaptation.
5. Public participation and consultation in research planning and oversight, assessments, and development of decision-making mechanisms and processes must be provided to ensure consideration of the international and intergenerational implications of climate engineering.[19]

To what extent are these five principles adequate? How are they linked to concerns for sustainability? To what extent do they apply in different ways to science and to engineering? What are their implications, if any, for science that is not associated with geoengineering?

Questions for research and discussion

1. Reflect on the relationships acknowledged as relevant to engineering ethics (relationships among engineers, between engineers and employers or clients, and between engineers and society – as well as between engineers and the natural environment). To what extent are these relationships similarly conceived and operative in the ethics of science?
2. The linear model vision of science promoting national health, economic prosperity, and military security may apply more to science translated into engineering than it does to science itself. Consider this suggestion in relation to the professional engineering ethics obligations to the protection of public safety, health, and welfare. What are the overlaps? What are the relationships? What might these in turn suggest about relationships among science, engineering, and ethics?
3. Investigate the concept of a "technological fix." To what extent is a technological fix a kind of engineering for policy?
4. What further arguments can be developed for or against a duty *plus respicere*? What might be its implications, positive and negative? How might it apply differently in different types of engineering or science?

[19] Asilomar Scientific Organizing Committee 2010, p. 9.

Further reading about the cases

Goodell, Jeff (2010) *How to Cool the Planet: Geoengineering and the Audacious Quest to Fix Earth's Climate*. Boston: Houghton Mifflin.

Kintisch, Eli (2010) *Hack the Planet: Science's Best Hope – or Worst Nightmare – for Averting Climate Catastrophe*. Hoboken, NJ: John Wiley & Sons.

Launder, Brian, and Michael Thompson, eds. (2010) *Geo-Engineering Climate Change: Environmental Necessity or Pandora's Box?* Cambridge University Press.

McDonald, Allan, and James Hansen (2009) *Truth, Lies, and O-Rings: Inside the Space Shuttle Challenger Disaster*. Tallahassee, FL: University Press of Florida.

Pinkus, Rosa Lynn, Larry Shuman, Norman Hummon, and Harvey Wolfe (1997) *Engineering Ethics: Balancing Cost, Schedule, and Risk – Lessons Learned from the Space Shuttle*. Cambridge University Press.

Vaughan, Diane (1996) *The Challenger Launch Decision: Risky Technology, Culture, and Deviance at NASA*. University of Chicago Press.

Epilogue: Looking back, leaning forward

The moral character of scientists

By way of conclusion, let us briefly meditate on a central paradox in the development of modern science. We first state it bluntly and then unpack it a bit, but we intentionally leave loose ends to discourage any temptation to think there are easy answers.

Here is the paradox. When science was a more personal matter, conducted by amateurs on the margins of society, scientists were imbued with a more public sense of responsibility. But just when science became more public – when it was enrolled into institutions of commerce and politics, money and power – scientists shrunk their sense of responsibility. In short, just when science became a powerful social force scientists became parochial laborers, responsible only to a narrow community of disciplinary peers. This mismatch, we believe, must be rectified. Scientists must reclaim a broader moral responsibility and rediscover a sense of science as a higher calling, a vocation, and not just another job.

The transition of science from vocation to job was traced and lamented in the 1925 novel by Sinclair Lewis, *Arrowsmith*. It was the first major novel to ruminate on the place of a newly powerful science in society. The crucial monologue by the medical scientist Max Gottlieb decries the shrinking of the scientist's role to that of a worker just like anyone else:

> To be a scientist – it is not just a different job, so that a man should choose between being a scientist and being an explorer or a bond-salesman or a physician or a king or a farmer. It is a tangle of very obscure emotions, like mysticism, or wanting to write poetry; it makes its victim all different from the good normal man. The normal man, he does not care much what he does except that he should eat and sleep and make love. But the scientist is intensely religious – he is so religious that he will not accept quarter truths, because they are an insult to his faith ... To be a scientist is like being a Goethe: it is born in you.[1]

[1] Lewis 1925, p. 279.

The routinization of science escalated after World War II, to the point where some began to worry about its effects on the character of scientists. For example, the mathematician Norbert Wiener lamented "the degradation of the scientist as an independent worker and thinker to that of morally irresponsible stooge in a science-factory." He called for scientists to resist becoming the "milk cows of power."[2] Should scientists think of science as just another job? Is it just a means to a paycheck, health insurance, and a pension? Does it matter who is writing the paycheck or in what causes one's scientific work is enrolled?

Consider this line from a song by the American songwriter, musician, and satirist Tom Lehrer: "'Once the rockets are up, who cares where they come down? That's not my department,' says Wernher von Braun."[3] Von Braun was a German rocket scientist who led the development of the V-2 combat rocket used by the Nazis during World War II. The V-2 is estimated to have killed or injured nearly 10,000 people in London during the war. After the war, von Braun worked for the US government and supervised development of the Saturn V booster rocket, which was used to land the first person on the Moon. In 1975, he received the US National Medal of Science.

Von Braun's career models the image of science as neutral tool and the scientist as the on-tap worker. He can work for Nazis building weapons to kill people or he can work for Americans building rockets to take people to the Moon. What is the difference as long as he has institutional support and the money to pursue his ideas? We should also wonder why he should be praised for peaceful uses of rockets but not blamed for the violent ones. Can a scientist take credit for the good outcomes of research, but disown the bad outcomes as "not in my department"? What are the responsibilities of scientists? What, exactly, is in their department?

Since World War II – just when science became world-transforming – the answer to this question has been circumscribed: scientists are responsible solely to their community of peers. They should do honest work that is deposited into a reservoir of knowledge. Society may use that knowledge for ill but that is not the scientists' responsibility. Scientists are morally exempt from the consequences of their research. Yet, oddly, their work is funded based on a general belief that scientific progress, as guided and judged by peers seeking only to advance their specialty, is somehow automatically good for society.

[2] In Shapin 2008, p. 82.

[3] A 1965 performance of the song, *Wernher von Braun*, by Lehrer can be found on the YouTube website, www.youtube.com/watch?v=kTKn1aSOyOs.

But as we lean forward into the future, that belief is wearing thin. Society is increasingly demanding that scientists think through the broader social and ethical implications of their research. Scientists are being asked to match their world-transforming technical powers with a proportional power of moral imagination.

This requires rethinking the notion that science is just another job, or what the historian of science Steven Shapin called "moral equivalence": scientists are just ordinary people doing ordinary jobs. It is commonplace by now to suppose that scientists possess no special claim to moral wisdom or virtuous character. Doing good science, we all tend to think, does not require one to be a good person, to possess a special talent for ethical reflection, or to have a privileged insight into what makes a good society.

The sociologist of science Robert K. Merton maintained that there was nothing special about scientists as people. They are not "recruited from the ranks of those who exhibit an unusual degree of moral integrity."[4] This is acceptable as long as the essential task of science is "the extension of certified knowledge," that is, producing research that passes muster with one's peers. This is only instrumental rationality – finding the best means for given ends. Insofar as science is divorced from the ends, scientists need not consider them.

But the task of science is being broadened. Scientific rationality now increasingly includes moral cognition about what ought to be. For example, scientists seeking funding from the US NSF (National Science Foundation) must give equal consideration both to the intellectual quality and to the broader social impacts of their work. Additionally, scientists conducting research with human subjects must design experiments that are not just intellectually but also ethically fruitful. Part of science entails reflecting on what is the right thing to do.

If scientists are to undertake broader ethical inquiry as part and parcel of scientific rationality, then they need to be more than just instrumental technicians. We need our scientists to be virtuous. Because they possess tremendous powers to shape our beliefs, actions, and world, they must shoulder a proportional duty to take more into account. They need to be good at ethical judgment and moral imagination.

There are precedents for the moral leadership of scientists. Aristotle thought the possession of natural knowledge improves the character of the knower. Joseph Priestley, the eighteenth-century Unitarian chemist, similarly believed

[4] Merton 1973, pp. 275–276.

"a Philosopher ought to be something greater and better than another man."[5] For Aristotle, the natural world was bound up with the moral world – contemplation of the former yielded insights into the latter. For Priestley, the natural world was God's second book – studying it both required and conferred a nobility of character.

But modern science pictures what Max Weber called a "disenchantment of the world" – mere matter in motion. Knowing about this world can help us to manipulate it instrumentally to serve various ends. But the ends, the values, are extrinsic to the science. Scientists have no business there. If science is merely instrumental, divorced from considerations of ends, then we face the very real possibility of rational irresponsibility. We may, for example, very rationally make deadly rockets or design a civilization-ending pathogen. The latter, as we continue to lean forward, is something that could well be done in a garage from supplies ordered over the Internet. As a mere instrument, peer review just ensures the efficacy of the bomb or the virulence of the disease.

Do we need to abandon the modern image of nature as mere stuff to be instrumentally manipulated? Or can we still think that way but nonetheless conceive of science again as a noble vocation that requires and cultivates moral wisdom? Somehow, we need to go beyond the mentality displayed by the physicist Richard Feynman when he celebrated the "social irresponsibility" of the scientist. The questions a scientist can answer, he argued, are limited to the kinds "you can put this way: 'if I do this, what will happen?' Questions like, 'should I do this?' and 'what is the value of this?' are not of the same kind ... That is the step the scientist cannot take."[6]

Scientists may nevertheless have to take that step and make the consideration of ends intrinsic to scientific reasoning. In a world constantly transformed by technoscience, the scientist, perforce, becomes the scientist-ethicist. Rationality, perhaps through expanded forms of "peer" review, becomes substantive (considering ends) and not just instrumental (limited to means).

This is additional cognitive labor, but if scientists do not do it, someone else will do it for them. Social control will increase, "ethics experts" will clog laboratories, and new rules will proliferate. This is why Alvin Weinberg, a nuclear physicist who helped administer the Manhattan Project, wrote, "As much out of prudent concern for their own survival as for any loftier motive ...

[5] Quoted from Shapin 2008, p. 24.

[6] Feynman 1998, pp. 16–17. Feynman was not surprisingly a defender of the moral equivalence of the scientist. Even though he became somewhat of a scientific celebrity, he claimed to be just an ordinary person working hard. See Shapin 2008, p. 83.

scientists must acquire the habit of scrutinizing what they do from a broader point of view than has been their custom."[7]

But how far can we stretch this responsibility of the scientist to take more into account? After all, just about anything could potentially be used by nefarious actors to cause harm. Reflecting on all the potential bad outcomes that might one day arise indirectly from one's work would cause total paralysis. This poses what the philosopher Stanley Rosen calls "the ultimate absurdity of the attack against the enlightenment." In short, "all fundamental aspects of the natural sciences ... may lead to the destruction of the human race ... Whereas no one would argue the wisdom of attempting to prevent a nuclear holocaust or the biochemical pollution of the environment, not many are prepared to admit that the only secure way in which to protect ourselves against science is to abolish it entirely."[8]

If we are to avoid this absurd conclusion and continue to live with the ambiguous outcomes of the Enlightenment, then nonscientists too must shoulder a broader set of responsibilities. We all form beliefs and take actions on the basis of what we take to be scientific authority. We all use and build our lives around the technologies that science helps make possible. We all, then, have a duty to take more into account when we form our view of the world and take action in it. It is not sufficient to delegate this cognitive responsibility to the experts in an act of blind faith. We must get involved in the technoscientific activities that are transforming our world.

In his essay "What is Enlightenment?" Immanuel Kant argued that enlightenment simply means "Dare to know!" Enlightenment is emerging from immaturity, or the inability to use understanding without guidance from others. Yet too often, in a supposedly enlightened era, we encounter the dogmatic slumbers of people who refuse to think for themselves. They assume too readily in a technocratic and bureaucratic age that someone else – someone with a degree and certification – has it all figured out and will tell them what to do. This is a threat to enlightenment and democracy.

We must not let others do the thinking for us. We must question scientists and experts of all stripes. Insofar as we can be up to that challenge, we will be participating in the essential activity shared by science and ethics: thinking for one's self rather than conforming.

[7] Weinberg 1963, p. 171. [8] Rosen 1989, p. 8.

Appendix: Ethics codes

This appendix contains information for accessing a wide range of influential science ethics codes and declarations. In addition to the websites listed, many of these documents and other related codes, statements, and declarations can be found in appendix V in volume IV (pp. 2158–2296) of Mitcham (2005).

1 Hippocratic Oath (fifth century BCE)

Ancient oath requiring physicians to swear upon a number of healing gods and to uphold certain professional ethical standards. The National Library of Medicine, nlm.nih.gov/hmd/greek/greek_oath.html.

2 The Nuremberg Code (1947)

The first and perhaps most influential code outlining ethical guidelines for the treatment of human subjects of medical research. National Institutes of Health, http://ohsr.od.nih.gov/guidelines/nuremberg.html.

3 World Medical Association: Declaration of Geneva or International Code of Medical Ethics (1948)

A declaration of the physician's dedication to the humanitarian goals of medicine. Updated in 1968, 1984, 1994, 2005, and 2006. World Medical Association, www.wma.net/en/30publications/10policies/c8/index.html.

4 The Einstein-Russell Manifesto (1955)

A statement calling on scientists to convene a conference to consider the perils that have arisen as a result of nuclear arms proliferation. Pugwash Conference on Science and World Affairs, www.pugwash.org/about/manifesto.htm.

5 World Medical Association: Declaration of Helsinki (1964) and (2008)

A set of ethical principles for human experimentation developed by the medical community. Widely regarded as one of the most influential statements on the issue. Revised multiple times, most significantly in 1975 and 2000. World Medical Association, www.wma.net/en/30publications/10policies/b3/index.html.

6 The National Commission for the Protection of Human Subjects of Biomedical and Behavioral Research: The Belmont report (1979)

A set of ethical principles for human experimentation developed by the first US federal-level bioethics committee. Directly informed the development of US law on this matter. National Institutes of Health, http://ohsr.od.nih.gov/guidelines/belmont.html.

7 Association for Computing Machinery: Code of Ethics and Professional Conduct (1992)

A code consisting of twenty-four imperatives that identify the key elements of ethical conduct for computing professionals. Association for Computing Machinery, www.acm.org/about/code-of-ethics.

8 American Chemical Society: The Chemist's Code of Conduct (1994)

A statement of principles to guide the conduct of society members. American Chemical Society, http://portal.acs.org/portal/acs/corg/content?_nfpb=true&_pageLabel=PP_ARTICLEMAIN&node_id=1095&content_id=CNBP_023290&use_sec=true&sec_url_var=region1&__uuid=e54c88f1-9337-4c11-8afc-b484915e3080.

9 Association for Computing Machinery and Institute for Electrical and Electronic Engineers Computer Society Software Engineering Code of Ethics and Professional Practice (1999)

Statement of both aspirations to guide conduct and details of how the aspirations shape professional roles and activities. Association of Computing Machinery, www.acm.org/about/se-code.

10 UNESCO World Conference on Science: Declaration on Science and the Use of Scientific Knowledge (1999)

Statement of broad principles to guide the conduct of science in a globalizing context. United Nations Educational, Scientific and Cultural Organization, www.unesco.org/science/wcs/eng/declaration_e.htm.

11 Definition of Research Misconduct from the US Federal Register (2000)

The official definition of fabrication, falsification, or plagiarism. United States Department of Health and Human Services, http://ori.hhs.gov/policies/fed_research_misconduct.shtml.

12 Rio de Janeiro Declaration on Ethics in Science and Technology (2003)

Recommendations for the ethical conduct of science and technology in a global context with emphasis on education and access to knowledge. United Nations Educational, Scientific and Cultural Organization, http://portal.unesco.org/shs/en/files/6753/10981096191Declaration_eng.pdf/Declaration_eng.pdf.

13 Swiss Academy of Medical Sciences and Swiss Academy of Natural Sciences: Ethical Principles and Guidelines for Experiments on Animals (2005)

Outlines principles for conducting ethical experimentation with animals. Swiss Academy of Medical Science, www.samw.ch/dms/en/Ethics/Ethics-of-Animal.../e_RL_Tierethik.pdf.

14 UNESCO: Universal Declaration on Bioethics and Human Rights (2005)

Statement of principles to guide the application of biomedical science and technology to human beings. United Nations Educational, Scientific and Cultural Organization, http://portal.unesco.org/en/ev.php-URL_ID=31058&URL_DO=DO_TOPIC&URL_SECTION=201.html.

15 American Anthropological Association: Code of Ethics (2009)

A code to foster discussion and education about anthropologists' many involvements and obligations. The American Anthropological Association, www.aaanet.org/_cs_upload/issues/policy-advocacy/27668_1.pdf.

16 World Conference on Research Integrity: Singapore Statement on Research Integrity (2010)

Outlines four principles and fourteen responsibilities essential to the integrity of research. The Singapore Statement website, www.singaporestatement.org/statement.html.

Bibliography

Allenby, Brad (2005) *Reconstructing Earth: Technology and Environment in the Age of Humans*. Washington, DC: Island Press.

Allenby, Bradn, and Daniel Sarewitz (2011) *The Techno-Human Condition*. Cambridge, MA: MIT Press.

Appiah, Kwame Anthony (2008) *Experiments in Ethics*. Cambridge, MA: Harvard University Press.

Arnhart, Larry (1998) *Darwinian Natural Right: The Biological Ethics of Human Nature*. Albany, NY: SUNY Press.

(2010) "Darwinian Conservatism versus Metaphysical Conservatism," *Intercollegiate Review*, vol. 45, nos. 1–2, pp. 22–32.

Asilomar Scientific Organizing Committee (2010) *The Asilomar Conference Recommendations on Principles for Research into Climate Engineering Techniques*. Washington, DC, Climate Institute, http://climateresponsefund.org/images/Conference/finalfinalreport.pdf.

Ask Amy (2010) "Reader Explains Why Men Cheat," *Chicago Tribune*, August 17.

Ayer, A.J. (1936) *Language, Truth and Logic*. London: Gollancz.

Babbage, Charles (1830) *Reflections on the Decline of Science in England, and on Some of Its Causes*. London: B. Fellowes.

Balsamo, Anne, and Carl Mitcham (2010) "Ethics," in Robert Frodeman, ed., *The Oxford Handbook of Interdisciplinarity*. Oxford University Press, pp. 259–272.

Barbour, Ian (1990) *Religion in an Age of Science*. London: SCM Press.

Barenblatt, Daniel (2004) *A Plague upon Humanity: The Hidden History of Japan's Biological Warfare Program*. New York: Harper Collins Perennial.

Beecher, Henry K. (1955) "The Powerful Placebo," *Journal of the American Medical Association*, vol. 159, no. 17, pp. 1602–1606.

(1961) "Surgery as Placebo: A Quantitative Study of Bias," *Journal of the American Medical Association*, vol. 176 (July), pp. 1102–1107.

(1966) "Ethics and Clinical Research," *New England Journal of Medicine*, vol. 274, no. 24, pp. 1354–1360.

Begley, Glenn, and Lee Ellis (2012) "Drug Development: Raise Standards for Preclinical Cancer Research," *Nature*, vol. 483, pp. 531–533.

Begley, Sharon (2009) "Anatomy of a Scare," *Newsweek*, February 21.

(2010) "Who Owns Your DNA? Why Patenting Genes Is a Bad Idea," *Newsweek*, February 3.

Ben-David, Joseph (1984) *The Scientist's Role in Society*. University of Chicago Press.

Benedict, Ruth (1946) *The Chrysanthemum and the Sword: Patterns of Japanese Culture*. Boston: Houghton Mifflin.

Bennett, Burton (2005) "Most Radiation-Related Deaths Happened in 1945," *Nature*, vol. 437, pp. 610–611.

Berg, Paul, et al. (1974) "Potential Biohazards of Recombinant DNA Molecules," *Science*, vol. 185, no. 4148, p. 303.

Biddle, Wayne (2009) *Dark Side of the Moon: Wernher von Braun, the Third Reich, and the Space Race*. New York: W.W. Norton.

Bloor, David (1991) *Knowledge and Social Imagery*. University of Chicago Press.

Boas, Franz (1919) "Scientists as Spies," *Nation*, December 20.

Briggle, Adam (2010) *A Rich Bioethics: Public Policy, Biotechnology, and the Kass Council*. Notre Dame, IN: University of Notre Dame Press.

Broad, William, and Nicholas Wade (1983) *Betrayers of the Truth: Fraud and Deceit in the Halls of Science*. New York: Simon & Schuster.

Bronowski, Jacob (1956) *Science and Human Values*. New York: Harper & Row.

Brower, Kenneth (2010) "The Danger of Cosmic Genius," *Atlantic Monthly*, December.

Brown, Mark B. (2009) *Science in Democracy: Expertise, Institutions, and Representation*. Cambridge, MA: MIT Press.

Bucchi, Massimiano (1998) *Science and the Media: Alternative Routes in Scientific Communication*. London: Routledge.

Buchanan, Elizabeth, ed. (2004) *Readings in Virtual Research Ethics: Issues and Controversies*. London: Information Science Publishing.

Bush, Vannevar (1945) *Science – The Endless Frontier: A Report to the President on a Program for Postwar Scientific Research*. Washington, DC: National Science Foundation, www.nsf.gov/od/lpa/nsf50/vbush1945.htm.

Cao, Cong (2010) "Climate for Scientific Misconduct in China," *UPI Asia.com*, January 26.

Caplan, Arthur (1983) "Beastly Conduct: Ethical Issues in Animal Experimentation," *Annals of the New York Academy of Science*, vol. 406 (June), pp. 159–169.

Carroll, Sean (2005) "Purity of Essence," *Preposterous Universe* blog, April 18, http://preposterousuniverse.blogspot.ca/2005/04/purity-of-essence.html.

Carson, Rachel (1962) *Silent Spring*. Boston: Houghton Mifflin.

Casebeer, William D. (2003a) *Natural Ethical Facts: Evolution, Connectionism, and Moral Cognition*. Cambridge, MA: MIT Press.

(2003b) "Moral Cognition and Its Neural Constituents," *Nature Reviews: Neurosciences*, vol. 4, pp. 841–846.

Charter, David (2008) "AstraZeneca Row as Corruption Claims Engulf Nobel Prize," *Times* (London), December 19.

Cho, Mildred, Glenn McGee, and David Magnus (2006) "Lessons of the Stem Cell Scandal," *Science*, vol. 311, no. 5761, pp. 614–615.

Chubin, D.R., and E.J. Hackett (1990) *Peerless Science: Peer Review and US Science Policy*. Albany, NY: SUNY Press.

Clifford, W.K. (1877) "The Ethics of Belief," *Contemporary Review*, vol. 29, pp. 289–309.

(1999) *The Ethics of Belief and Other Essays*. New York: Prometheus Books.

Cohen, Baruch C. (1990) "The Ethics of Using Medical Data from Nazi Experiments," *Journal of Halacha and Contemporary Society*, vol. 19, pp. 103–126.

Collingridge, David (1980) *The Social Control of Technology*. New York: St. Martin's Press.

Collins, Harry, and Robert Evans (2002) "The Third Wave in Science Studies: Studies of Expertise and Experience," *Social Studies of Science*, vol. 32, no. 2, pp. 235–296.

Committee for the Update of the Guide for the Care and Use of Laboratory Animals, National Research Council (2011) *Guide for the Care and Use of Laboratory Animals*, 8th edn. Washington, DC: National Academies Press.

Congressional Budget Office (2008) "Technological Change and the Growth of Health Care Spending," Congressional Budget Office, www.cbo.gov/ftpdocs/89xx/doc8947/01-31-TechHealth.pdf.

Couzin, Jennifer (2006) "And How the Problems Eluded Peer Reviewers and Editors," *Science*, vol. 311, no. 5757, pp. 23–24.

Crease, Robert, and Evan Selinger, eds. (2006) *The Philosophy of Expertise*. New York: Columbia University Press.

Curci, Jonathan (2010) *The Protection of Biodiversity and Traditional Knowledge in International Law of Intellectual Property*. Cambridge University Press.

Cutcliffe, Stephen, and Carl Mitcham, eds. (2001) *Visions of STS: Counterpoints in Science, Technology, and Society Studies*. Albany, NY: SUNY Press.

Darwin, Charles ([1871] 1981) *Descent of Man and Selection in Relation to Sex*. Princeton University Press.

Davis, Michael (2002) *Profession, Codes and Ethics*. Burlington, VT: Ashgate.
(2005) "Conflict of Interest," in Carl Mitcham, ed., *Encyclopedia of Science, Technology, and Ethics*. Detroit, MI: Macmillan Reference USA, vol. 1, pp. 402–405.
Dawkins, Richard (1998) *Unweaving the Rainbow: Science, Delusion, and the Appetite for Wonder*. Boston: Houghton Mifflin.
(2006) *The Selfish Gene*, 30th anniversary edn. Oxford University Press.
(2007) *The God Delusion*. New York: Bantam Books.
de Chardin, Pierre Teilhard (1959) *The Phenomenon of Man*. New York: Harper & Brothers.
de Santillana, Giorgio (1955) *The Crime of Galileo*. University of Chicago Press.
de Solla Price, Derek (1963) *Little Science, Big Science*. New York: Columbia University Press.
Deer, Brian (2004) "Revealed: The MMR Research Scandal," *Sunday Times* (London), February 22.
Dewey, John (1916) *Democracy and Education*. New York: Free Press.
([1929] 1960) *The Quest for Certainty: A Study of the Relation of Knowledge and Action*. New York: Capricorn.
Diamond, Cora (1978) "Eating Meat and Eating People," *Philosophy*, vol. 53, no. 206, pp. 465–479.
Donovan, Claire (2007) "The Qualitative Future of Research Evaluation," *Science and Public Policy*, vol. 34, no. 8, pp. 585–597.
Douglas, Heather (2003) "The Moral Responsibilities of Scientists (Tensions between Autonomy and Responsibility)," *American Philosophical Quarterly*, vol. 40, no. 1, pp. 59–68.
(2009) *Science, Policy, and the Value-Free Ideal*. University of Pittsburgh Press.
Downey, Gary Lee, Juan C. Lucena, and Carl Mitcham (2007) "Engineering Ethics and Identity: Emerging Initiatives in Comparative Perspective," *Science and Engineering Ethics*, vol. 13, no. 4, pp. 463–487.
Drake, Stillman (1957) *Discoveries and Opinions of Galileo*. Garden City, NY: Doubleday Anchor.
Dyson, Freeman (2008) "The Question of Global Warming," *New York Review of Books*, June 12.
Easterbrook, Gregg (2003) *The Progress Paradox: How Life Gets Better While People Feel Worse*. New York: Random House.
Edsall, John (1975) "Scientific Freedom and Responsibility: Report of the AAAS Committee on Scientific Freedom and Responsibility," *Science*, vol. 188, no. 4189, pp. 687–693.
Einstein, Albert (1946) "'The Real Problem Is in the Hearts of Men': Professor Einstein Says a New Type of Thinking Is Needed to Meet the Challenge of

the Atomic Bomb," interview by Michael Amrine, *New York Times Sunday Magazine*, June 23, SM4.

(1968) *Einstein on Peace*, ed. Otto Nathan and Heinz Norden. New York: Random House.

European Commission (2007) *Ethics, Research and Globalization: Europe and Its Partners Building Capacity in Research Ethics*. Luxembourg: Office for Official Publications of the European Communities.

(2009) *Global Governance of Science: Report of the Expert Group on Global Governance of Science to the Science, Economy and Society Directorate, Directorate-General for Research, European Commission*. Luxembourg: Office for the Official Publications of the European Communities.

Eyerman, Ron, and Andrew Jamison (1991) *Social Movements: A Cognitive Approach*. University Park, PA: Pennsylvania State University Press.

Ezrahi, Yaron (1990) *The Descent of Icarus: Science and the Transformation of Contemporary Democracy*. Cambridge, MA: Harvard University Press.

Faden, Ruth R., and Tom L. Beauchamp (1986) *A History and Theory of Informed Consent*. Oxford University Press.

Fahie, John (2005) *Galileo, His Life and Work*. Whitefish, MT: Kessinger Publishing.

Fanelli, Daniele (2009) "How Many Scientists Fabricate and Falsify Research? A Systematic Review and Meta-Analysis of Survey Data," *PLoS ONE*, vol. 4, no. 5, e5738, www.plosone.org/article/info:doi%2F10.1371%2Fjournal.pone.0005738.

Fealing, Kaye Husbands, Julia Lane, John Marburger III, and Stephanie Shipp, eds. (2011) *The Science of Science Policy: A Handbook*. Stanford University Press.

Feynman, Richard (1998) *The Meaning of It All: Thoughts of a Citizen-Scientist*. Reading, MA: Perseus.

Flanagan, Owen (1991) *Varieties of Moral Personality: Ethics and Psychological Realism*. Cambridge, MA: Harvard University Press.

Frodeman, Robert, ed. (2010) *The Oxford Handbook of Interdisciplinarity*. Oxford University Press.

Frodeman, Robert, and Adam Briggle (2012) "The Dedisciplining of Peer Review," *Minerva*, vol. 50, no. 1, pp. 3–19.

Frodeman, Robert, and Carl Mitcham (2000) "Beyond the Social Contract Myth: Integrating Science and the Common Good," *Issues in Science and Technology*, vol. 16, no. 4, pp. 37–41.

Fuchs, Victor (1979) "Economics, Health, and Post-Industrial Society," *Milbank Memorial Fund Quarterly*, vol. 57, no. 2, pp. 153–182.

Funtowicz, Silvio, and Jerome Ravetz (1993) "Science for the Post-Normal Age," *Futures*, vol. 25, no. 7, pp. 735–755.

Gauthier, David (1986) *Morals by Agreement*. Oxford University Press.

Gawande, Atul (2010) *The Checklist Manifesto: How to Get Things Right*. New York: Metropolitan.

Gert, Bernard (1998) *Morality: Its Nature and Justification*. Oxford University Press. (First published as *The Moral Rules: A New Rational Foundation for Morality*. New York: Harper & Row, 1970.)

Gert, Bernard, et al. (1996) *Morality and the New Genetics: A Guide for Students and Health Care Providers*. Subdury, MA: Jones & Bartlett.

Gert, Bernard, Charles M. Culver, and K. Danner Clouser (1997) *Bioethics: A Return to Fundamentals*. Oxford University Press.

Gille, Bertrand (1966) *Engineers of the Renaissance*. Cambridge, MA: MIT Press.

Gilligan, Carol (1982) *In a Different Voice: Psychological Theory and Women's Development*. Cambridge, MA: Harvard University Press.

Glenn, David (2006) "Blood Feud," *Chronicle of Higher Education*, vol. 52, no. 26, p. A14.

Glenn, David, and Thomas Bartlett (2009) "Rebuttal of Decade-Old Accusations against Researchers Roils Anthropology Meeting Anew," *Chronicle of Higher Education*. December 3.

Goes, L.G. (2009) "The Miseducation of Sharon Begley: One Parent's Reaction to Irresponsible Journalism," *Age of Autism*, March 27, www.ageofautism.com/2009/03/the-miseducation-of-sharon-begley-one-parents-reaction-to-irresponsible-journalism.html.

Golden, Frederic (1999) "Albert Einstein: Person of the Century," *Time*, December 31, www.time.com/time/magazine/article/0,9171,993017,00.html.

Goodstein, David (2000) "In Defense of Robert Andrews Millikan," *Engineering and Science*, vol. 63, no. 4, pp. 30–38.

Goujon, P., and Hériard Dubreuil (2001) *Technology and Ethics: A European Quest for Responsible Engineering*. Leuven, Belgium: Peeters.

Gould, Stephen Jay (1996) *The Mismeasure of Man*. New York: W.W. Norton.

(1999) *Rocks of Ages: Science and Religion in the Fullness of Life*. New York: Ballantine.

(2002) *The Structure of Evolutionary Theory*. Cambridge, MA: Belknap Press.

Grady, Denise, and William Broad (2011) "Seeing Terror Risks, US Asks Journals to Cut Flu Study Facts," *New York Times*, December 20, www.nytimes.com/2011/12/21/health/fearing-terrorism-us-asks-journals-to-censor-articles-on-virus.html?pagewanted=all.

Grandin, Temple (2002) "Animals Are Not Things: A View of Animal Welfare Based on Neurological Complexity," research paper presented in 2002 at the Department of Psychology, Harvard University, www.grandin.com/welfare/animals.are.not.things.html.

Greenberg, Daniel S. (2001) *Science, Money, and Politics: Political Triumph and Ethical Erosion*. University of Chicago Press.

Griffin, Marcus (2007) "Research to Reduce Bloodshed," *Chronicle of Higher Education*, November 30, vol. 54, no. 14, p. B10.

Grinspoon, David (2004) "Is Mars Ours? The Logistics and Ethics of Colonizing the Red Planet," *Slate*, January 7.

Grossman, Wendy (2005) "Decoding Bees' Wild Waggle Dances," *Wired Magazine*, May 13.

Guston, David (2000) *Between Politics and Science: Assuring the Integrity and Productivity of Research*. Cambridge University Press.

Haber, L.F. (1986) *The Poisonous Cloud: Chemical Warfare in the First World War*. Oxford: Clarendon Press.

Habermas, Jürgen (1970) "Technology and Science as 'Ideology,'" in *Toward a Rational Society: Student Protest, Science, and Politics*, trans. Jeremy J. Shapiro. Boston: Beacon Press, pp. 91–92.

Haddick, Robert (2009) "This Week at War," No. 18, *Foreign Policy*, May 29, 2009, www.foreignpolicy.com/articles/2009/05/28/this_week_at_war_no_18.

Haidt, Jonathan, and Corey L.M. Keyes (2002) *Flourishing: Positive Psychology and the Life Well Lived*. Washington, DC: American Psychological Association.

Hao, Xin (2008) "You Say You Want a Revolution," *Science*, vol. 322, no. 5902, pp. 664–666.

Haraway, Donna (1990) *Simians, Cyborgs, and Women: The Reinvention of Nature*. London: Routledge.

(1997) *Modest_Witness@Second_Millennium. FemaleMan_Meets_OncoMouse: Feminism and Technoscience*. New York: Routledge.

(2003) *Companion Species Manifesto: Dogs, People, and Significant Otherness*. Chicago: Prickly Paradigm Press.

Harding, Sandra (1991) *Whose Science? Whose Knowledge? Thinking from Women's Lives*. Ithaca, NY: Cornell University Press.

Harremoës, Paul, ed. (2002) *The Precautionary Principle in the 20th Century: Late Lessons from Early Warnings*. London: Earthscan.

Harris, Sam (2010) *The Moral Landscape: How Science Can Determine Human Values*. New York: Free Press.

Harrison, Ruth (1964) *Animal Machines: The New Factory Farming Industry*. London: V. Stuart.

Hastings Center (1980) *The Teaching of Ethics in Higher Education: A Report by the Hastings Center*. Hastings-on-Hudson, NY: Institute of Society, Ethics, and the Life Sciences.

Hawkins, Jennifer, and Ezekiel Emanuel, eds. (2008) *Exploitation and Developing Countries: The Ethics of Clinical Research*. Princeton University Press.

Hayward, J.S., and J.D. Erickson (1984) "Physiological Responses and Survival Time Prediction for Humans in Ice Water," *Aviation, Space, and Environmental Medicine*, vol. 55, no. 3, pp. 206–211.

Heller, Jean (1972a) "America's Dirty Little Secret," *Washington Star*, July 25, p. X.

(1972b) "Syphilis Victims in the US Study Went Untreated for 40 Years," *New York Times*, July 26, pp. 1 and 8.

Hempel, Carl (1960) "Science and Human Values," in R.E. Spiller, ed., *Social Control in a Free Society*. Philadelphia, PA: University of Pennsylvania Press, pp. 39–64.

(1966) *Philosophy of Natural Science*. Englewood Cliffs, NJ: Prentice Hall.

Hixson, Joseph R. (1976) *The Patchwork Mouse*. New York: Anchor Press.

Holbrook, J. Britt (2005) "Assessing the Science–Society Relation: The Case of the US National Science Foundation's Second Merit Review Criterion," *Technology in Society*, vol. 27, no. 4, pp. 437–451.

(2009) Editor's Introduction to *US National Science Foundation's Broader Impacts Criterion*, special issue of *Social Epistemology*, vol. 23, nos. 3–4, pp. 177–181.

Holden, Constance (2005) "Korean Cloner Admits Lying about Oocyte Donations," *Science*, vol. 310, no. 5753, pp. 1402–1403.

Hollander, Rochelle, ed. (2009) *Ethics Education and Scientific and Engineering Research: What's Been Learned? What Should Be Done? Summary of a Workshop*. Washington, DC: National Academies Press.

Holton, Gerald (1998) *The Scientific Imagination*. Cambridge, MA: Harvard University Press.

Hough, Susan (2010) "A Seismological Retrospective of the Brady–Spence Prediction," *Seismological Research Letters*, vol. 81, no. 1, pp. 113–117.

Howard, Jennifer (2011) "Despite Warnings, Biomedical Scholars Cite Hundreds of Retracted Papers." *Chronicle of Higher Education*, April 10, http://chronicle.com/article/Hot-Type-Despite-Warnings/127050/.

Hróbjartsson, A., and P.C. Gøtzsche (2001) "Is the Placebo Powerless? An Analysis of Clinical Trials Comparing Placebo with No Treatment," *New England Journal of Medicine*, vol. 344, no. 21, pp. 1594–1602.

Hume, David ([1739] 2000) *A Treatise of Human Nature*, ed. David Fate Norton and Mary J. Norton. Oxford University Press.

Hundley, Kris (2008) "The Latest Industry Being Outsourced to India: Clinical Drug Trials," *St. Petersburg Times*, December 14.

Huning, A., and Carl Mitcham (1993) "The Historical and Philosophical Development of Engineering Ethics in Germany," *Technology in Society*, vol. 15, no. 4, pp. 427–439.

Huntington, Samuel P. (1996) *The Clash of Civilizations: Remaking the World Order.* New York: Simon & Schuster.

Huxley, Thomas Henry (1893) *Evolution and Ethics*. New York: Macmillan.

Hwang Woo-Suk, et al. (2004) "Evidence of a Pluripotent Human Embryonic Stem Cell Line Derived from a Cloned Blastocyst," *Science*, vol. 303, no. 5664, pp. 1669–1674.

(2005) "Patient-Specific Embryonic Stem Cells Derived from Human SCNT Blastocysts," *Science*, vol. 308, no. 5729, pp. 1777–1783.

Illich, Ivan (1987) *Toward a History of Needs*. Berkeley, CA: Heyday Books.

Institute of Medicine and National Research Council (2002) *Integrity in Scientific Research: Creating an Environment That Promotes Responsible Conduct.* Washington, DC: National Academies Press.

Ioannidis, John P.A. (2005) "Why Most Published Research Findings Are False," *PLoS Medicine*, vol. 2, no. 8, pp. 696–701.

Isaacson, Walter (2007) *Einstein: His Life and Universe*. New York: Simon & Schuster.

Ivanhoe, Philip, trans. (2002) *The Daodejing of Laozi*. Indianapolis, IN: Hackett.

James, William (1896) "The Will to Believe," *New World*, vol. 5, pp. 327–347.

Jasanoff, Sheila (1997) *Science at the Bar: Law, Science, and Technology in America*. Cambridge, MA: Harvard University Press.

Jonas, Hans (1966) *The Phenomenon of Life: Toward a Philosophical Biology*. University of Chicago Press.

(1969) "Philosophical Reflections on Experimenting with Human Subjects," *Daedalus*, vol. 98, pp. 219–247.

(1984) *The Imperative of Responsibility*. University of Chicago Press.

Jordan-Young, Rebecca M. (2010) *Brain Storm: The Flaws in the Science of Sex Differences*. Cambridge, MA: Harvard University Press.

Joshi, S.C., and B.S. Rajput (2002) "Axion-Dilation Black Holes with SL(2, Z) Symmetry through APT-FGP Model," *Europhysics Letters*, vol. 57, p. 639.

Joy, Bill (2000) "Why the Future Doesn't Need Us," *Wired*, vol. 8, no. 4, www.wired.com/wired/archive/8.04/joy.html?pg=1&topic=&topic_set=.

Juengst, Eric T. (1996) "Self-Critical Federal Science? The Ethics Experiment within the US Human Genome Project," *Social Philosophy and Policy*, vol. 13, no. 2, pp. 63–95.

Kahneman, Amos, and Daniel Tversky (1982) *Judgment Under Uncertainty: Heuristics and Biases*. Cambridge University Press.

Kant, Immanuel (1784) "An Answer to the Question: What Is Enlightenment?" Columbia University website, www.columbia.edu/acis/ets/CCREAD/etscc/kant.html.

(1993) *Grounding for the Metaphysics of Morals*, 3rd edn., trans. James W. Ellington. Indianapolis: Hackett.

Kass, Leon (1988) *Toward a More Natural Science*: New York: Simon & Schuster.

Katz, D., A.L. Caplan, and J.F. Merz (2003) "All Gifts Large and Small: Toward an Understanding of the Ethics of Pharmaceutical Industry Gift-Giving," *American Journal of Bioethics*, vol. 3, no. 3, pp. 39–46.

Katz, Jay (1987) "The Regulation of Human Experimentation in the United States - A Personal Odyssey," *IRB: Ethics and Human Research*, vol. 9, pp. 1–6.

Kazmi, S.M.A. (2002) "Kumaun Prof Says She Blew Plagiarism Whistle on V-C, So He Suspended Her," *Indian Express*, October 4, www.indianexpress.com/storyOld.php?storyId=10730.

Kegley, Jacquelyn Ann K. (2004) "Challenges to Informed Consent," *EMBO Reports*, vol. 5, no. 9, pp. 832–836.

Kemp, Kenneth (1989) "Conducting Scientific Research for the Military as a Civic Duty," *Annals of the New Academy of Sciences*, vol. 577, pp. 115–121.

Kennedy, Donald (2002) "More Questions about Research Misconduct," *Science*, vol. 297, no. 5578, p. 13.

Kevles, Daniel J. (1998) *The Baltimore Case: A Trial of Politics, Science, and Character.* New York: W.W. Norton & Company.

Keynes, Geoffrey, ed. (1956) *The Letters of William Blake*. London: Rupert Hart-Davis.

King, Martin Luther, Jr. (1963) "Letter from a Birmingham Jail," African Studies Center, University of Pennsylvania, www.africa.upenn.edu/Articles_Gen/Letter_Birmingham.html.

Kitcher, Philip (2001) *Science, Truth, and Democracy.* Oxford University Press.

Kohlberg, Lawrence (1981) *Essays on Moral Development*, vol. I: *The Philosophy of Moral Development*. San Francisco, CA: Harper & Row.

Kohlberg, Lawrence, Charles Levine, and Alexandra Hewer (1983) *Moral Stages: A Current Formulation and a Response to Critics.* Basel and New York: Karger.

Kroeber, A.L., and Clyde Kluckhohn (1952) *Culture: A Critical Review of Concepts and Definitions.* New York: Vintage.

Kuhn, Thomas (1962) *The Structure of Scientific Revolutions.* University of Chicago Press.

(1977) "Objectivity, Value Judgment, and Theory Choice," in *The Essential Tension*. University of Chicago Press, pp. 320–339.

Lane, Robert (2000) *The Loss of Happiness in Market Democracies.* New Haven, CT: Yale University Press.

Latour, Bruno (2004) *Politics of Nature: How to Bring the Sciences into Democracy*, trans. Catherine Porter. Cambridge, MA: Harvard University Press.

Latour, Bruno, and Steven Woolgar (1986) *Laboratory Life: The Construction of Scientific Facts.* Princeton University Press.

Lattuca, Lisa R., Patrick T. Terenzini, and J. Fredricks Volkwein (2006) *Engineering Change: A Study of the Impact of EC2000*. Baltimore, MD: ABET.

Lazerson, Marvin (2010) "The Making of Corporate U.," *Chronicle of Higher Education*, October 17.

Lenk, Hans (1983) "Notes on Extended Responsibility and Increased Technological Power," in Paul T. Durin and Friedrich Rapp, eds., *Philosophy and Technology, Boston Studies in the Philosophy of Science*, vol. 80. Boston: D. Reidel.

Lewis, Sinclair (1925) *Arrowsmith*. San Diego, CA: Harcourt, Brace & Company.

Lily, John (1987) *Communication between Man and Dolphin*. New York: Julian Press.

Lippmann, Walter (1922) *Public Opinion*. New York: Harcourt Brace.

Lomborg, Bjørn (2001) *The Skeptical Environmentalist: Measuring the Real State of the World*. Cambridge University Press.

Longino, Helen (1990) *Science as Social Knowledge: Values and Objectivity in Scientific Inquiry*. Princeton University Press.

Loring, L.L. (1955) "Lag in Ethics," *Los Angeles Times*, April 10, pp. B4, 10.

Lucchi, Nicola (2006) *Digital Media and Intellectual Property*. London: Springer.

McFadden, Robert D. (2010) "Samuel T. Cohen, Neutron Bomb Inventor, Dies at 89," *New York Times*, December 1.

McGinn, Robert (1994) "Technology, Demography, and the Anachronism of Traditional Rights," *Journal of Applied Philosophy*, vol. 11, no. 1, 57–70.

Macilwain, Colin (2000) "AAAS Members Fret over Links with Theological Foundation," *Nature*, vol. 403, p. 819.

MacIntyre, Alasdair (2007) *After Virtue: A Study in Moral Theory*, 3rd edn. Notre Dame, IN: University of Notre Dame Press.

McKie, Robin (2004) "Icelandic DNA Project Hit by Privacy Storm," *Observer*, May 16, www.guardian.co.uk/science/2004/may/16/genetics.research.

McMullin, Ernan (1993) "Indifference Principle and Anthropic Principle in Cosmology," *Studies in History and Philosophy of Science*, vol. 24, no. 3, pp. 359–389.

McShea, Daniel W., and Robert N. Brandon (2010) *Biology's First Law: The Tendency for Diversity and Complexity to Increase in Evolutionary Systems*. University of Chicago Press.

Martin, Mike, and Roland Schinzinger (1989) *Ethics in Engineering*, 2nd edn. New York: McGraw-Hill.

Mazlish, Bruce (1995) *The Fourth Discontinuity: The Co-Evolution of Humans and Machines*. New Haven, CT: Yale University Press.

Merton, Robert (1942) "The Normative Structure of Science," in Robert K. Merton, *The Sociology of Science: Theoretical and Empirical Investigations*. University of Chicago Press, 1973, pp. 267–278.

(1973) *The Sociology of Science: Theoretical and Empirical Investigations*. University of Chicago Press.

Minkel, J.R. (2002) "Reality Check," *Scientific American*, vol. 287, no. 5, pp. 20–21.

Mirowski, Philip (2011) *Science Mart: Privatizing American Science*. Cambridge, MA: Harvard University Press.

Mitcham, Carl (1994) "Engineering Design Research and Social Responsibility," in K.S. Shrader-Frechette, *Ethics of Scientific Research*. Totowa, NJ: Rowman & Littlefield, pp. 153–168.

ed. (2005) *Encyclopedia of Science, Technology, and Ethics*. 4 vols. Detroit, MI: Macmillan Reference USA.

Mitcham, Carl, and David Muñoz (2010) *Humanitarian Engineering*. San Rafael, CA: Morgan & Claypool.

Moe, Kristine (1984) "Should the Nazi Research Data Be Cited?" *Hastings Center Report*, vol. 14, no. 6, pp. 5–7.

Moore, G.E. (1903) *Principia Ethica*. Cambridge University Press.

Moreno, Jonathan (2001) *Undue Risk: Secret State Experiments on Humans*. New York: Routledge.

Mulder, Karel (2006) *Sustainable Development for Engineers: A Handbook and Resource Guide*. Sheffield: Greenleaf.

Nagel, Thomas (1989) *The View from Nowhere*. Oxford University Press.

National Academy of Sciences, National Academy of Engineering, and Institute of Medicine (1992) *Responsible Science – Ensuring the Integrity of the Research Process*. Washington, DC: National Academies Press.

(2007) *Rising above the Gathering Storm: Energizing and Employing America for a Brighter Economic Future*. Washington, DC: National Academies Press.

(2009) *On Being a Scientist*, 3rd edn. Washington, DC: National Academies Press.

Neelakantan, Shailaja (2008) "India to Double Spending on Scientific Research," *Chronicle Review of Higher Education*, December 4.

Nelkin, Dorothy (1995) *Selling Science: How the Press Covers Science and Technology*. New York: W.H. Freeman.

Nerlich, Brigitte, Richard Elliott, and Brendon Larson (2009) *Communicating Biological Sciences: Ethical and Metaphorical Dimensions*. Burlington, VT: Ashgate.

New York Times (1931) "Einstein Sees Lack in Applying Science," *New York Times*, February 16.

Newman, John Henry ([1852] 1996) *The Idea of a University*, ed. Frank Turner. New Haven, CT: Yale University Press.

Newsweek Online (2009) "Pharma's Facebook: Research 2.0: How Drug Companies Are Using Social Networks to Recruit Patients for Clinical

Research," *Newsweek*, March 10, www.newsweek.com/2009/03/10/pharma-s-facebook.html.

Normile, Dennis (2007) "An Asian Tiger's Bold Experiment," *Science*, vol. 316, no. 5821, pp. 38–41.

Nuffield Council on Bioethics (2005) *The Ethics of Research Involving Animals*. London: Nuffield Council on Bioethics.

Oakeshott, Michael (2004) *What Is History? And Other Essays*, ed. Luke O'Sullivan. Charlottesville, VA: Imprint Academic.

Olson, Richard G. (2008) *Science and Scientism in Nineteenth-Century Europe*. Chicago: University of Illinois Press.

Olson, Richard S., B. Podesta, and J.M. Nigg (1989) *The Politics of Earthquake Prediction*. Princeton University Press.

Oppenheimer, J. Robert (1947) *Physics in the Contemporary World*, Arthur D. Little Memorial Lecture at MIT, November 25.

Oreskes, Naomi, and Erik Conway (2010) *Merchants of Doubt: How a Handful of Scientists Obscured the Truth on Issues from Tobacco Smoke to Global Warming*. New York: Bloomsbury.

Palmer, Craig, and Randy Thornhill (2000) *A Natural History of Rape: Biological Bases of Sexual Coercion*. Cambridge, MA: MIT Press.

Pappworth, D.H. (1968) *Human Guinea Pigs*. Boston: Beacon Press.

Parsons, Keith, ed. (2003) *The Science Wars: Debating Scientific Knowledge and Technology*. Amherst, NY: Prometheus Books.

Petroski, Henry (1985) *To Engineer Is Human: The Role of Failure in Successful Design*. New York: St. Martin's Press.

Piaget, Jean (1932) *The Moral Judgment of the Child*. London: Kegan Paul.

Pielke, Roger, Jr. (2004) "When Scientists Politicize Science: Making Sense of the Controversy over *The Skeptical Environmentalist*," *Environmental Science and Policy*, vol. 7, no. 5, pp. 405–417.

(2006) "When Scientists Politicize Science," *Regulation*, vol. 29, no. 1, pp. 28–34.

(2007) *The Honest Broker: Making Sense of Science in Policy and Politics*. Cambridge University Press.

Pielke, Roger, Jr., and Rad Byerly (1998) "Beyond Basic and Applied," *Physics Today*, vol. 51, no. 2, pp. 42–46.

Pogge, Thomas (2008) *World Poverty and Human Rights: Cosmopolitan Responsibilities and Reforms*, 2nd edn. Cambridge: Polity Press.

Polanyi, Michael (1962) "The Republic of Science: Its Political and Economic Theory," *Minerva*, vol. 1, pp. 54–74.

Popper, Karl (1945) *The Open Society and Its Enemies*. 2 vols. London: Routledge.

(1959) *The Logic of Scientific Discovery*. London: Hutchinson.

President's Council on Bioethics (2005) *Alternative Sources of Pluripotent Stem Cells*. Washington, DC: US Government Printing Office.

Presidential Commission on the Space Shuttle Challenger Disaster, The (1986) Vol. 1. Washington, DC: US Government Printing Office.

Proctor, Robert N. (1995) *Cancer Wars: How Politics Shapes What We Know and Don't Know about Cancer*. New York: Basic Books.

(2012) *Golden Holocaust: Origins of the Cigarette Catastrophe and the Case for Abolition*. Berkeley, CA: University of California Press.

Proctor, Robert N., and Londa Schiebinger, eds. (2008) *Agnotology: The Making and Unmaking of Ignorance*. Stanford University Press.

Qin, Zhu (2010) "Engineering Ethics Studies in China: Dialogue between Traditionalism and Modernism," *Engineering Studies*, vol. 2, no. 2, pp. 85–107.

Rahner, Karl (1965) *Hominisation: The Evolutionary Origin of Man as a Theological Problem*, trans. W.J. O'Hara. New York: Herder & Herder.

Raj, N. Gopal (2002) "Scientific Misconduct," *Hindu*, October 11.

Ramachandran, R. (2002) "The Physics of Plagiarism," *Frontline*, vol. 19, no. 22, http://frontlineonnet.com/fl1922/stories/20021108003508400.htm.

Rawls, John (1971) *A Theory of Justice*. Cambridge, MA: Harvard University Press.

Regan, Tom (1980) "Animal Rights, Human Wrongs," *Environmental Ethics*, vol. 2, no. 2, pp. 99–120.

Reich, Eugenie Samuel (2009) *Plastic Fantastic: How the Biggest Fraud in Physics Shook the Scientific World*. New York: Palgrave Macmillan.

Reilly, Jerome (2010) "Sex Harassment Row Sparks Global Debate," *Independent.ie*, May 23.

Reiss, Michael (1999) "Teaching Ethics in Science," *Studies in Science Education*, vol. 34, pp. 115–140.

Rennie, John (2002) "Misleading Math about the Earth: Science Defends Itself against *The Skeptical Environmentalist*," *Scientific American*, vol. 286, no. 1, p. 61.

Resnik, David. B. (1998) *The Ethics of Science: An Introduction*. London: Routledge.

Rhodes, Richard (1986) *The Making of the Atomic Bomb*. New York: Simon & Schuster.

Ridker, Paul, and Jose Torres (2006) "Reported Outcomes in Major Cardiovascular Clinical Trials Funded by For-Profit and Not-for-Profit Organizations: 2000–2005," *Journal of the American Medical Association*, vol. 295, no. 19, p. 2270–2274.

Ringach, Dario, and David Jentsch (2009) "We Must Face the Threats," *Journal of Neuroscience*, vol. 29, no. 37, pp. 11417–11418.

Roberts, Seth, and Allen Neuringer (1998) "Self-Experimentation," in Kennon A. Lattal and Michael Perone, eds., *Handbook of Research Methods in Human Operant Behavior.* New York: Plenum, pp. 619–656.

Robinson, Kim Stanley (1992) *Red Mars.* New York: Bantam Books.

(1993) *Green Mars.* New York: Bantam Books.

(1996) *Blue Mars.* New York: Bantam Books.

Rollin, Bernard (2006) *Science and Ethics.* Cambridge University Press.

Rorty, Richard (1981) *Philosophy and the Mirror of Nature.* Princeton University Press.

Rosen, Christine (2004) *Preaching Eugenics: Religious Leaders and the American Eugenics Movement.* Oxford University Press.

Rosen, Stanley (1989) *The Ancients and the Moderns.* New Haven, CT: Yale University Press.

Ross, W.D. (1954) *Kant's Ethical Theory.* Oxford University Press.

Rothman, K.J., and K.B. Michels (1994) "The Continuing Unethical Use of Placebo Controls," *New England Journal of Medicine*, vol. 331, no. 6, pp. 394–398.

Rothman, Tony (2003) *Everything's Relative: And Other Fables from Science and Technology.* Hoboken, NJ: John Wiley & Sons.

Russell, W.M.S., and R.L. Burch (1959) *The Principles of Humane Experimental Technique.* London: Methuen.

Ryder, Richard (2000) *Animal Revolution: Changing Attitudes towards Speciesism.* Oxford: Berg.

Sandel, Michael (2012) *What Money Can't Buy: The Moral Limits of Markets.* New York: Farrar, Straus & Giroux.

Sarewitz, Daniel (1996) *Frontiers of Illusion: Science, Technology, and the Politics of Progress.* Philadelphia, PA: Temple University Press.

(1997) "Science and Environmental Policy: An Excess of Objectivity," in Robert Frodeman, ed., *Earth Matters: The Earth Sciences, Philosophy, and the Claims of Community.* Upper Saddle River, NJ: Prentice Hall, pp. 79–98.

(2004) "How Science Makes Environmental Controversies Worse," *Environmental Science and Policy*, vol. 7, no. 5, pp. 385–403.

Sax, Boria (2000) *Animals in the Third Reich: Pets, Scapegoats, and the Holocaust.* New York: Continuum.

Schattschneider, E.E. (1960) *The Semisovereign People: A Realist's View of Democracy in America.* New York: Holt, Rinehart & Winston.

Schienke, Erich, Seth D. Baum, Nancy Tuana, Kenneth J. Davis, and Klaus Keller (2010) "Intrinsic Ethics Regarding Integrated Assessment Models for Climate Management," *Science and Engineering Ethics*, vol. 17, no. 3, pp. 503–523.

Schwartz, John, and Andrew Pollack (2010) "Judge Invalidates Human Gene Patent," *New York Times*, March 29, www.nytimes.com/2010/03/30/business/30gene.html.

Schweber, Silvan (2000) *In the Shadow of the Bomb: Oppenheimer, Bethe, and the Moral Responsibility of the Scientist*. Princeton University Press.

Shabecoff, Philip (1988) "Head of EPA Bars Nazi Data in Study on Gas," *New York Times*, March 23.

Shamoo, A. E., and Resnik, D. B. (2009) *Responsible Conduct of Research*, 2nd edn. Oxford University Press.

Shane, Scott, and Mark Mazzetti (2009) "In Adopting Harsh Tactics, No Look at Past Use," *New York Times*, April 22, p. A1.

Shapin, Steven (2008) *The Scientific Life: A Moral History of a Late Modern Vocation*. University of Chicago Press.

Shapin, Steven, and Simon Schaffer (1985) *Leviathan and the Air-Pump: Hobbes, Boyle, and the Experimental Life*. Princeton University Press.

Shapiro, T. Rees (2010) "Search for More Humane Nuclear Weapon Led to Neutron Bomb," *Washington Post*, December 1.

Shattuck, Roger (1997) *Forbidden Knowledge: From Prometheus to Pornography*. San Diego, CA: Harcourt Brace.

Shrader-Frechette, Kristin (1994) *Ethics of Scientific Research*. Boston: Rowman & Littlefield.

Singer, Peter (1975) *Animal Liberation: A New Ethic for the Treatment of Animals*. New York: New York Review.

(2011) *Practical Ethics*, 3rd edn. Cambridge University Press.

Smith, John Maynard (1993) *The Theory of Evolution*, 3rd edn. Cambridge University Press.

Snow, C.P. (1959) *The Two Cultures and the Scientific Revolution*. Cambridge University Press.

(1961) *Science and Government*. Cambridge, MA: Harvard University Press.

(1963) *The Two Cultures and a Second Look*. New York: New American Library.

Sol, Ayhan, and Halil Turan (2004) "The Ethics of Earthquake Prediction," *Science and Engineering Ethics*, vol. 10, no. 4, pp. 655–666.

Spencer, Herbert ([1873] 1961) *The Study of Sociology*. reprint Ann Arbor, MI: University of Michigan Press.

Stern, Robert (1994) "Drug Promotion for an Unlabeled Indication – The Case of Topical Tretinoin," *New England Journal of Medicine*, vol. 331, no. 20, pp. 1348–1349.

Stokes, Donald (1997) *Pasteur's Quadrant: Basic Science and Technological Innovation*. Washington, DC: Brookings Institution.

Stolley, Paul, and Tamar Lasky (1992) "Johannes Fibiger and His Nobel Prize for the Hypothesis That a Worm Causes Stomach Cancer," *Annals of Internal Medicine*, vol. 116, no. 9, pp. 765–769.

Strauss, Leo (1953) *Natural Right and History*. University of Chicago Press.

(1959) *Thoughts on Machiavelli*. University of Chicago Press.

Sun, Marjorie (1988) "EPA Bars Use of Nazi Data," *Science*, vol. 240, no. 4848, p. 21.

Sutz, Judith (1993) "The Social Implications of Information Technologies: A Latin American Perspective," in Carl Mitcham, ed., *Spanish Language Contributions to the Philosophy of Technology*. Boston: Kluwer.

Tan, Min, et al (2009) "Fellatio by Fruit Bats Prolongs Copulation Time," *PLoS ONE*, vol. 4, no. 10.

Tierney, Patrick (2000) *Darkness in El Dorado: How Scientists and Journalists Devastated the Amazon*. New York: W.W. Norton & Company.

Toulmin, Stephen (1982) "How Medicine Saved the Life of Ethics," *Perspectives on Biology and Medicine*, vol. 25, no. 4 (Summer), pp. 736–750.

Tumpey, Terrence, et al. (2005) "Characterization of the Reconstructed 1918 Spanish Influenza Pandemic Virus," *Science*, vol. 310, no. 5745, pp. 77–80.

van de Poel, Ibo, and Lamber Royakkers (2011) *Ethics, Technology, and Engineering: An Introduction*. Malden, MA: Wiley-Blackwell.

Varmus, Harold (2000) "Squeeze on Science," *Washington Post*, October 4, p. A33.

Vaughan, Diane (1996) *The Challenger Launch Decision: Risky Technology, Culture, and Deviance at NASA*. University of Chicago Press.

VDI (Verein Deutscher Ingenieure), ed. (1991) *Technikbewertung: Begriffe und Grundlagen*, VDI-Richtlinie 3780, Düsseldorf: VDI.

Veblen, Thorstein ([1921] 2009) *The Engineers and the Price System*. Repr. New York: Viking Press.

Vine, David (2007) "Enabling the Kill Chain," *Chronicle of Higher Education*, vol. 54, no. 14, pp. B9–B10.

Vogel, Gretchen (2005) "Landmark Paper Has an Image Problem," *Science*, vol. 310, no. 5754, p. 1595.

von Schomberg, René (2011) "Prospects for Technology Assessment in a Framework of Responsible Research and Innovation," in M. Dusseldorp and R. Beecroft, eds., *Technikfolgen abschätzen Lehren: Bildungspotenziale transdisciplinärer Methoden*. Wiesbaden: VS Verlag, 39–61.

Vreeland, Leslie (1989) "The Selling of Retin-A," *Money*, April 1, http://money.cnn.com/magazines/moneymag/moneymag_archive/1989/04/01/85047/index.htm.

Wade, Nicholas (1981) "The Rise and Fall of a Scientific Superstar," *New Scientist*, vol. 91, no. 1272, pp. 781–782.

(2010) "A Decade Later, Genetic Map Yields Few New Cures," *New York Times*, June 12.

Wakefield, Andrew, et al. (1998) RETRACTED "Ileal-lymphoid-nodular Hyperplasia, Non-Specific Colitis, and Pervasive Developmental Disorder in Children," *Lancet*, vol. 351, no. 9103, pp. 637–641.

Walsh, John (2010) "Lecturer Fights Sanctions after Showing Colleague Bat-Sex Article," *Independent.ie*, May 17.

Washburn, Jennifer (2005) *University, Inc.: The Corporate Corruption of Higher Education*. New York: Basic Books.

Watson, Judith, and David Torgerson (2006) "Increasing Recruitment to Randomised Trials: A Review of Randomised Controlled Trials," *BMC Medical Research Methodology*, vol. 6, no. 34, pp. 1–9.

Weber, Max (1919) *Wissenschaft als Beruf*. Munich and Leipzig: Duncker & Humblot.

Weinberg, Alvin M. (1961) "Impact of Large-Scale Science on the United States," *Science*, vol. 134, no. 3473, pp. 161–164.

(1963) "Criteria for Scientific Choice," *Minerva*, vol. 1, no. 2, pp. 159–171.

(1992) "The Axiology of Science," *Nuclear Reactions: Science and Trans-Science*. New York: American Institute of Physics, pp. 51–64.

Weiner, Joseph S. (2003) *The Piltdown Forgery: The Classic Account of the Most Famous and Successful Hoax in Science*. Oxford University Press.

Weiss, J.S., C.N. Ellis, J.T. Headington, T. Tincoff, T.A. Hamilton, and J.J. Voorhees (1988) "Topical Tretinoin Improves Photoaged Skin," *Journal of the American Medical Association*, vol. 259, pp. 527–532.

Whewell, William (1840) *Philosophy of the Inductive Sciences*. 2 vols. London.

Whitehead, Alfred North ([1929] 1979) *Process and Reality: An Essay in Cosmology*, corrected edn., ed. David Ray Griffin and Donald W. Sherburne. New York: Free Press.

Wiener, Norbert (1948) "A Rebellious Scientist after Two Years," *Bulletin of the Atomic Scientists*, vol. 4, no. 11, pp. 338–340.

Wilson, E.O. (1978) *On Human Nature*. Cambridge, MA: Harvard University Press.

(1998) *Consilience: The Unity of Knowledge*. New York: Vintage.

(2000) *Sociobiology: The New Synthesis – 25th Anniversary Edition*. Cambridge, MA: Belknap Press.

Wilson, Robin (2011) "One Animal Researcher Refuses to Hide," *Chronicle of Higher Education*, February 20.

Wittgenstein, Ludwig (1965) "Lecture on Ethics," *Philosophical Review*, vol. 74, no. 1, pp. 3–12.

Wolff, Robert Paul (1992) *The Ideal of the University.* New Brunswick, NJ: Transaction.

Wood, Graeme (2009) "Re-Engineering the Earth," *Atlantic*, July/August.

Wynne, Brian (1991) "Knowledges in Context," *Science, Technology, & Human Values*, vol. 16, no. 1, pp. 111–121.

Index